SHORTCAKE CAKE

STORY AND ART BY

suu Morishita

Characters

SHORTCAKE CAKE

NEKOCHIYA HIGH SCHOOL

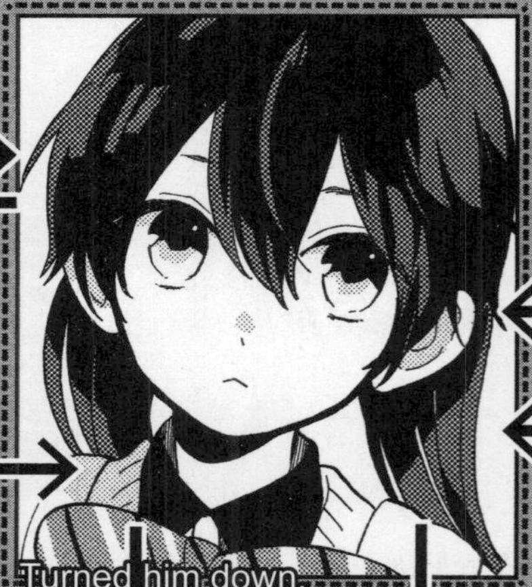

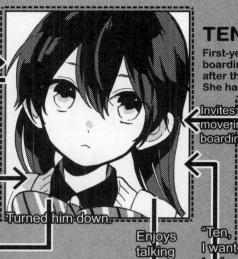

TEN

First-year. She moved into the boardinghouse about a month after the new school year started. She has pluck.

Invites Ten to move into the boardinghouse.

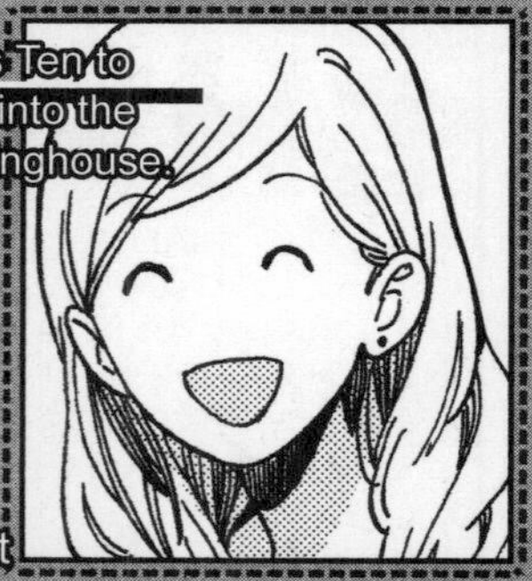

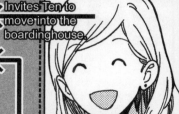

AGEHA

First-year. She attended the same junior high school as Ten.

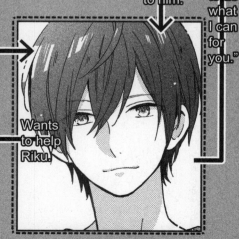

Turned him down.

Enjoys talking to him.

"Ten, I want to do what I can for you."

Wants to help Riku.

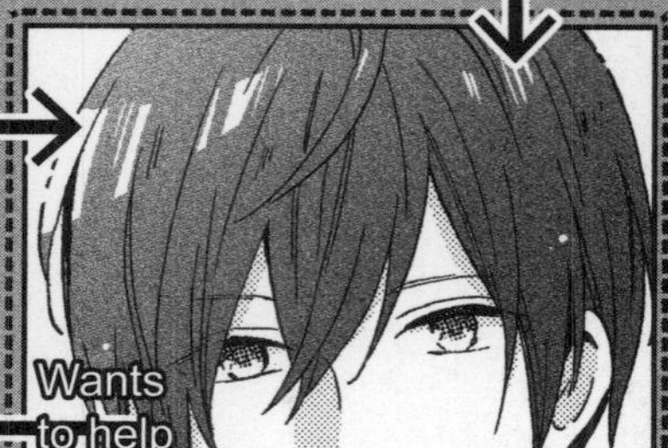

CHIAKI

First-year. A gorgeous guy who loves reading books.

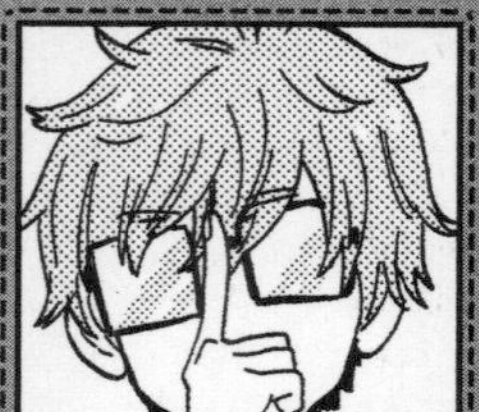

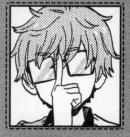

YUTO

Second-year. He tutors Ten and the other first-years.

REI

Age 16. The son of the owner of Hoshino Boardinghouse.

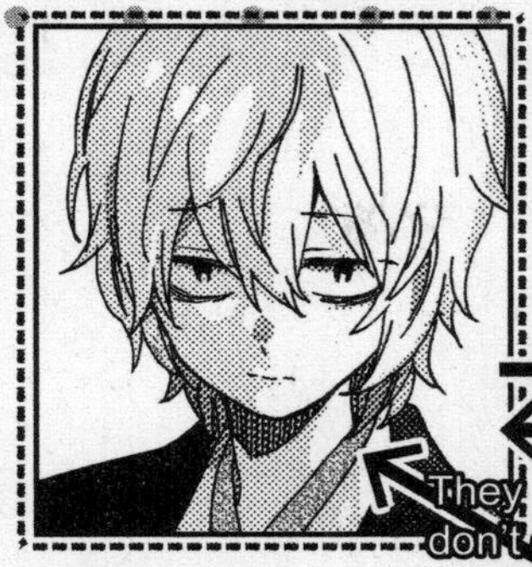

SHIRAOKA

Rei's driver. What's his connection to Ran?

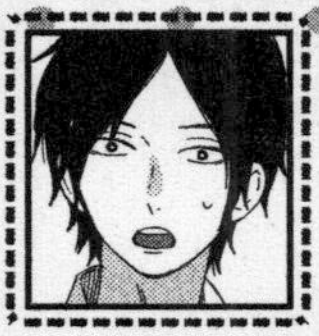

Hoshino Boardinghouse

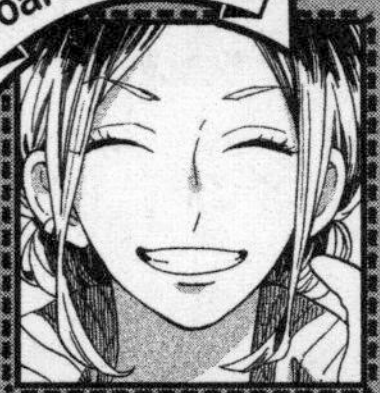

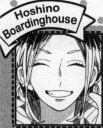

RAN

House mom. She likes cooking and cars.

"Be my girlfriend."

She thinks he's weird.

They don't get along.

NEKOCHIYA SHOGYO HIGH SCHOOL

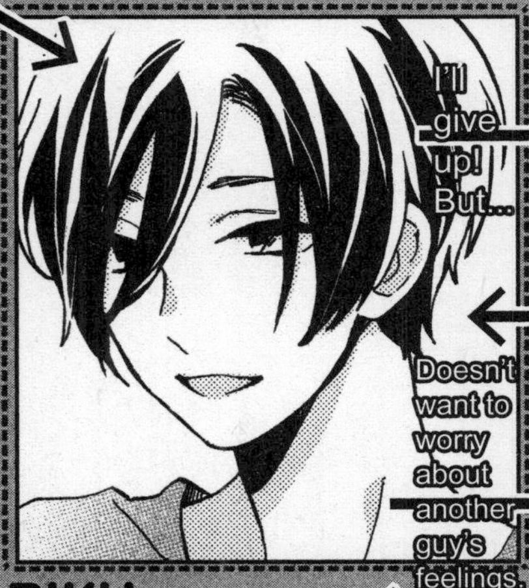

I'll give up! But...

Doesn't want to worry about another guy's feelings.

RIKU

First-year. Lives in the boardinghouse though he grew up nearby. Very friendly with girls.

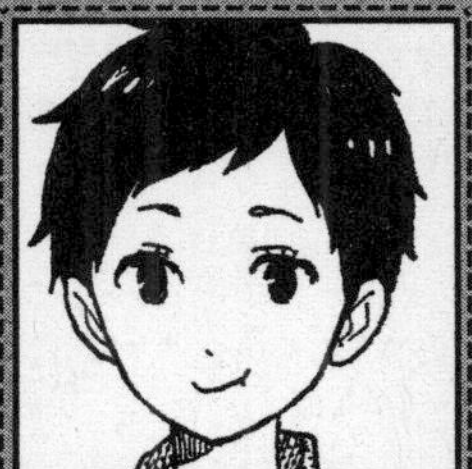

AOI

Third-year. She's the oldest in the boardinghouse. Likes talking about relationships.

Story Thus Far

Ten is a first-year in high school who lives in a boardinghouse with boys. When she runs into Rei, he asks her to be his girlfriend. He pursues her aggressively, so Ten and Chiaki pretend to be dating to dissuade Rei. Meanwhile, Riku finds himself in an awkward position because he still likes Ten after she turned him down.

On the night of a big storm, lightening knocks the power out at Hoshino Boardinghouse. Riku and Ten head into the darkness in search of batteries. Ten has Riku on her mind, so when their hands accidentally brush, she involuntarily throws the smartphone she was using as a flashlight. The phone hits Riku on the head, and she touches him to make sure he's okay. As lightning strikes, Riku leans in and kisses her...

SHORTCAKE CAKE

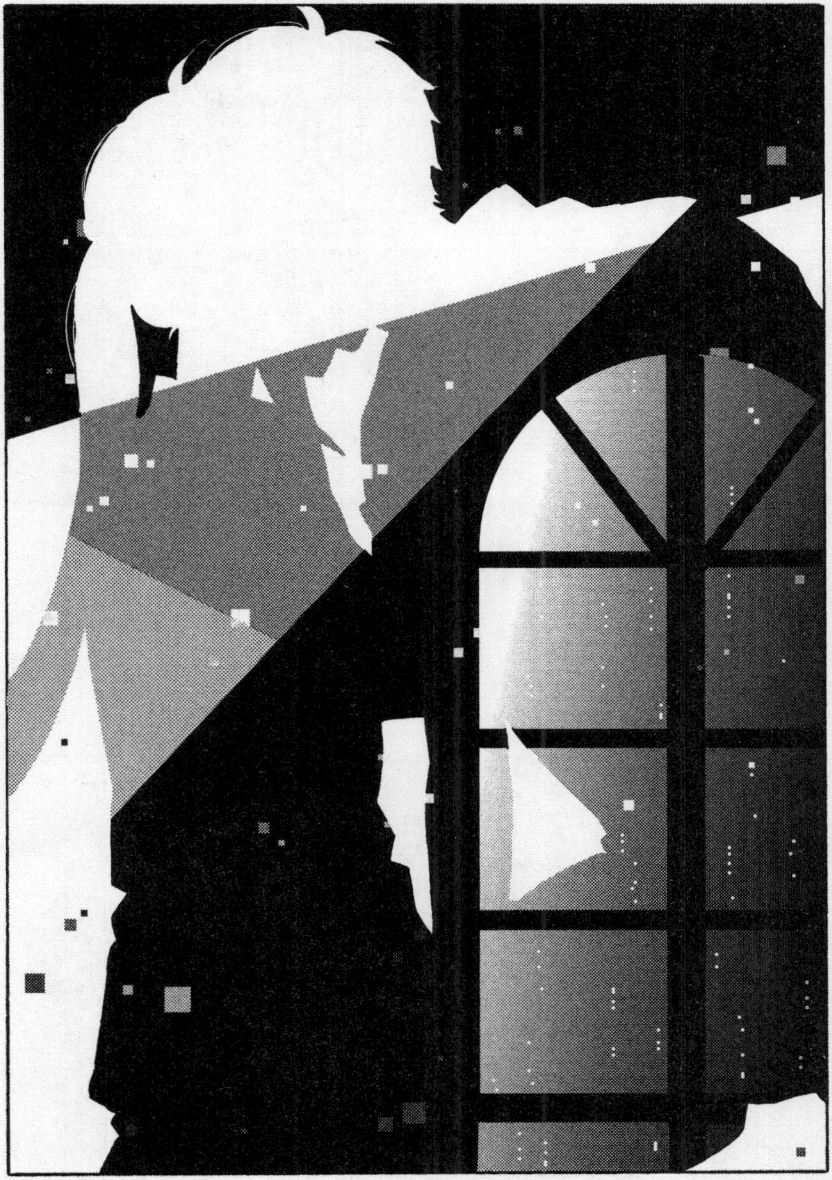

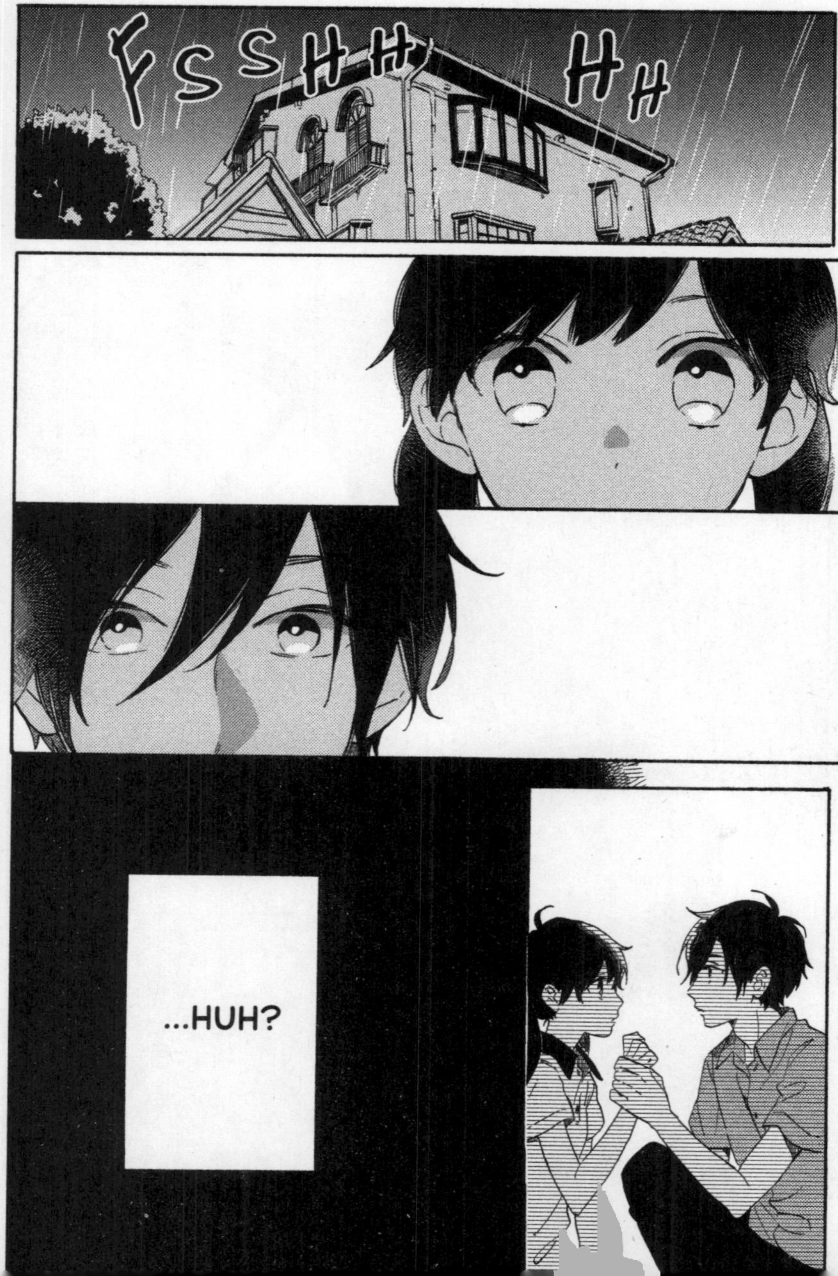
FSSHH HH
...HUH?

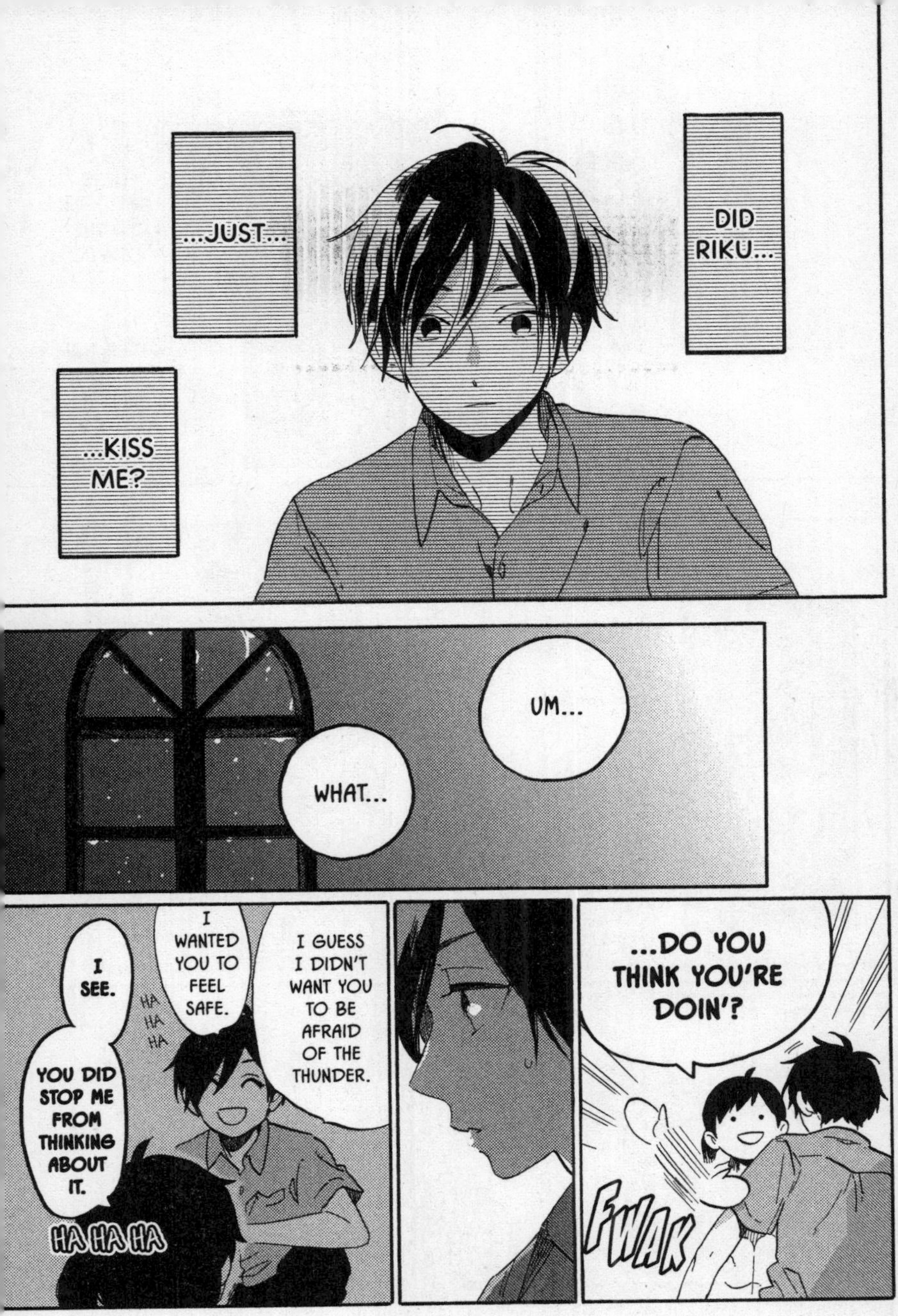
DID RIKU...
...JUST...
...KISS ME?
UM...
WHAT...
...DO YOU THINK YOU'RE DOIN'?
FWAK
I GUESS I DIDN'T WANT YOU TO BE AFRAID OF THE THUNDER.
I WANTED YOU TO FEEL SAFE.
I SEE.
HA HA HA
YOU DID STOP ME FROM THINKING ABOUT IT.
HA HA HA

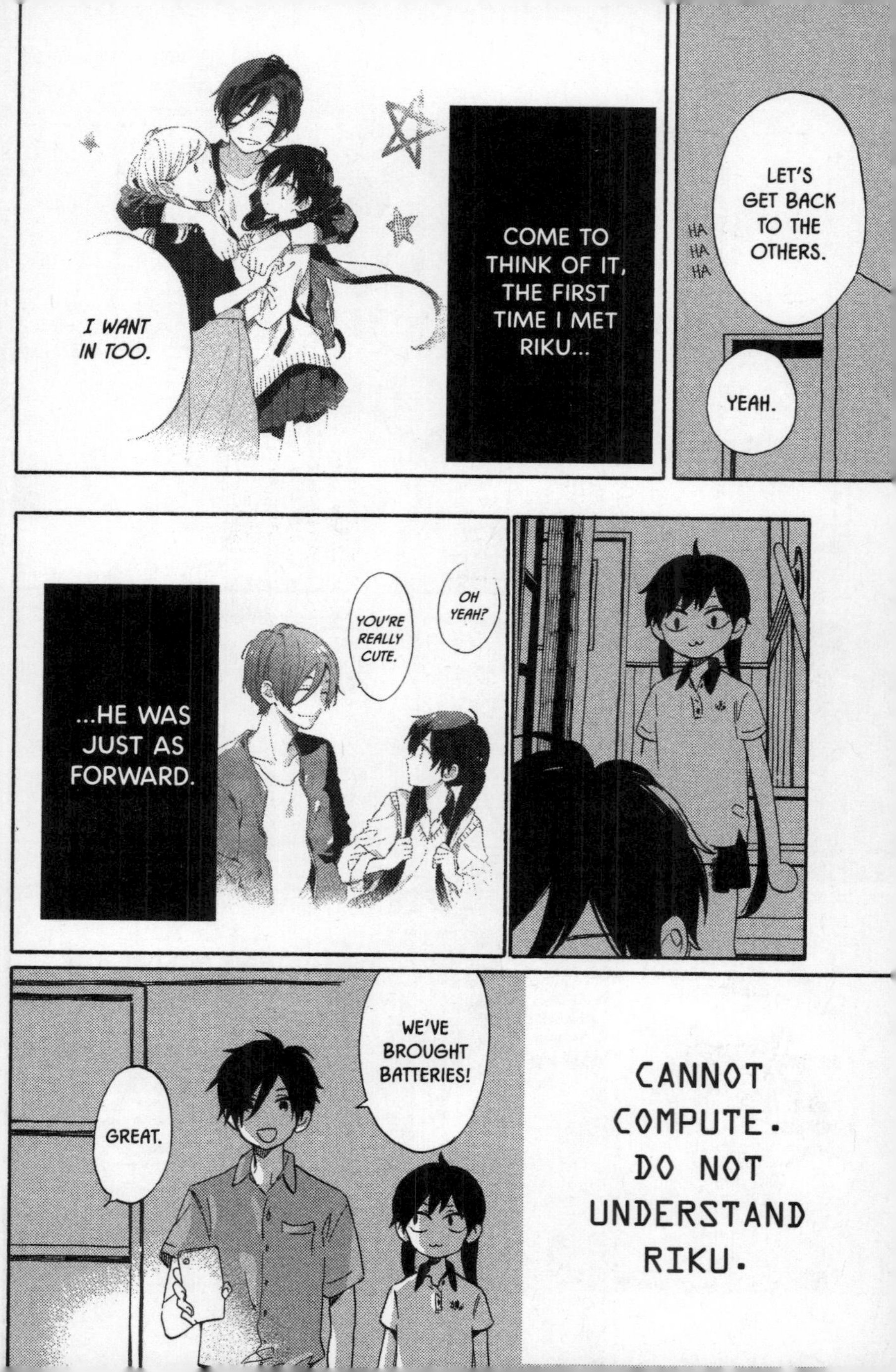
LET'S GET BACK TO THE OTHERS.
HA HA HA
YEAH.
COME TO THINK OF IT, THE FIRST TIME I MET RIKU...
I WANT IN TOO.
OH YEAH?
YOU'RE REALLY CUTE.
...HE WAS JUST AS FORWARD.
CANNOT COMPUTE. DO NOT UNDERSTAND RIKU.
WE'VE BROUGHT BATTERIES!
GREAT.

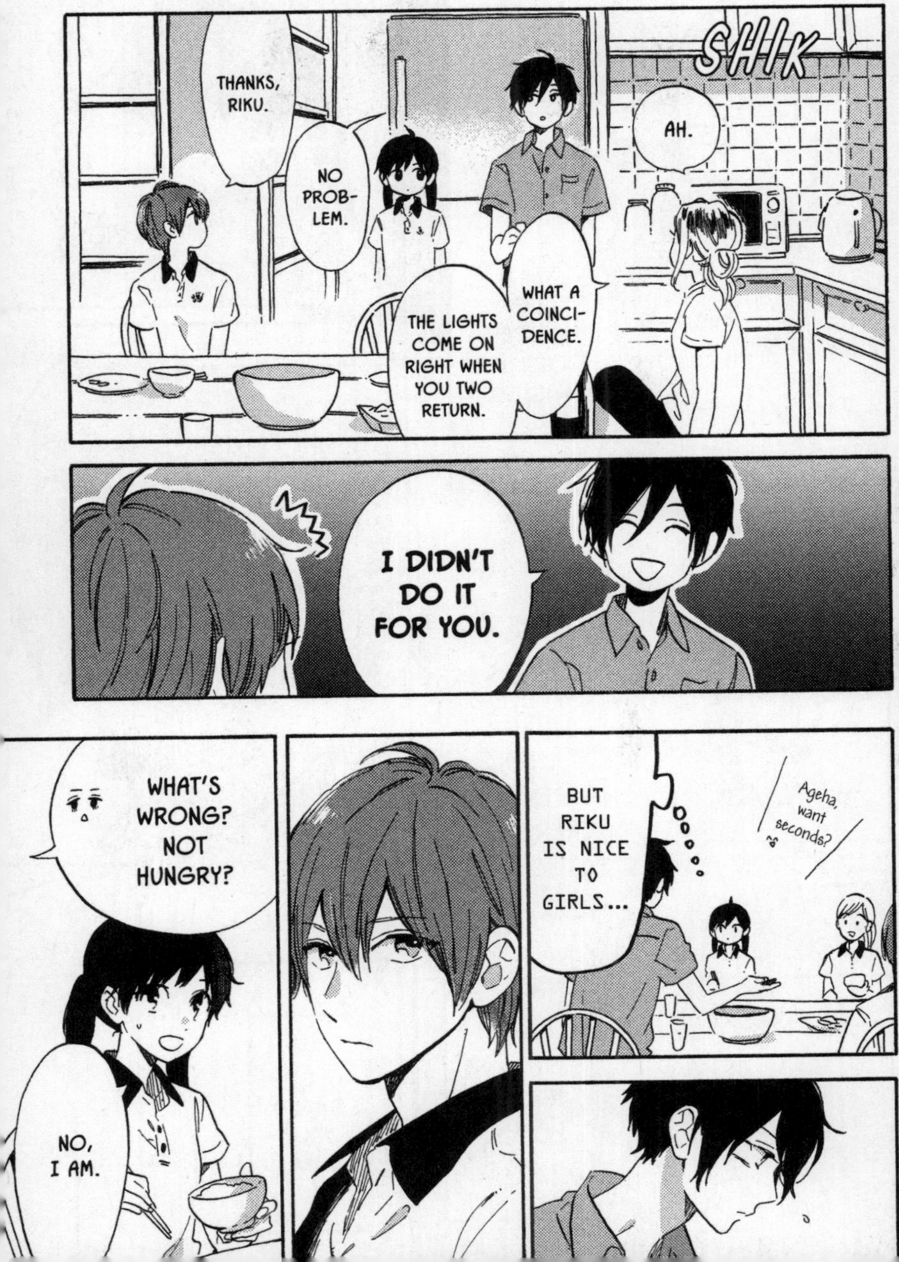
SHIK
AH.
WHAT A COINCIDENCE.
THE LIGHTS COME ON RIGHT WHEN YOU TWO RETURN.
THANKS, RIKU.
NO PROBLEM.
I DIDN'T DO IT FOR YOU.
Ageha, want seconds?
BUT RIKU IS NICE TO GIRLS...
WHAT'S WRONG? NOT HUNGRY?
NO, I AM.

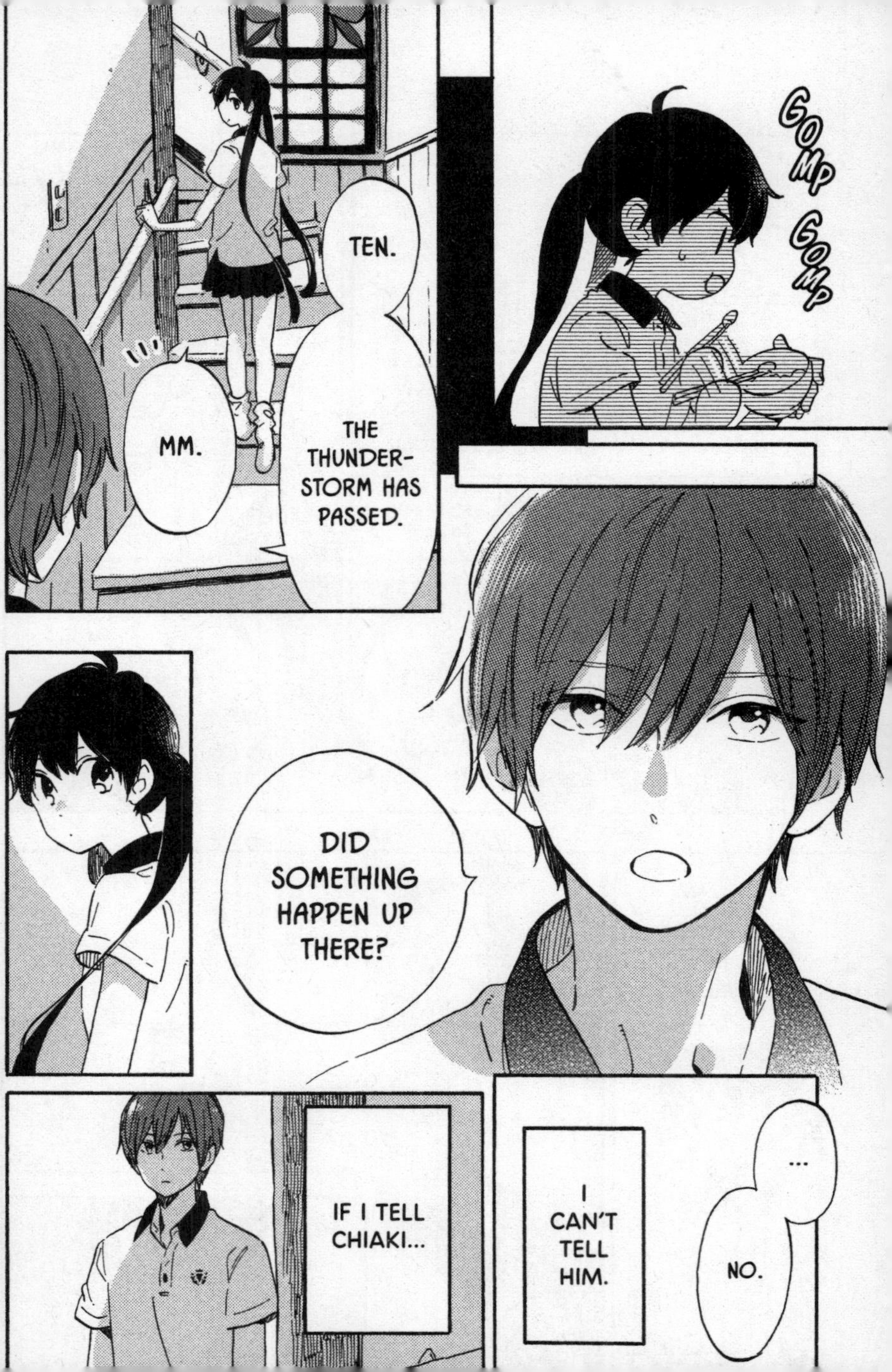
GOMP GOMP
TEN.
THE THUNDER-STORM HAS PASSED.
MM.
DID SOMETHING HAPPEN UP THERE?
...
NO.
I CAN'T TELL HIM.
IF I TELL CHIAKI...

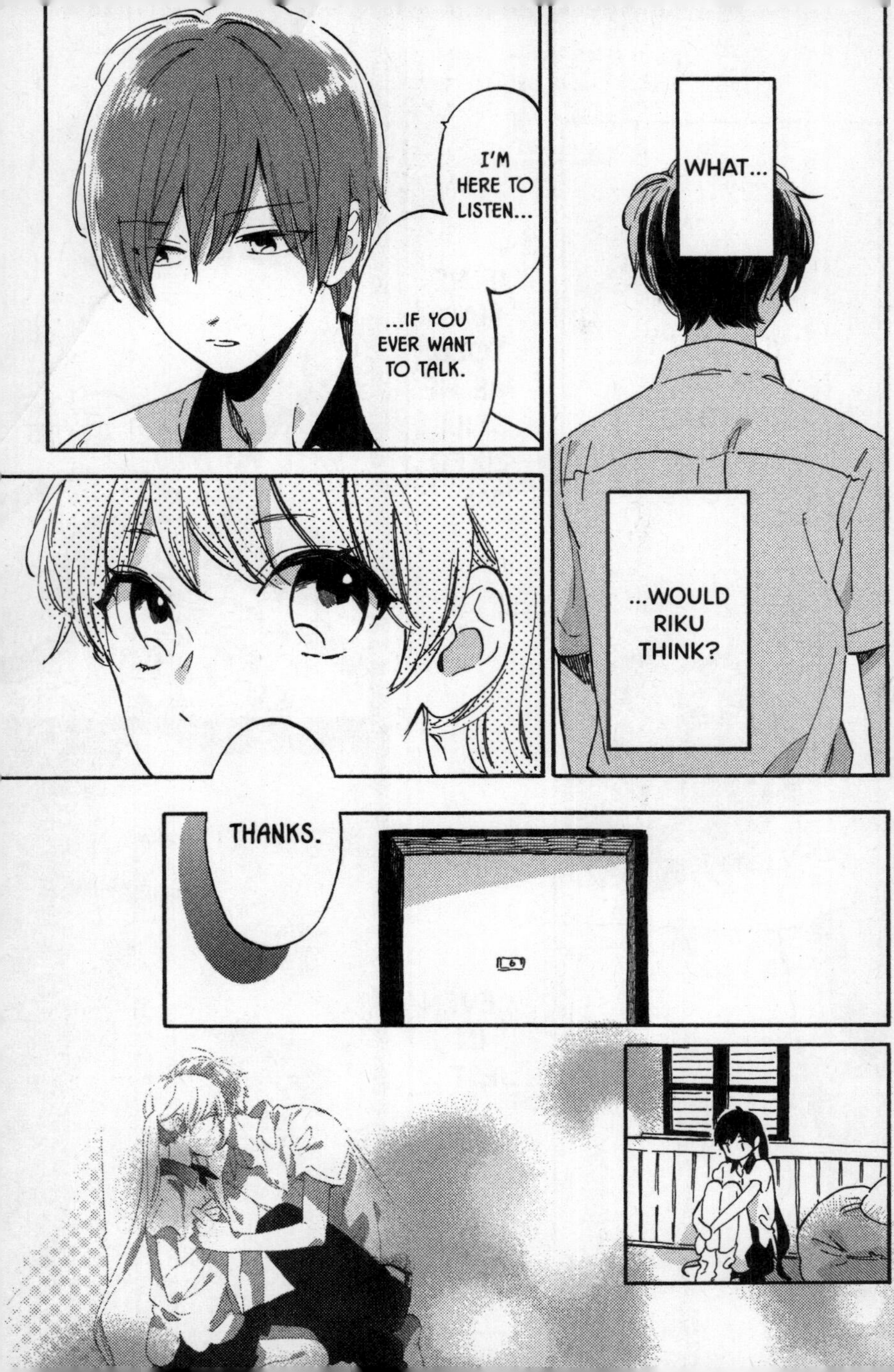
WHAT...
...WOULD RIKU THINK?
I'M HERE TO LISTEN...
...IF YOU EVER WANT TO TALK.
THANKS.

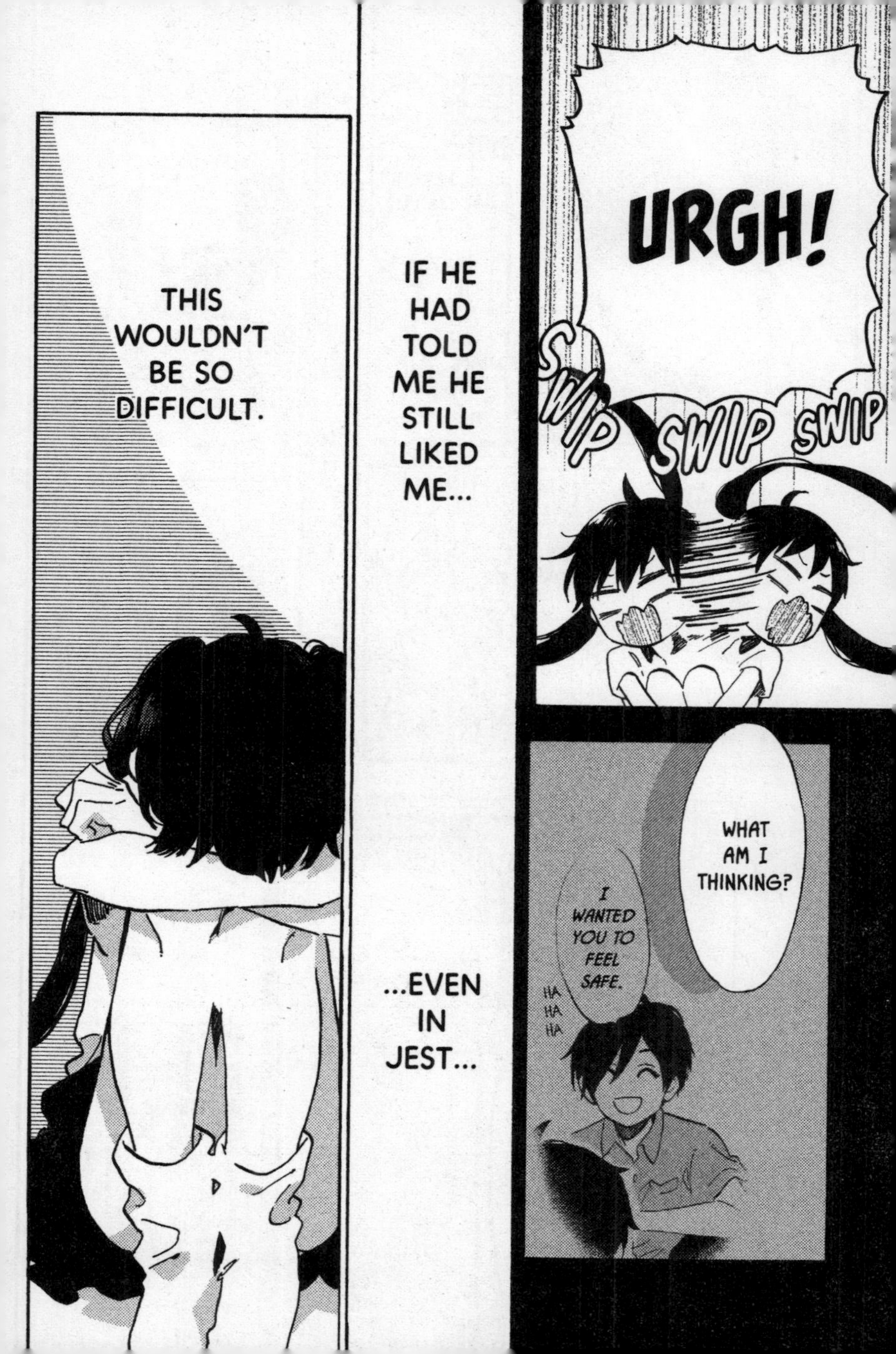
URGH!
SWIP SWIP SWIP
WHAT AM I THINKING?
I WANTED YOU TO FEEL SAFE.
HA HA HA
IF HE HAD TOLD ME HE STILL LIKED ME...
...EVEN IN JEST...
THIS WOULDN'T BE SO DIFFICULT.

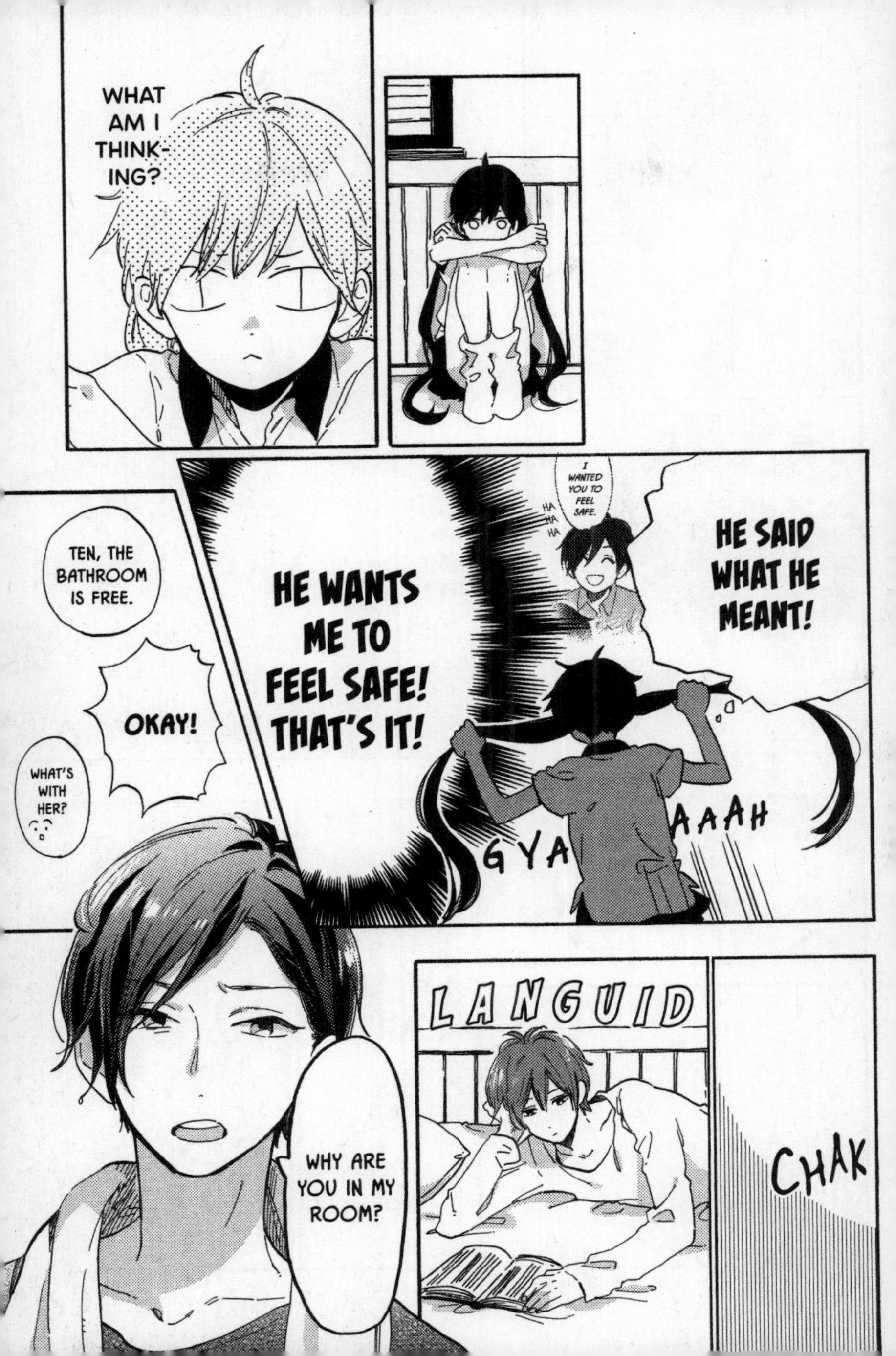
WHAT AM I THINKING?
HA HA HA
I WANTED YOU TO FEEL SAFE.
HE SAID WHAT HE MEANT!
HE WANTS ME TO FEEL SAFE! THAT'S IT!
GYAAAAH
TEN, THE BATHROOM IS FREE.
OKAY!
WHAT'S WITH HER?
CHAK
LANGUID
WHY ARE YOU IN MY ROOM?

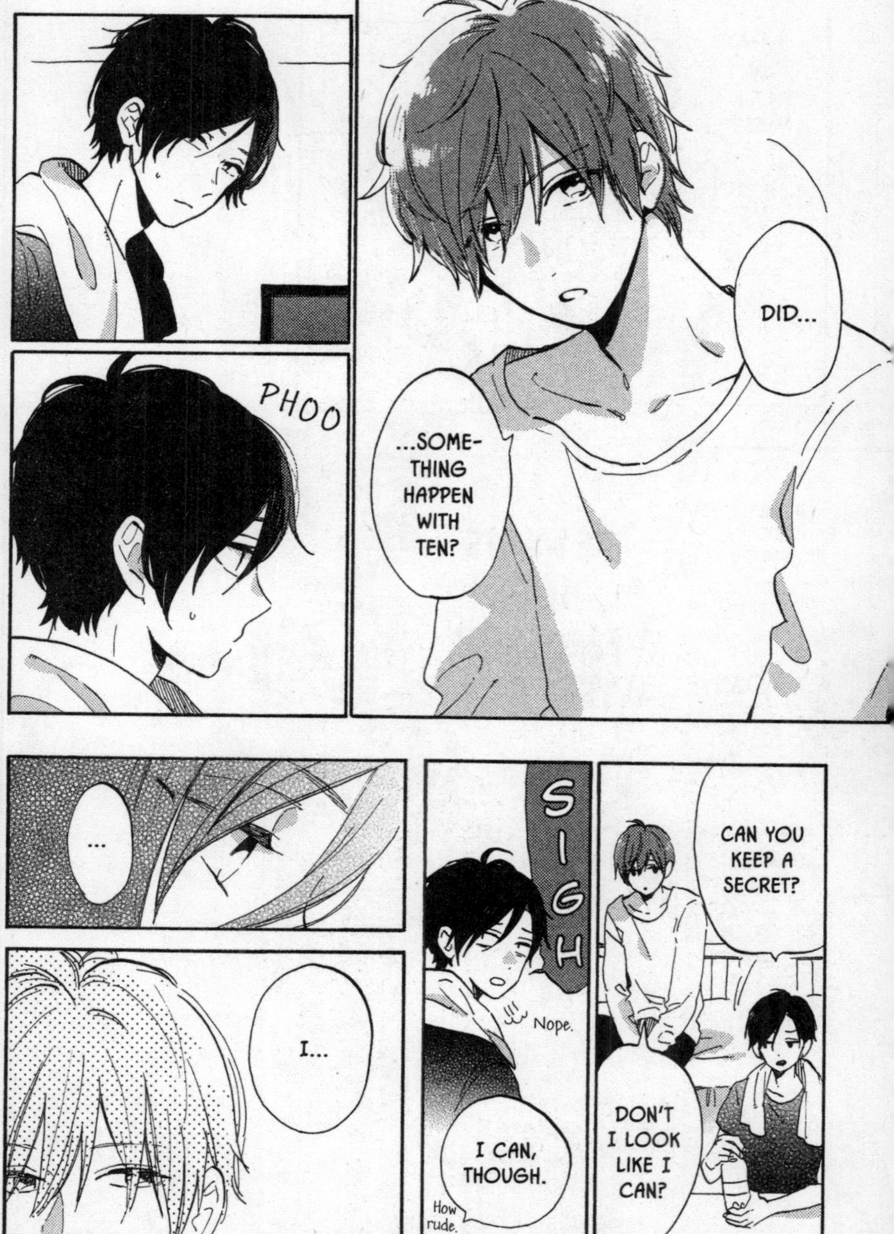
DID...
...SOME-THING HAPPEN WITH TEN?
PHOO
CAN YOU KEEP A SECRET?
DON'T I LOOK LIKE I CAN?
SIGH
Nope.
I CAN, THOUGH.
How rude.
...
I...

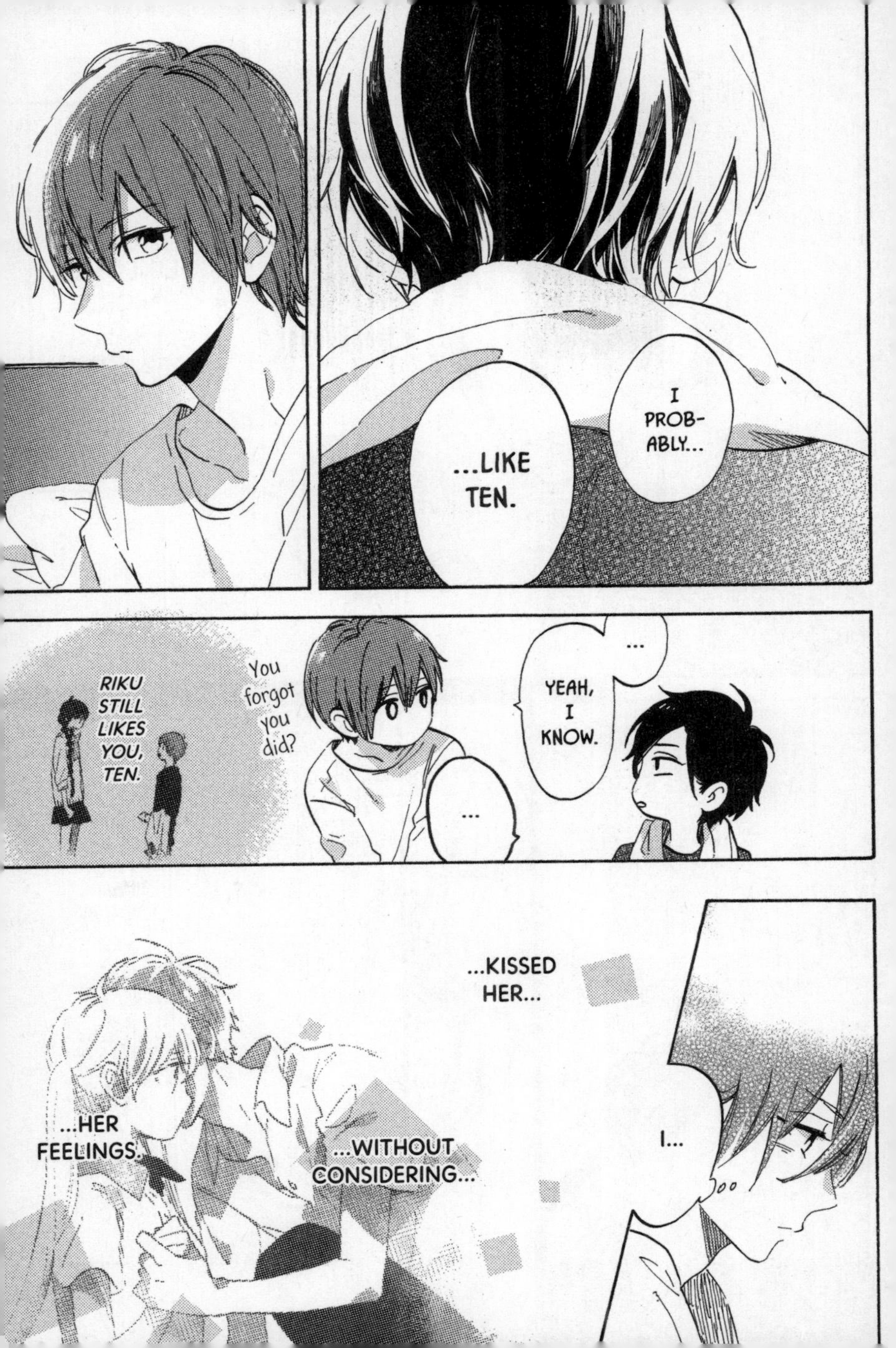
I PROBABLY...
...LIKE TEN.
...
YEAH, I KNOW.
...
You forgot you did?
RIKU STILL LIKES YOU, TEN.
I...
...KISSED HER...
...WITHOUT CONSIDERING...
...HER FEELINGS.

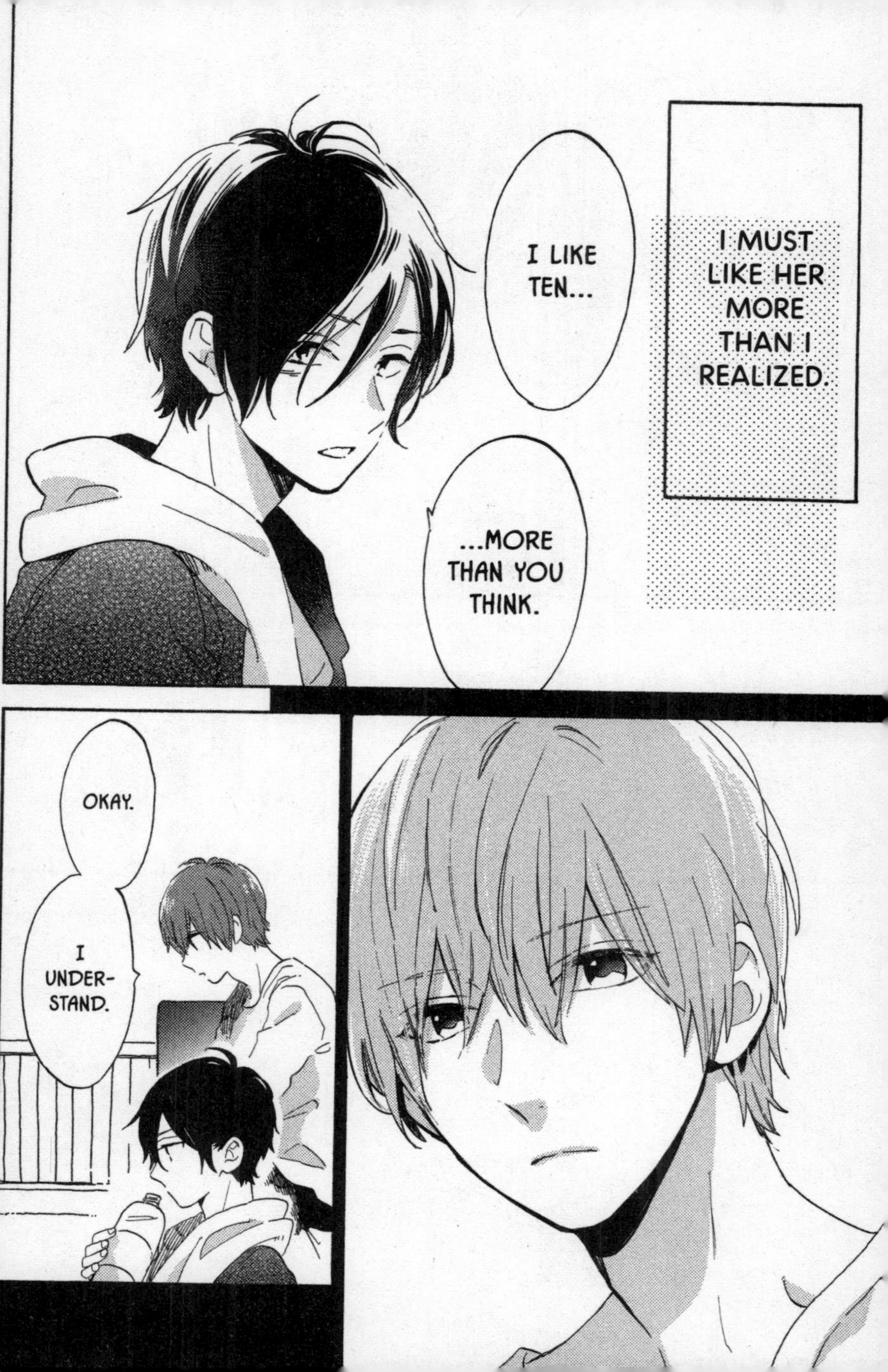
I MUST LIKE HER MORE THAN I REALIZED.
I LIKE TEN...
...MORE THAN YOU THINK.
OKAY.
I UNDER-STAND.

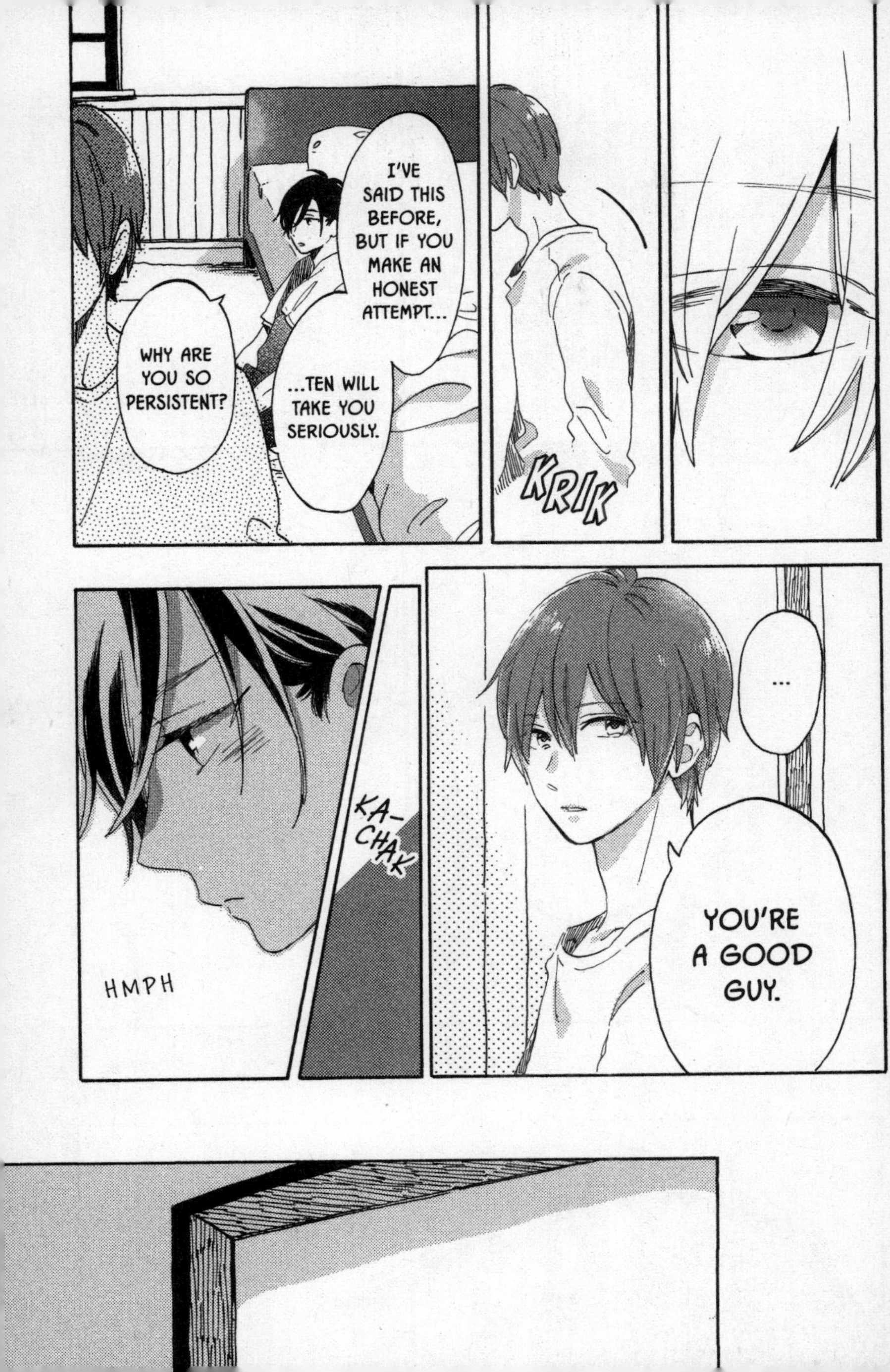
KRIK
I'VE SAID THIS BEFORE, BUT IF YOU MAKE AN HONEST ATTEMPT...
...TEN WILL TAKE YOU SERIOUSLY.
WHY ARE YOU SO PERSISTENT?
...
YOU'RE A GOOD GUY.
KA-CHAK
HMPH

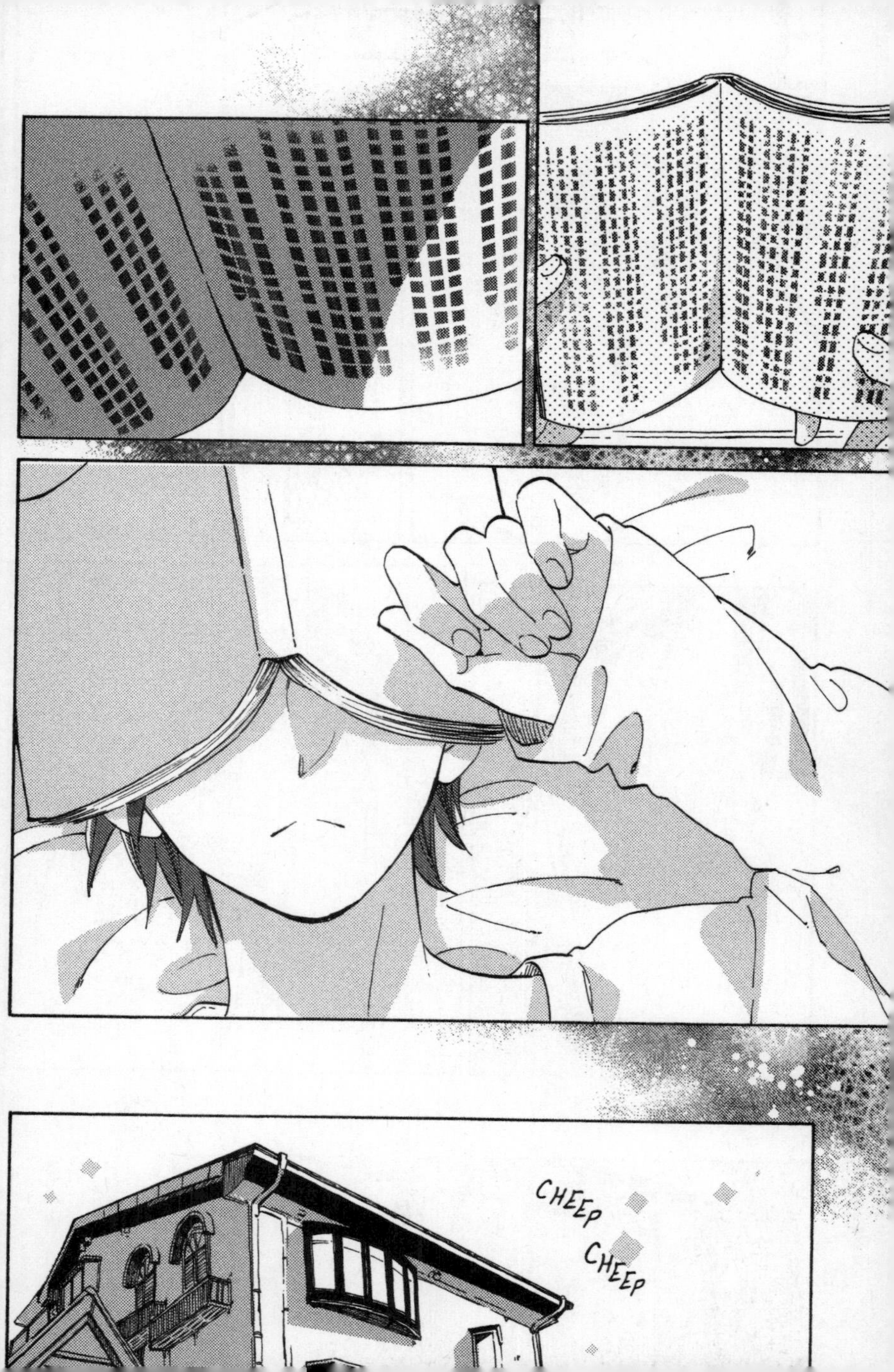
CHEEP
CHEEP

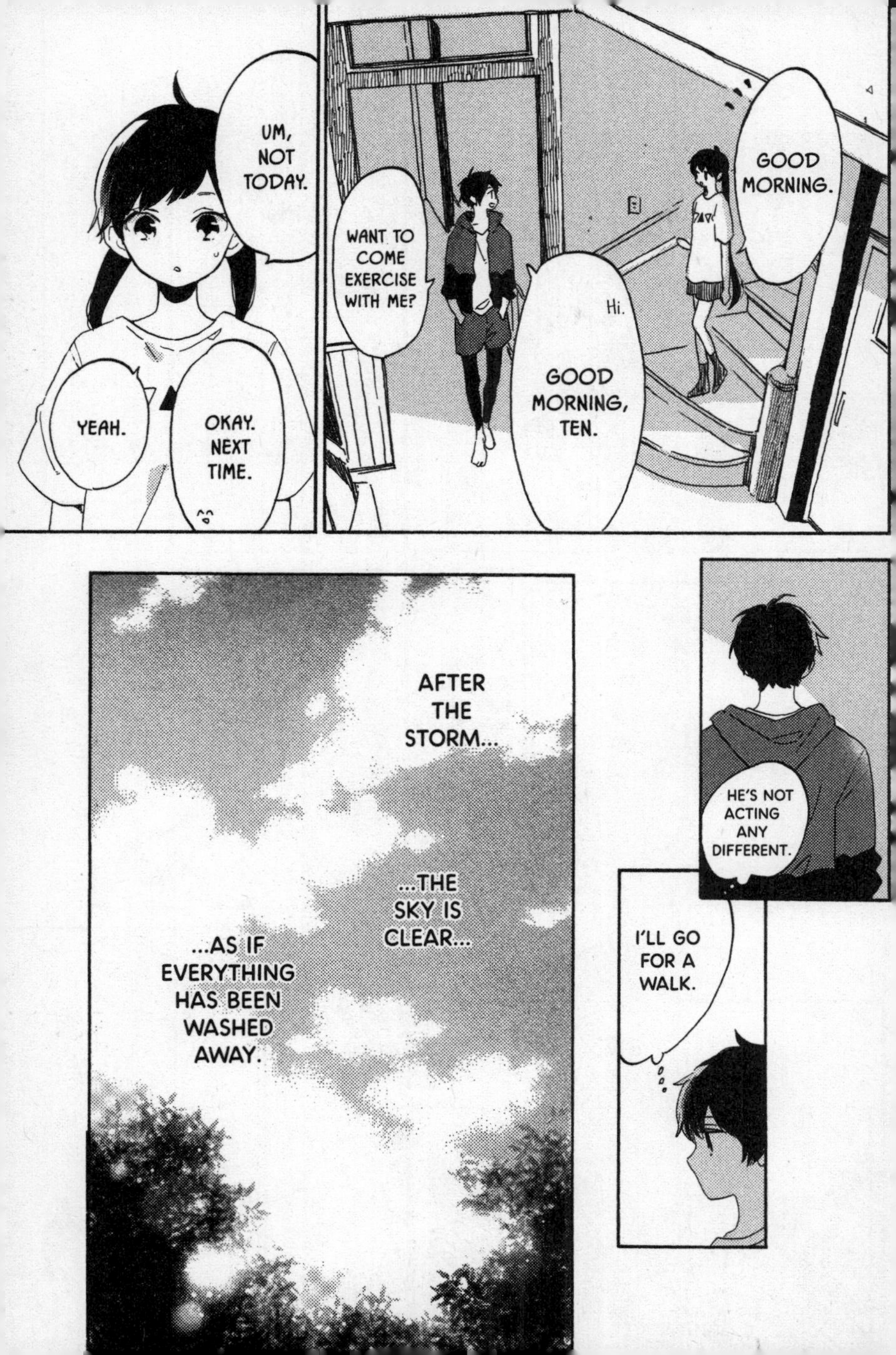
GOOD MORNING.
GOOD MORNING, TEN.
Hi.
WANT TO COME EXERCISE WITH ME?
UM, NOT TODAY.
OKAY. NEXT TIME.
YEAH.
HE'S NOT ACTING ANY DIFFERENT.
I'LL GO FOR A WALK.
AFTER THE STORM...
...THE SKY IS CLEAR...
...AS IF EVERYTHING HAS BEEN WASHED AWAY.

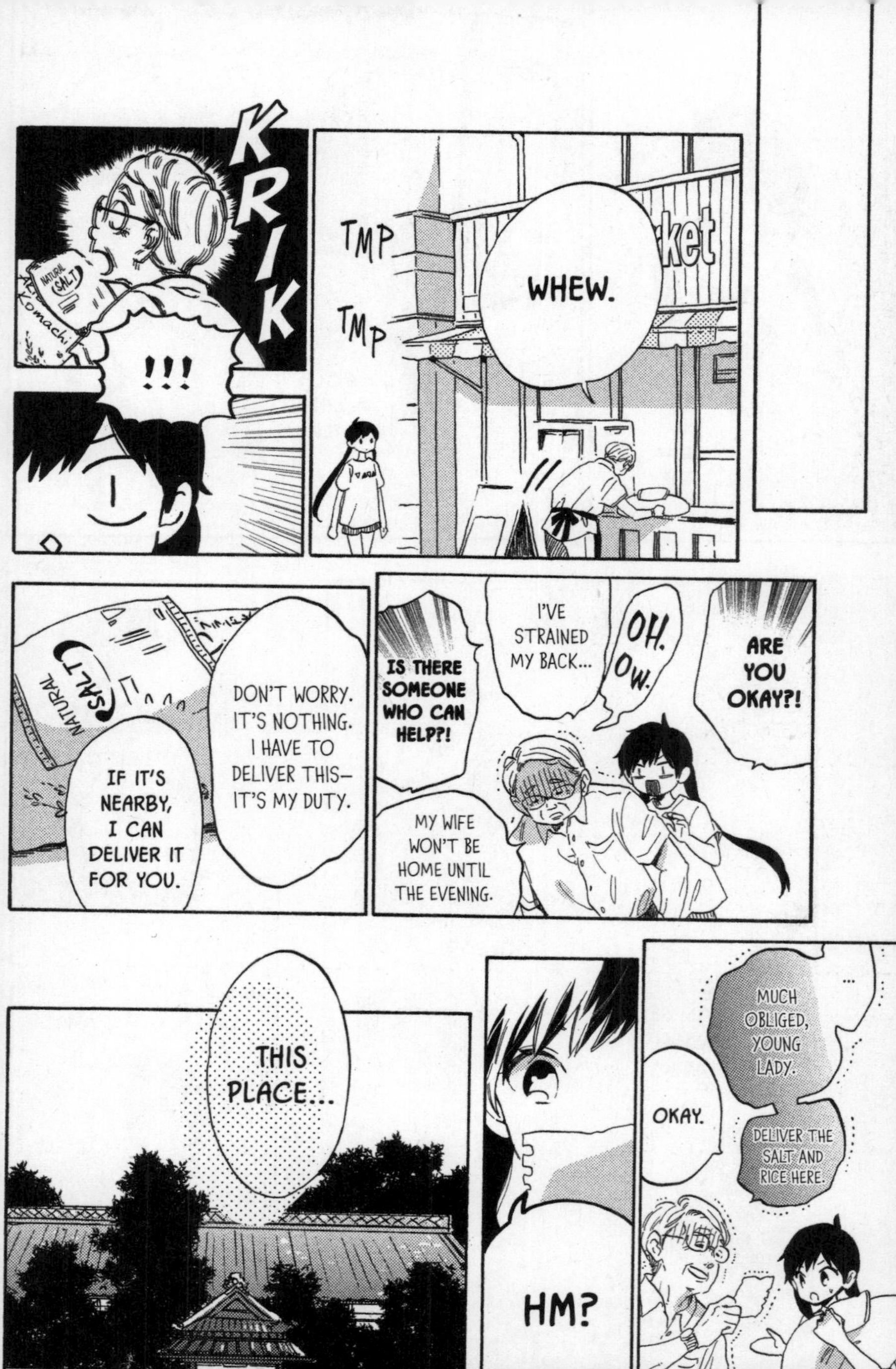

TMP
TMP
WHEW.
KRIK
NATURAL SALT
!!!
ARE YOU OKAY?!
OH. OW.
I'VE STRAINED MY BACK...
IS THERE SOMEONE WHO CAN HELP?!
MY WIFE WON'T BE HOME UNTIL THE EVENING.
DON'T WORRY. IT'S NOTHING. I HAVE TO DELIVER THIS— IT'S MY DUTY.
NATURAL SALT
IF IT'S NEARBY, I CAN DELIVER IT FOR YOU.
...
MUCH OBLIGED, YOUNG LADY.
OKAY.
DELIVER THE SALT AND RICE HERE.
HM?
THIS PLACE...

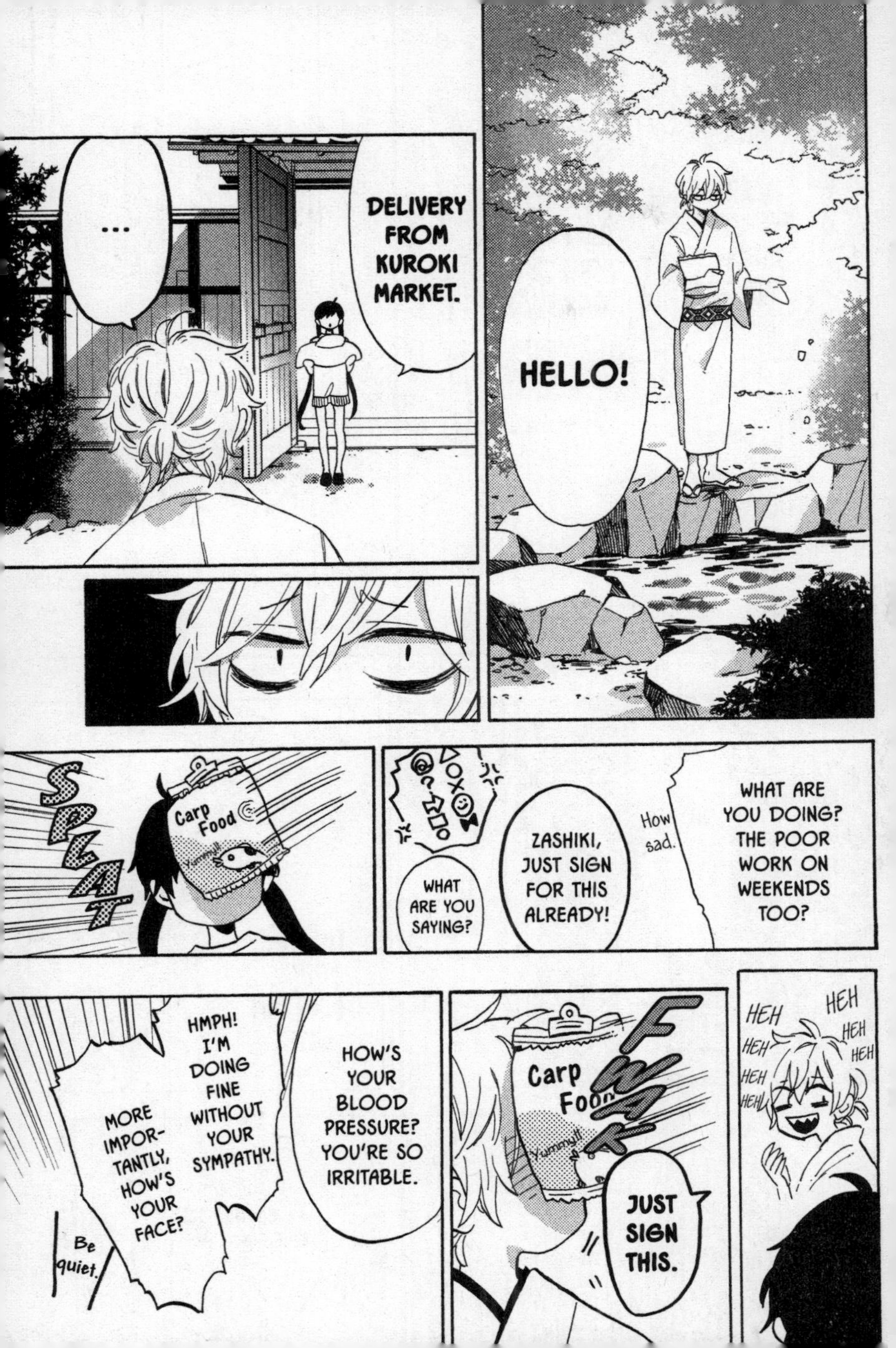
HELLO!
DELIVERY FROM KUROKI MARKET.
...
WHAT ARE YOU DOING? THE POOR WORK ON WEEKENDS TOO?
How sad.
ZASHIKI, JUST SIGN FOR THIS ALREADY!
WHAT ARE YOU SAYING?
SPLAT
Carp Food
Yummy!!
HEH HEH HEH HEH HEH HEH HEH
FWAK
Carp Foo
Yummy!!
JUST SIGN THIS.
HOW'S YOUR BLOOD PRESSURE? YOU'RE SO IRRITABLE.
HMPH! I'M DOING FINE WITHOUT YOUR SYMPATHY.
MORE IMPORTANTLY, HOW'S YOUR FACE?
Be quiet.

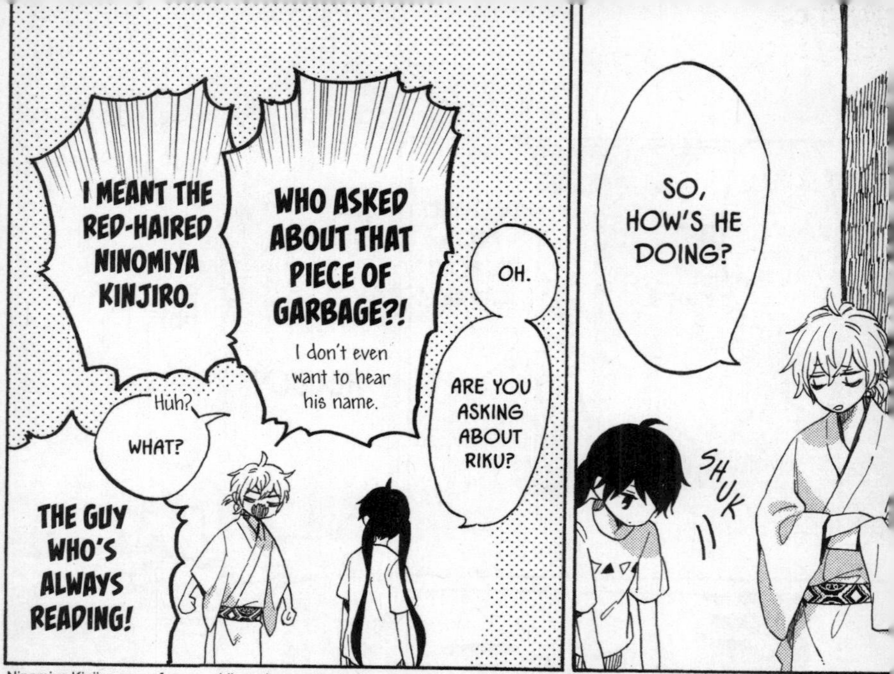
SO, HOW'S HE DOING?
SHUK
OH.
ARE YOU ASKING ABOUT RIKU?
WHO ASKED ABOUT THAT PIECE OF GARBAGE?!
I don't even want to hear his name.
I MEANT THE RED-HAIRED NINOMIYA KINJIRO.
Huh?
WHAT?
THE GUY WHO'S ALWAYS READING!

Ninomiya Kinjiro was a famous philosopher and agricultural leader who is usually depicted reading a book.

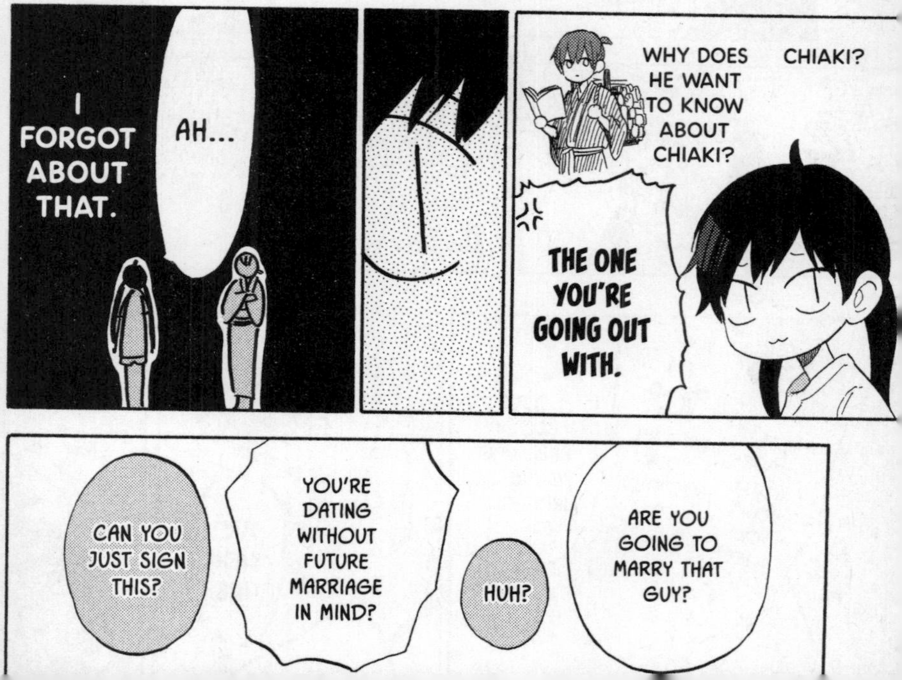
CHIAKI?
WHY DOES HE WANT TO KNOW ABOUT CHIAKI?
THE ONE YOU'RE GOING OUT WITH.
AH...
I FORGOT ABOUT THAT.
ARE YOU GOING TO MARRY THAT GUY?
HUH?
YOU'RE DATING WITHOUT FUTURE MARRIAGE IN MIND?
CAN YOU JUST SIGN THIS?

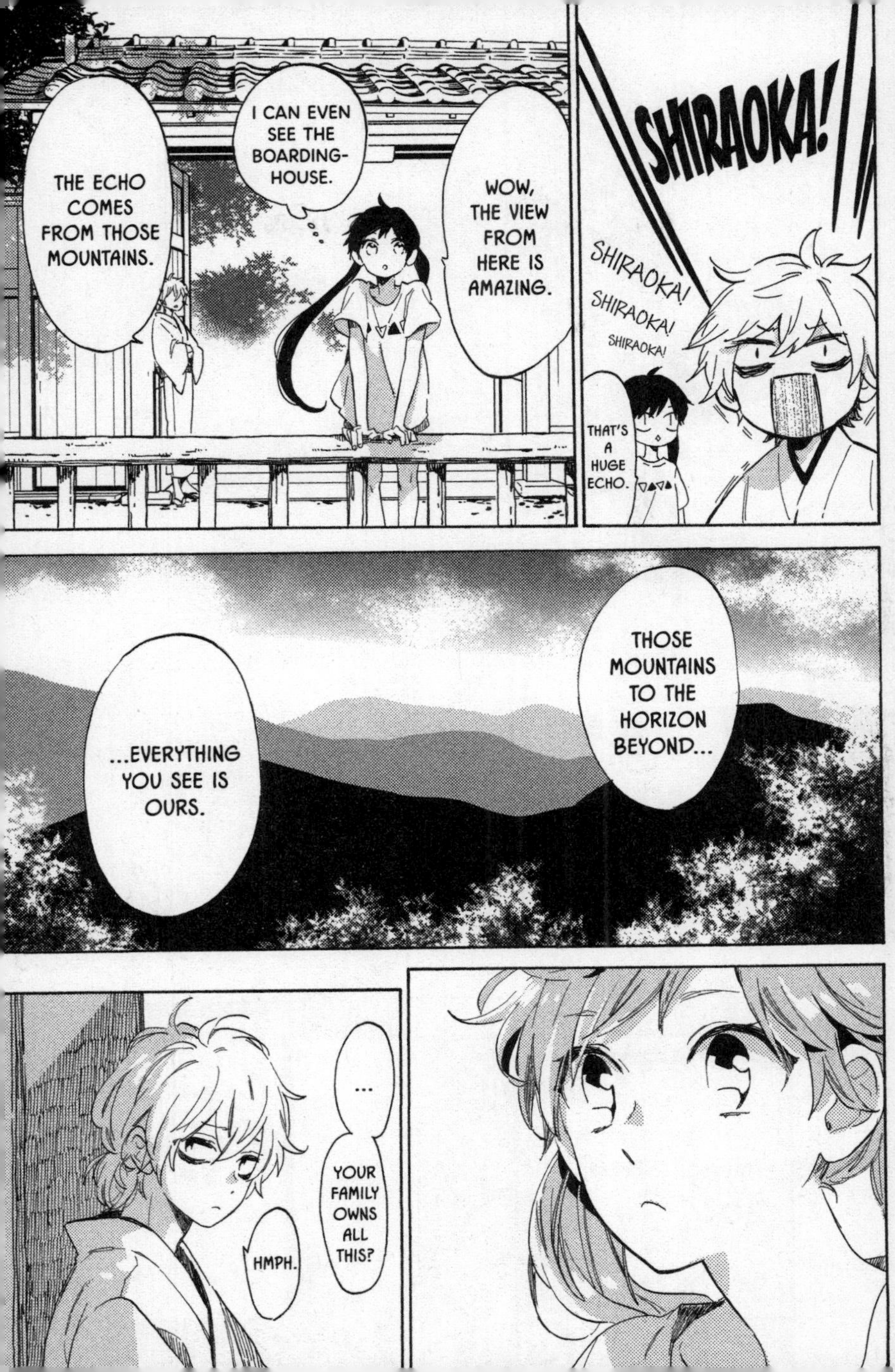
SHIRAOKA!
SHIRAOKA!
SHIRAOKA!
SHIRAOKA!
THAT'S A HUGE ECHO.
WOW, THE VIEW FROM HERE IS AMAZING.
I CAN EVEN SEE THE BOARDING-HOUSE.
THE ECHO COMES FROM THOSE MOUNTAINS.
THOSE MOUNTAINS TO THE HORIZON BEYOND...
...EVERYTHING YOU SEE IS OURS.
...
YOUR FAMILY OWNS ALL THIS?
HMPH.

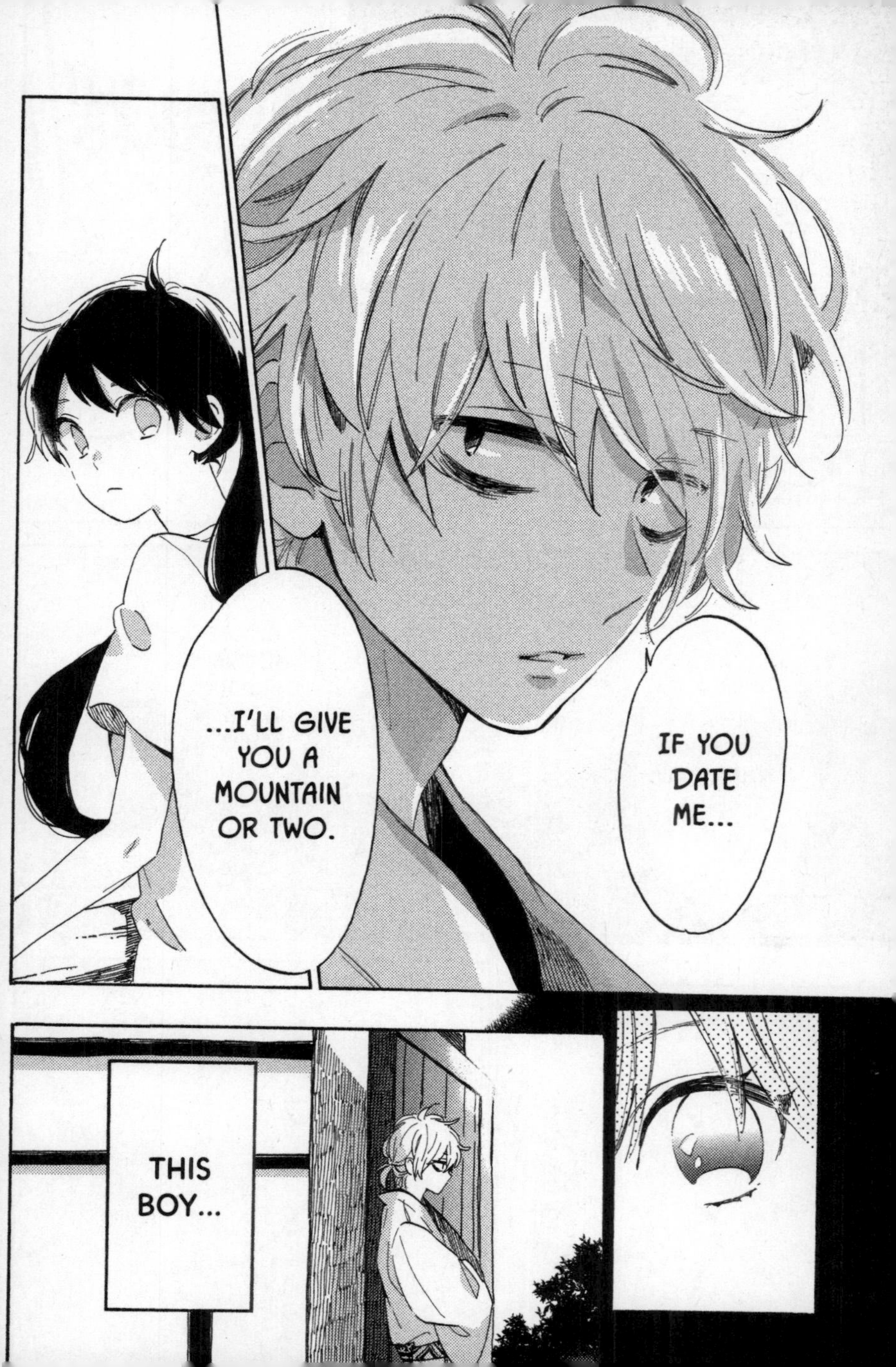
IF YOU DATE ME...
...I'LL GIVE YOU A MOUNTAIN OR TWO.
THIS BOY...

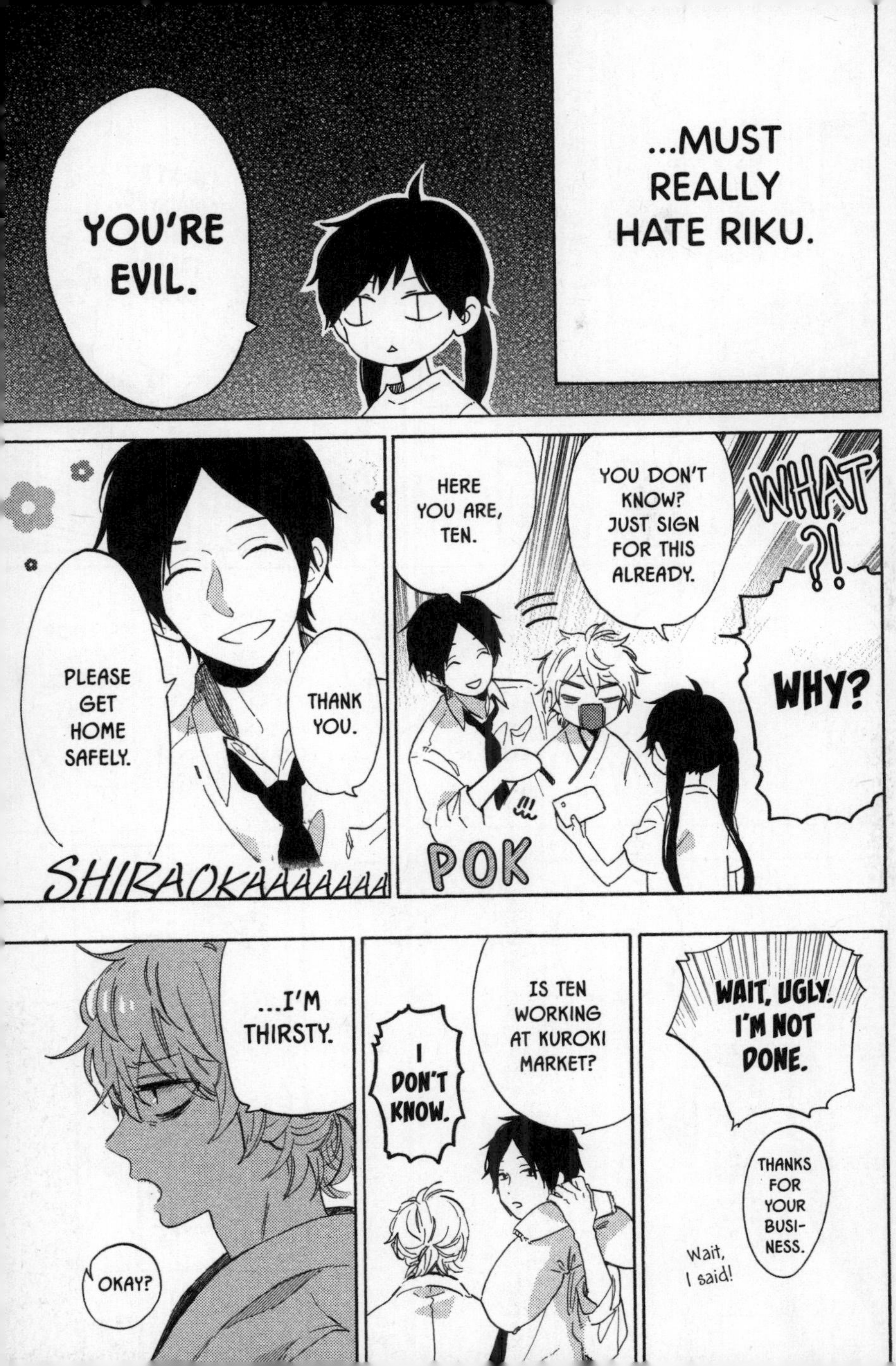
...MUST REALLY HATE RIKU.
YOU'RE EVIL.
WHAT?!
YOU DON'T KNOW? JUST SIGN FOR THIS ALREADY.
HERE YOU ARE, TEN.
WHY?
!!!
POK
THANK YOU.
PLEASE GET HOME SAFELY.
SHIRAOKAAAAAAA
WAIT, UGLY. I'M NOT DONE.
THANKS FOR YOUR BUSI-NESS.
Wait, I said!
IS TEN WORKING AT KUROKI MARKET?
I DON'T KNOW.
...I'M THIRSTY.
OKAY?

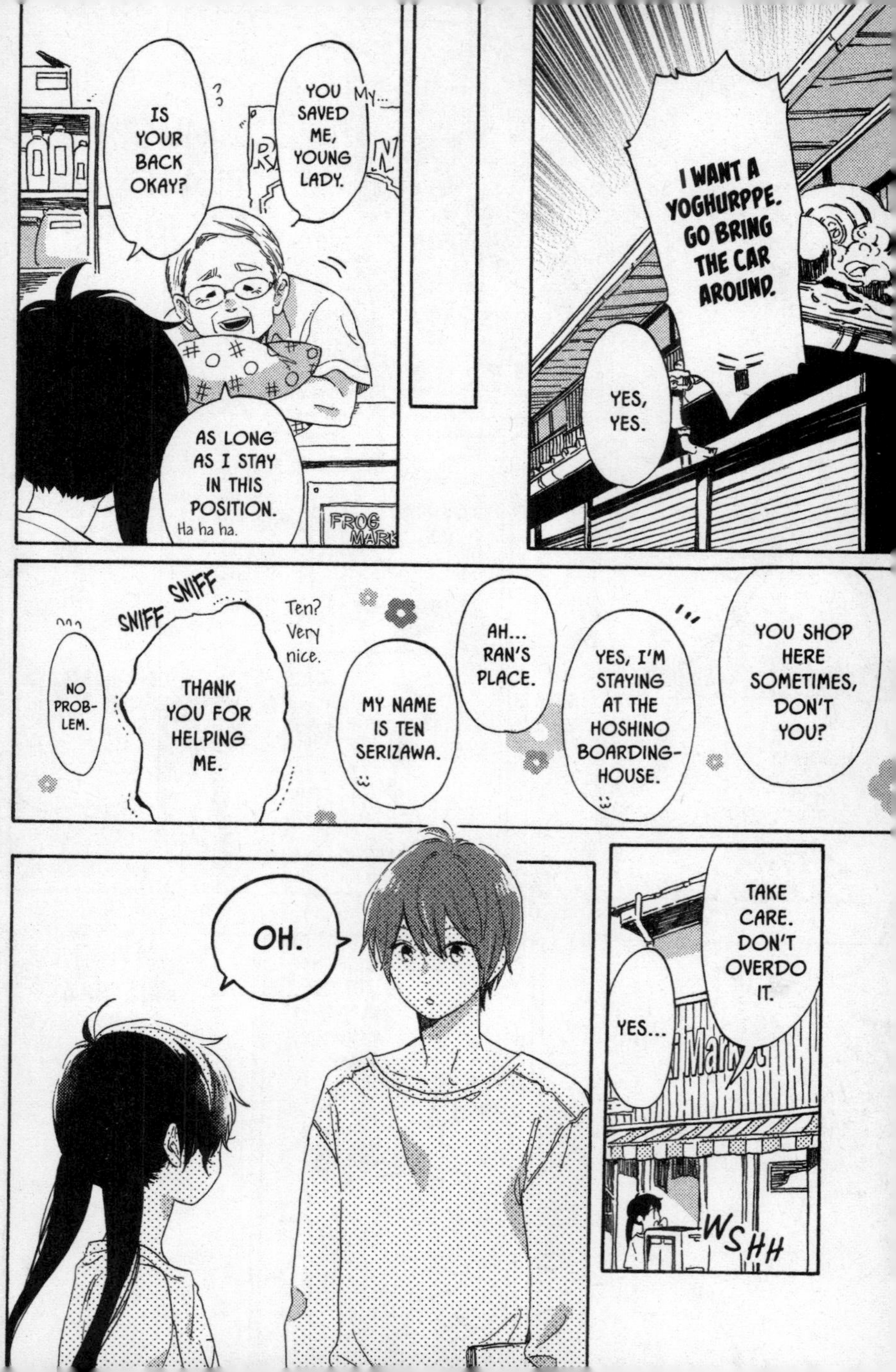
I WANT A YOGHURPPE. GO BRING THE CAR AROUND.
YES, YES.
YOU SAVED ME, YOUNG LADY.
My...
IS YOUR BACK OKAY?
AS LONG AS I STAY IN THIS POSITION.
Ha ha ha.
YOU SHOP HERE SOMETIMES, DON'T YOU?
YES, I'M STAYING AT THE HOSHINO BOARDING-HOUSE.
AH... RAN'S PLACE.
MY NAME IS TEN SERIZAWA.
Ten? Very nice.
SNIFF SNIFF
THANK YOU FOR HELPING ME.
NO PROB-LEM.
TAKE CARE. DON'T OVERDO IT.
YES...
WSHH
OH.

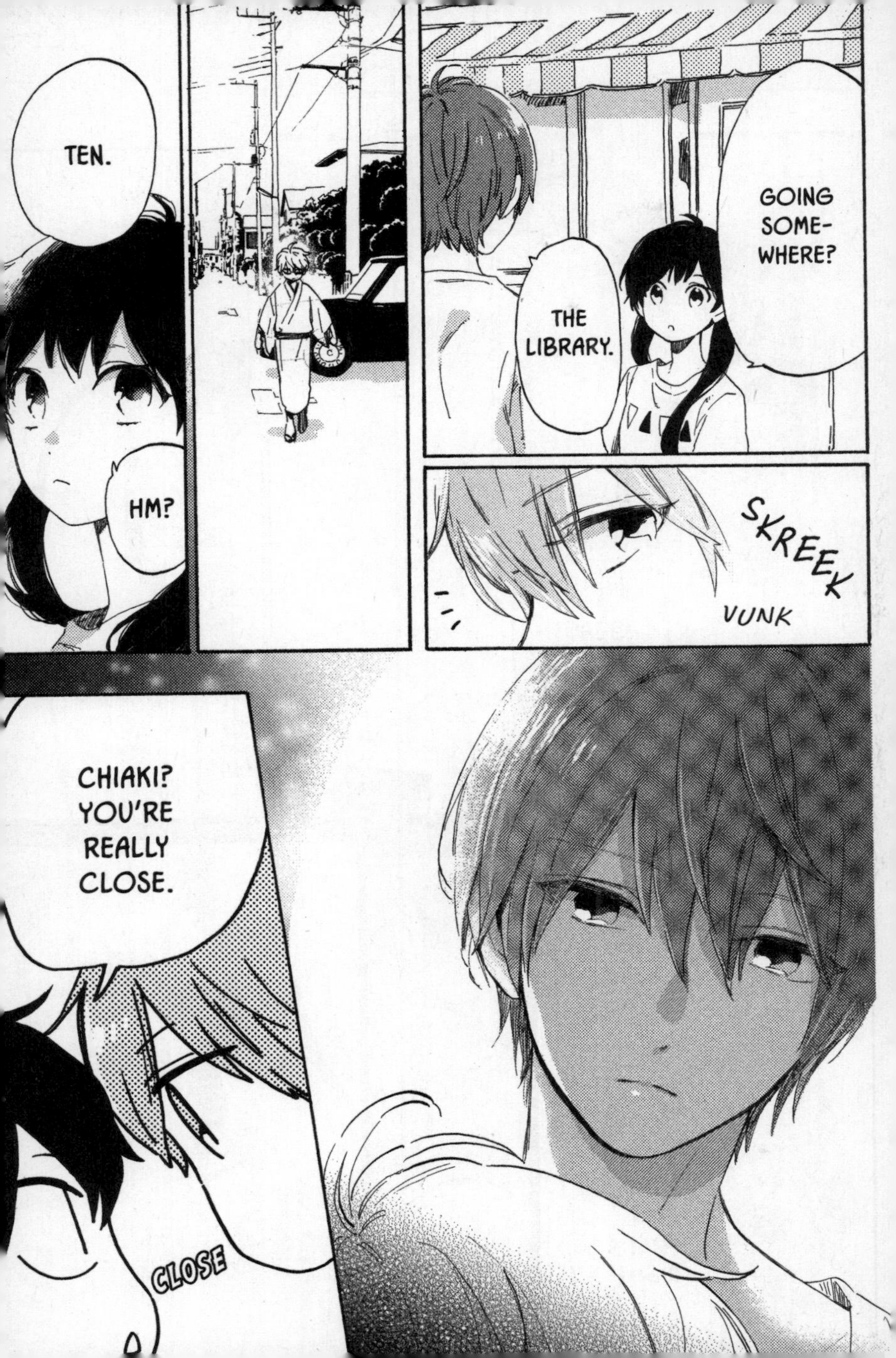
GOING SOME-WHERE?
THE LIBRARY.
SKREEK
VUNK
TEN.
HM?
CHIAKI? YOU'RE REALLY CLOSE.
CLOSE

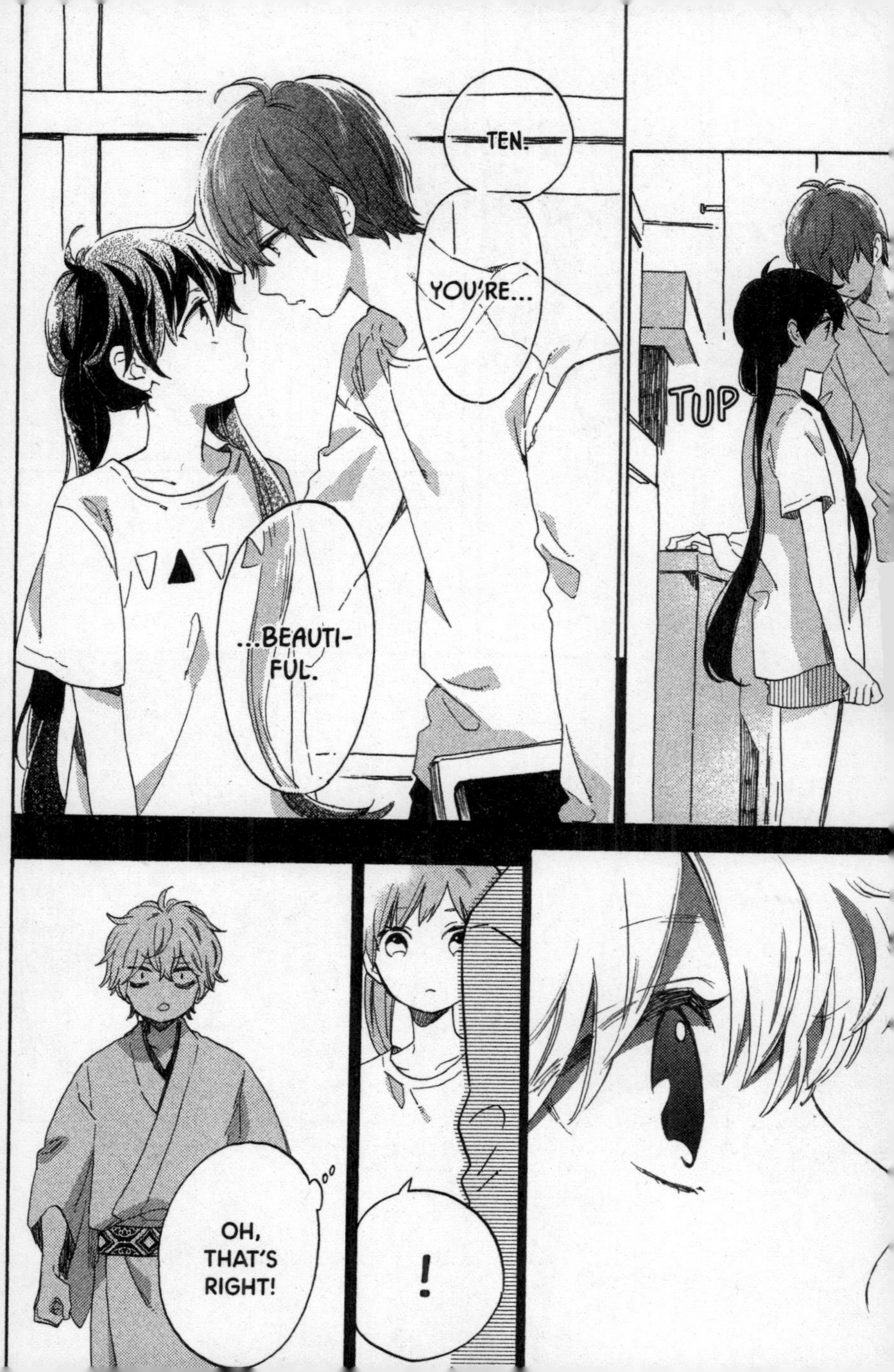
TUP
TEN.
YOU'RE...
...BEAUTI-
FUL.
!
OH,
THAT'S
RIGHT!

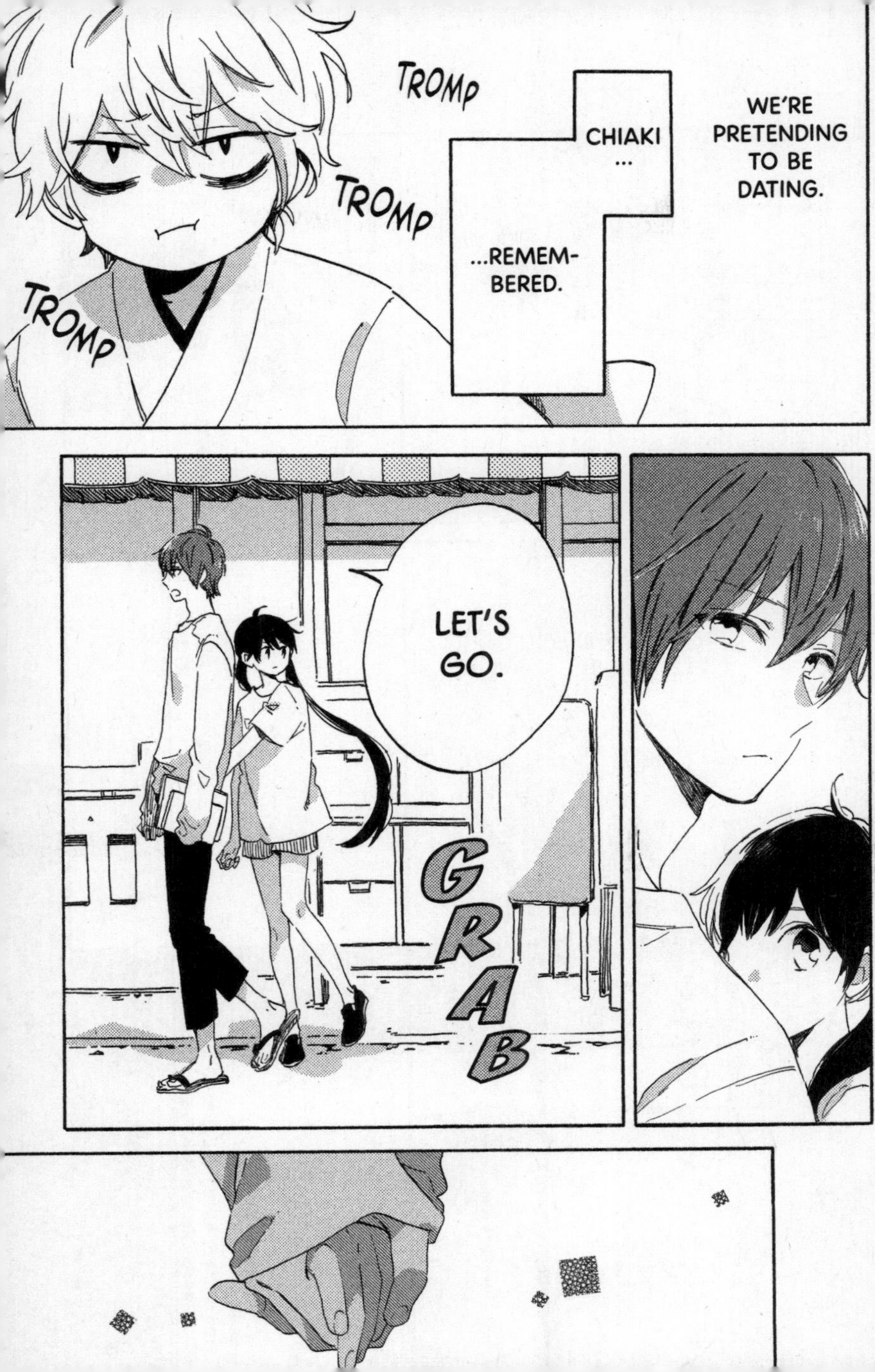
WE'RE PRETENDING TO BE DATING.
CHIAKI ...
...REMEM-BERED.
TROMP
TROMP
TROMP
LET'S GO.
GRAB

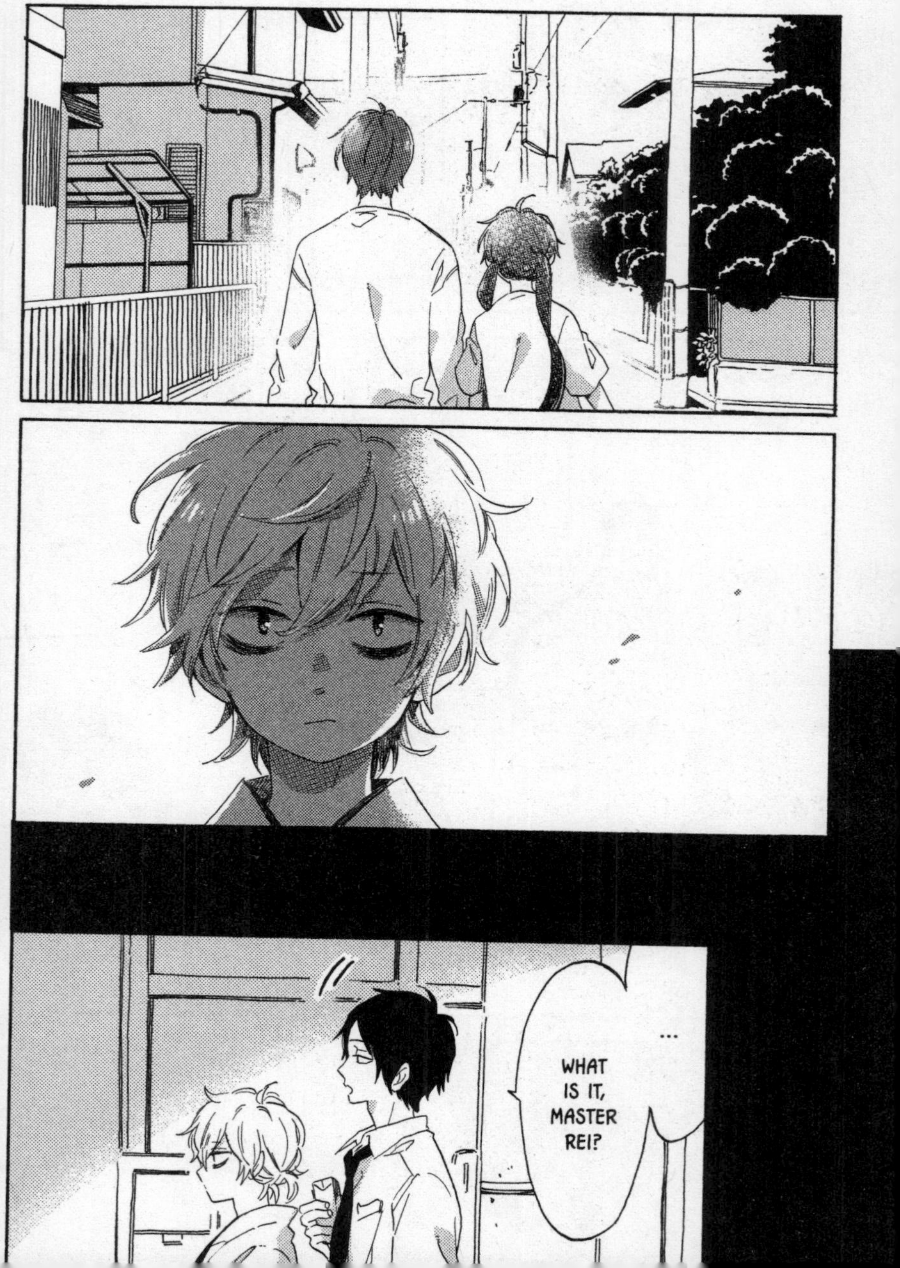

...
WHAT IS IT, MASTER REI?

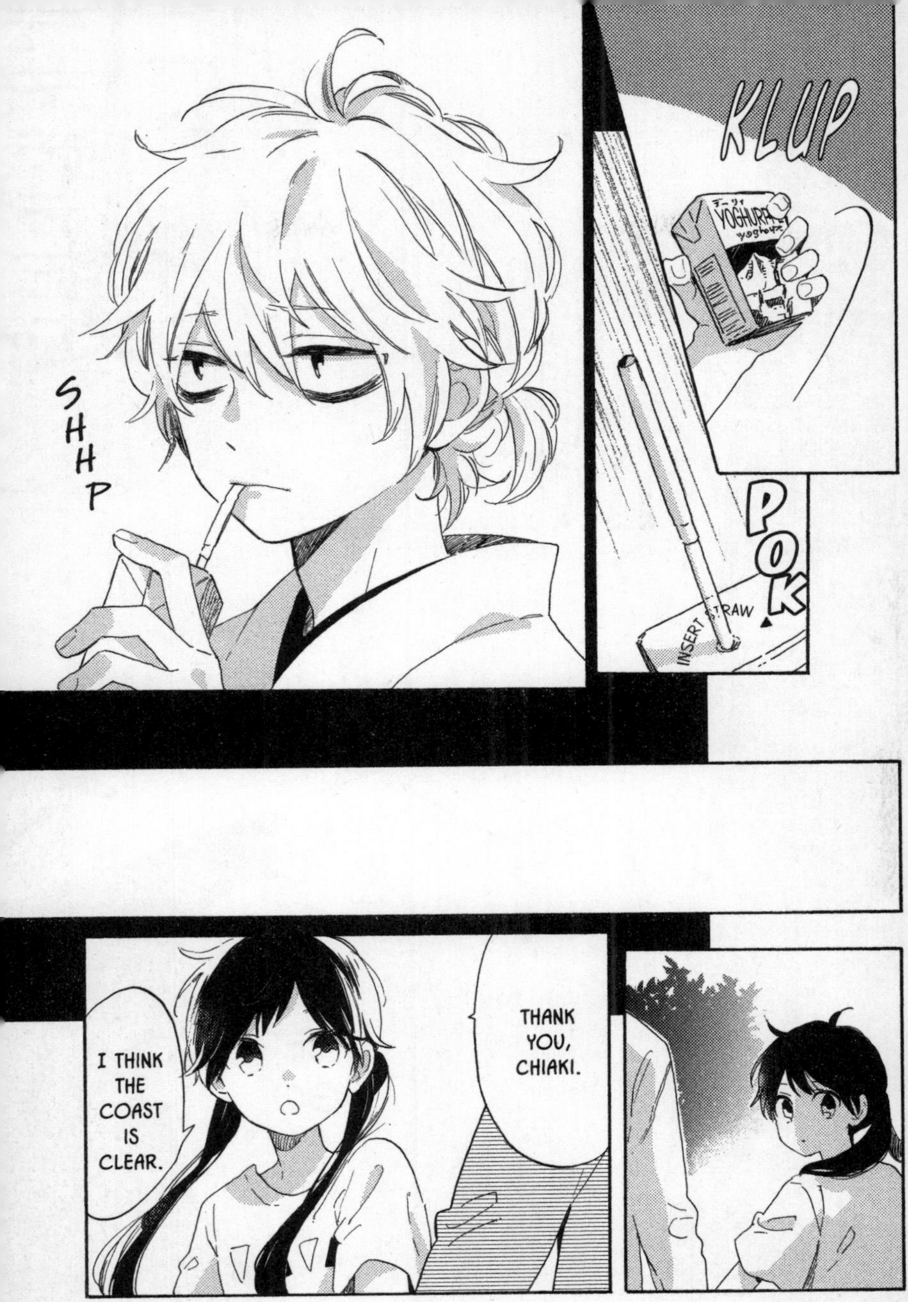
KLUP
POK
INSERT STRAW
SHHP
THANK YOU, CHIAKI.
I THINK THE COAST IS CLEAR.

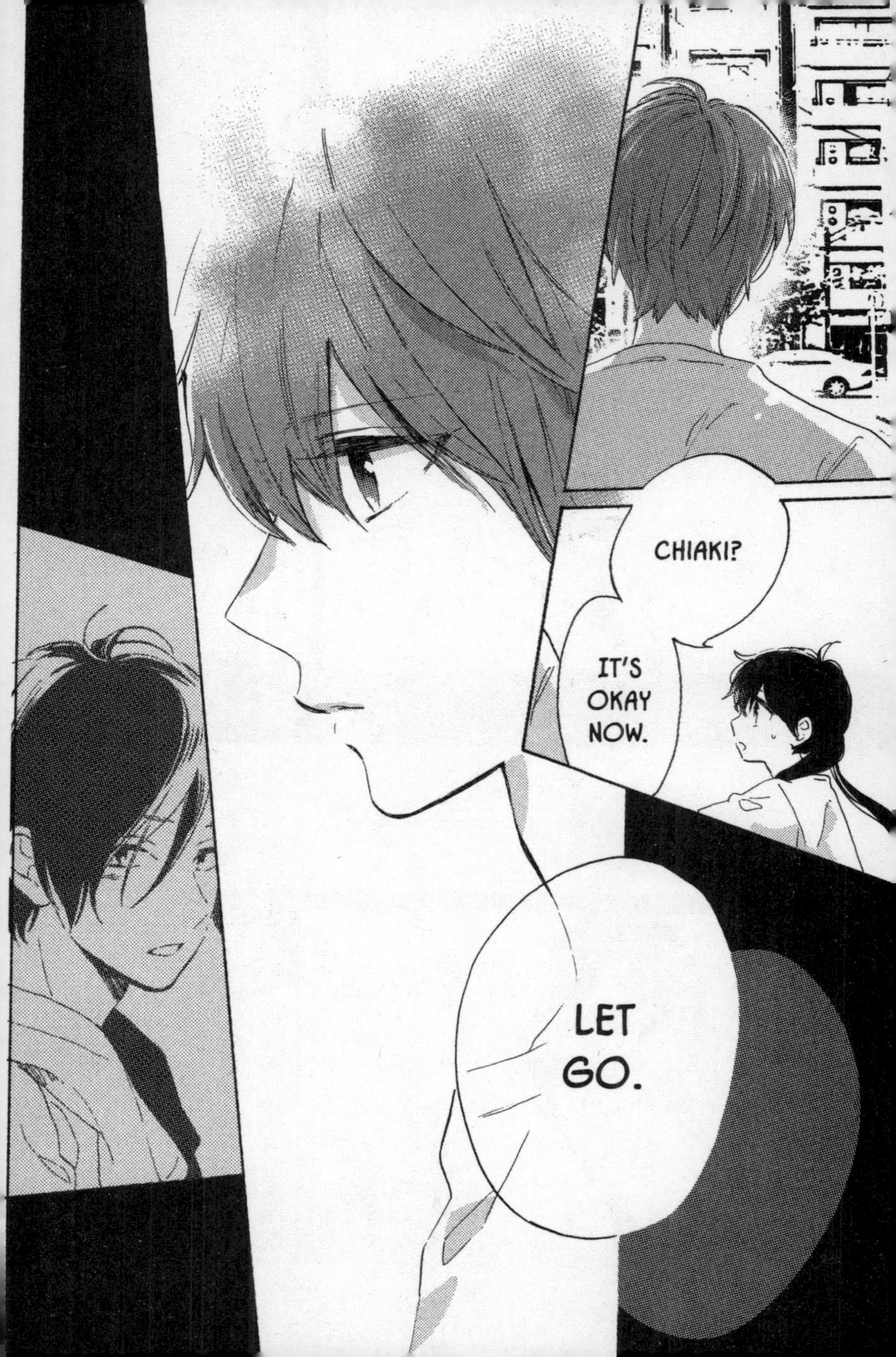
CHIAKI?
IT'S OKAY NOW.
LET GO.

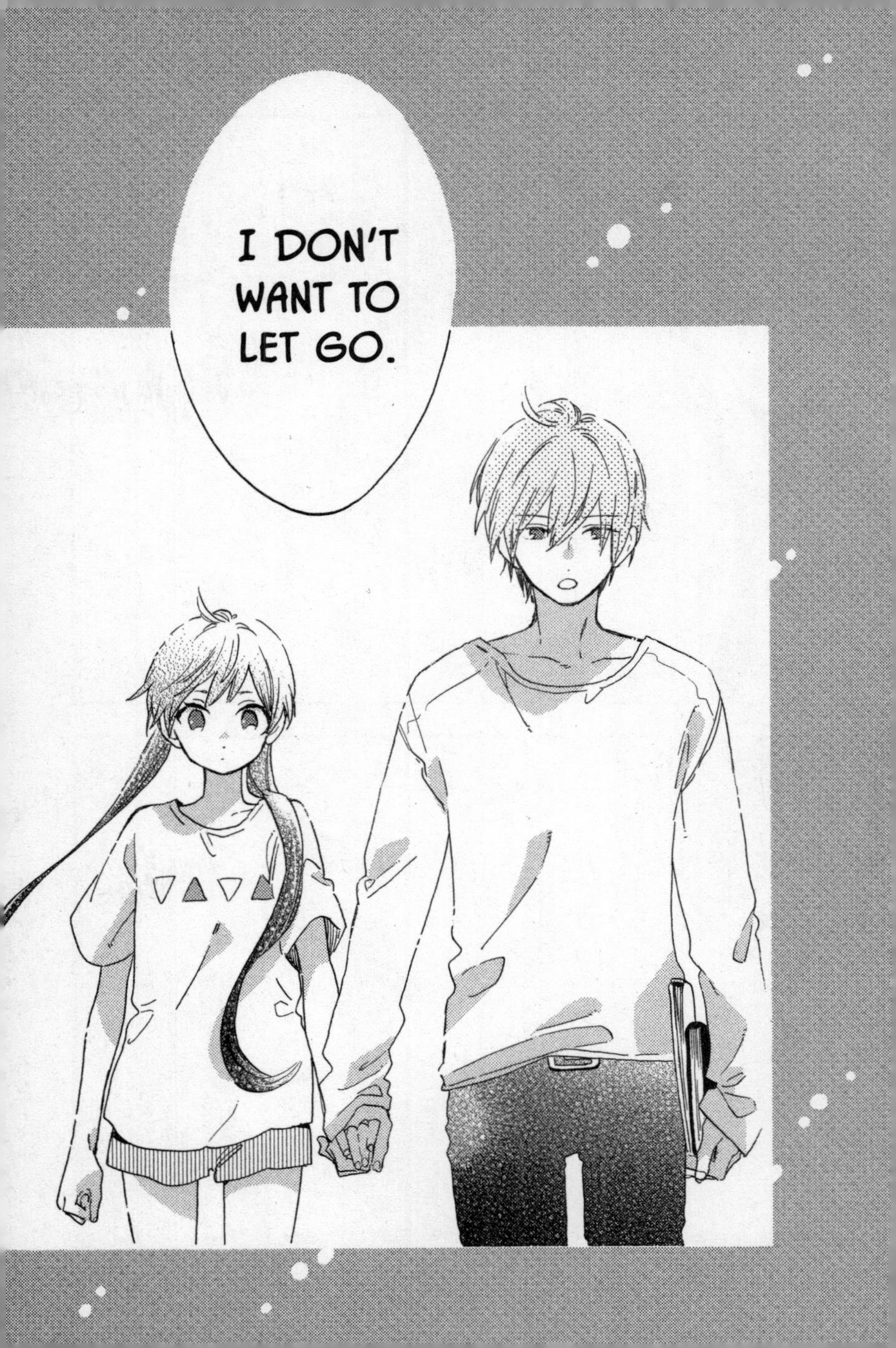
I DON'T WANT TO LET GO.

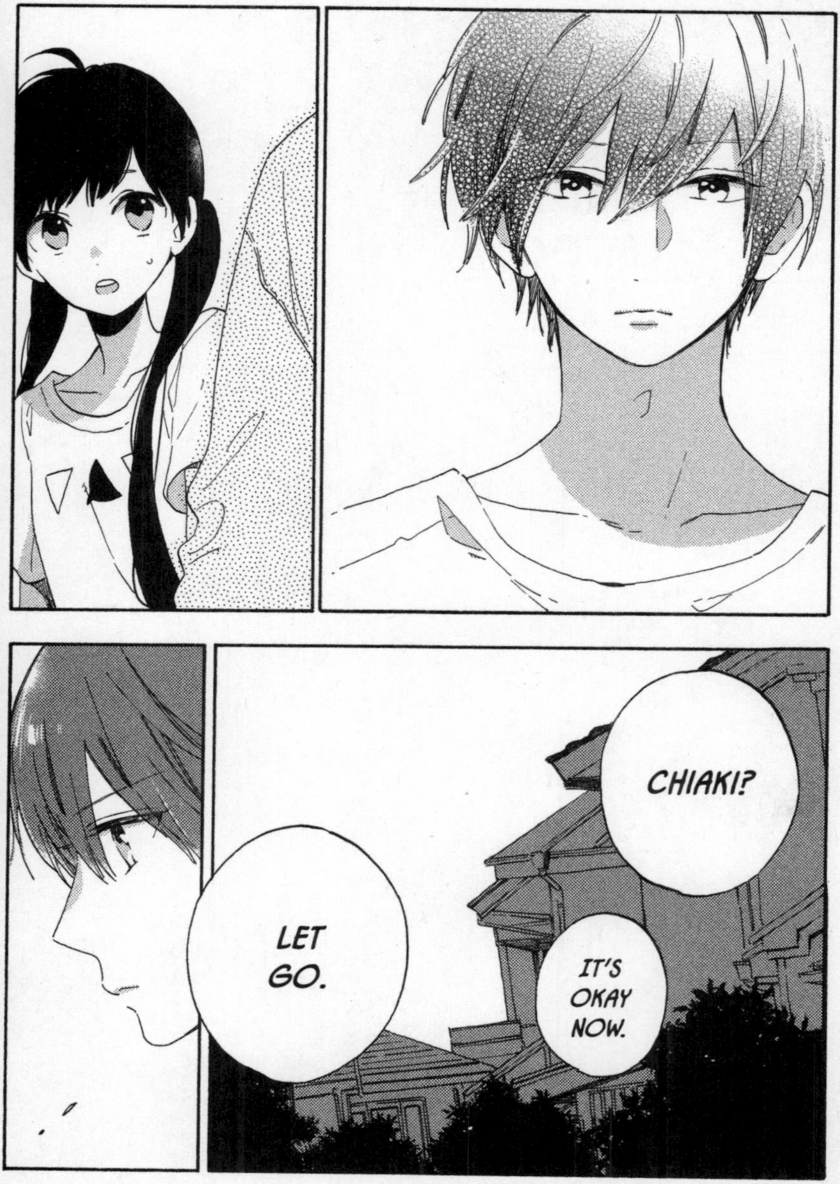
CHIAKI?
IT'S OKAY NOW.
LET GO.

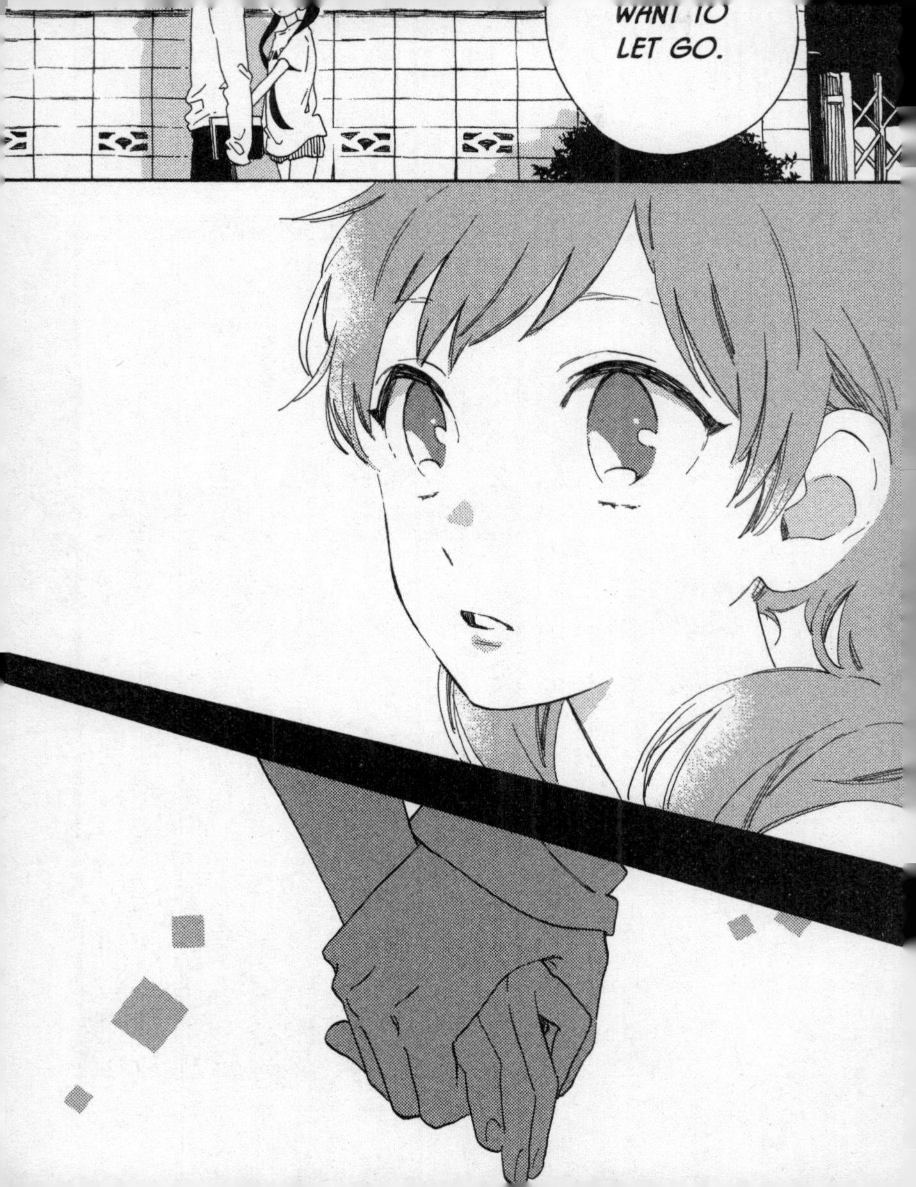WANT TO
LET GO.

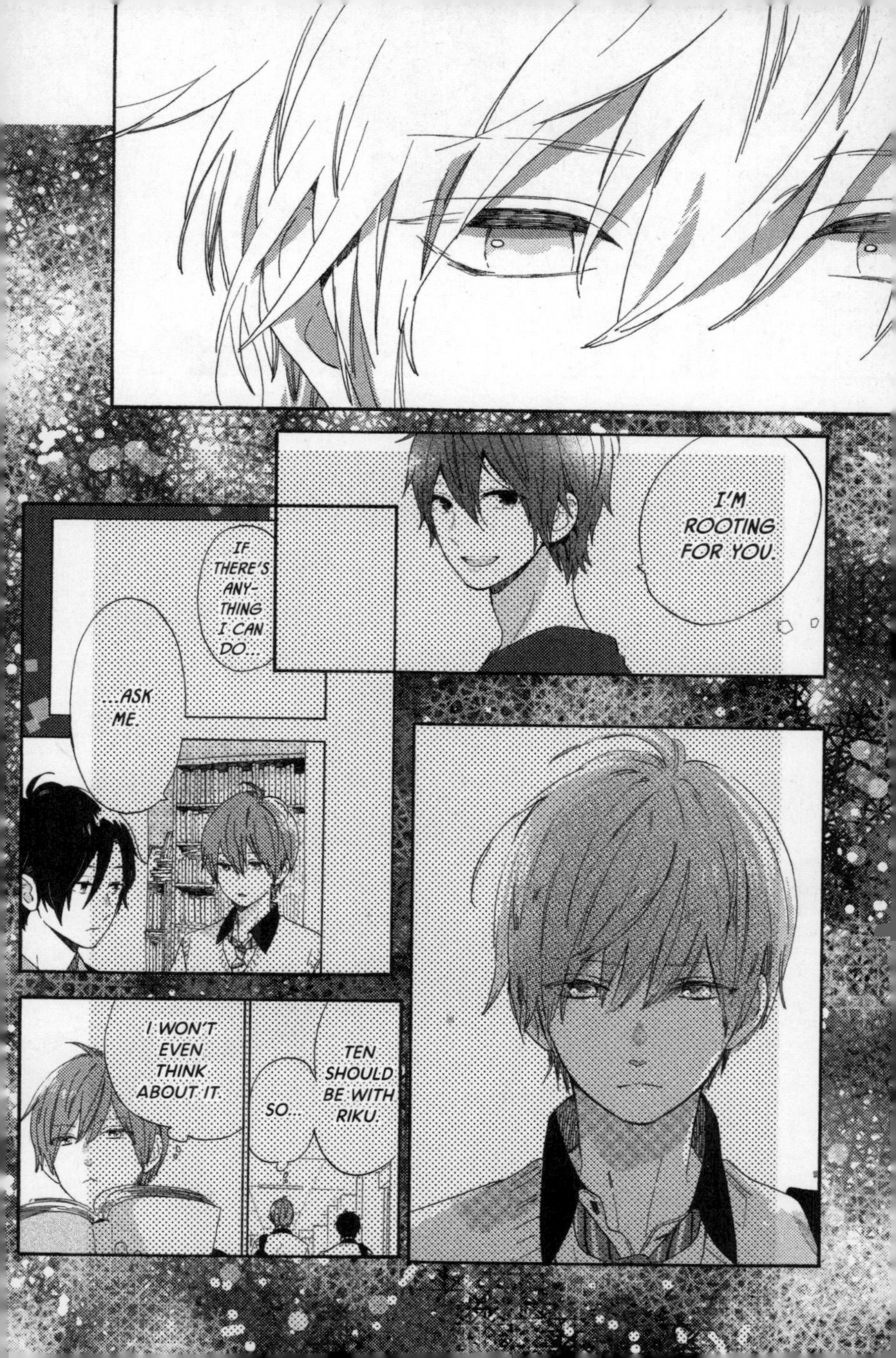
I'M ROOTING FOR YOU.
IF THERE'S ANY-THING I CAN DO...
...ASK ME.
TEN SHOULD BE WITH RIKU.
SO...
I WON'T EVEN THINK ABOUT IT.

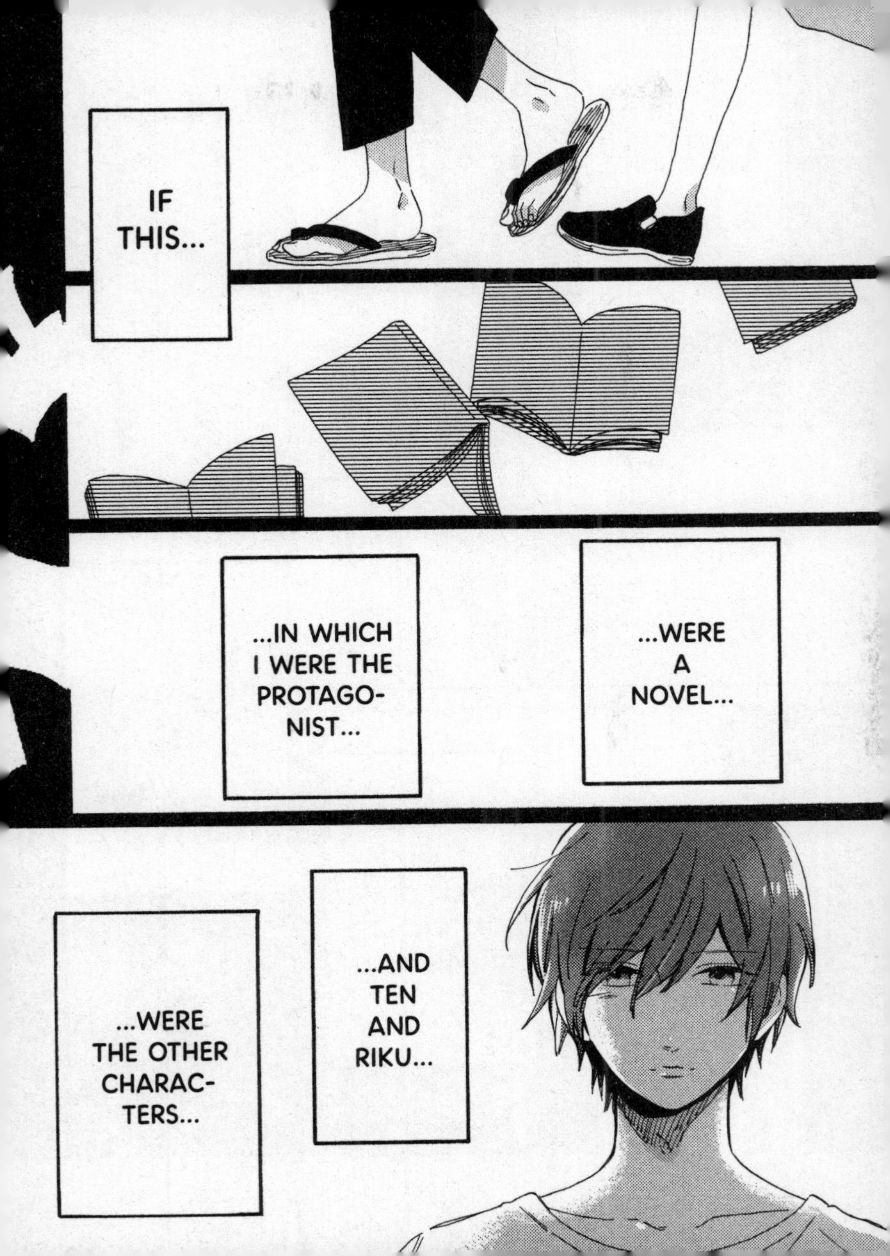
IF THIS...
...WERE A NOVEL...
...IN WHICH I WERE THE PROTAGONIST...
...AND TEN AND RIKU...
...WERE THE OTHER CHARACTERS...

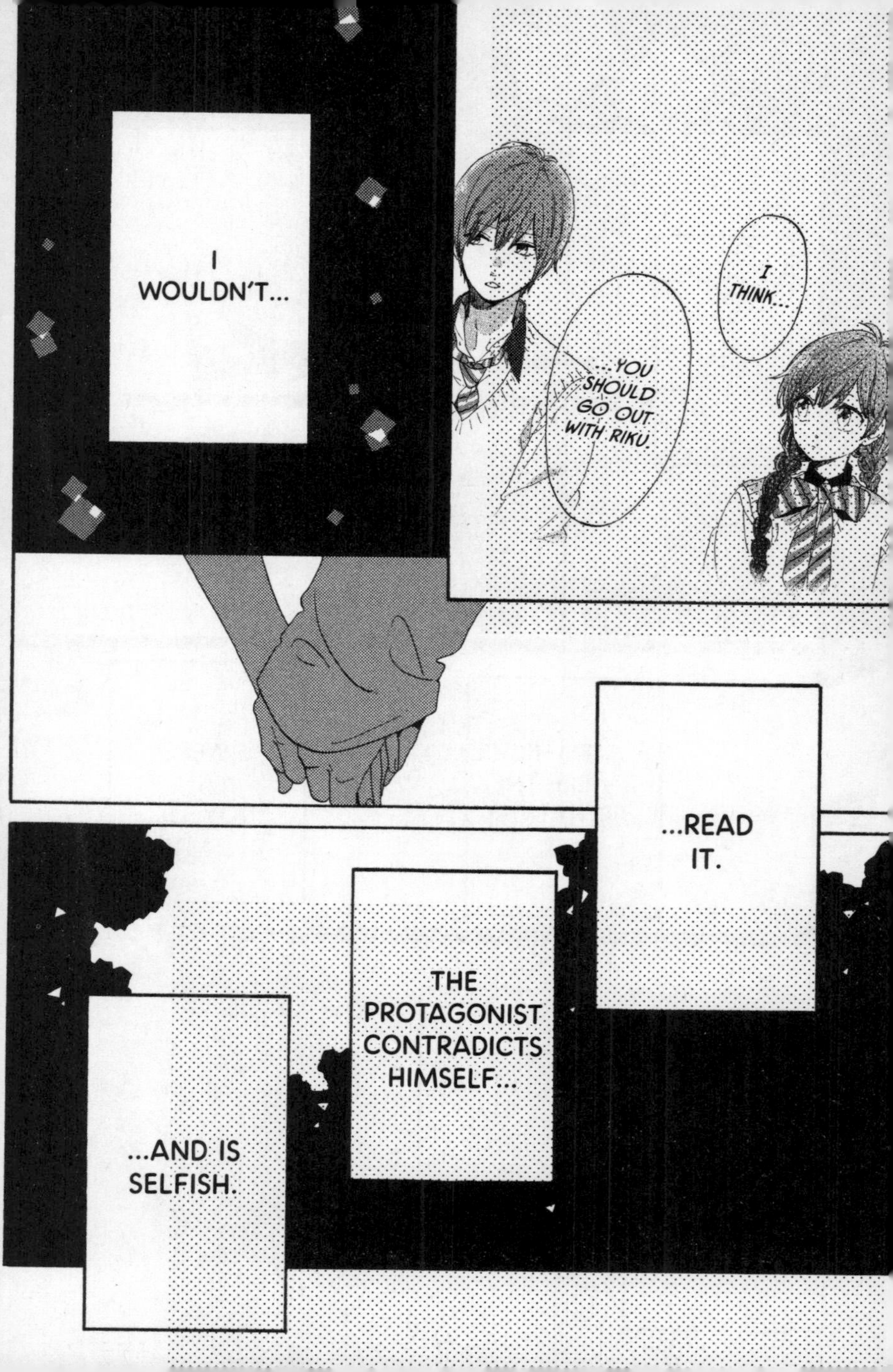
I THINK...
...YOU SHOULD GO OUT WITH RIKU.
I WOULDN'T...
...READ IT.
THE PROTAGONIST CONTRADICTS HIMSELF...
...AND IS SELFISH.

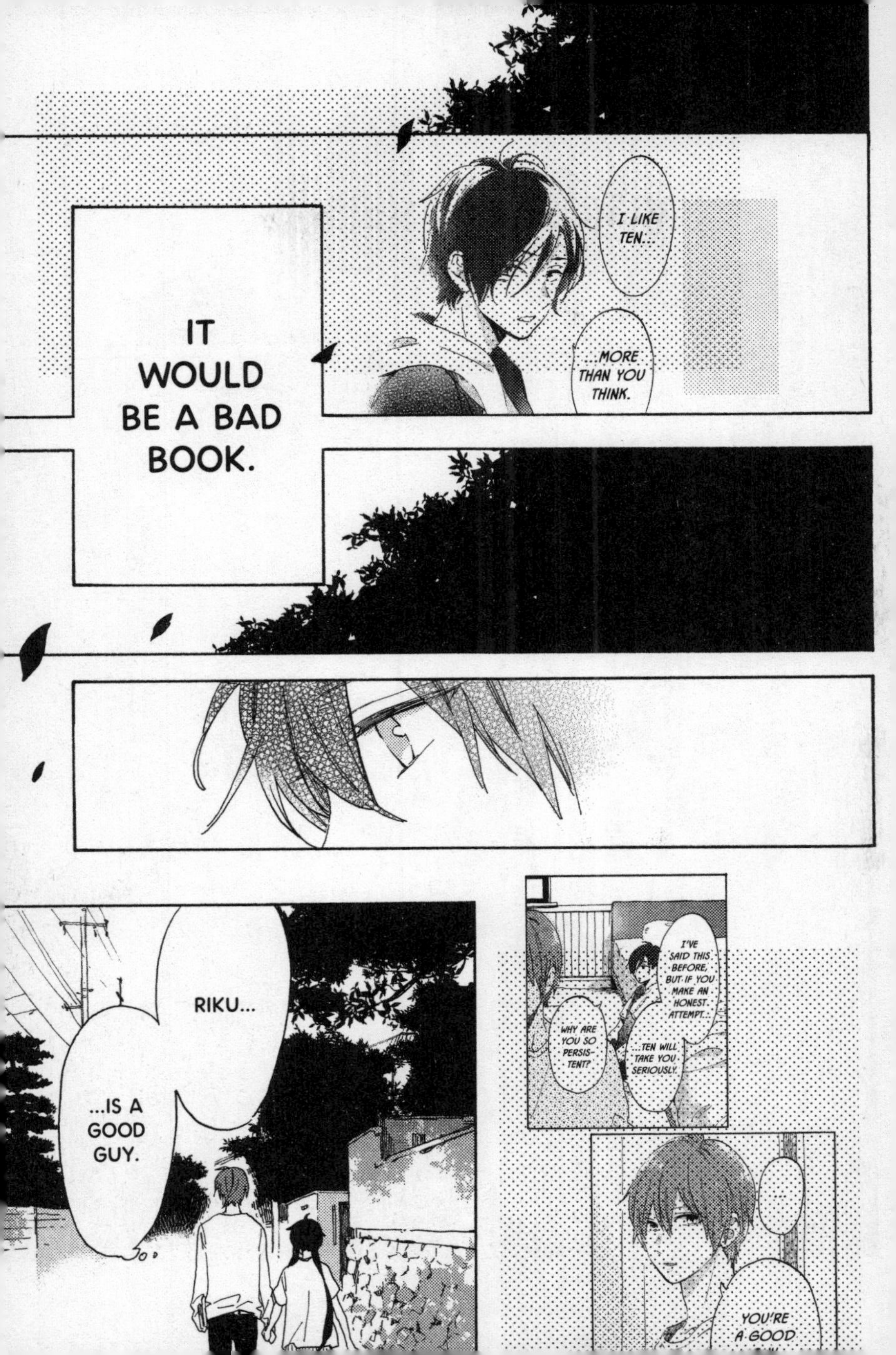
I LIKE TEN...
...MORE THAN YOU THINK.
IT WOULD BE A BAD BOOK.
I'VE SAID THIS BEFORE, BUT IF YOU MAKE AN HONEST ATTEMPT...
...TEN WILL TAKE YOU SERIOUSLY.
WHY ARE YOU SO PERSIS-TENT?
YOU'RE A GOOD
RIKU...
...IS A GOOD GUY.

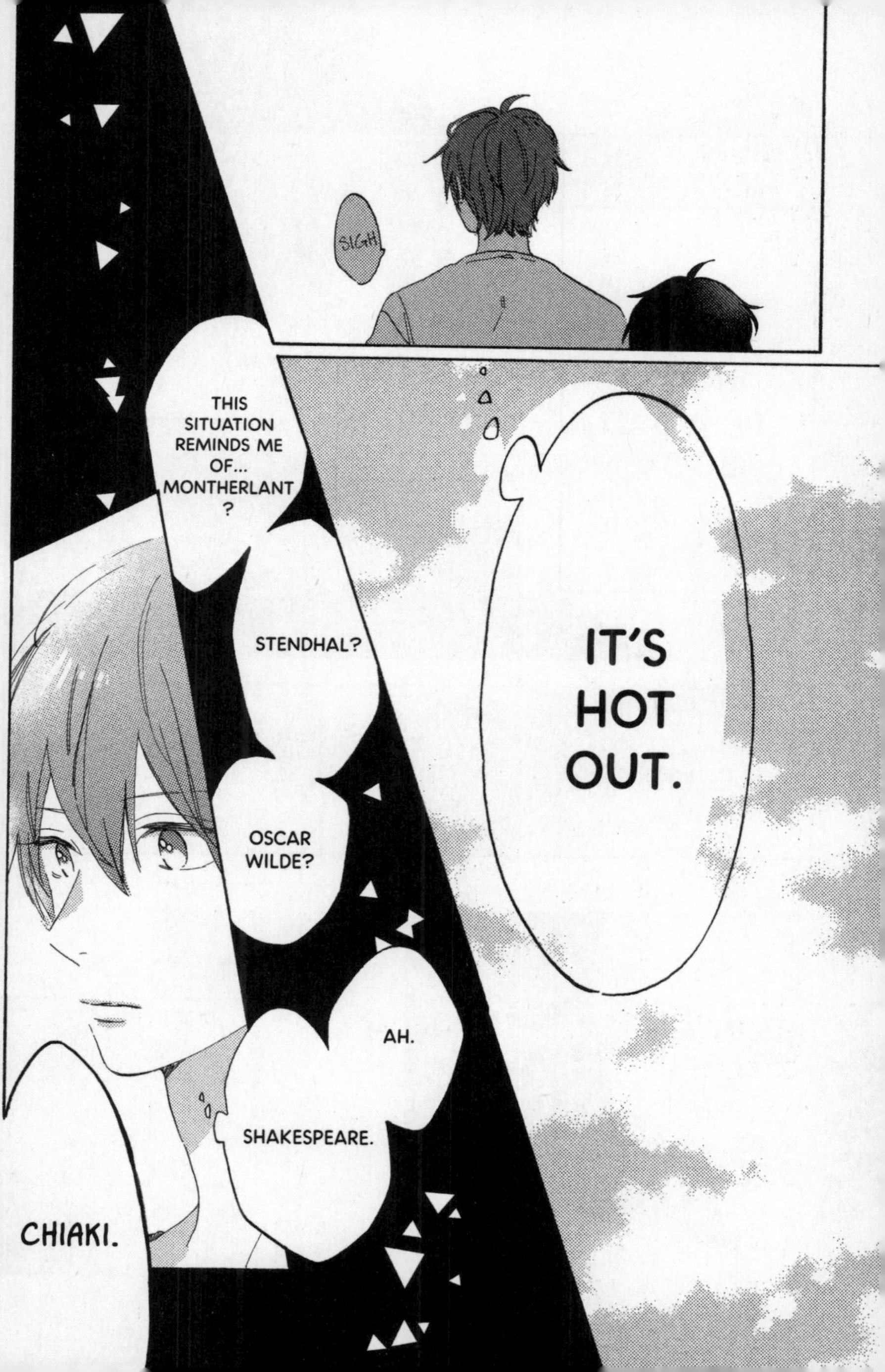
SIGH
IT'S HOT OUT.
THIS SITUATION REMINDS ME OF... MONTHERLANT?
STENDHAL?
OSCAR WILDE?
AH.
SHAKESPEARE.
CHIAKI.

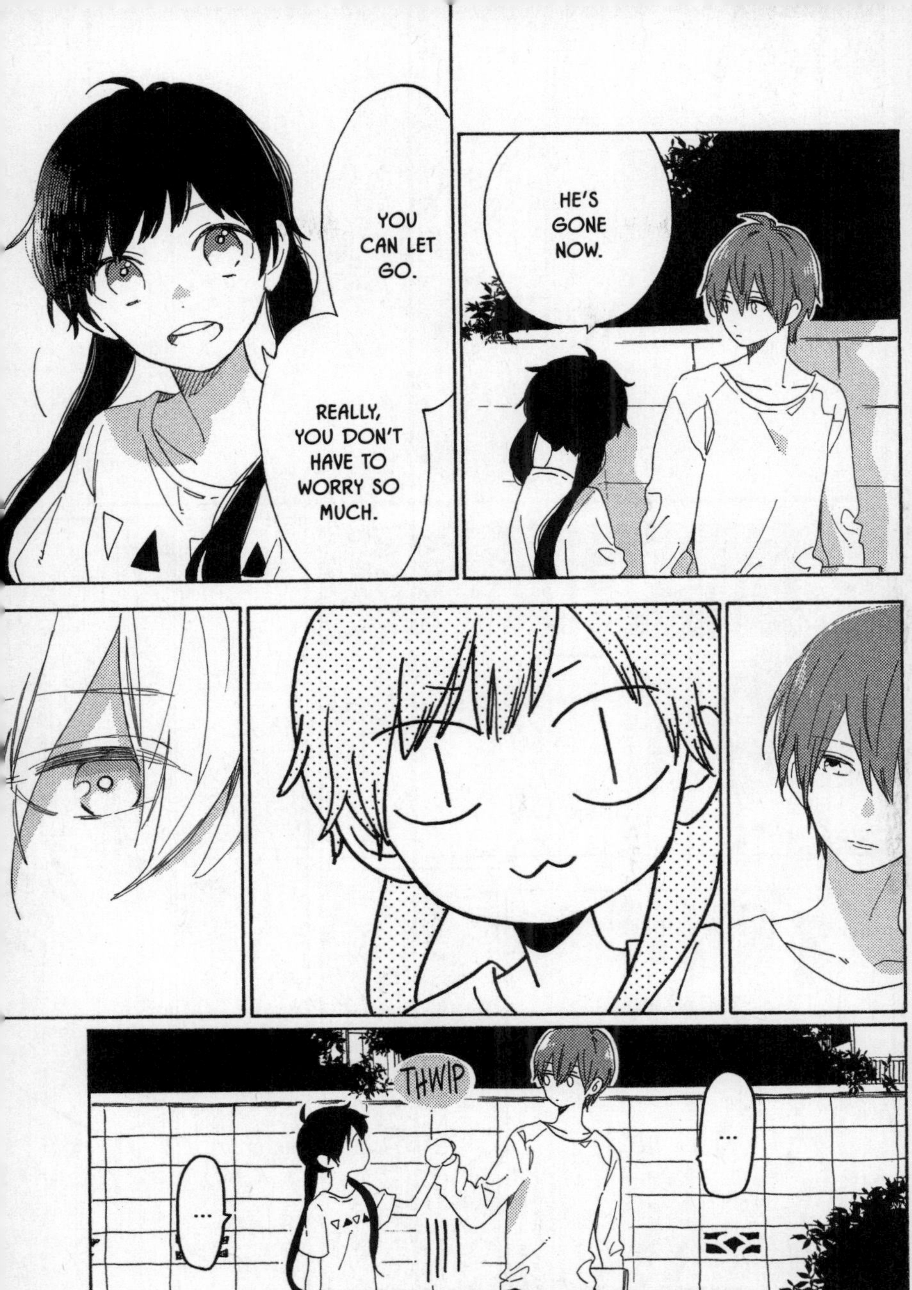
HE'S GONE NOW.
YOU CAN LET GO.
REALLY, YOU DON'T HAVE TO WORRY SO MUCH.
THWIP
...
...

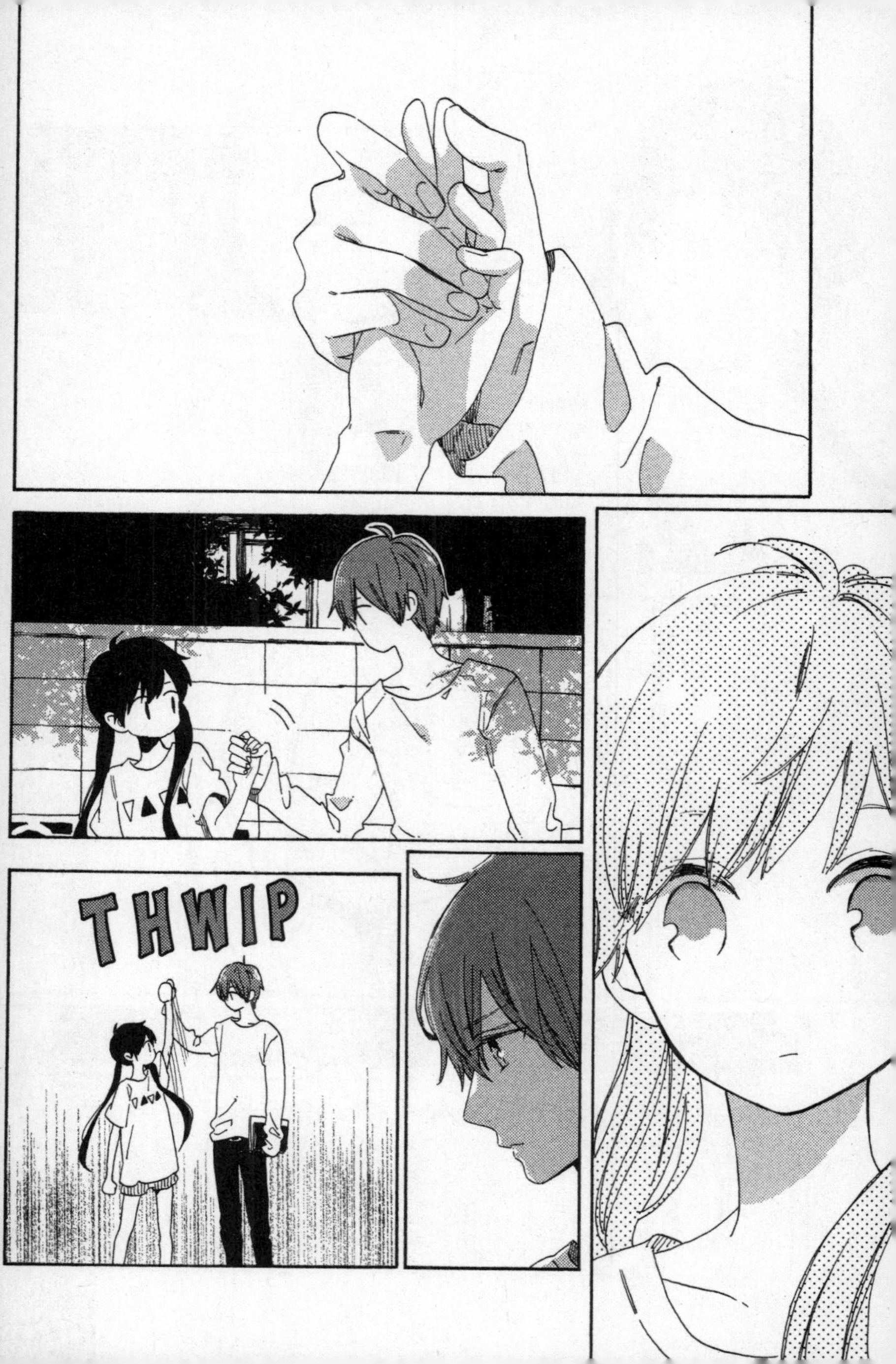
THWIP

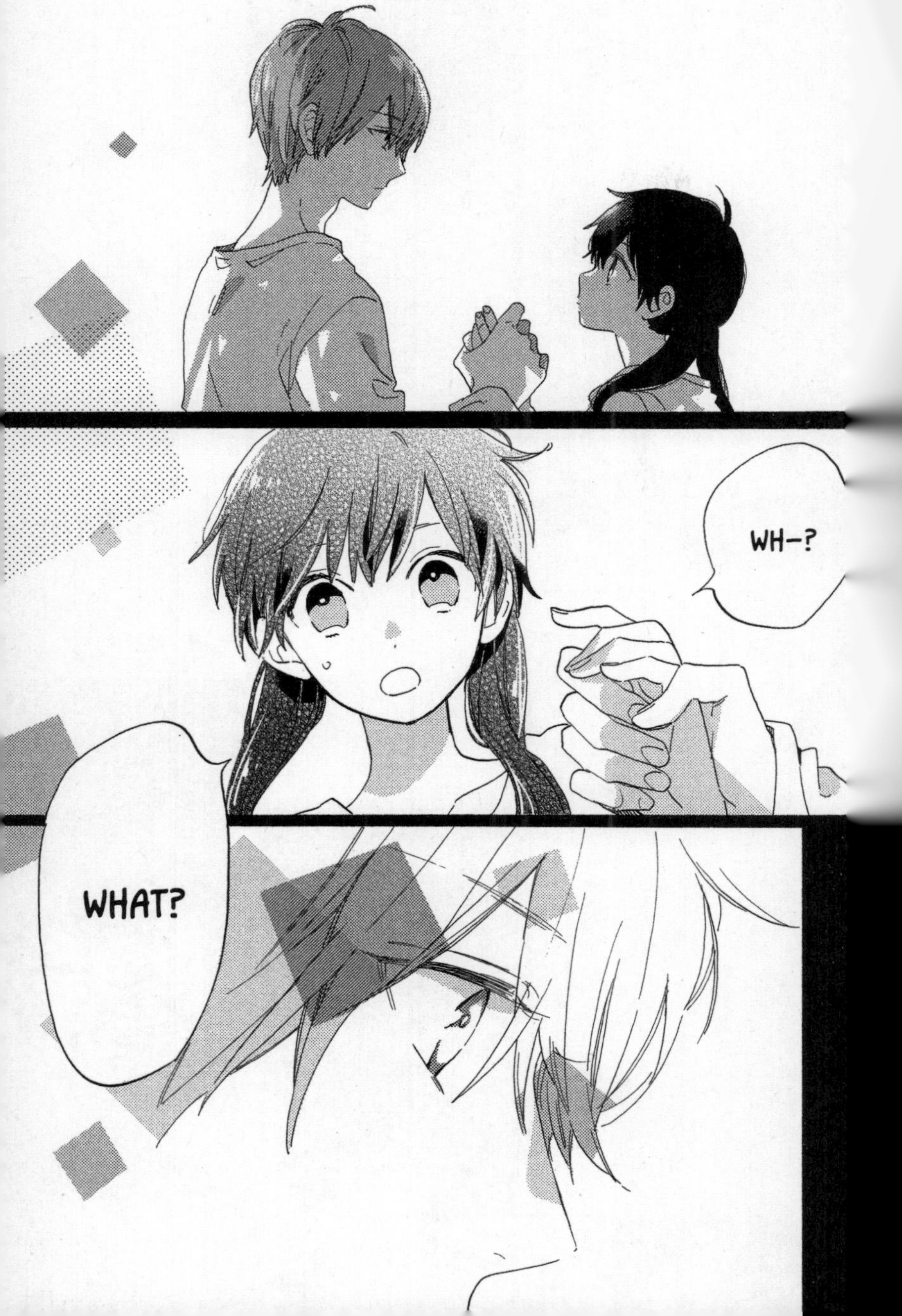
WH-?
WHAT?

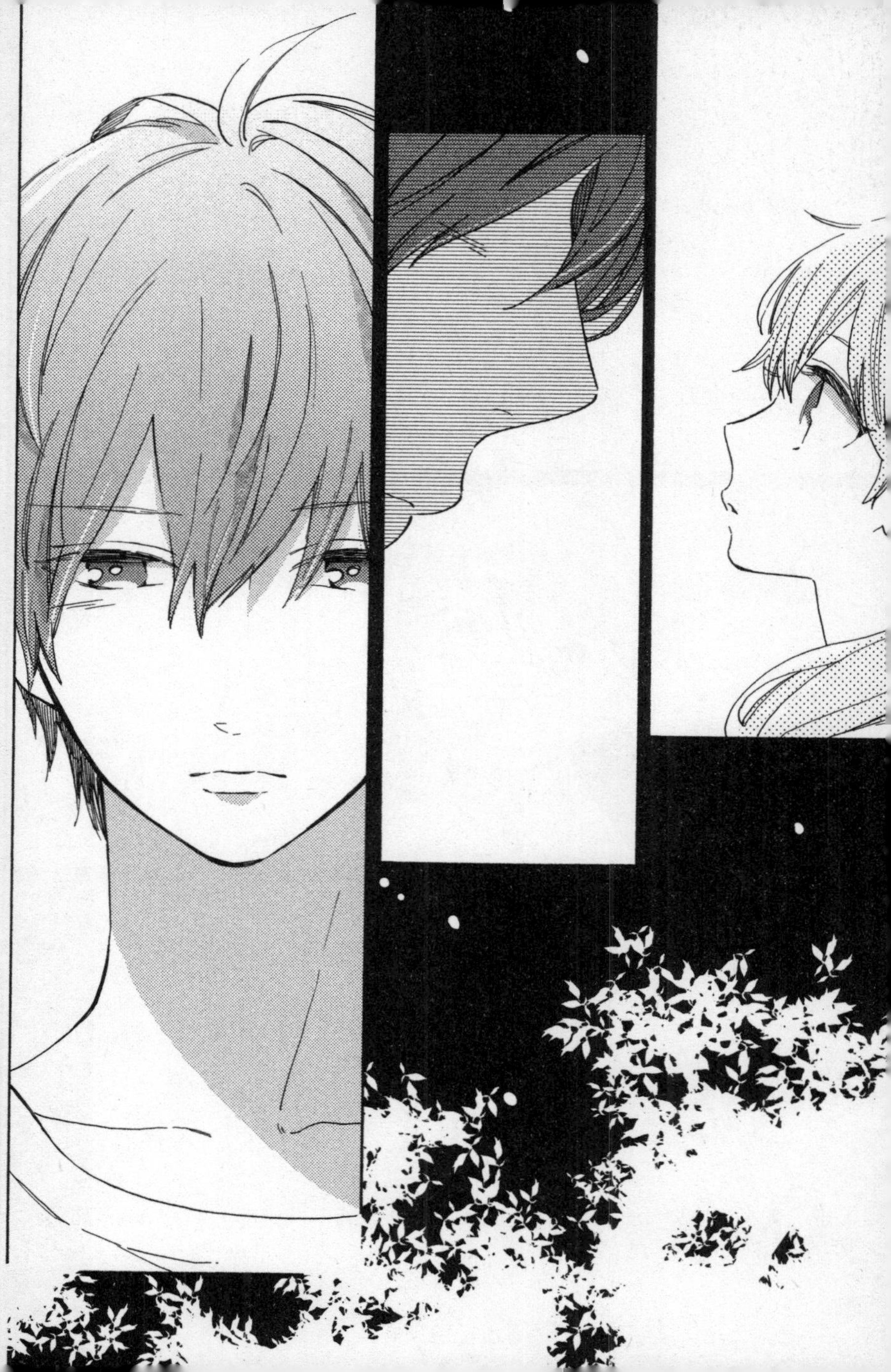

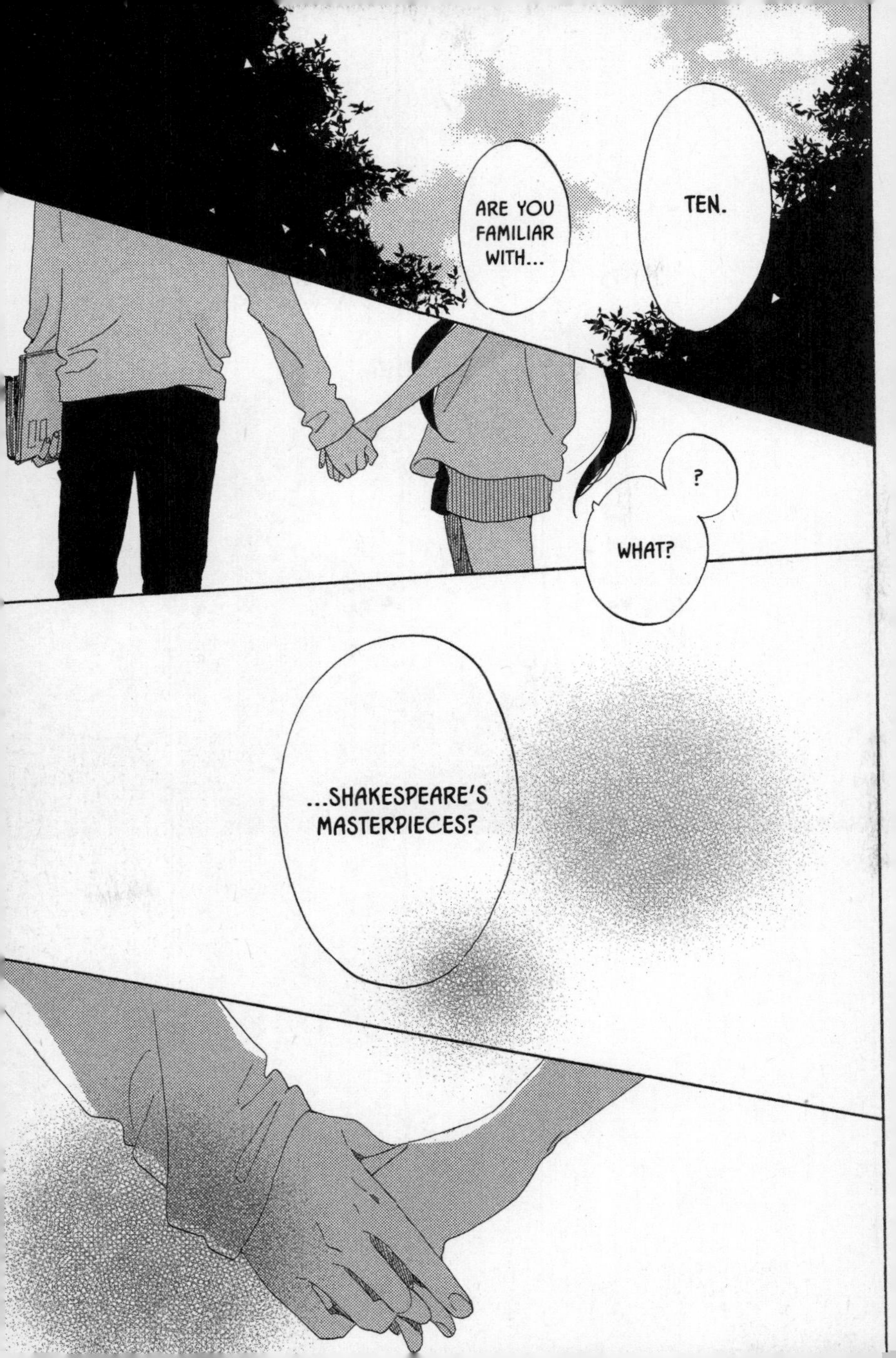
TEN.
ARE YOU FAMILIAR WITH...
?
WHAT?
...SHAKESPEARE'S MASTERPIECES?

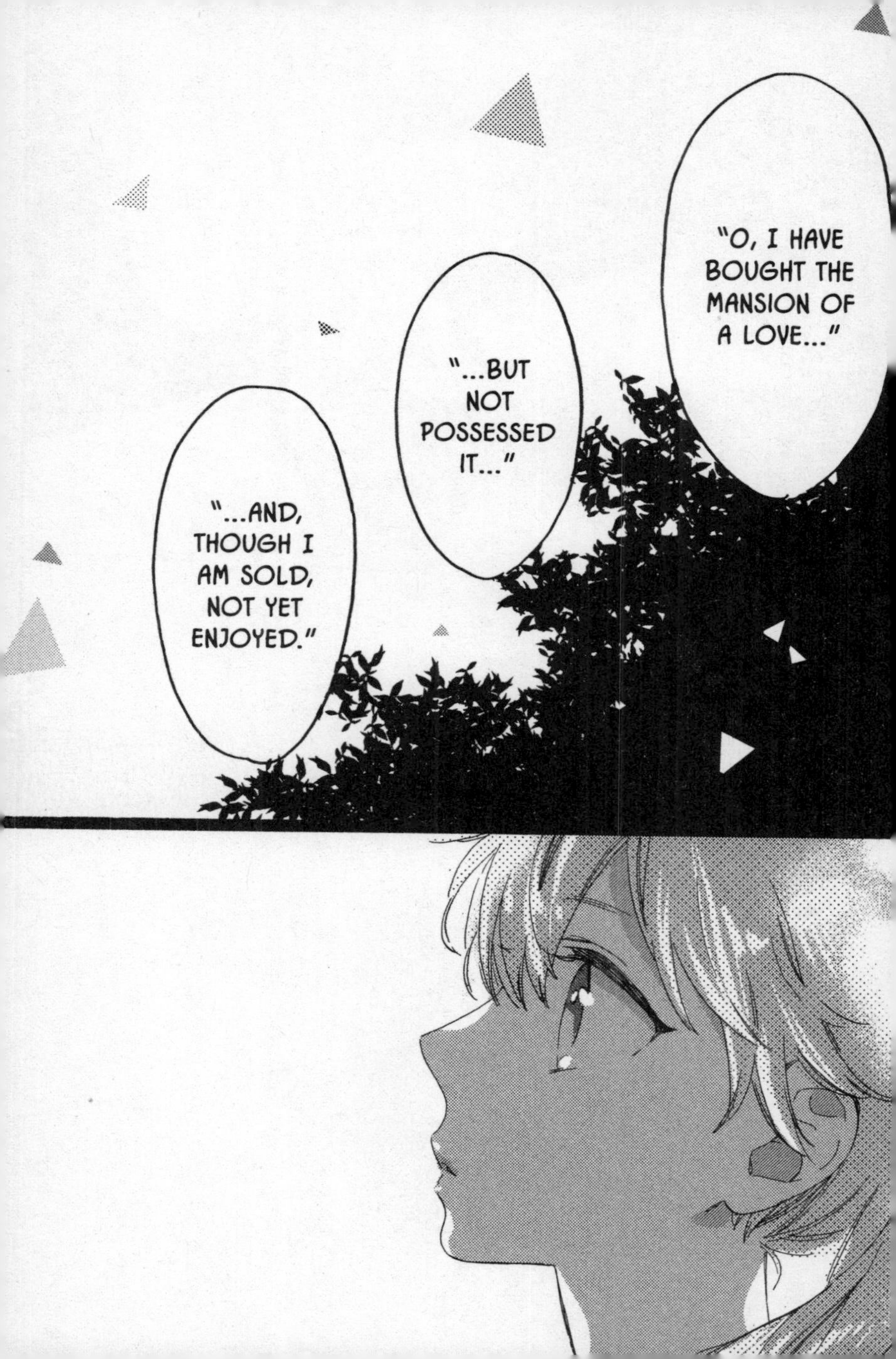
"O, I HAVE BOUGHT THE MANSION OF A LOVE..."
"...BUT NOT POSSESSED IT..."
"...AND, THOUGH I AM SOLD, NOT YET ENJOYED."

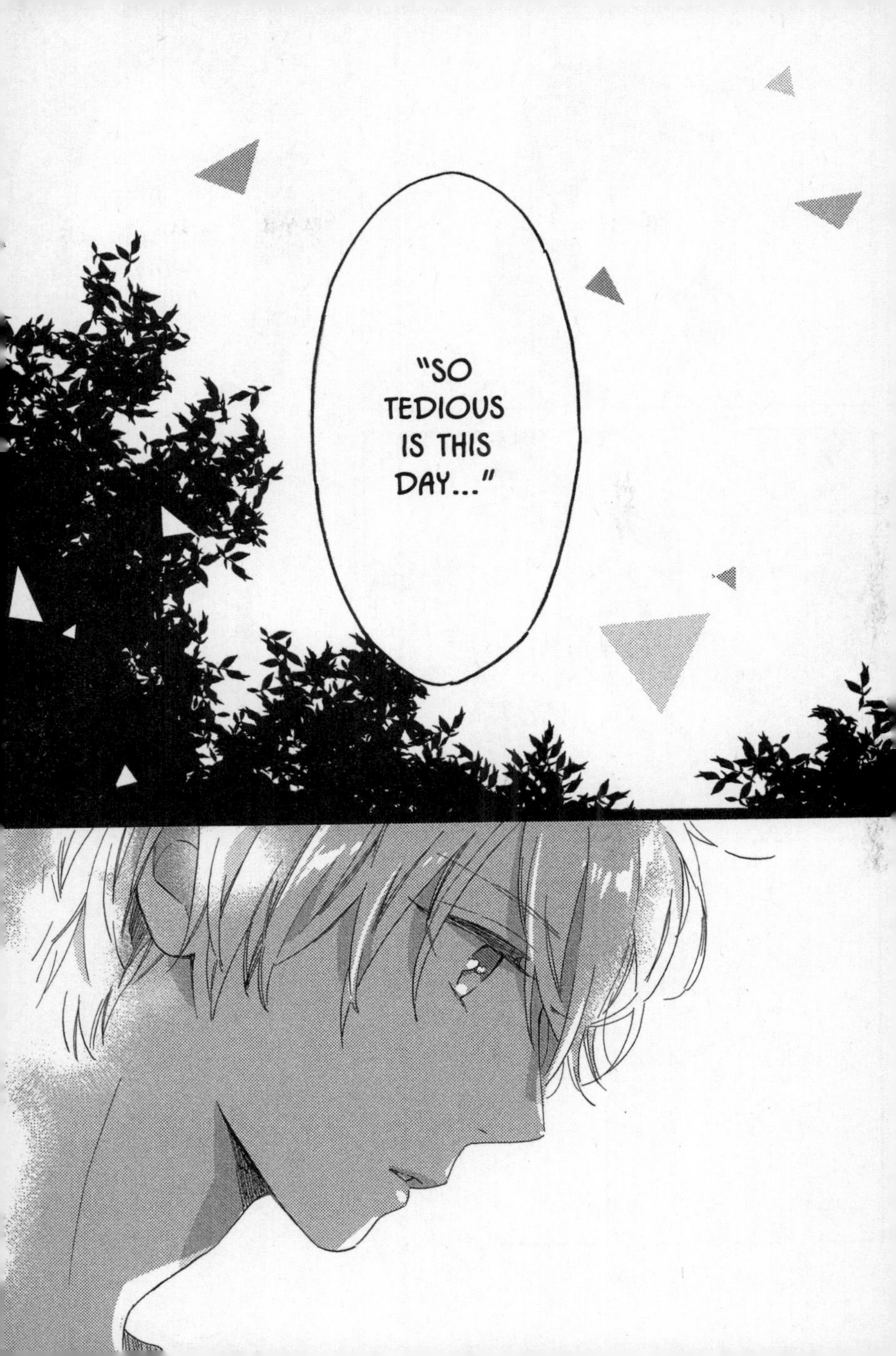
"SO TEDIOUS IS THIS DAY..."

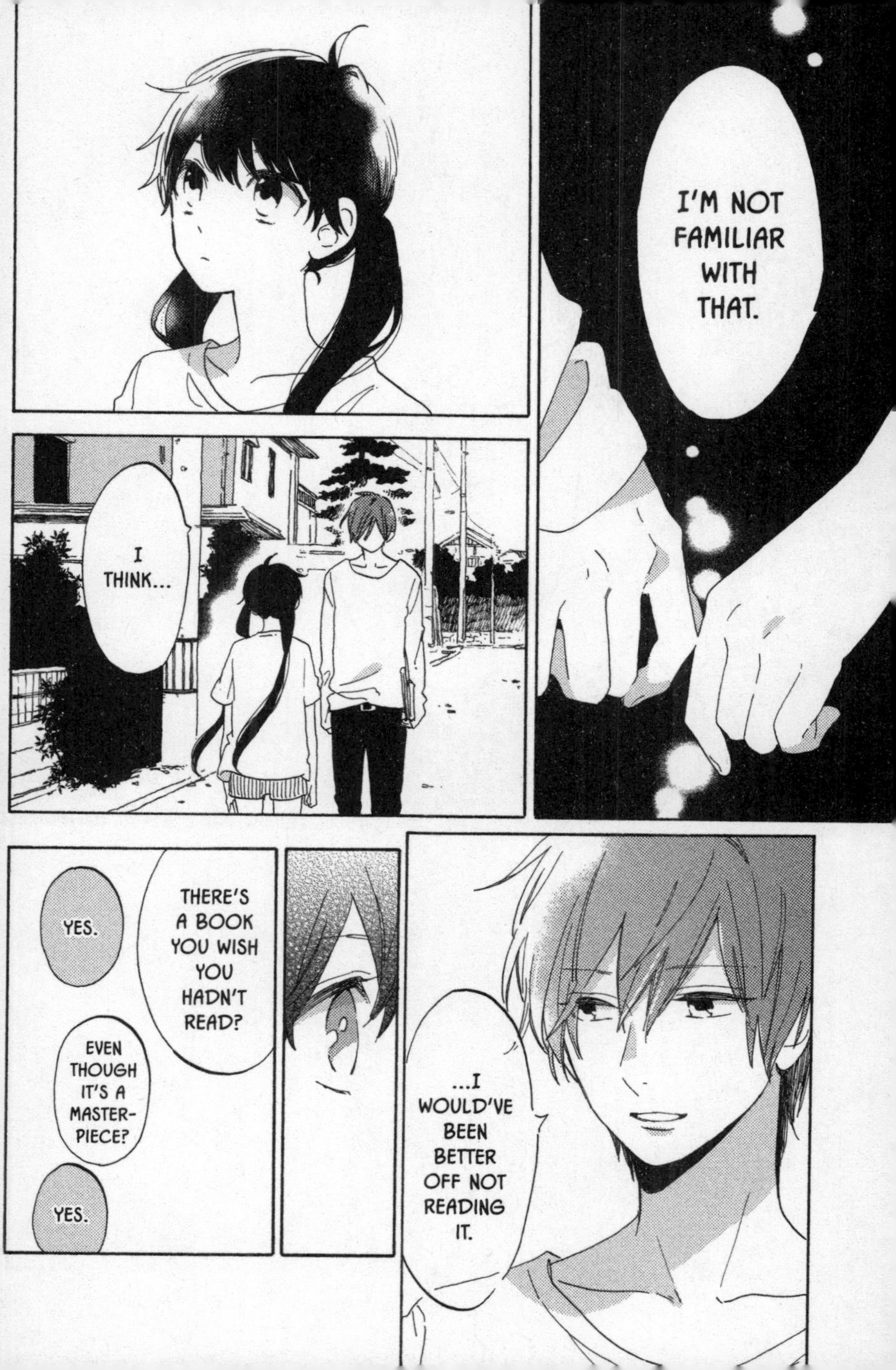
I'M NOT FAMILIAR WITH THAT.
I THINK...
...I WOULD'VE BEEN BETTER OFF NOT READING IT.
THERE'S A BOOK YOU WISH YOU HADN'T READ?
YES.
EVEN THOUGH IT'S A MASTER-PIECE?
YES.

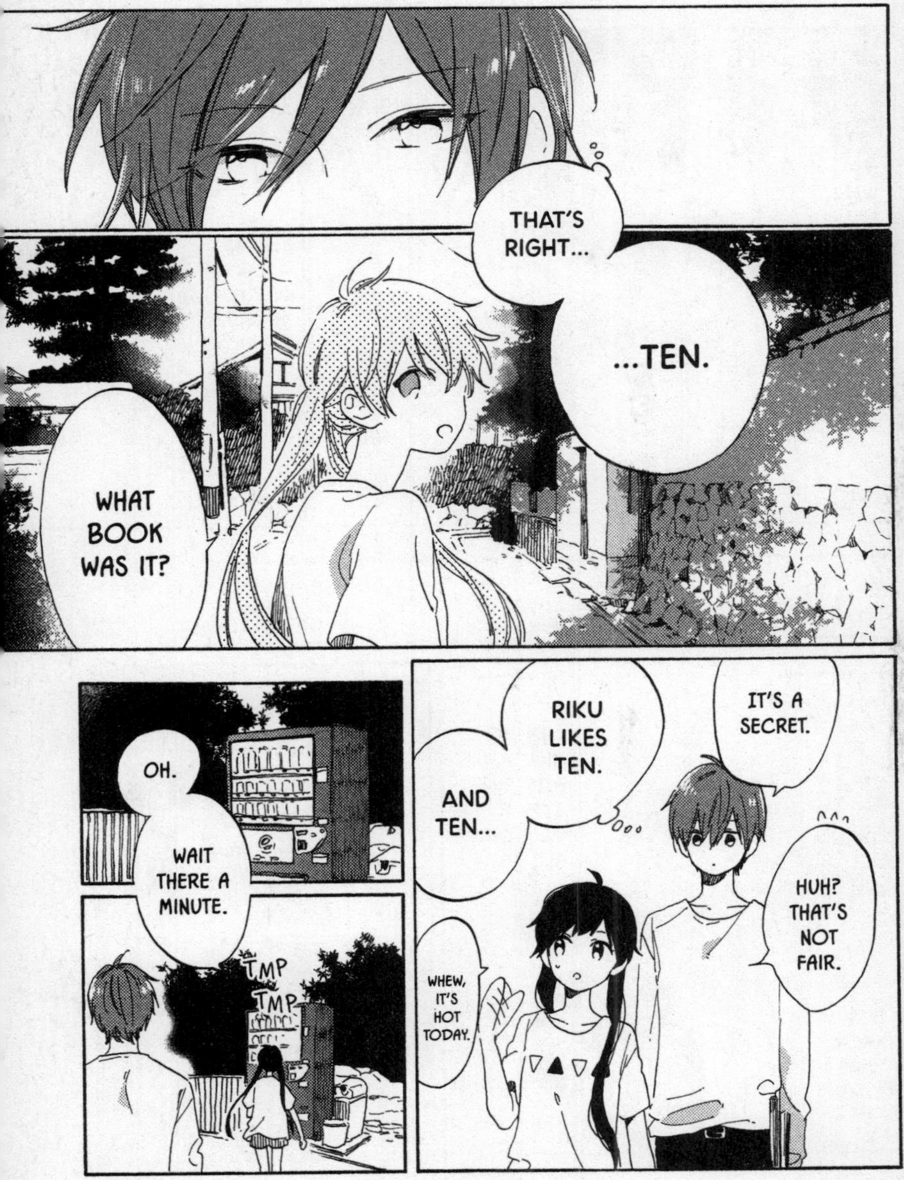
THAT'S RIGHT...
...TEN.
WHAT BOOK WAS IT?
IT'S A SECRET.
RIKU LIKES TEN.
AND TEN...
HUH? THAT'S NOT FAIR.
WHEW, IT'S HOT TODAY.
OH.
WAIT THERE A MINUTE.
TMP TMP

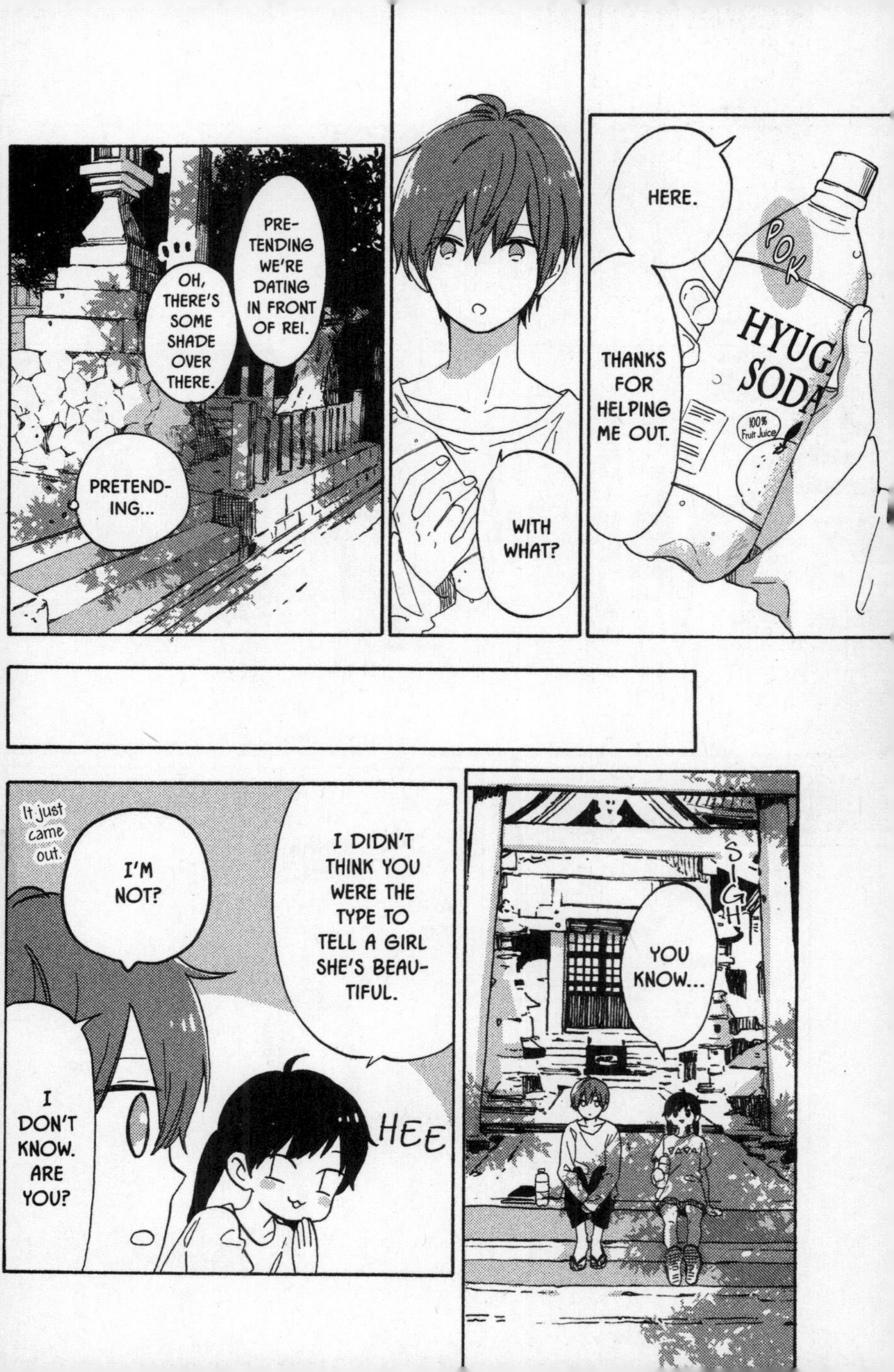
HERE.
POK
THANKS FOR HELPING ME OUT.
HYUG SODA
100% Fruit Juice
WITH WHAT?
PRE-TENDING WE'RE DATING IN FRONT OF REI.
...
OH, THERE'S SOME SHADE OVER THERE.
PRETEND-ING...
SIGH
YOU KNOW...
I DIDN'T THINK YOU WERE THE TYPE TO TELL A GIRL SHE'S BEAU-TIFUL.
I'M NOT?
It just came out.
HEE
I DON'T KNOW. ARE YOU?

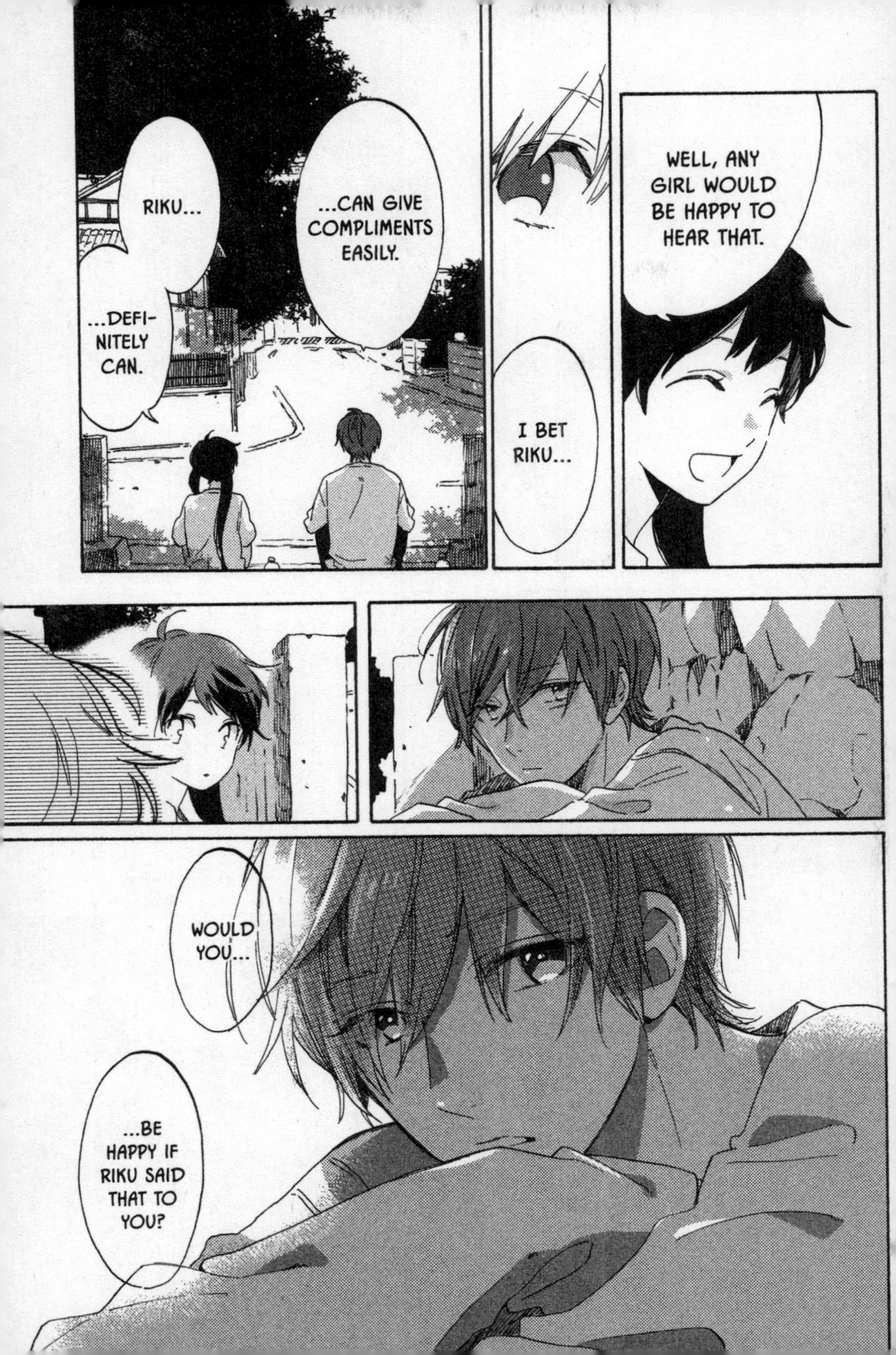
WELL, ANY GIRL WOULD BE HAPPY TO HEAR THAT.
I BET RIKU...
...CAN GIVE COMPLIMENTS EASILY.
RIKU...
...DEFINITELY CAN.
WOULD YOU...
...BE HAPPY IF RIKU SAID THAT TO YOU?

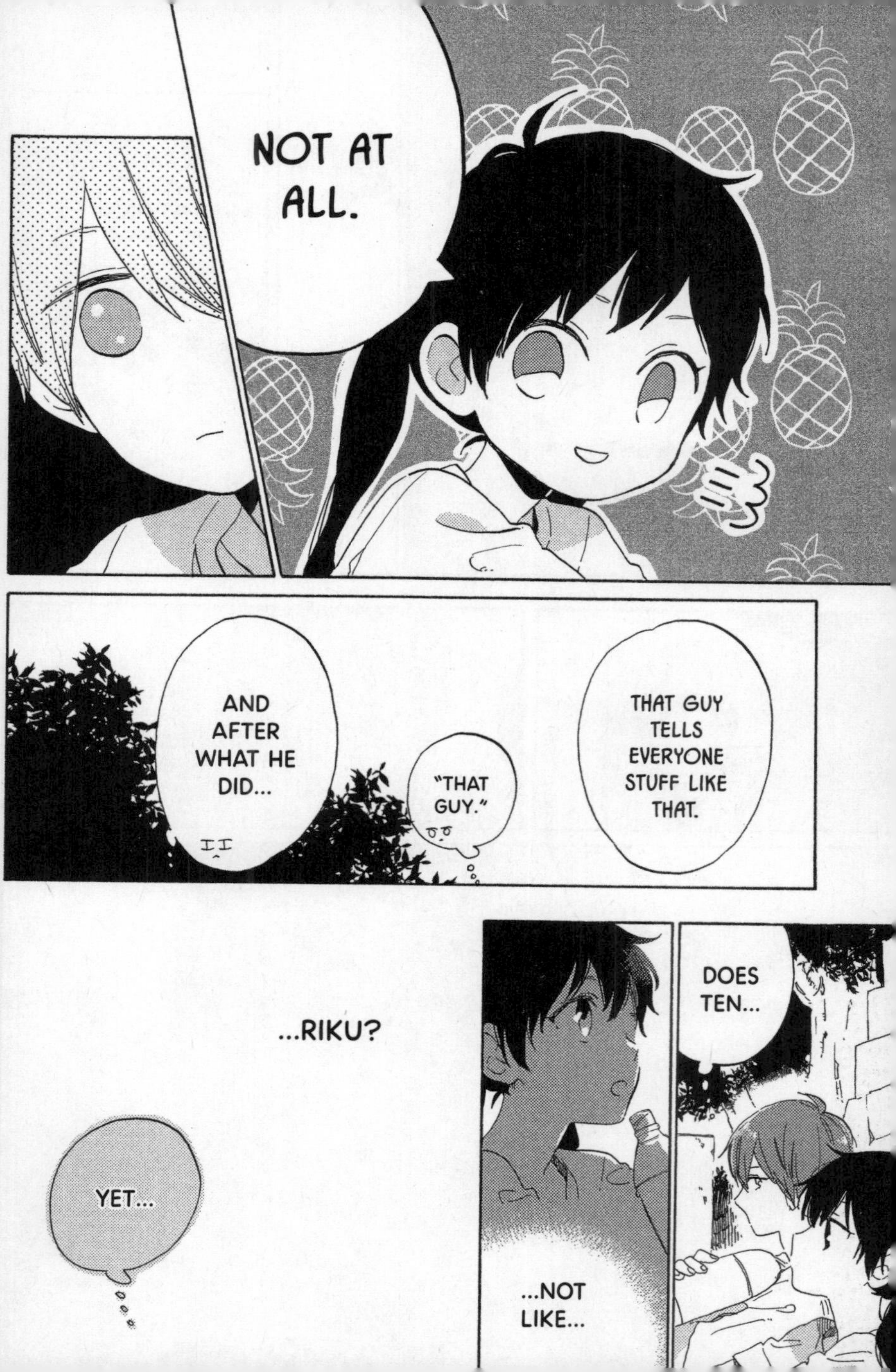
NOT AT ALL.
THAT GUY TELLS EVERYONE STUFF LIKE THAT.
"THAT GUY."
AND AFTER WHAT HE DID...
DOES TEN...
...NOT LIKE...
...RIKU?
YET...

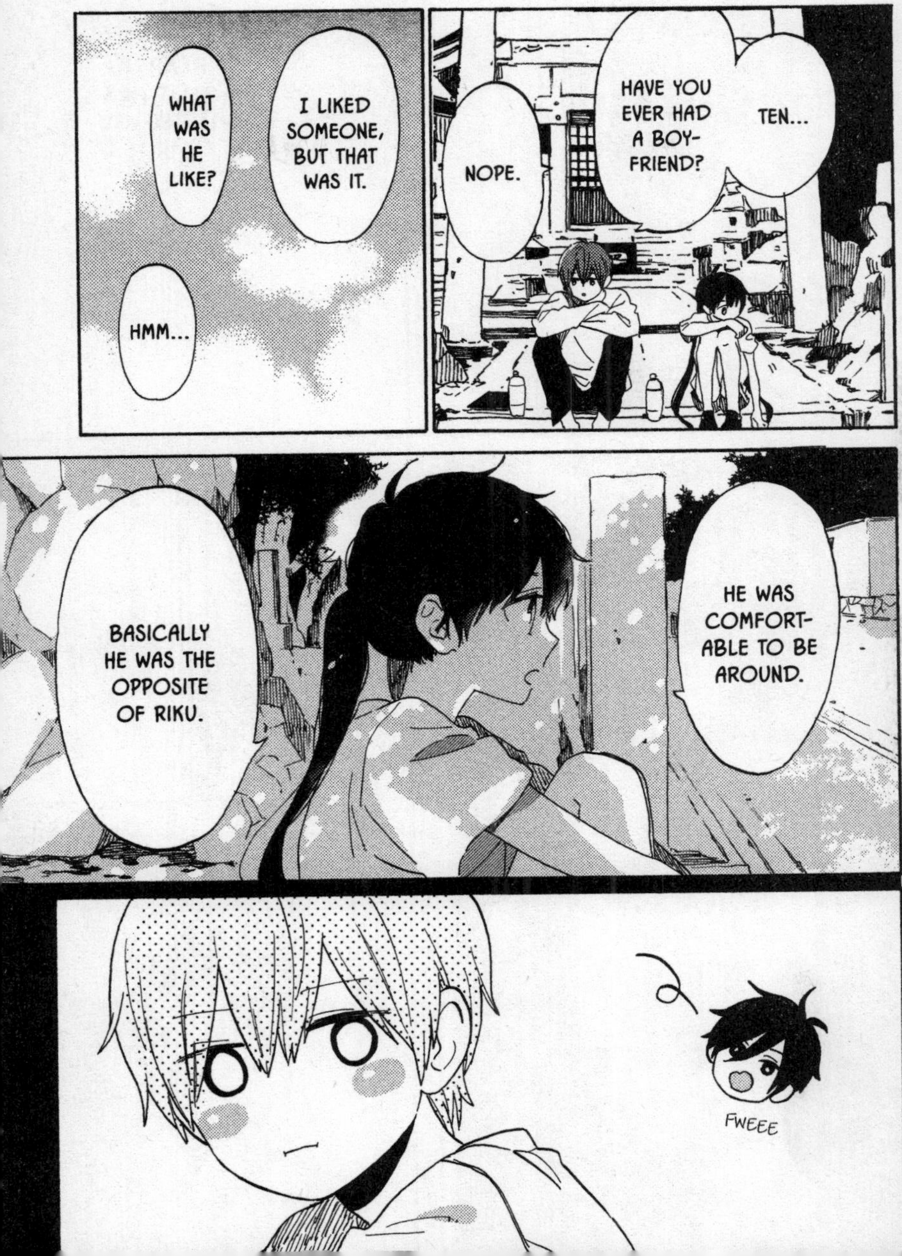
TEN...
HAVE YOU EVER HAD A BOY-FRIEND?
NOPE.
I LIKED SOMEONE, BUT THAT WAS IT.
WHAT WAS HE LIKE?
HMM...
HE WAS COMFORT-ABLE TO BE AROUND.
BASICALLY HE WAS THE OPPOSITE OF RIKU.
FWEEE

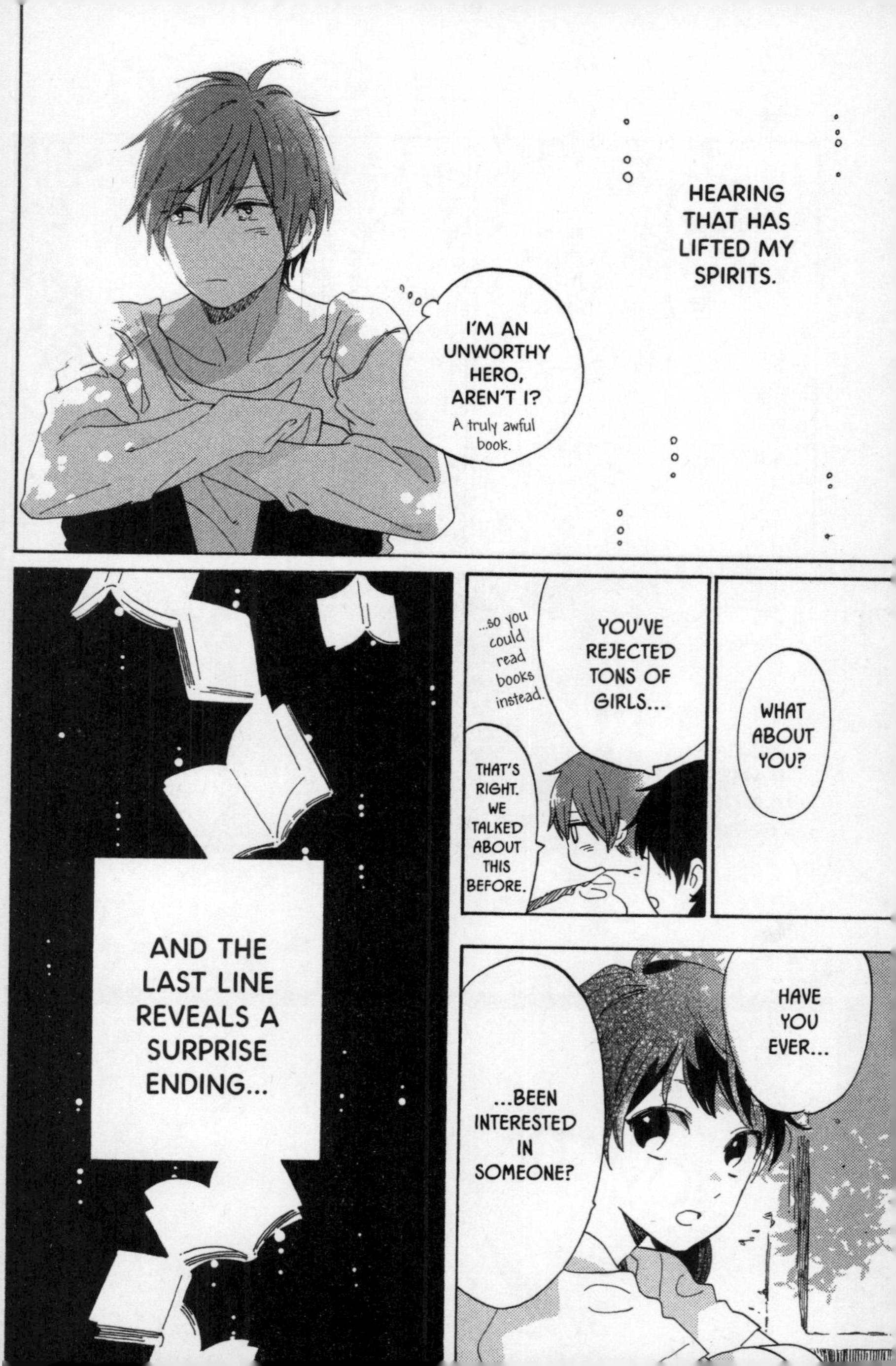
HEARING THAT HAS LIFTED MY SPIRITS.
I'M AN UNWORTHY HERO, AREN'T I?
A truly awful book.
WHAT ABOUT YOU?
YOU'VE REJECTED TONS OF GIRLS...
...so you could read books instead.
THAT'S RIGHT. WE TALKED ABOUT THIS BEFORE.
HAVE YOU EVER...
...BEEN INTERESTED IN SOMEONE?
AND THE LAST LINE REVEALS A SURPRISE ENDING...

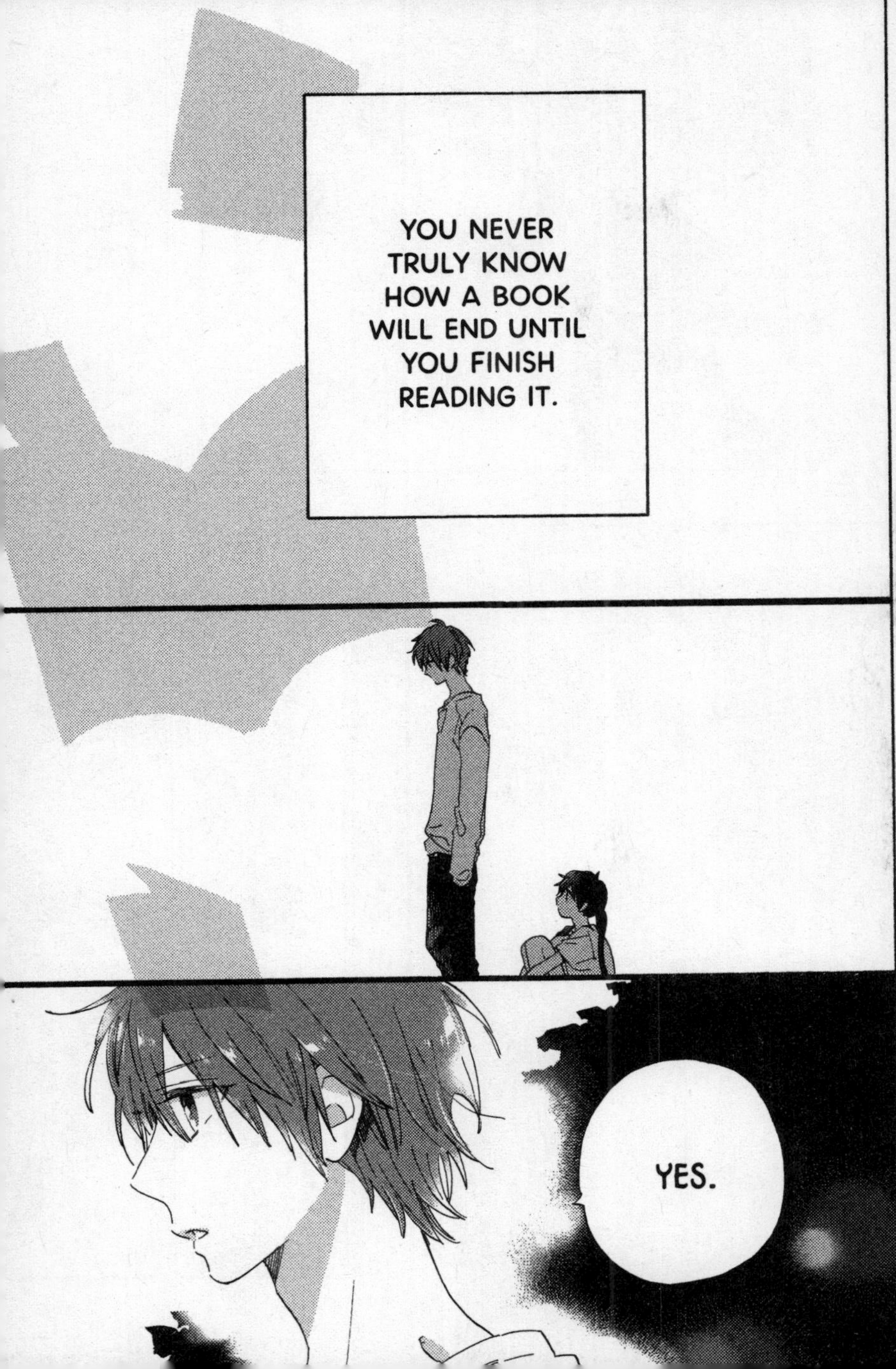
YOU NEVER TRULY KNOW HOW A BOOK WILL END UNTIL YOU FINISH READING IT.
YES.

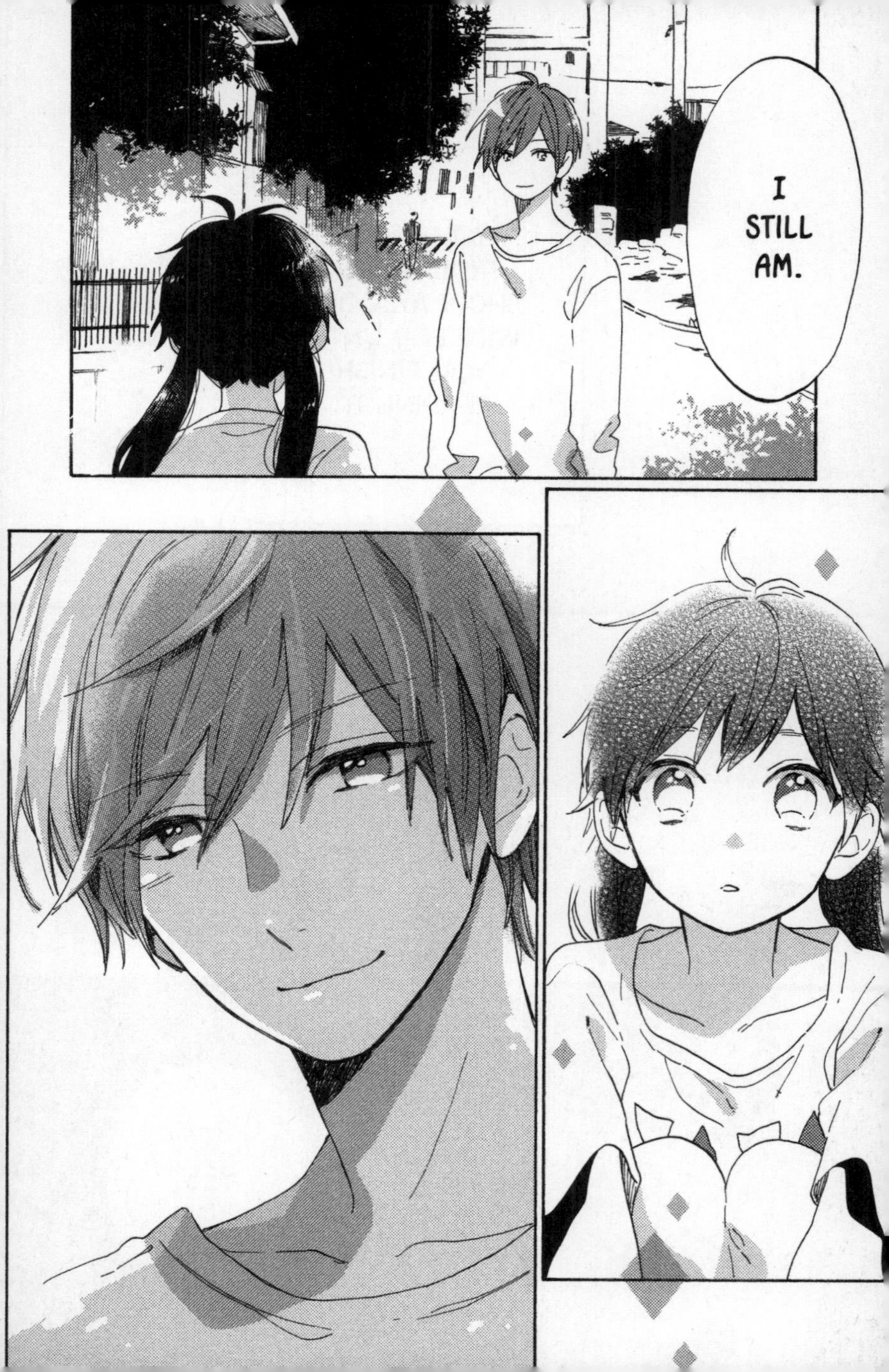
I STILL AM.

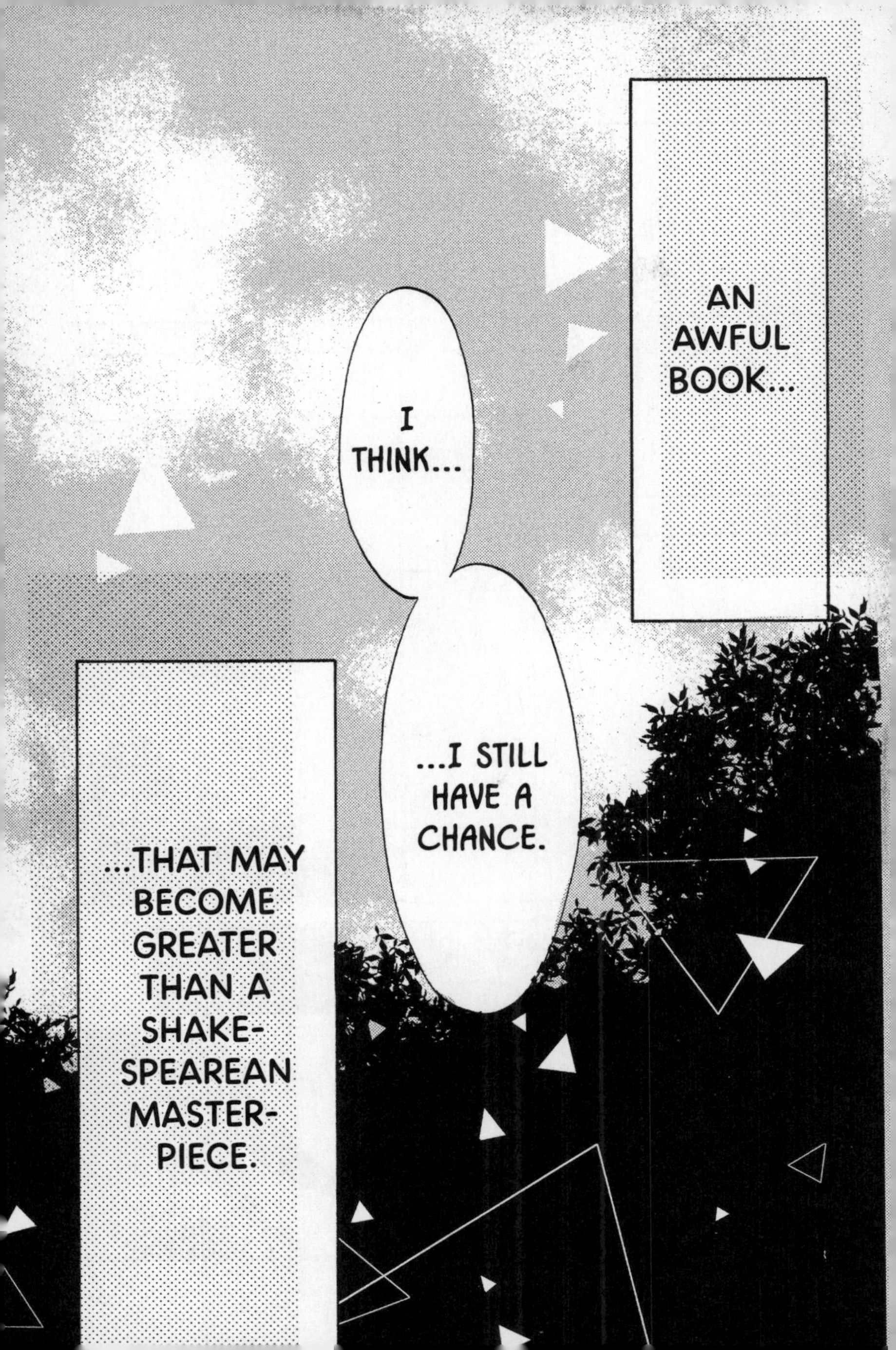
AN AWFUL BOOK...
I THINK...
...I STILL HAVE A CHANCE.
...THAT MAY BECOME GREATER THAN A SHAKE-SPEAREAN MASTER-PIECE.

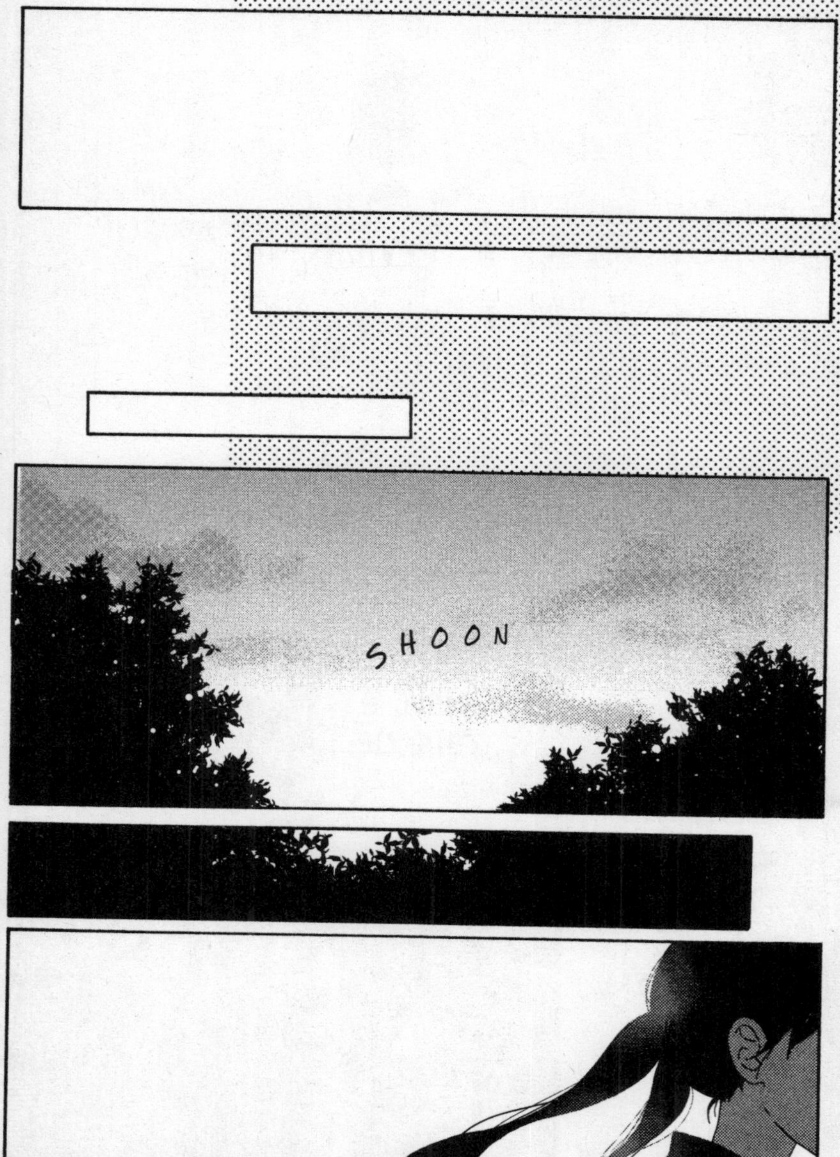
SHOON

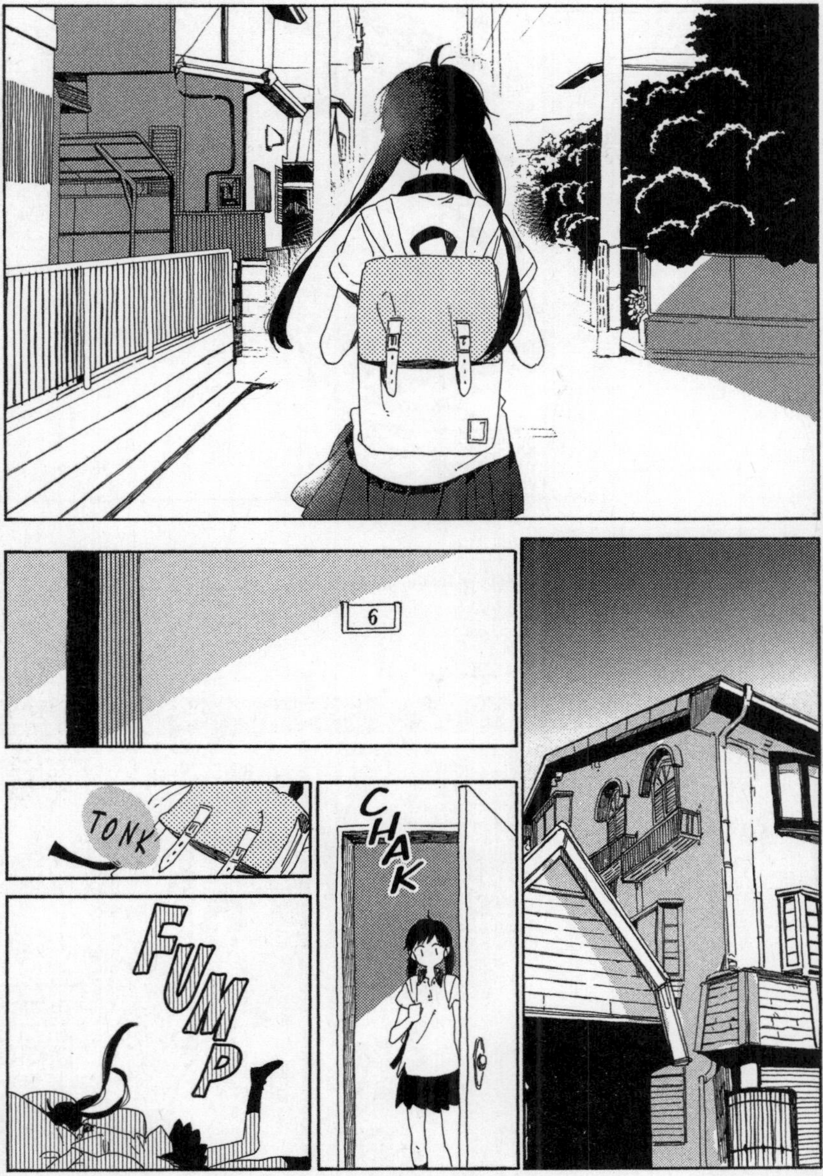
CHAK
TONK
FUMP

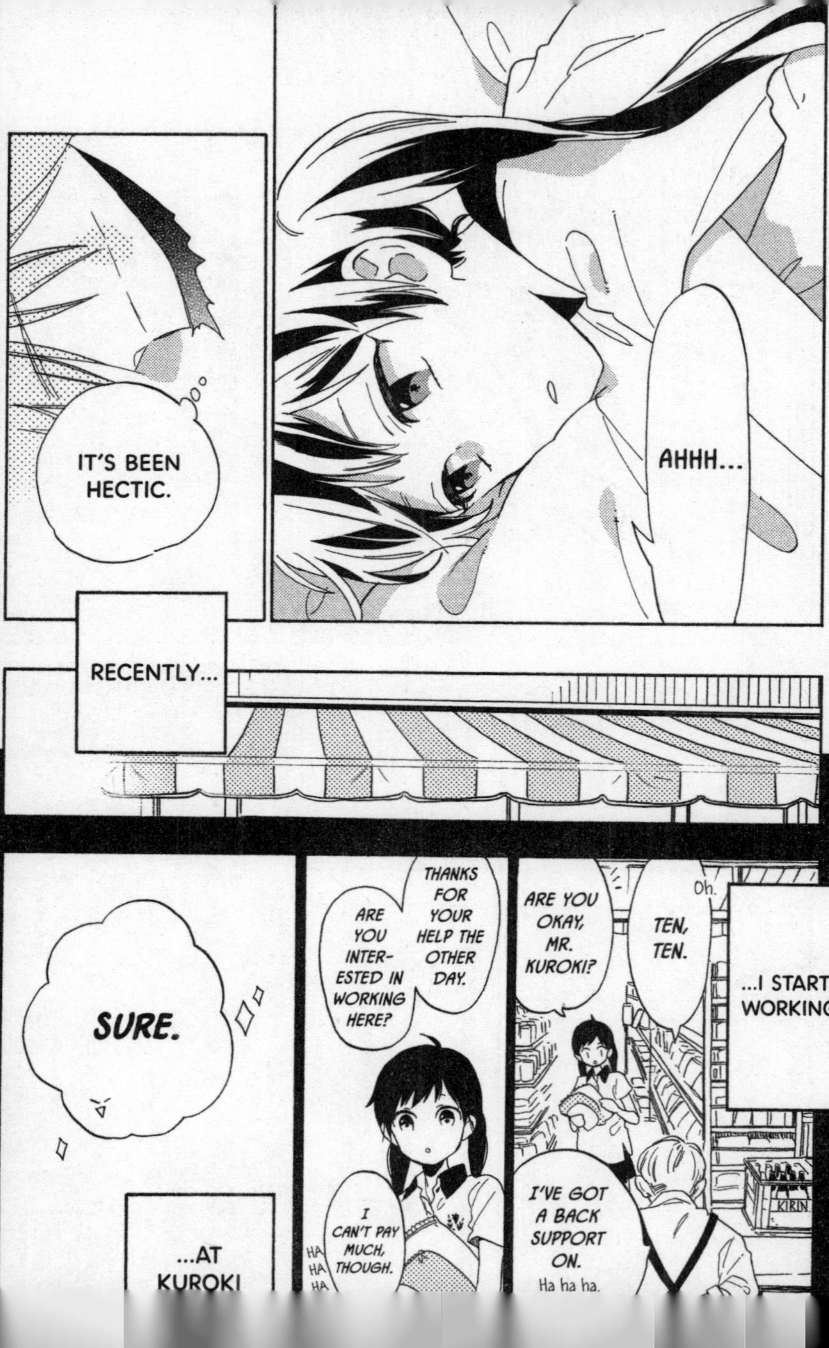
AHHH...
IT'S BEEN HECTIC.
RECENTLY...
...I STARTED WORKING...
Oh.
TEN, TEN.
ARE YOU OKAY, MR. KUROKI?
I'VE GOT A BACK SUPPORT ON.
Ha ha ha.
KIRIN
THANKS FOR YOUR HELP THE OTHER DAY.
ARE YOU INTER-ESTED IN WORKING HERE?
I CAN'T PAY MUCH, THOUGH.
HA HA HA
SURE.
...AT KUROKI

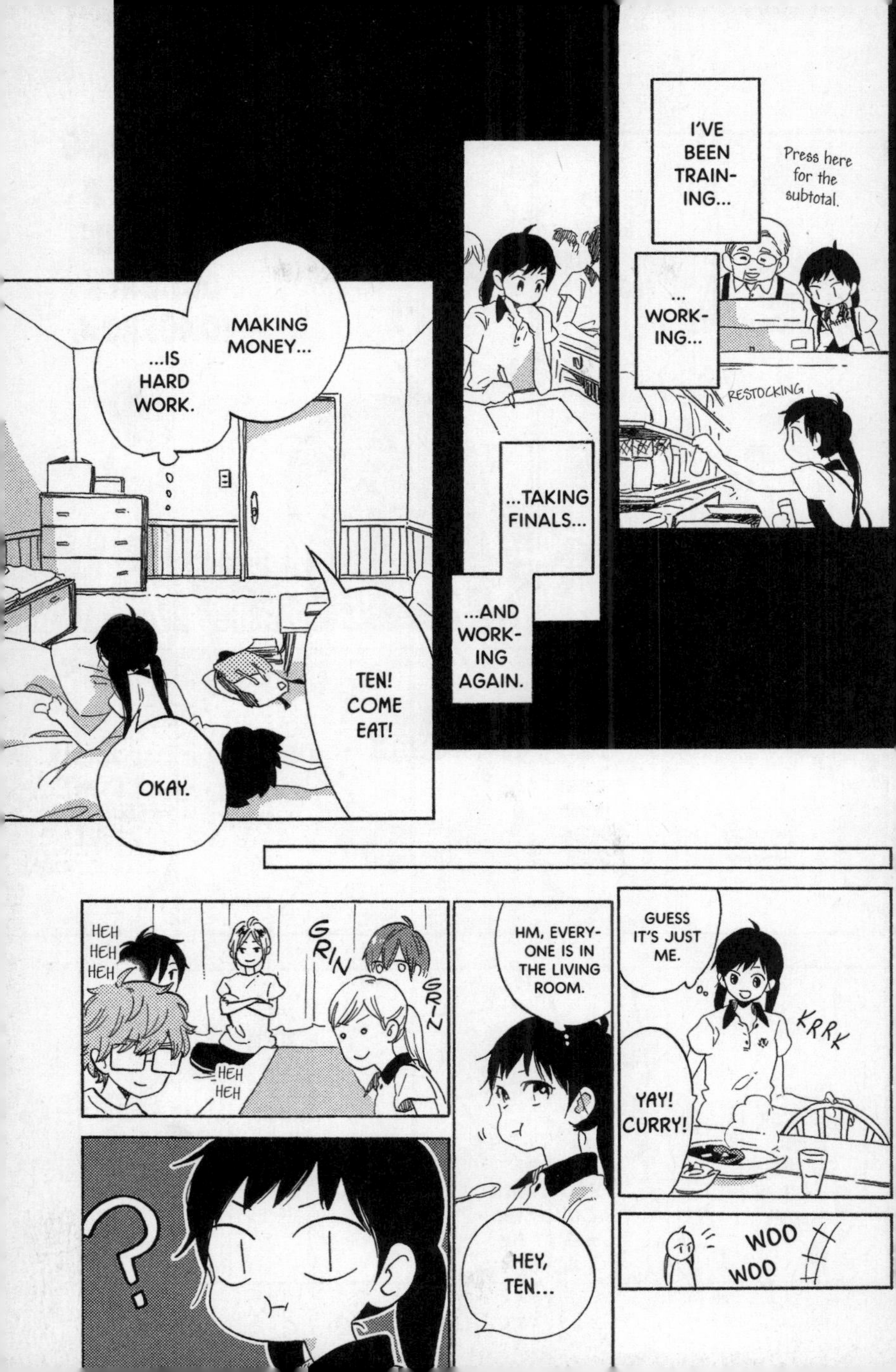
I'VE BEEN TRAIN-ING...
Press here for the subtotal.
... WORK-ING...
RESTOCKING
...TAKING FINALS...
...AND WORK-ING AGAIN.
MAKING MONEY...
...IS HARD WORK.
TEN! COME EAT!
OKAY.
GUESS IT'S JUST ME.
KRRK
YAY! CURRY!
WOO WOO
HM, EVERY-ONE IS IN THE LIVING ROOM.
HEY, TEN...
GRIN
GRIN
HEH HEH HEH
HEH HEH
?

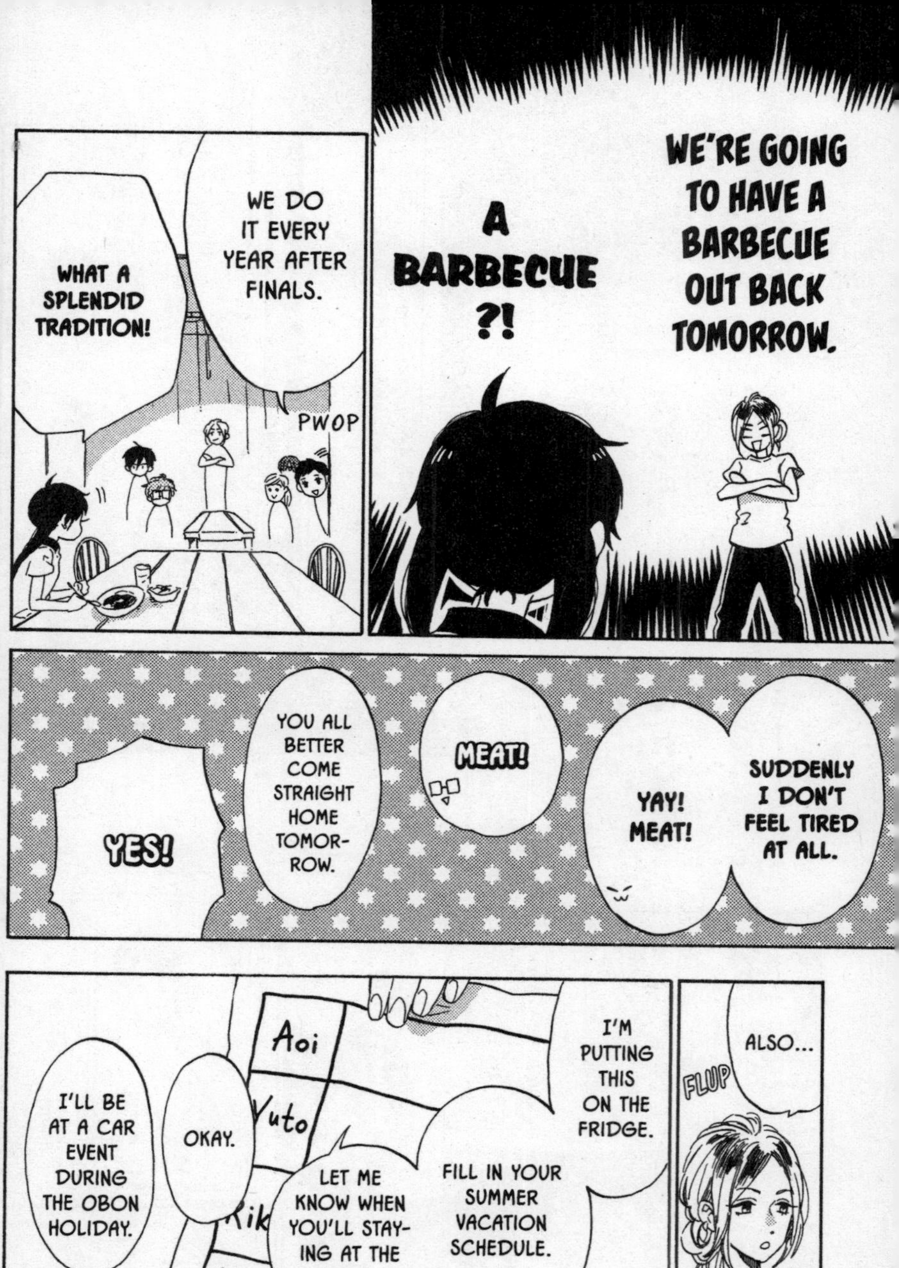
WE'RE GOING TO HAVE A BARBECUE OUT BACK TOMORROW.
A BARBECUE ?!
WE DO IT EVERY YEAR AFTER FINALS.
WHAT A SPLENDID TRADITION!
PWOP
SUDDENLY I DON'T FEEL TIRED AT ALL.
YAY! MEAT!
MEAT!
YOU ALL BETTER COME STRAIGHT HOME TOMOR-ROW.
YES!
ALSO...
FLUP
I'M PUTTING THIS ON THE FRIDGE.
FILL IN YOUR SUMMER VACATION SCHEDULE.
LET ME KNOW WHEN YOU'LL STAY-ING AT THE HOUSE.
Aoi
Yuto
OKAY.
I'LL BE AT A CAR EVENT DURING THE OBON HOLIDAY.

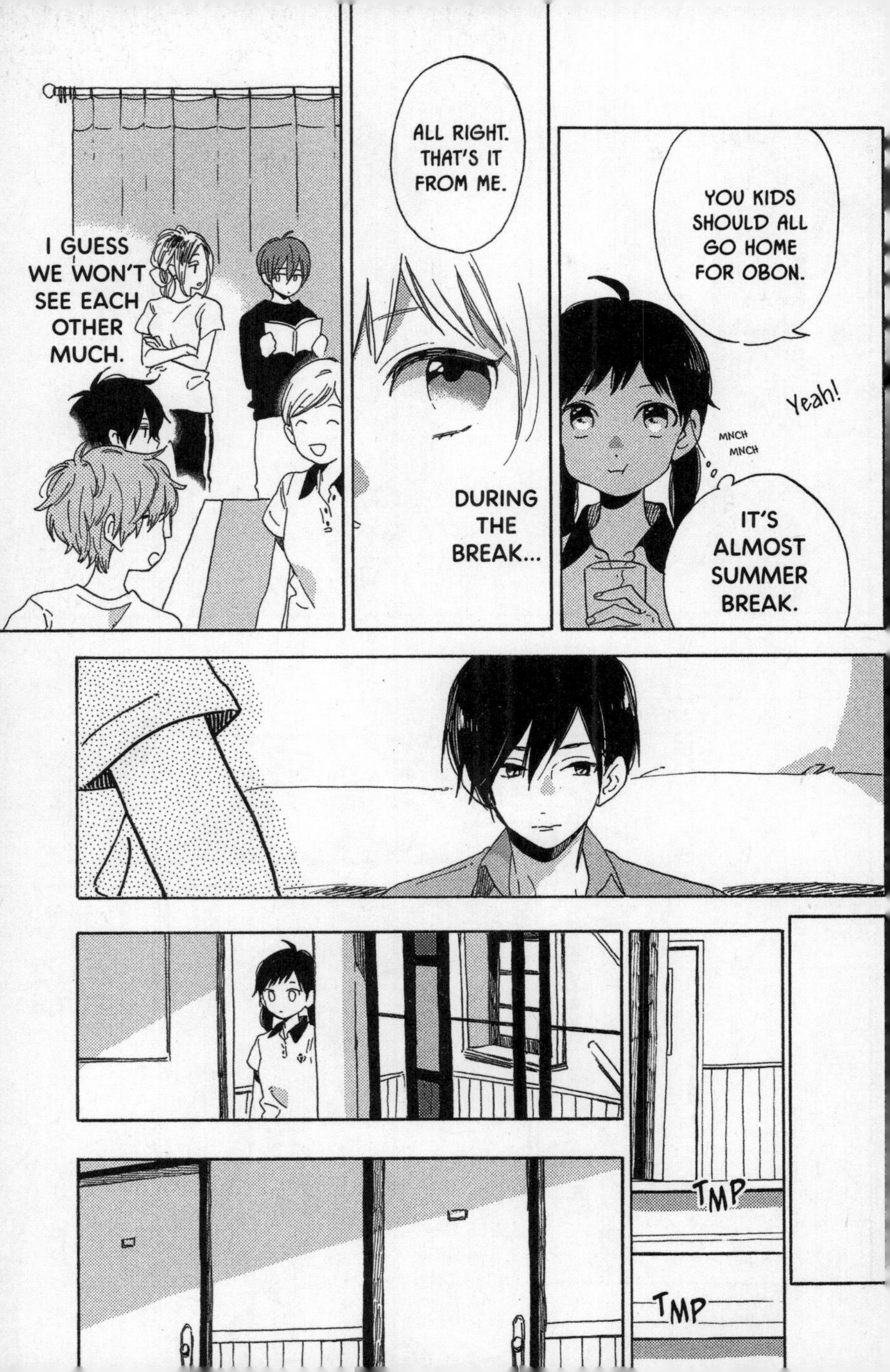
YOU KIDS SHOULD ALL GO HOME FOR OBON.
Yeah!
MNCH MNCH
IT'S ALMOST SUMMER BREAK.
ALL RIGHT. THAT'S IT FROM ME.
DURING THE BREAK...
I GUESS WE WON'T SEE EACH OTHER MUCH.
TMP
TMP

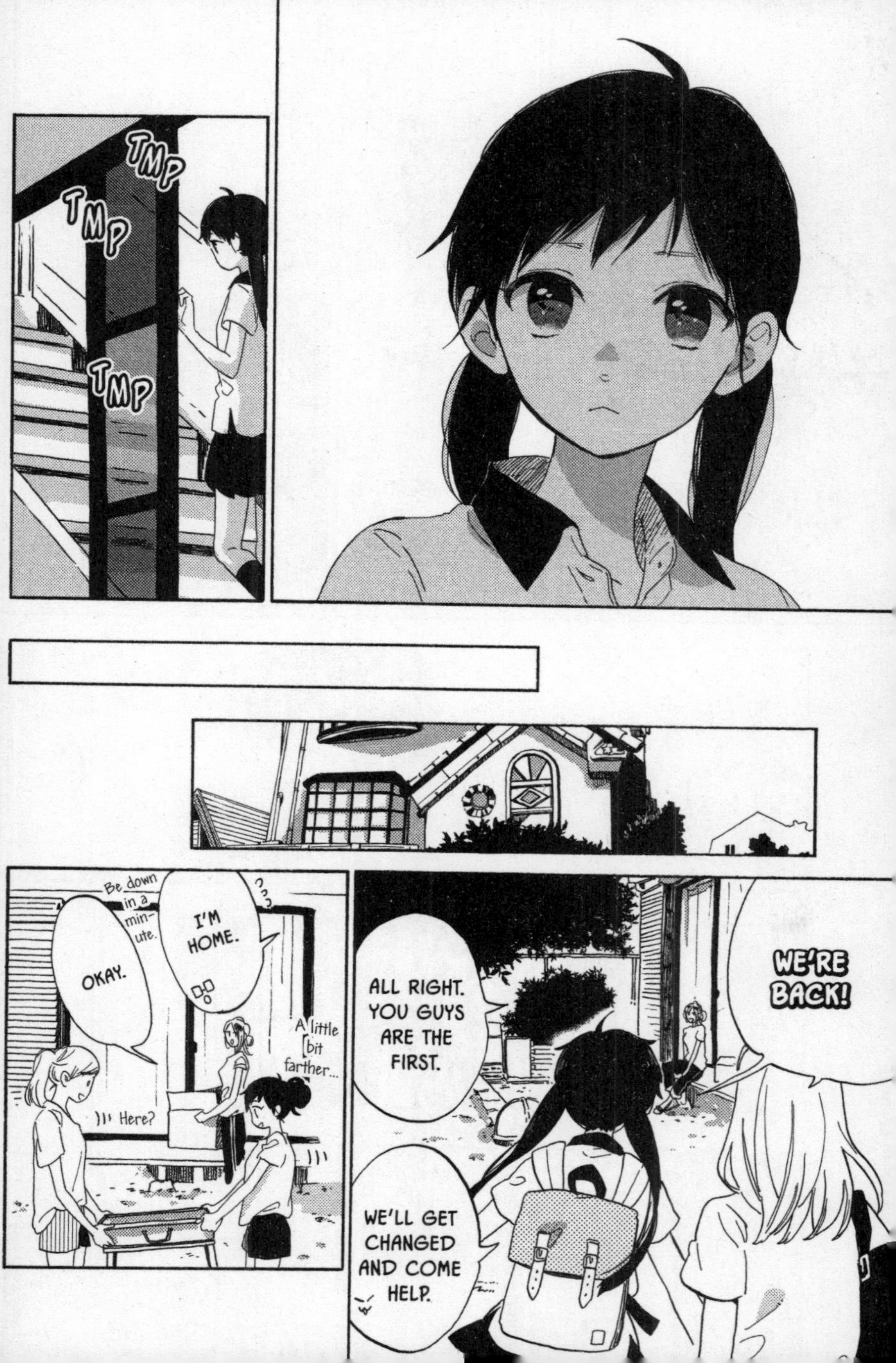
TMP
TMP
TMP
WE'RE BACK!
ALL RIGHT. YOU GUYS ARE THE FIRST.
WE'LL GET CHANGED AND COME HELP.
I'M HOME.
Be down in a min-ute.
OKAY.
A little bit farther...
Here?

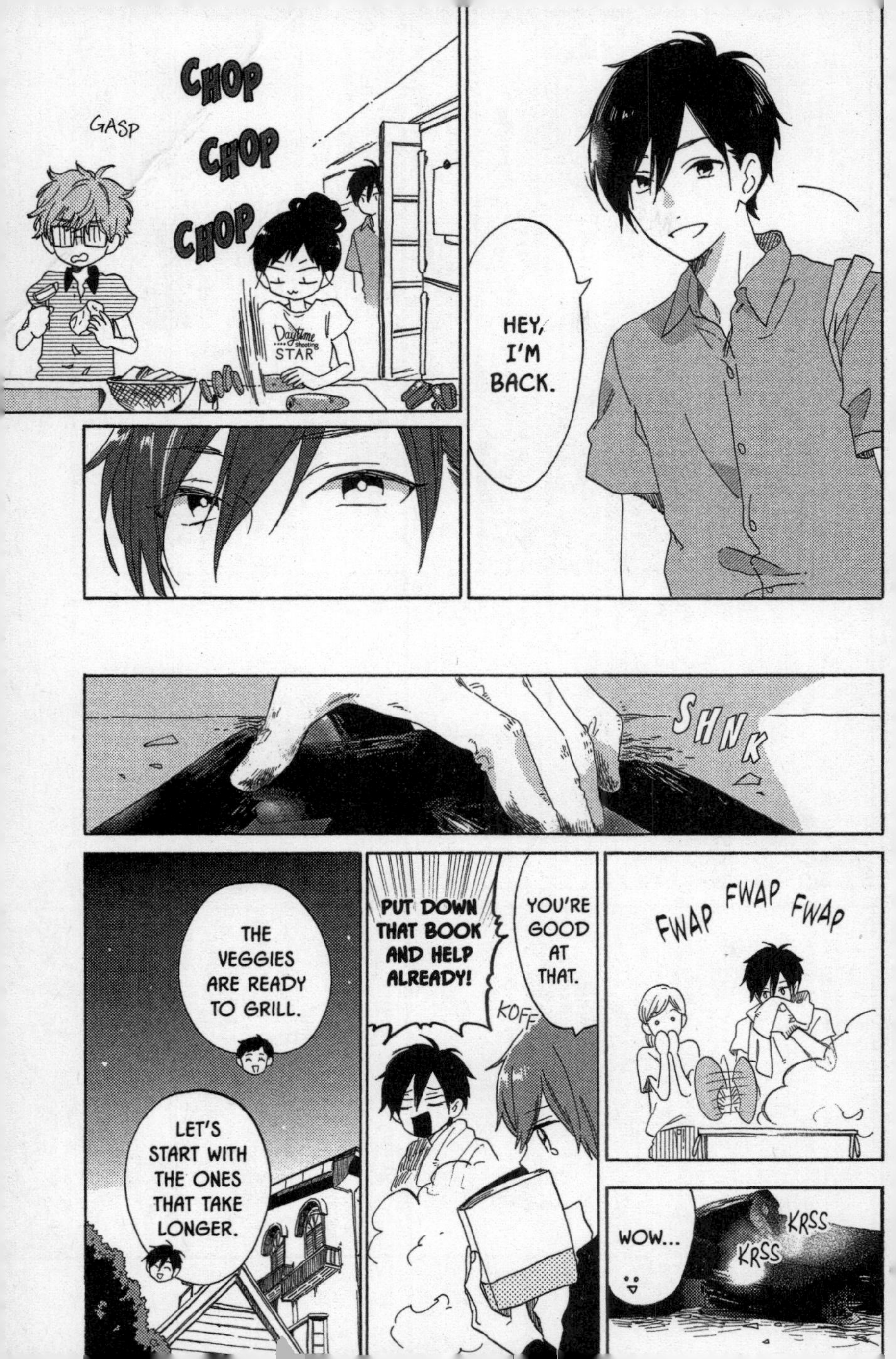
HEY, I'M BACK.
CHOP CHOP CHOP
GASP
Daytime Shooting STAR
SHNK
FWAP FWAP FWAP
WOW...
KRSS KRSS
YOU'RE GOOD AT THAT.
PUT DOWN THAT BOOK AND HELP ALREADY!
KOFF
THE VEGGIES ARE READY TO GRILL.
LET'S START WITH THE ONES THAT TAKE LONGER.

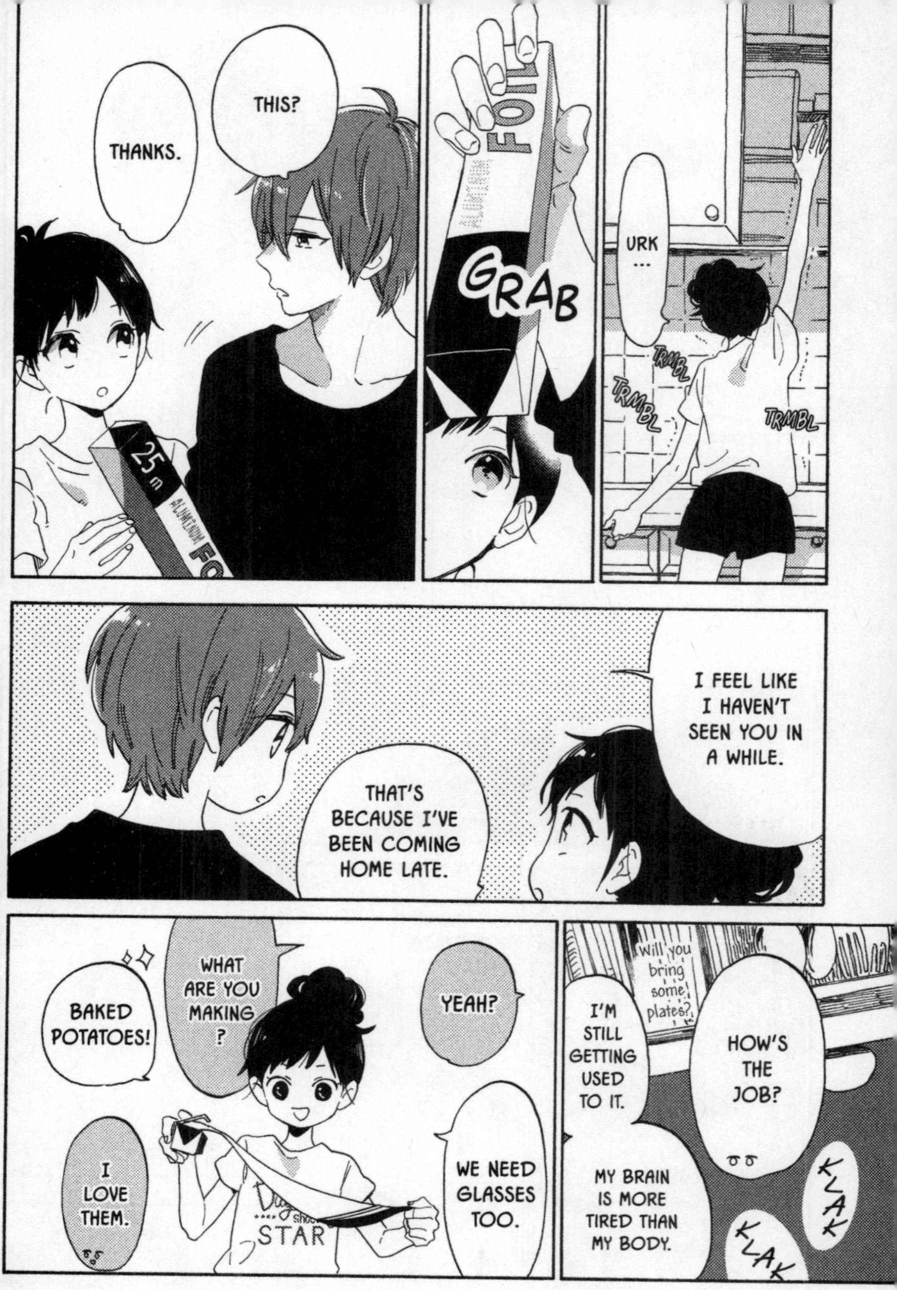
URK ...
TRMBL
TRMBL
TRMBL
GRAB
FOIL
THIS?
THANKS.
25 m
I FEEL LIKE I HAVEN'T SEEN YOU IN A WHILE.
THAT'S BECAUSE I'VE BEEN COMING HOME LATE.
HOW'S THE JOB?
Will you bring some plates?
I'M STILL GETTING USED TO IT.
MY BRAIN IS MORE TIRED THAN MY BODY.
KLAK
KLAK
YEAH?
WHAT ARE YOU MAKING?
BAKED POTATOES!
WE NEED GLASSES TOO.
STAR
I LOVE THEM.

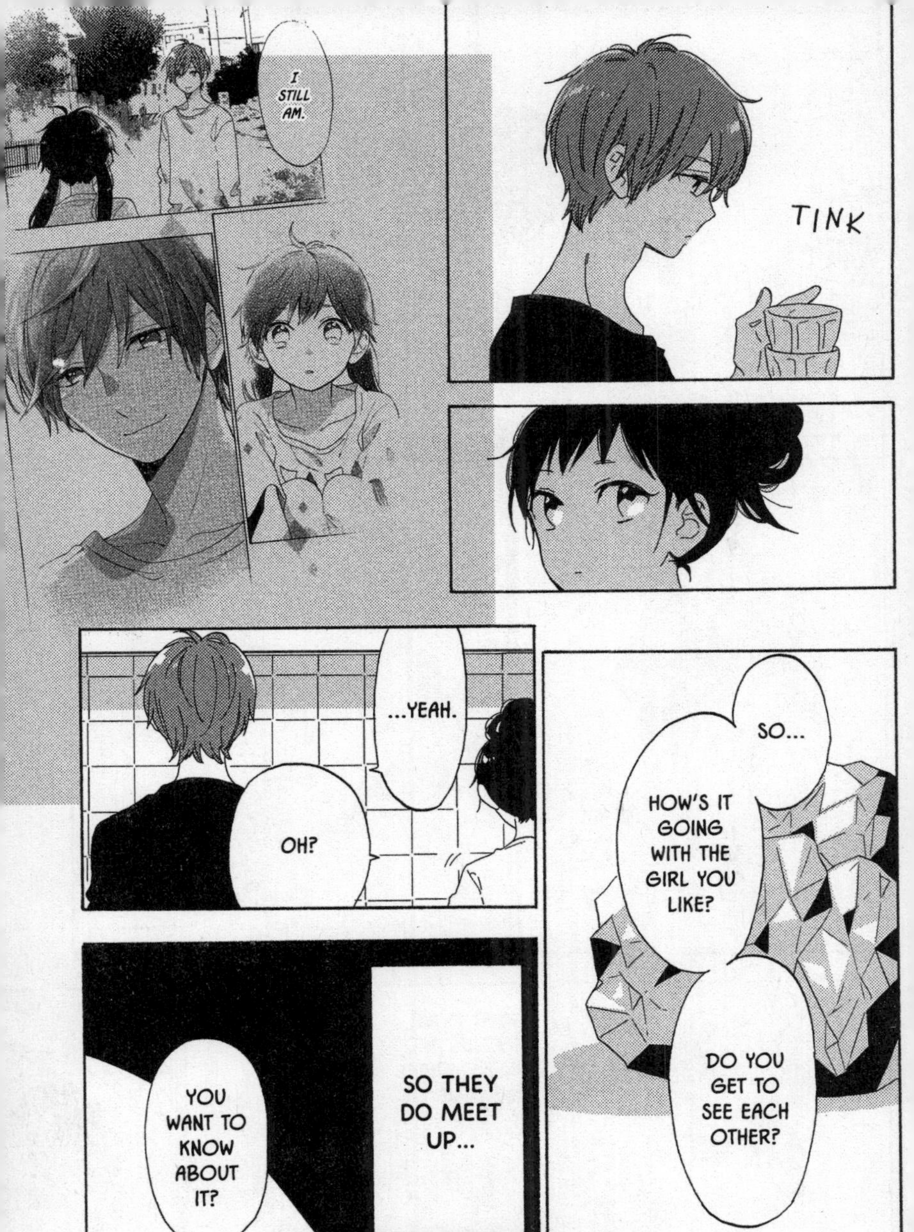
TINK
I STILL AM.
SO...
HOW'S IT GOING WITH THE GIRL YOU LIKE?
DO YOU GET TO SEE EACH OTHER?
...YEAH.
OH?
SO THEY DO MEET UP...
YOU WANT TO KNOW ABOUT IT?

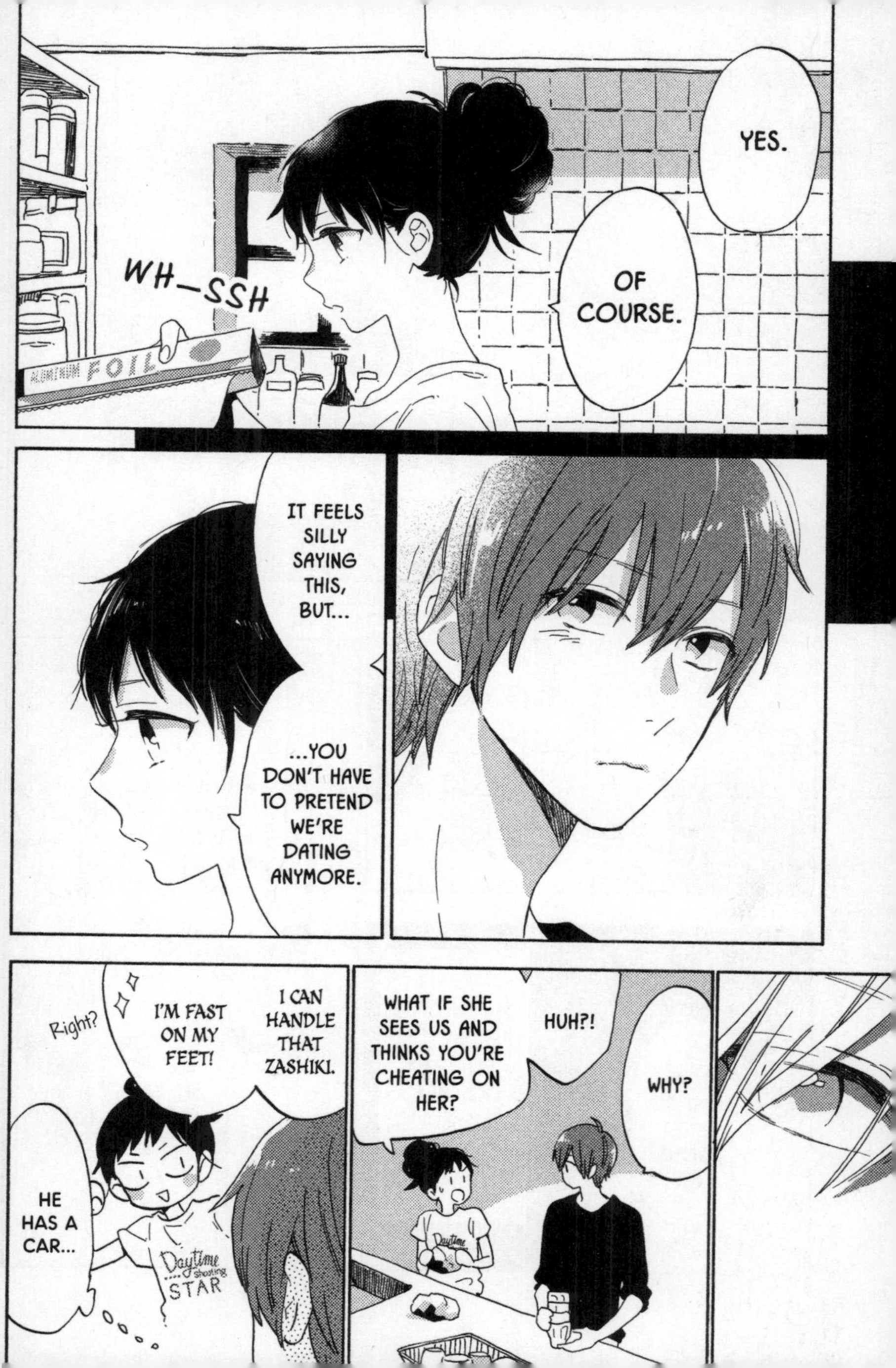
YES.
OF COURSE.
WH—SSH
ALUMINUM FOIL
IT FEELS SILLY SAYING THIS, BUT...
...YOU DON'T HAVE TO PRETEND WE'RE DATING ANYMORE.
HUH?!
WHY?
WHAT IF SHE SEES US AND THINKS YOU'RE CHEATING ON HER?
Daytime
I CAN HANDLE THAT ZASHIKI.
I'M FAST ON MY FEET!
Right?
HE HAS A CAR...
Daytime shooting STAR

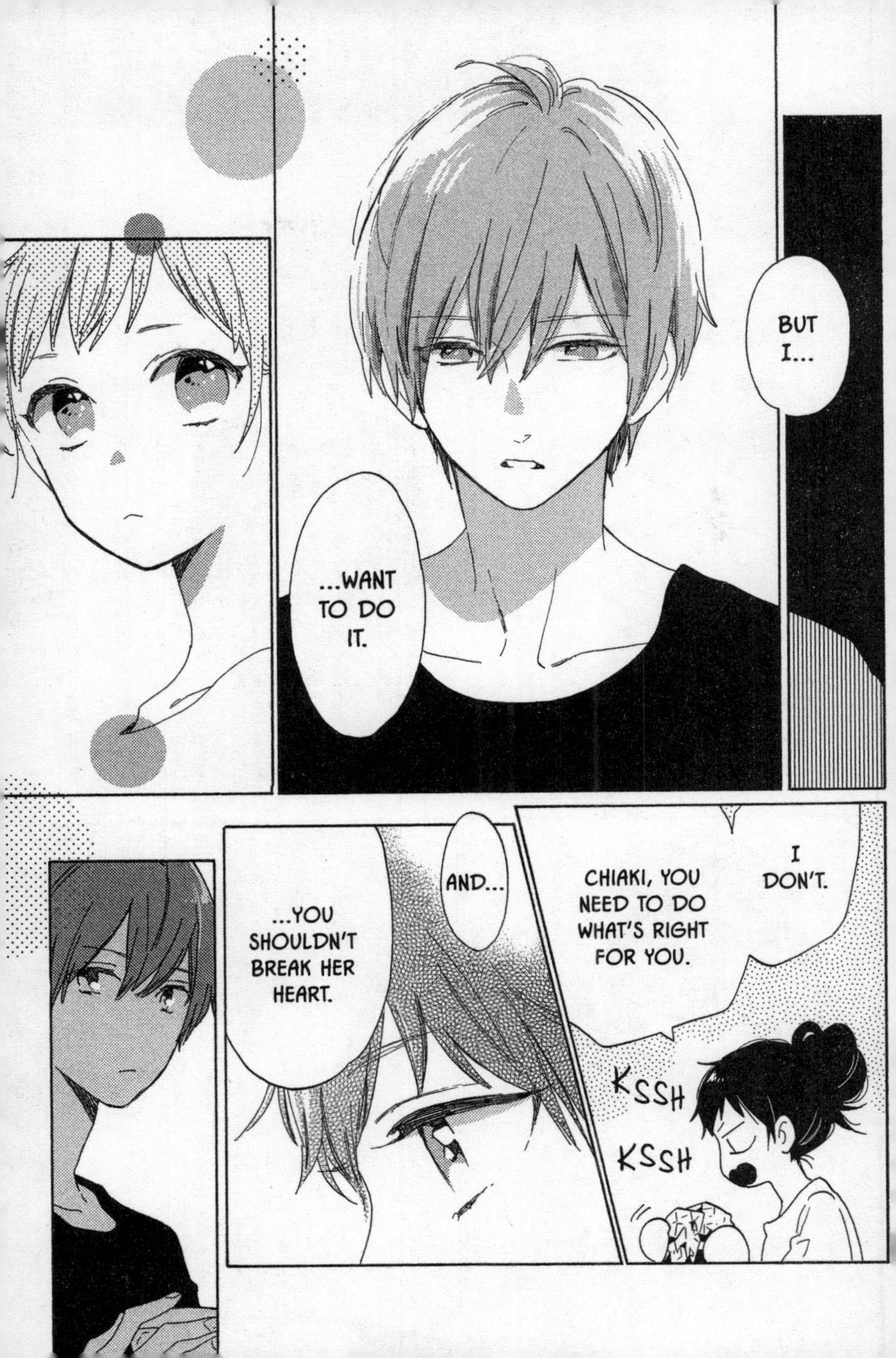
BUT I...
...WANT TO DO IT.
I DON'T.
CHIAKI, YOU NEED TO DO WHAT'S RIGHT FOR YOU.
KSSH
KSSH
AND...
...YOU SHOULDN'T BREAK HER HEART.

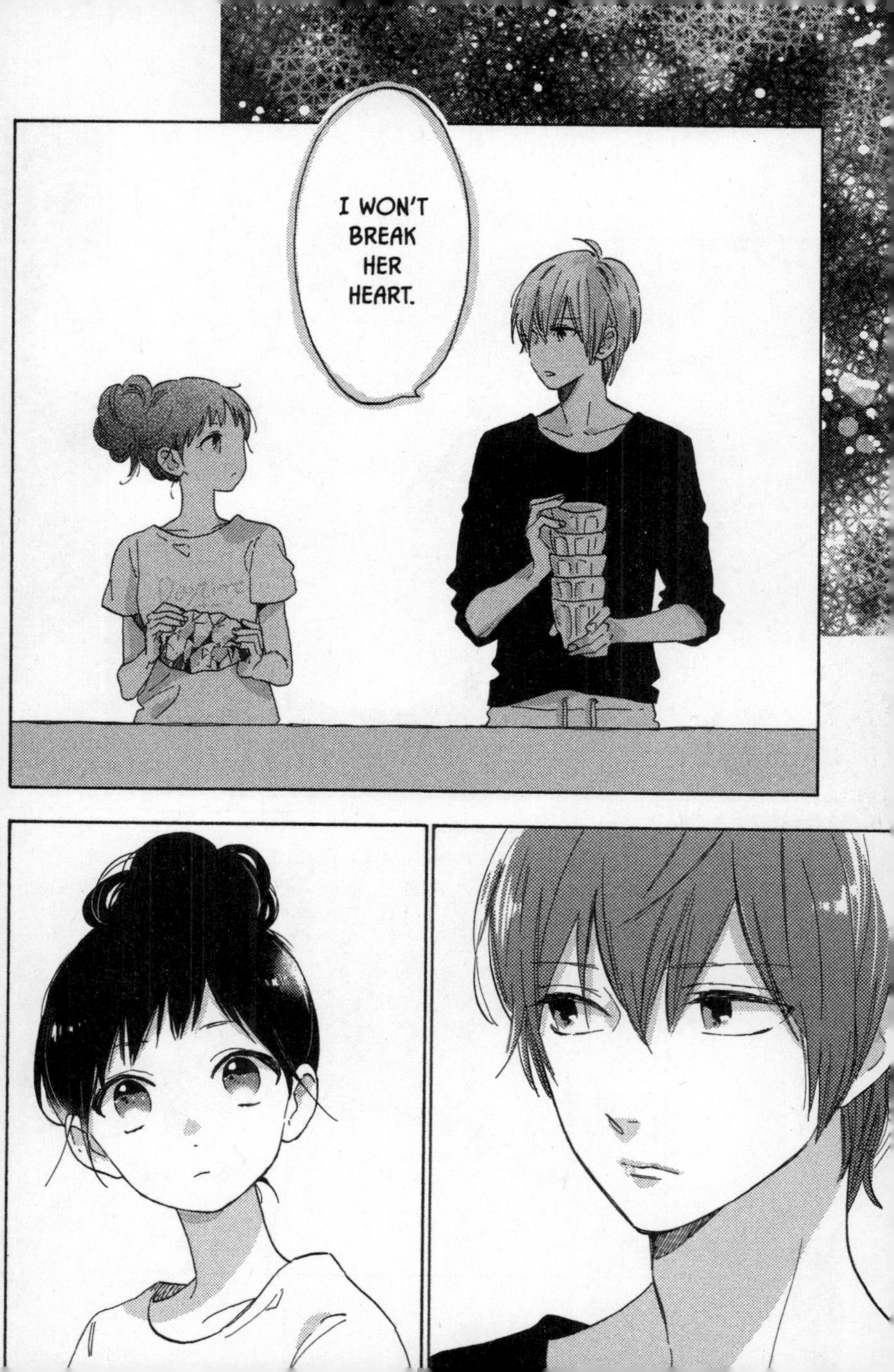
I WON'T BREAK HER HEART.

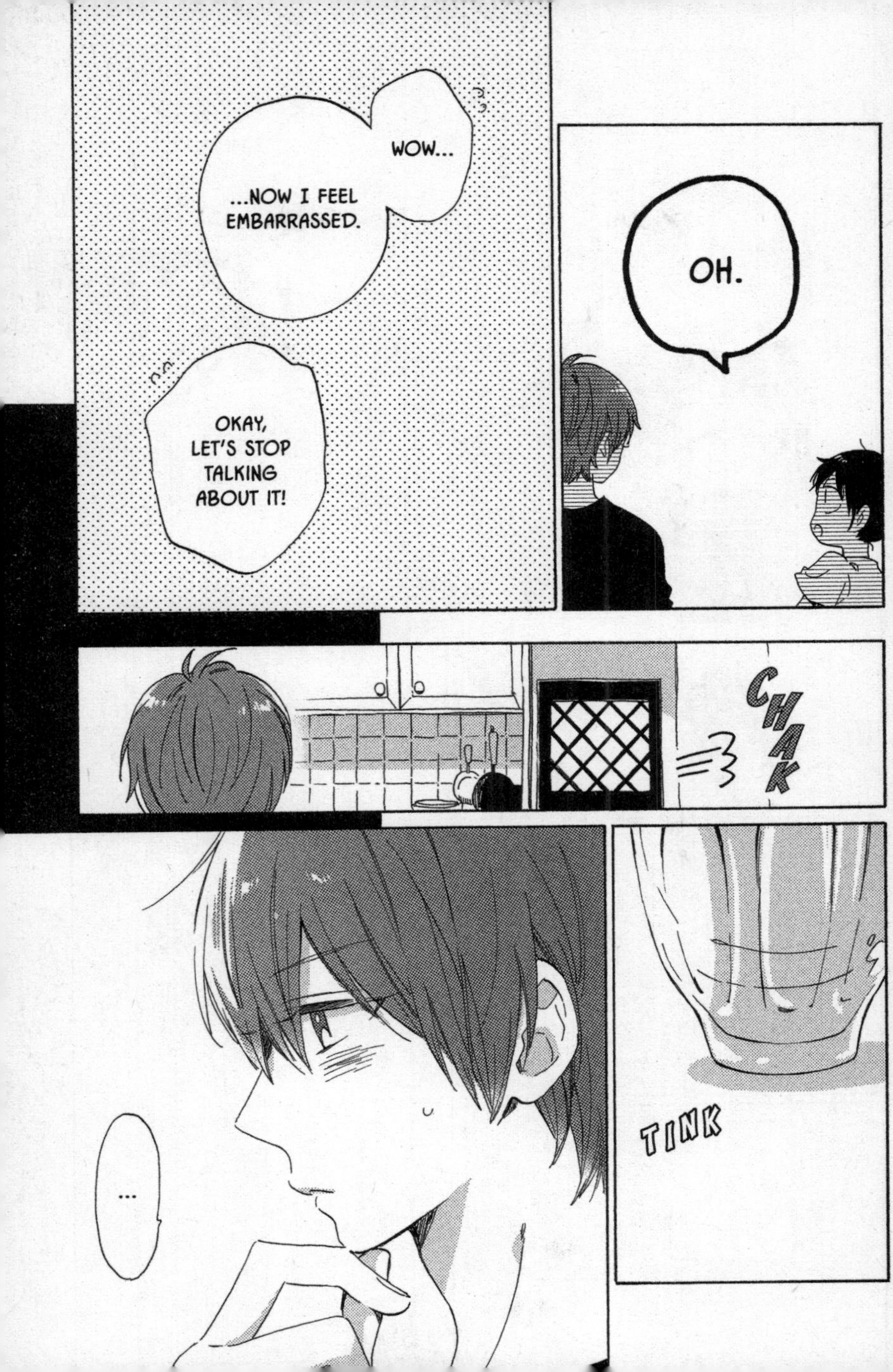
OH.
WOW...
...NOW I FEEL EMBARRASSED.
OKAY, LET'S STOP TALKING ABOUT IT!
CHAK
TINK
...

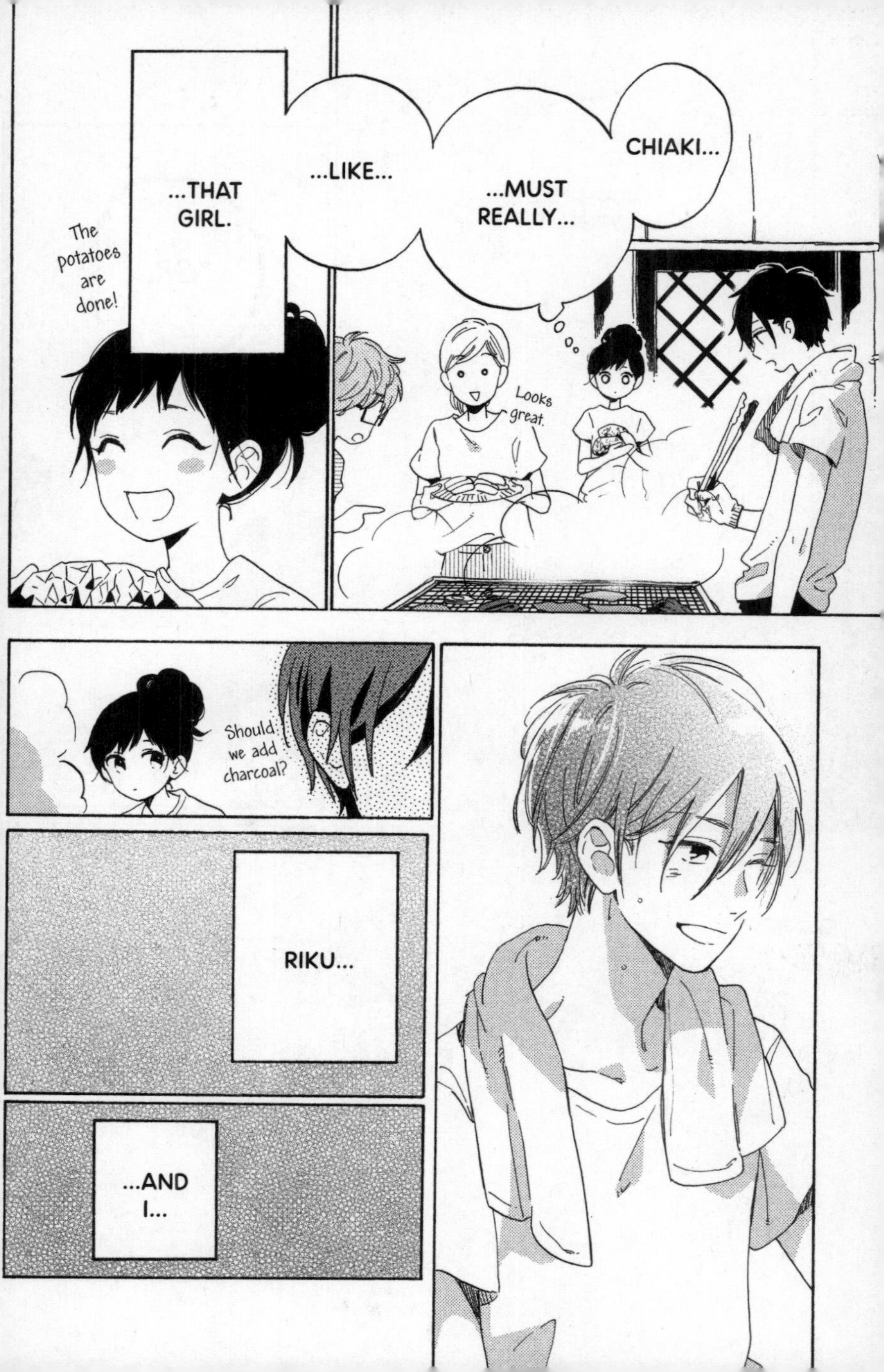
CHIAKI...
...MUST REALLY...
...LIKE...
Looks great.
...THAT GIRL.
The potatoes are done!
Should we add charcoal?
RIKU...
...AND I...

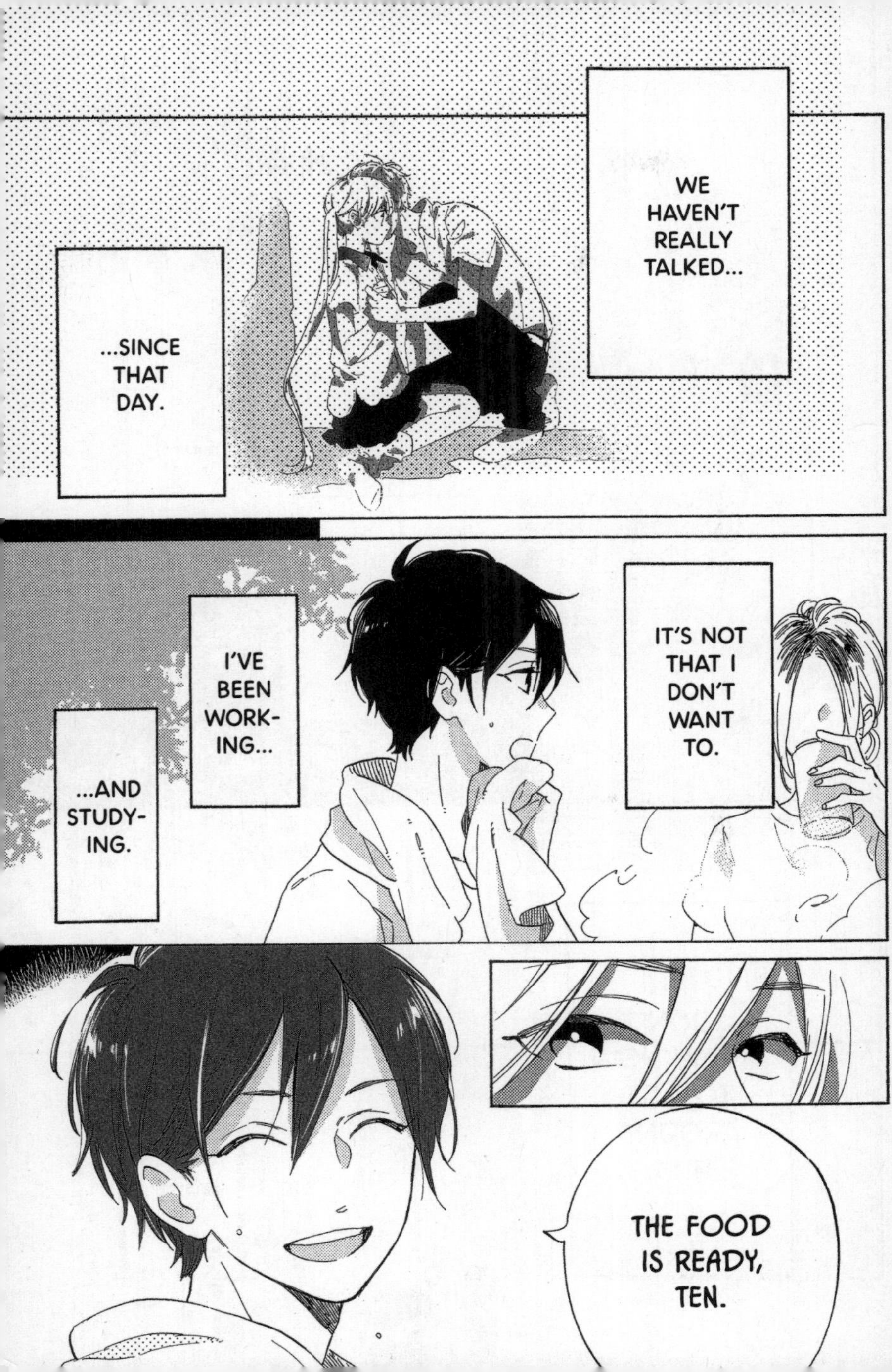
WE HAVEN'T REALLY TALKED...
...SINCE THAT DAY.
IT'S NOT THAT I DON'T WANT TO.
I'VE BEEN WORKING...
...AND STUDYING.
THE FOOD IS READY, TEN.

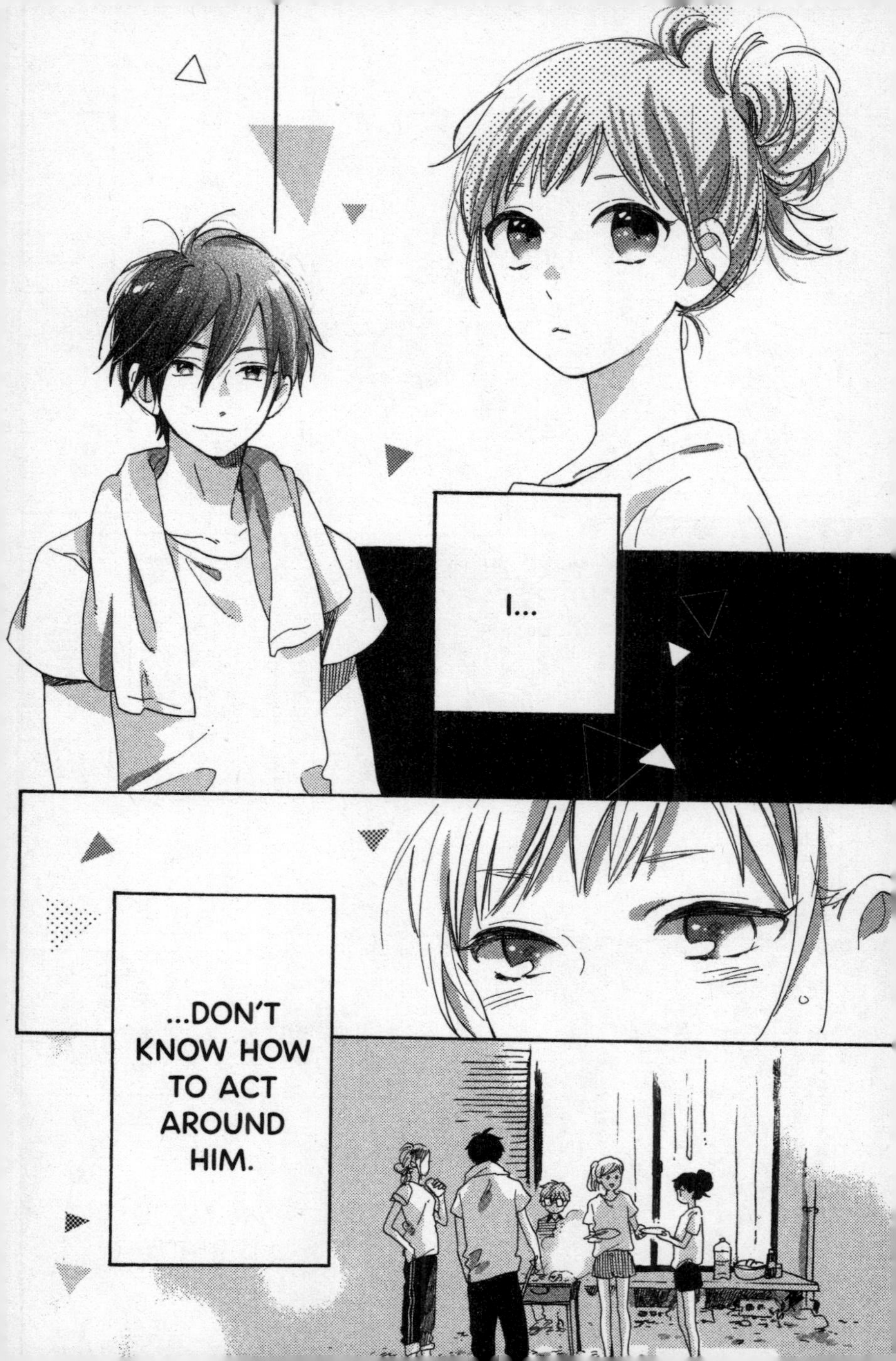
I...
...DON'T KNOW HOW TO ACT AROUND HIM.

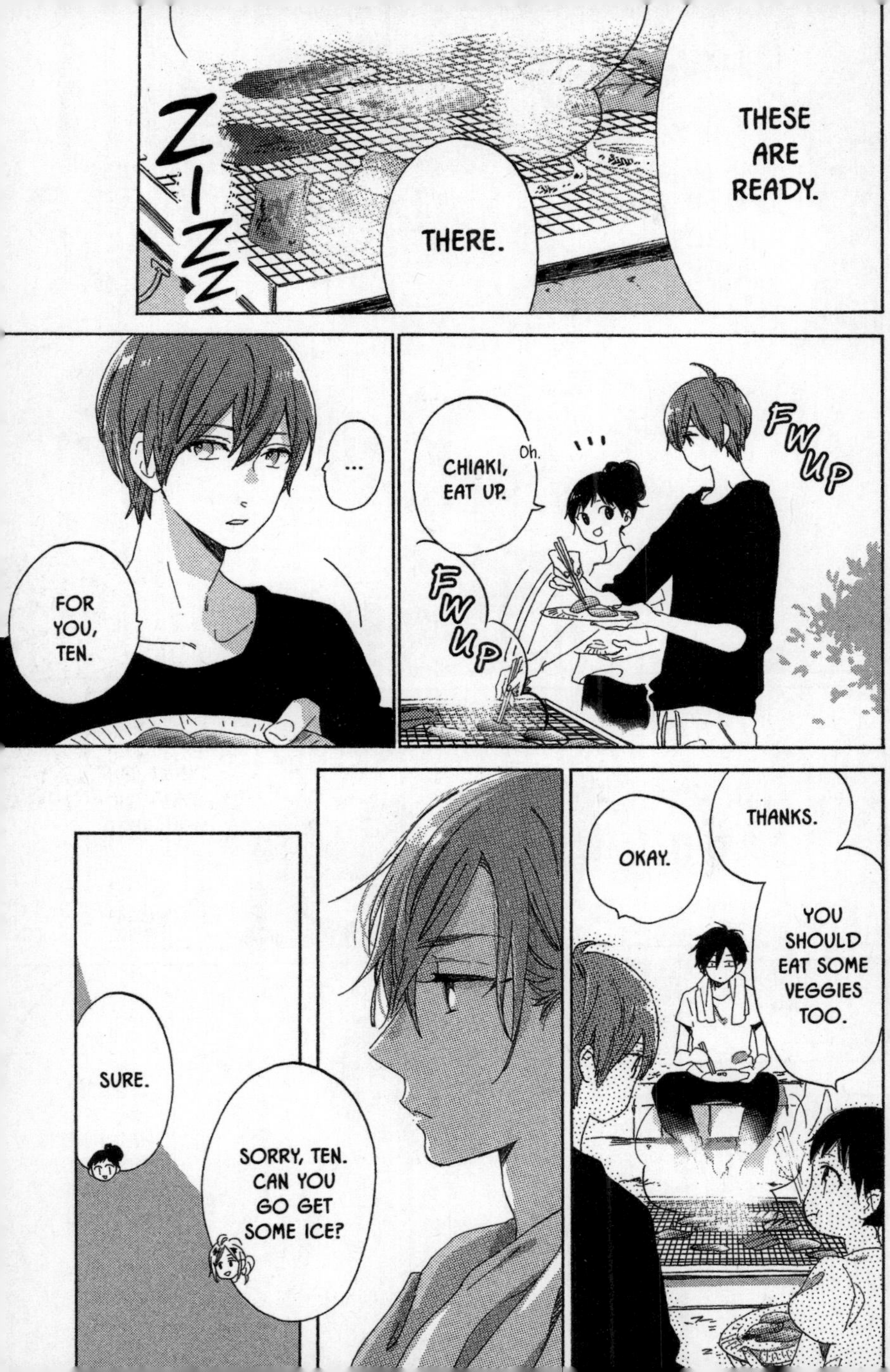
THESE ARE READY.
THERE.
ZIZZ
FWUP
CHIAKI, EAT UP.
Oh.
...
FWUP
...
FOR YOU, TEN.
THANKS.
OKAY.
YOU SHOULD EAT SOME VEGGIES TOO.
SORRY, TEN. CAN YOU GO GET SOME ICE?
SURE.

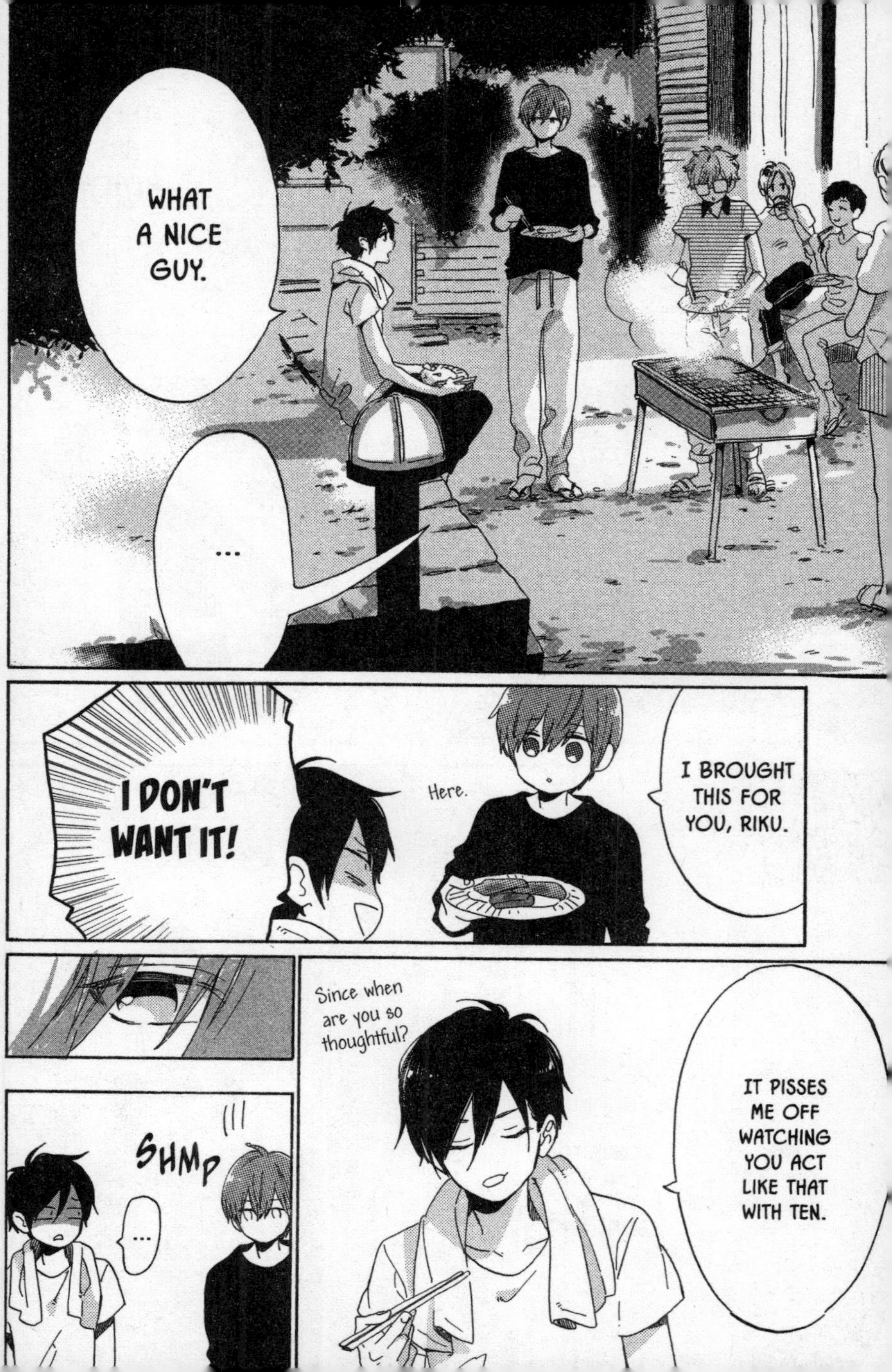
WHAT A NICE GUY.
...
I BROUGHT THIS FOR YOU, RIKU.
Here.
I DON'T WANT IT!
IT PISSES ME OFF WATCHING YOU ACT LIKE THAT WITH TEN.
Since when are you so thoughtful?
SHMP
...

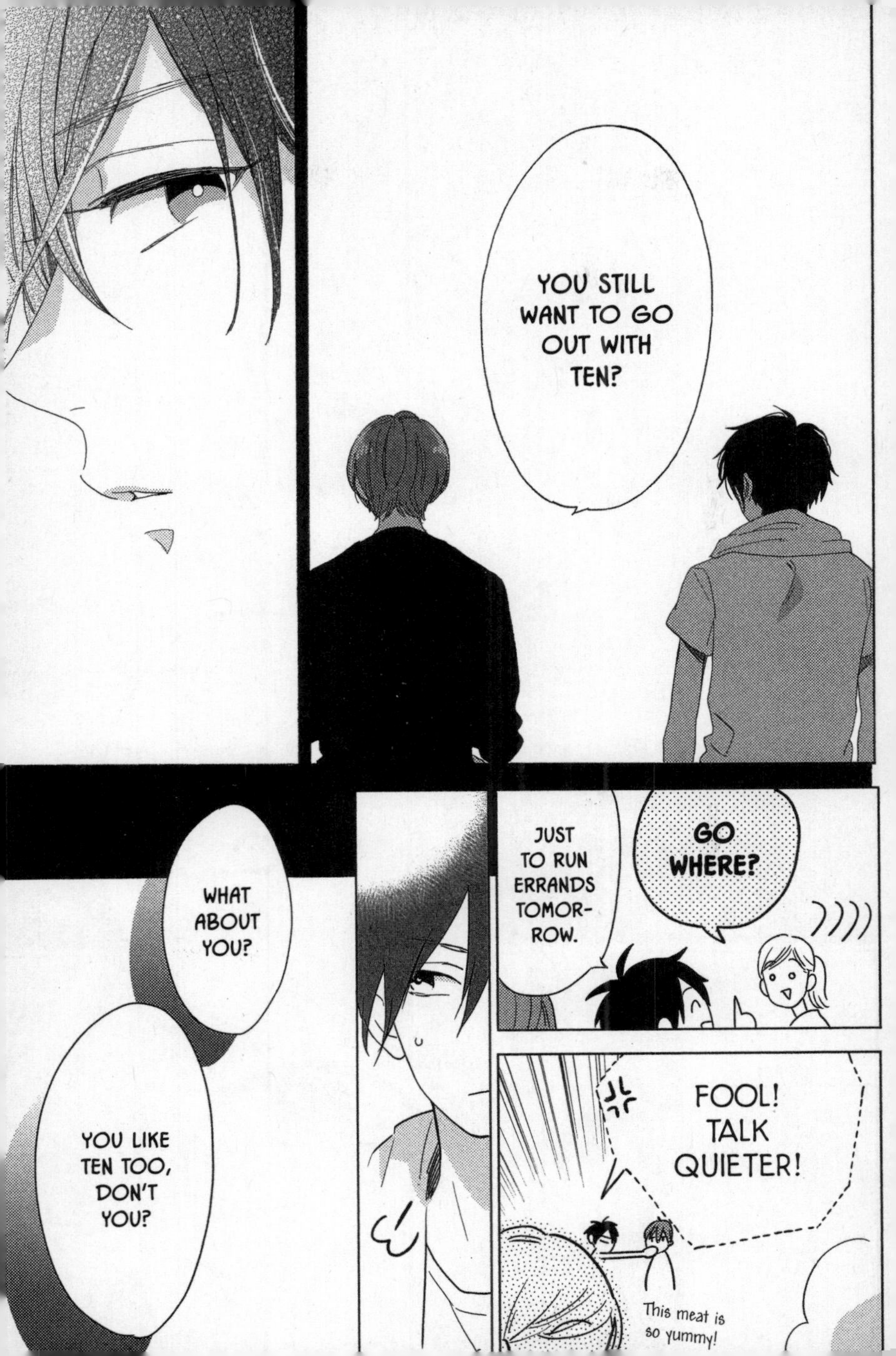
YOU STILL WANT TO GO OUT WITH TEN?
GO WHERE?
JUST TO RUN ERRANDS TOMORROW.
FOOL! TALK QUIETER!
This meat is so yummy!
WHAT ABOUT YOU?
YOU LIKE TEN TOO, DON'T YOU?

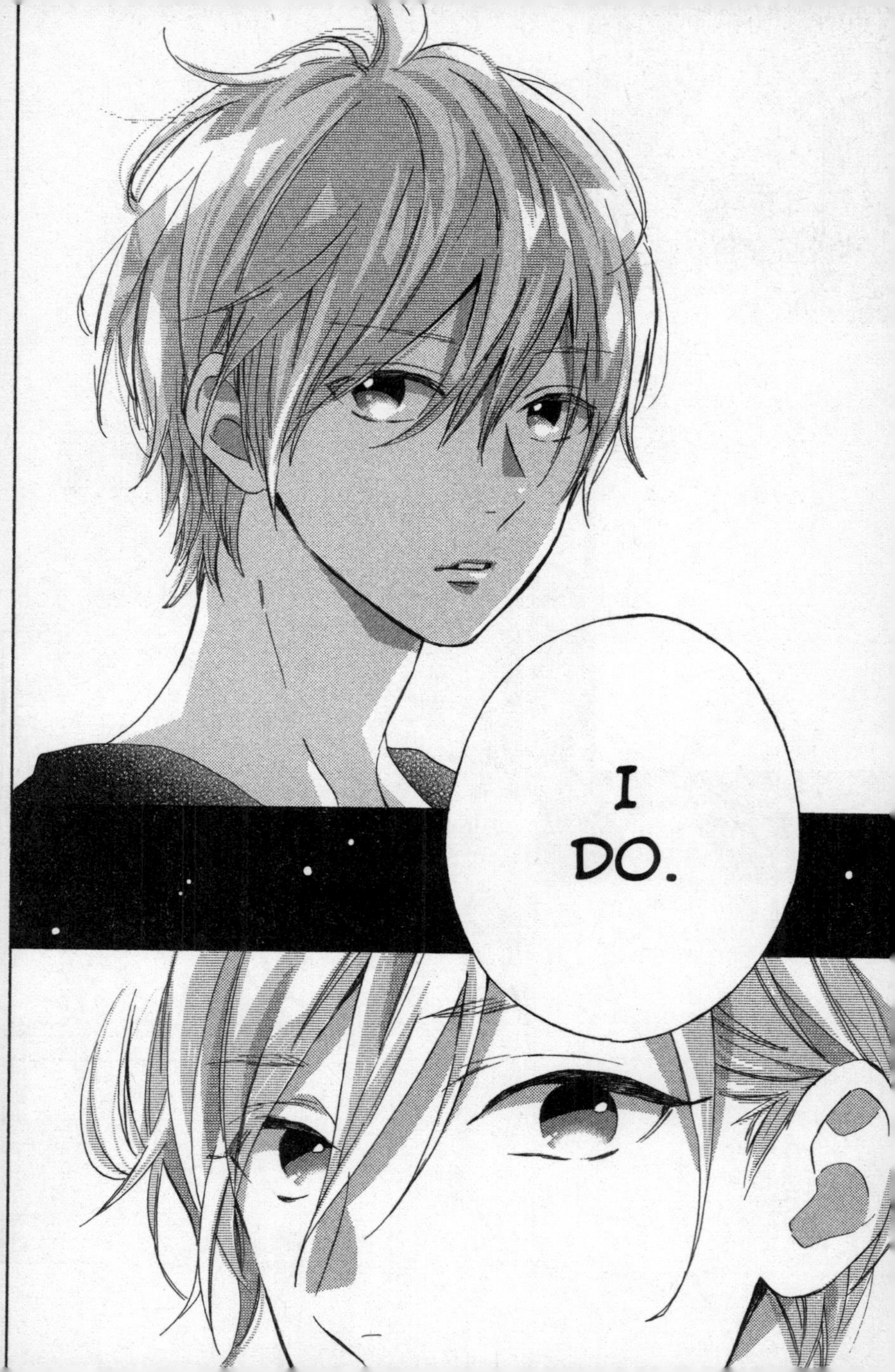
I DO.

KRIII

KRIII

KLINK

Yuto	7/25
Riku	7/25 ~ 8/31
Chiaki	7/25 ~ 8/12
Ageha	
Ten	

...ISN'T GOING HOME AT ALL.

RIKU...

OH.

IT'S ALL FILLED IN.

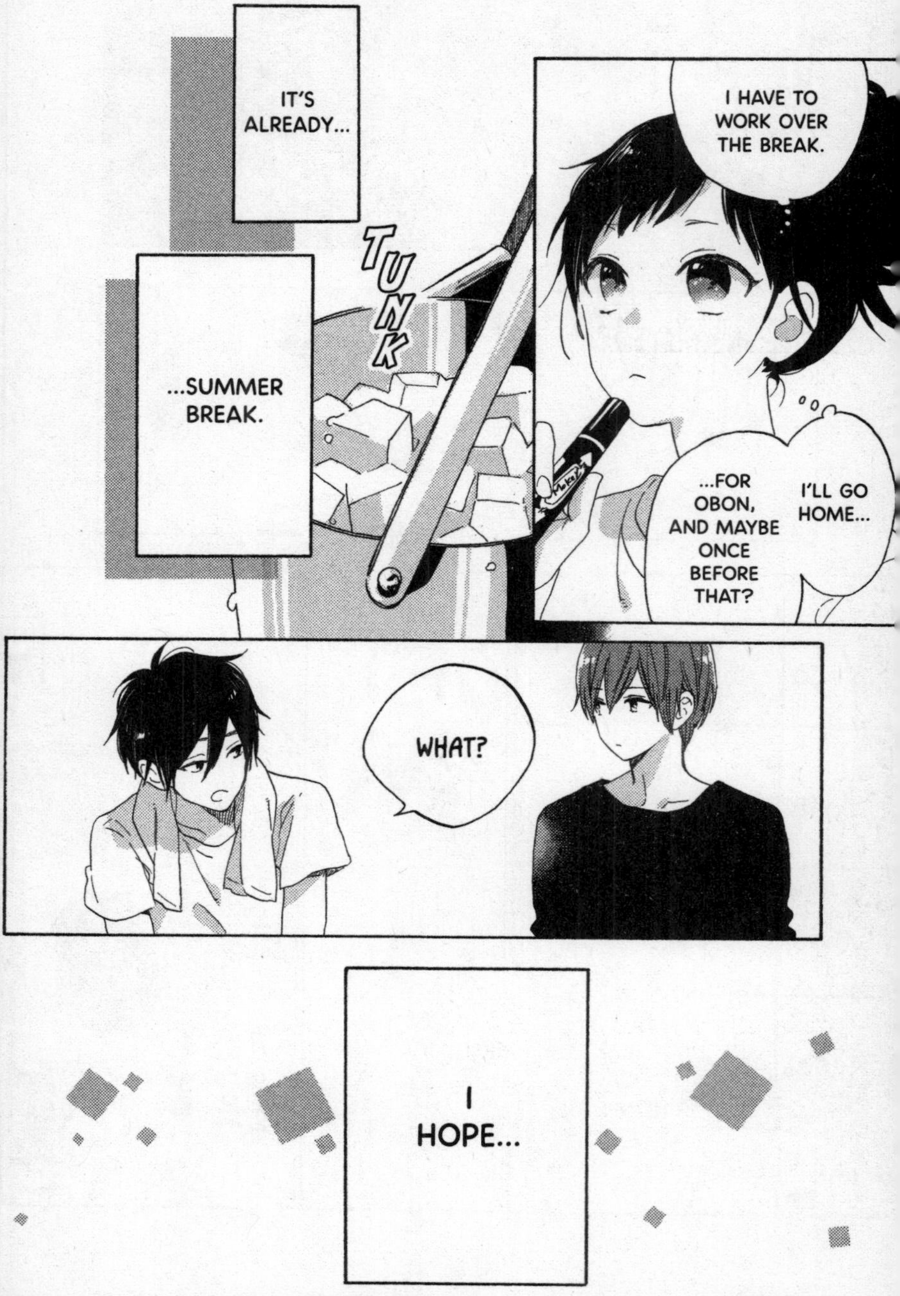
I HAVE TO WORK OVER THE BREAK.
I'LL GO HOME...
...FOR OBON, AND MAYBE ONCE BEFORE THAT?
IT'S ALREADY...
TUNK
...SUMMER BREAK.
WHAT?
I HOPE...

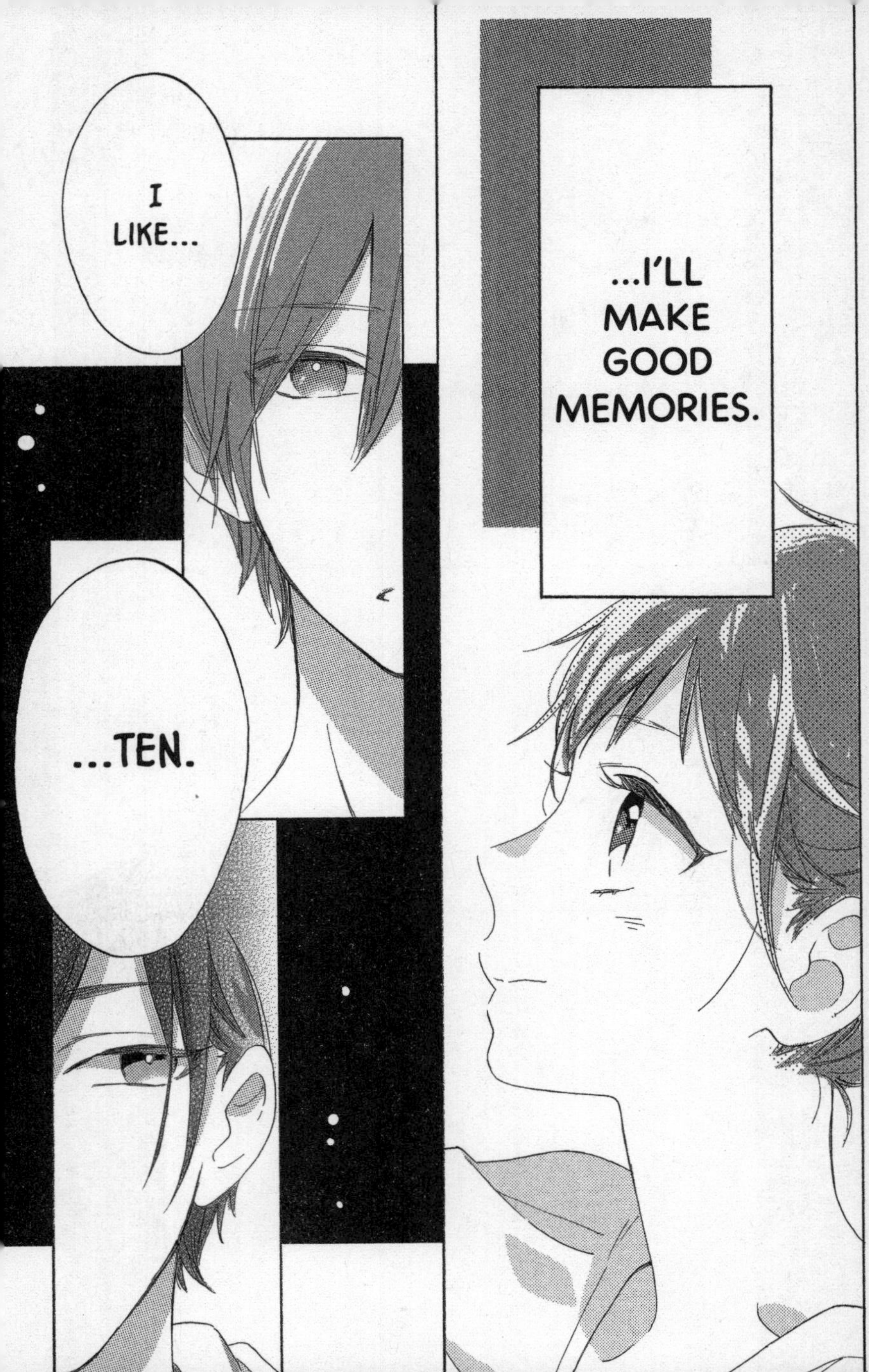
...I'LL MAKE GOOD MEMORIES.
I LIKE...
...TEN.

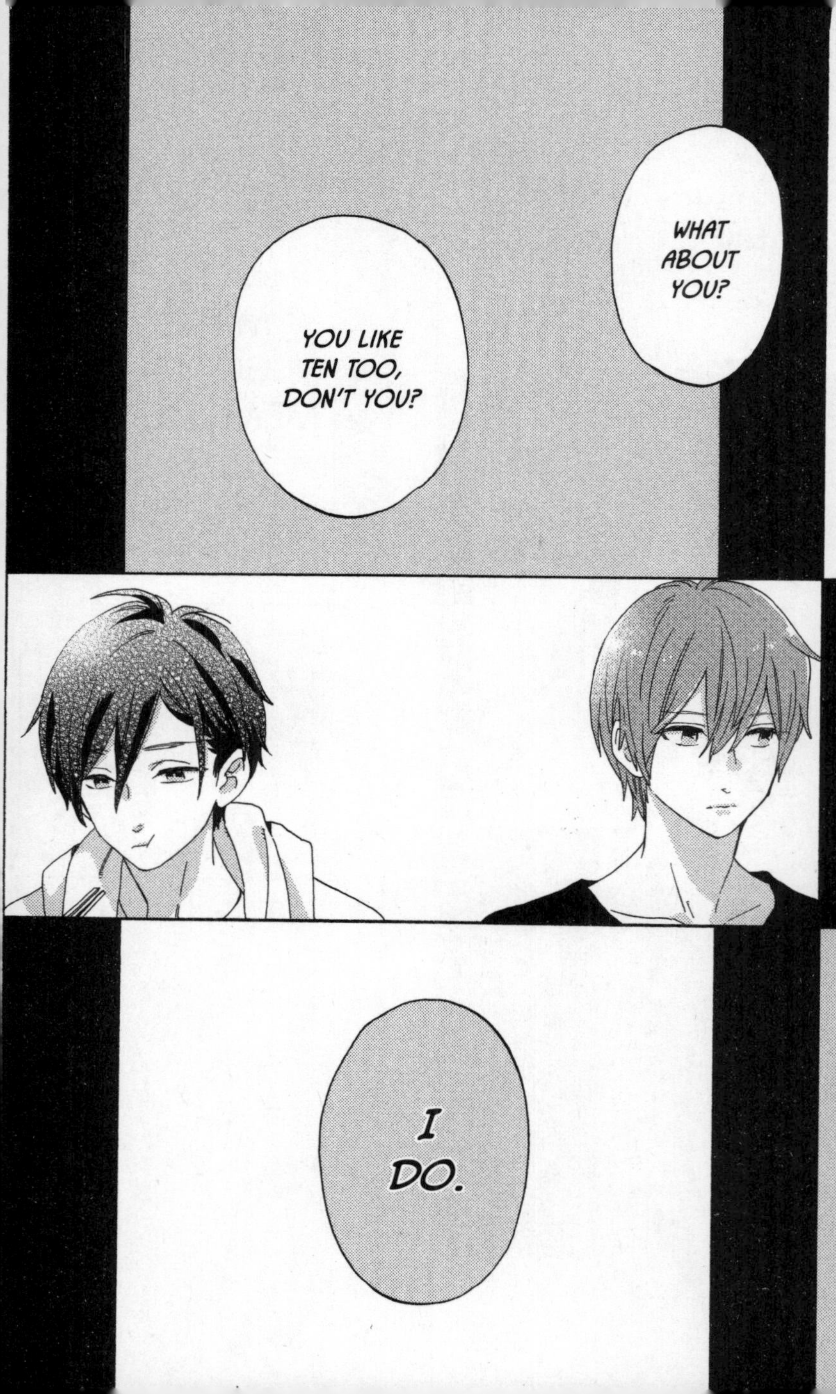
WHAT ABOUT YOU?
YOU LIKE TEN TOO, DON'T YOU?
I DO.

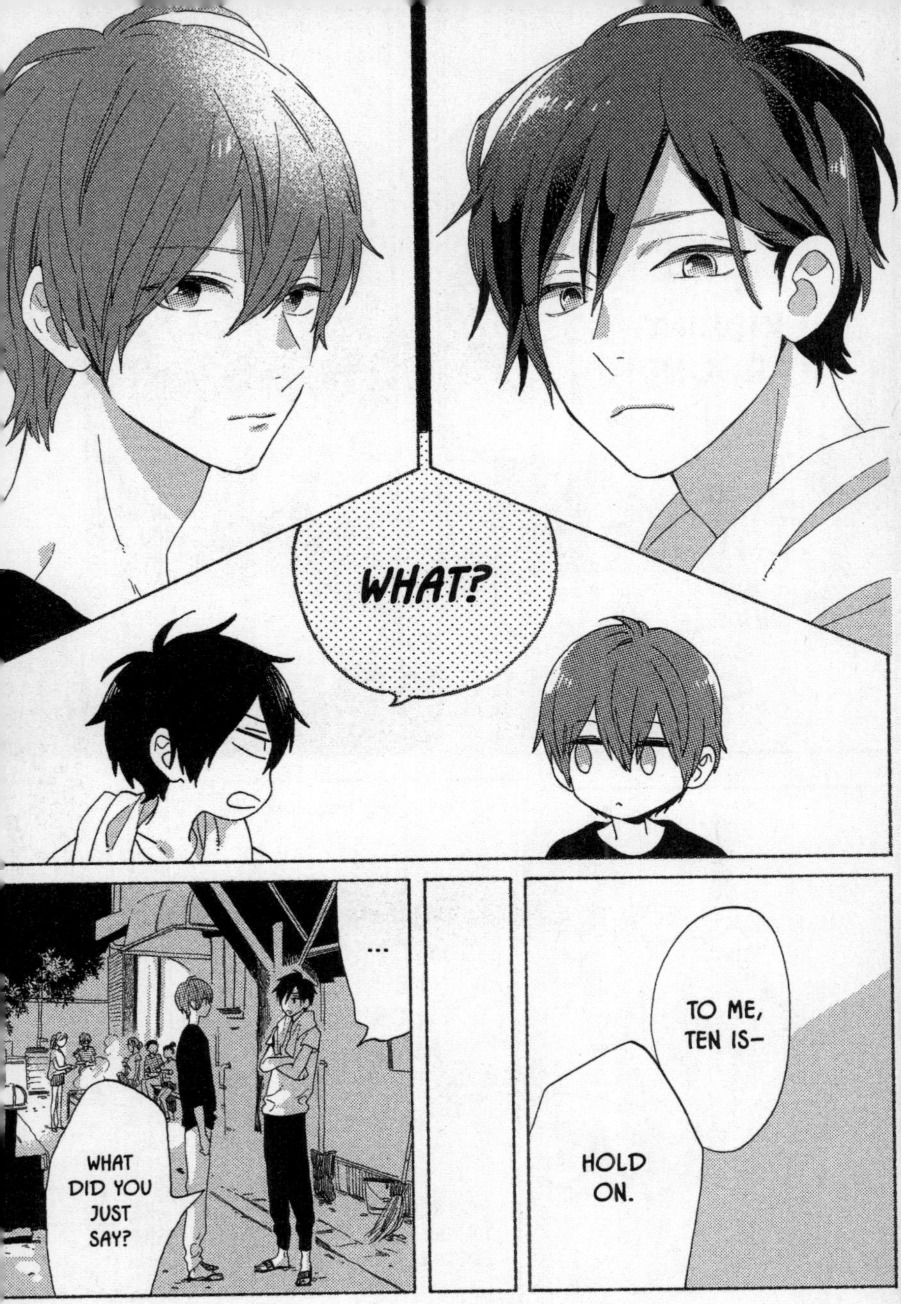
WHAT?
TO ME, TEN IS–
HOLD ON.
...
WHAT DID YOU JUST SAY?

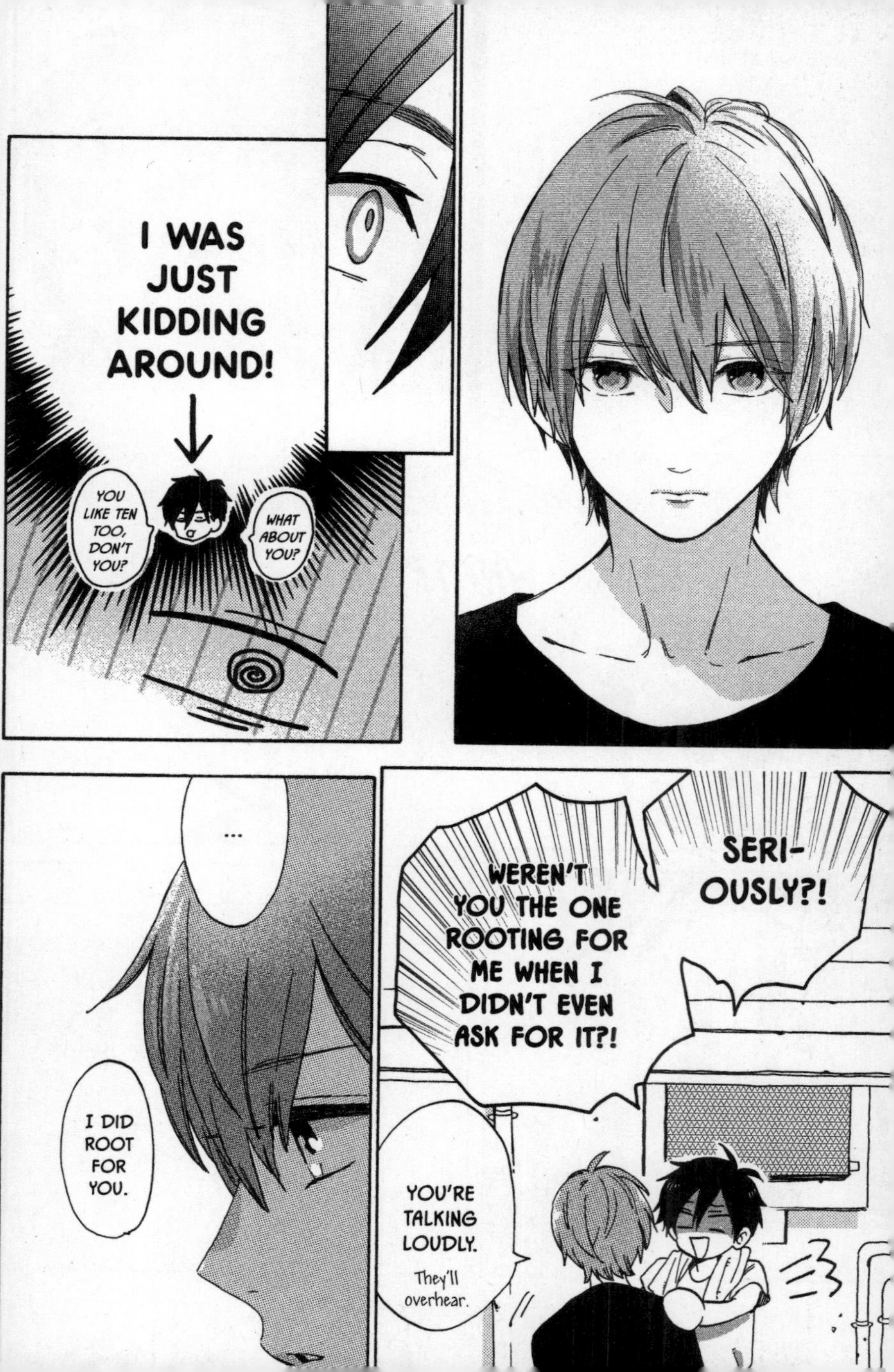
I WAS JUST KIDDING AROUND!
WHAT ABOUT YOU?
YOU LIKE TEN TOO, DON'T YOU?
SERI-OUSLY?!
WEREN'T YOU THE ONE ROOTING FOR ME WHEN I DIDN'T EVEN ASK FOR IT?!
YOU'RE TALKING LOUDLY.
They'll overhear.
...
I DID ROOT FOR YOU.

...I WANT TO BE UPFRONT WITH YOU.

THAT'S WHY...

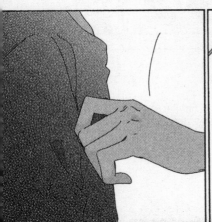

I CAN'T HANDLE THIS RIGHT NOW.

...

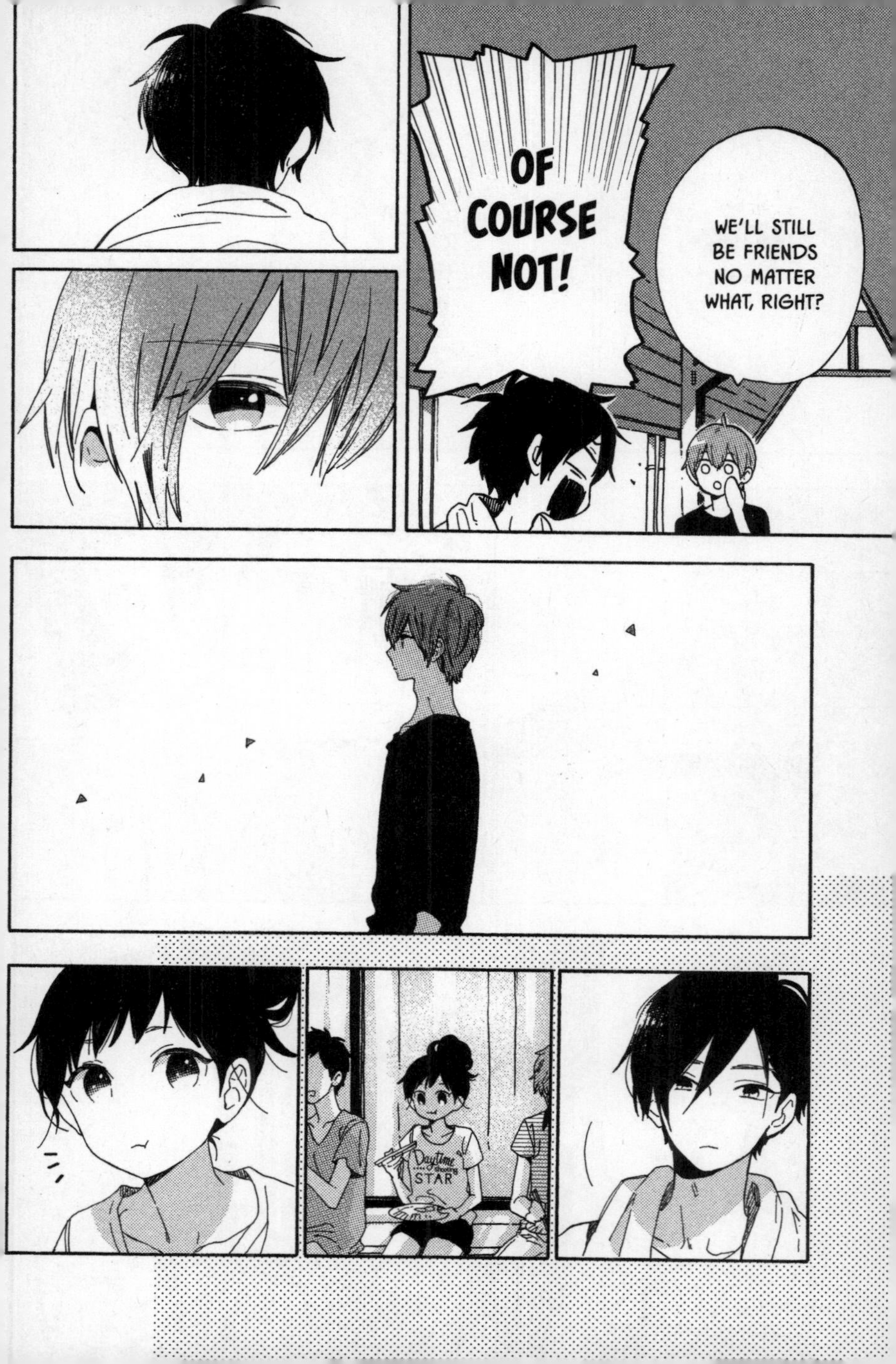
WE'LL STILL BE FRIENDS NO MATTER WHAT, RIGHT?
OF COURSE NOT!
Daytime shooting STAR

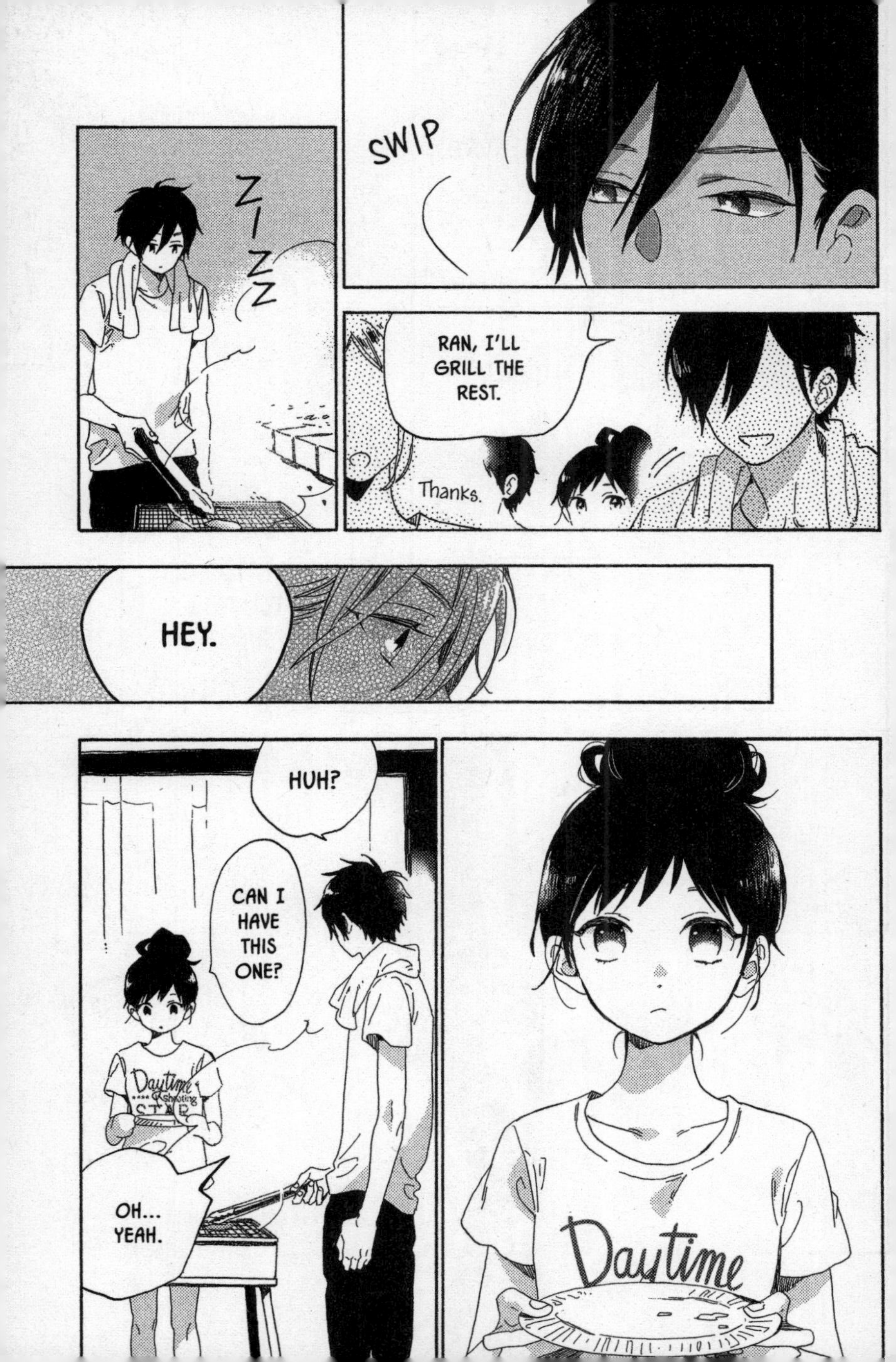
SWIP
RAN, I'LL GRILL THE REST.
Thanks.
ZIZZ
HEY.
Daytime
HUH?
CAN I HAVE THIS ONE?
OH... YEAH.

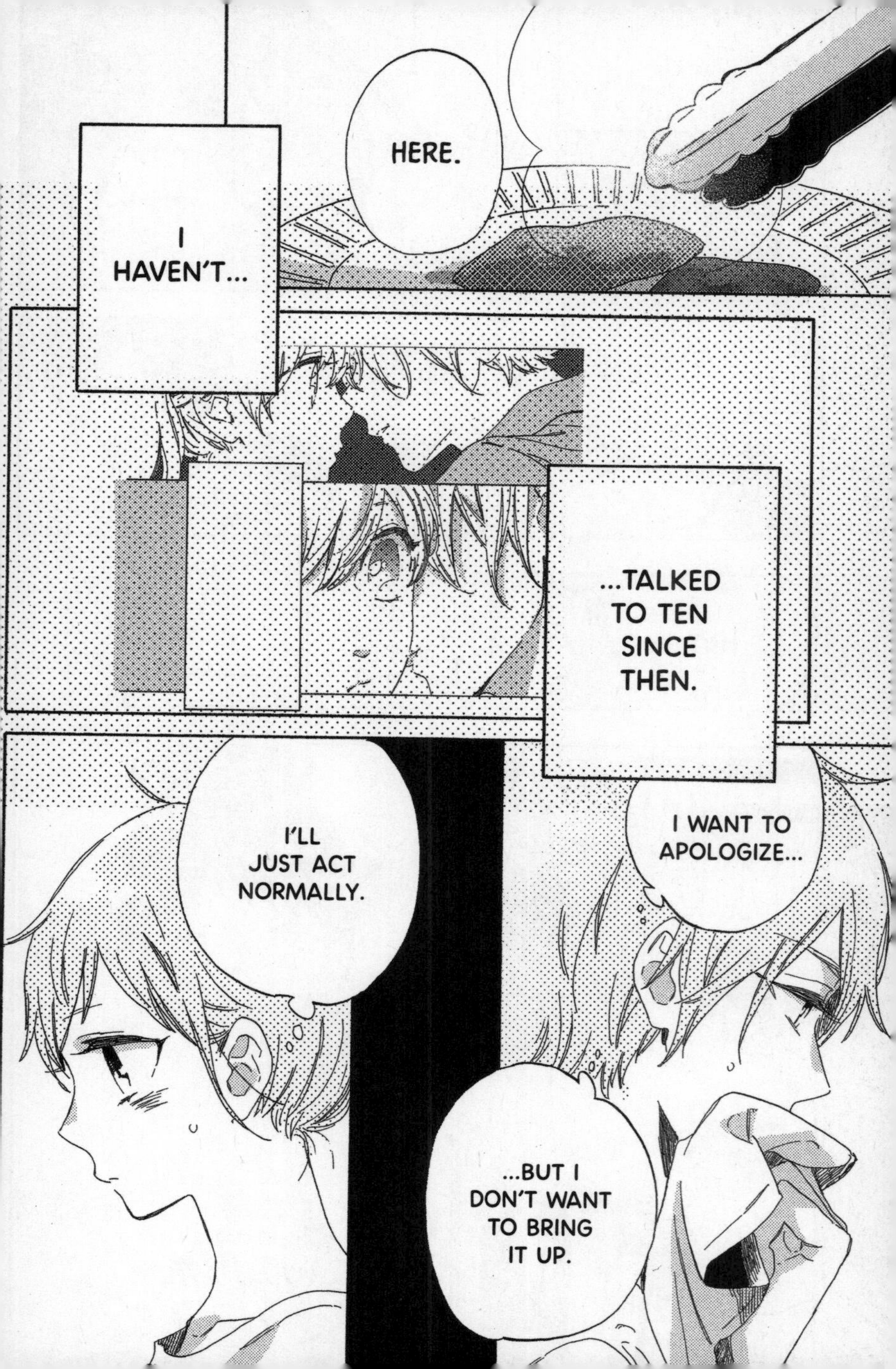
HERE.
I HAVEN'T...
...TALKED TO TEN SINCE THEN.
I WANT TO APOLOGIZE...
...BUT I DON'T WANT TO BRING IT UP.
I'LL JUST ACT NORMALLY.

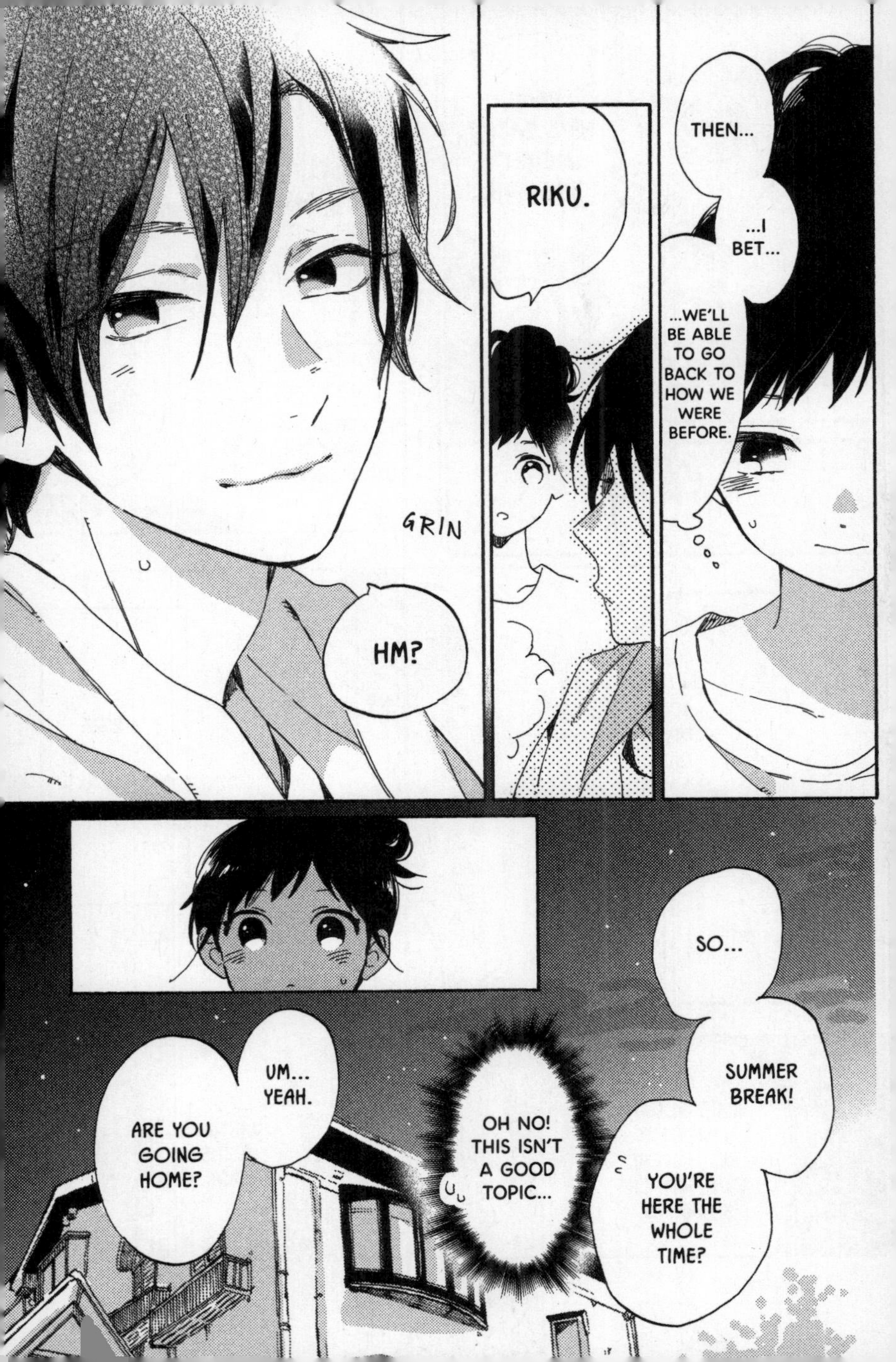
THEN...
...I BET...
...WE'LL BE ABLE TO GO BACK TO HOW WE WERE BEFORE.
RIKU.
GRIN
HM?
SO...
SUMMER BREAK!
YOU'RE HERE THE WHOLE TIME?
OH NO! THIS ISN'T A GOOD TOPIC...
UM... YEAH.
ARE YOU GOING HOME?

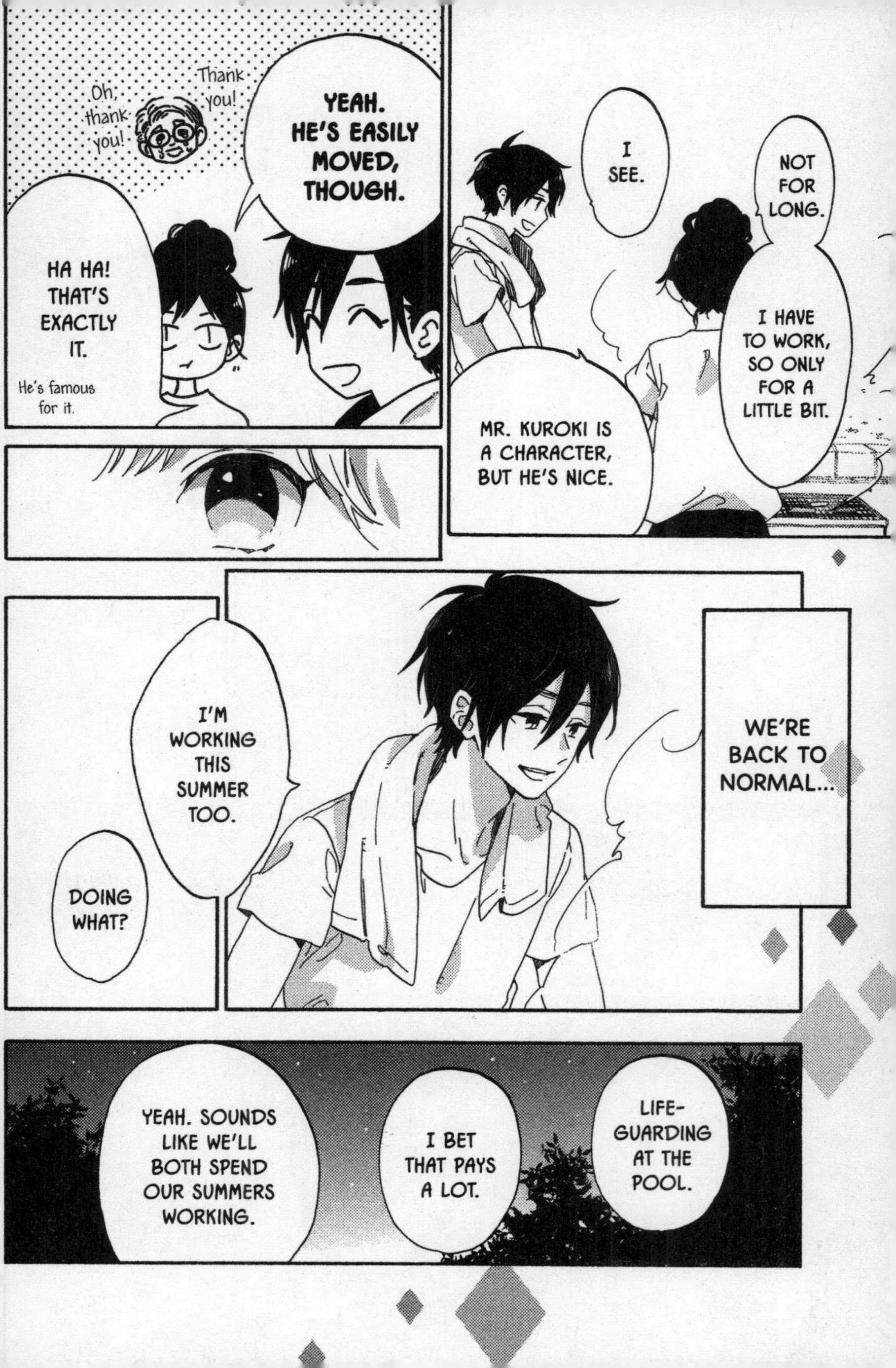
NOT FOR LONG.
I HAVE TO WORK, SO ONLY FOR A LITTLE BIT.
I SEE.
MR. KUROKI IS A CHARACTER, BUT HE'S NICE.
YEAH. HE'S EASILY MOVED, THOUGH.
Thank you!
Oh, thank you!
HA HA! THAT'S EXACTLY IT.
He's famous for it.
WE'RE BACK TO NORMAL...
I'M WORKING THIS SUMMER TOO.
DOING WHAT?
LIFE-GUARDING AT THE POOL.
I BET THAT PAYS A LOT.
YEAH. SOUNDS LIKE WE'LL BOTH SPEND OUR SUMMERS WORKING.

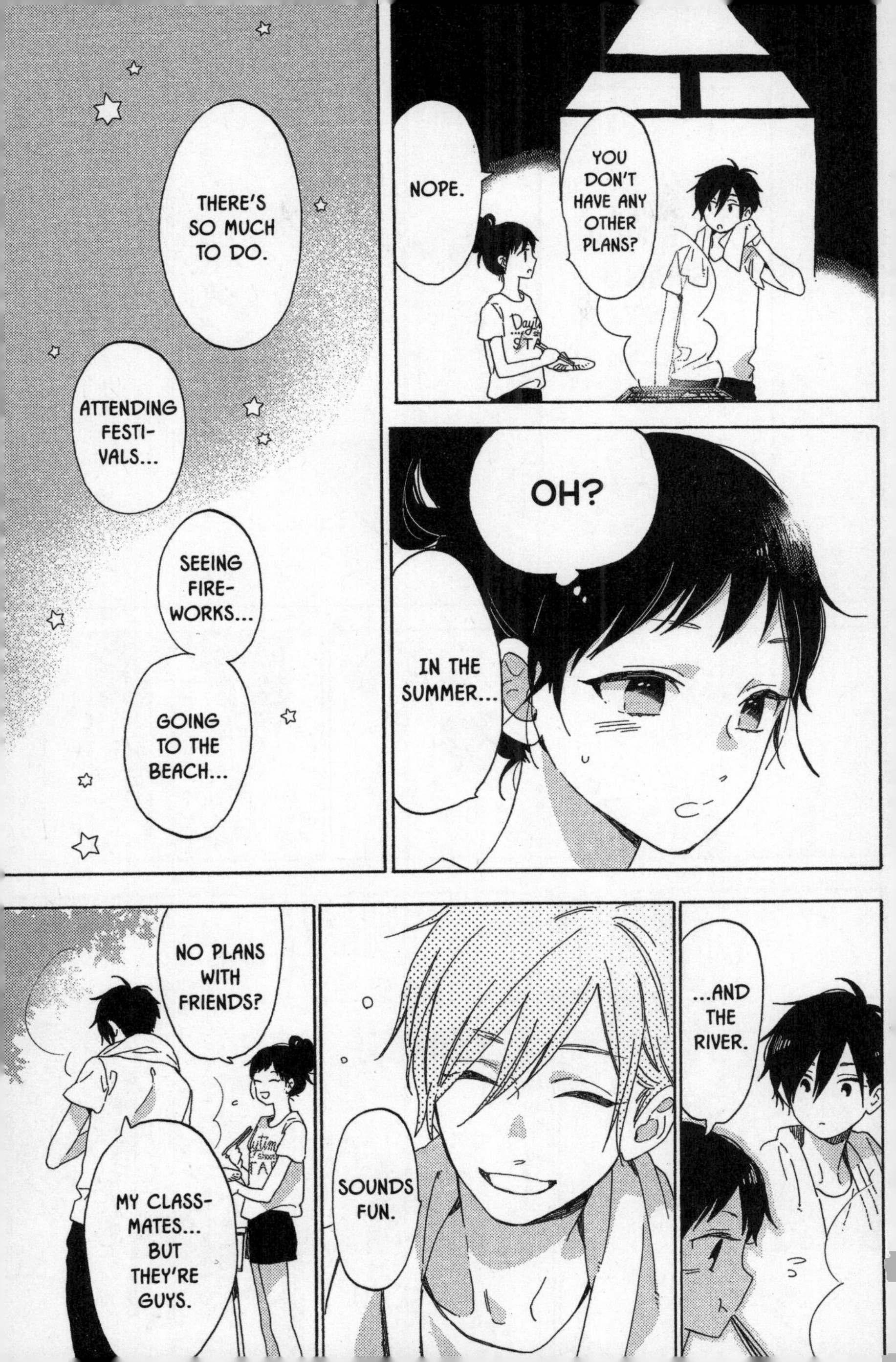
YOU DON'T HAVE ANY OTHER PLANS?
NOPE.
OH?
IN THE SUMMER...
THERE'S SO MUCH TO DO.
ATTENDING FESTI-VALS...
SEEING FIRE-WORKS...
GOING TO THE BEACH...
...AND THE RIVER.
SOUNDS FUN.
NO PLANS WITH FRIENDS?
MY CLASS-MATES... BUT THEY'RE GUYS.

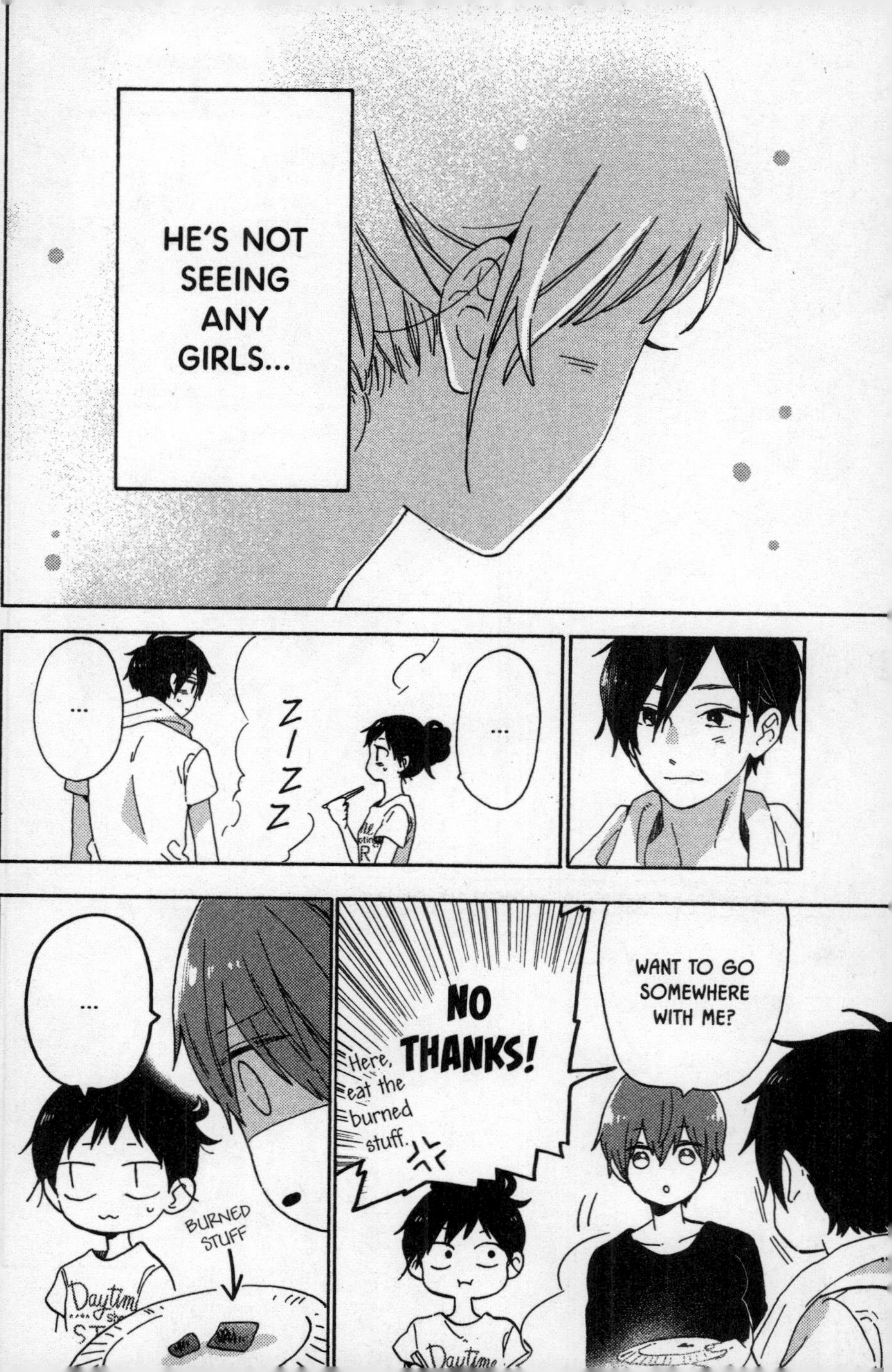
HE'S NOT SEEING ANY GIRLS...
...
...
ZIZZ
...
WANT TO GO SOMEWHERE WITH ME?
NO THANKS!
Here, eat the burned stuff.
...
BURNED STUFF

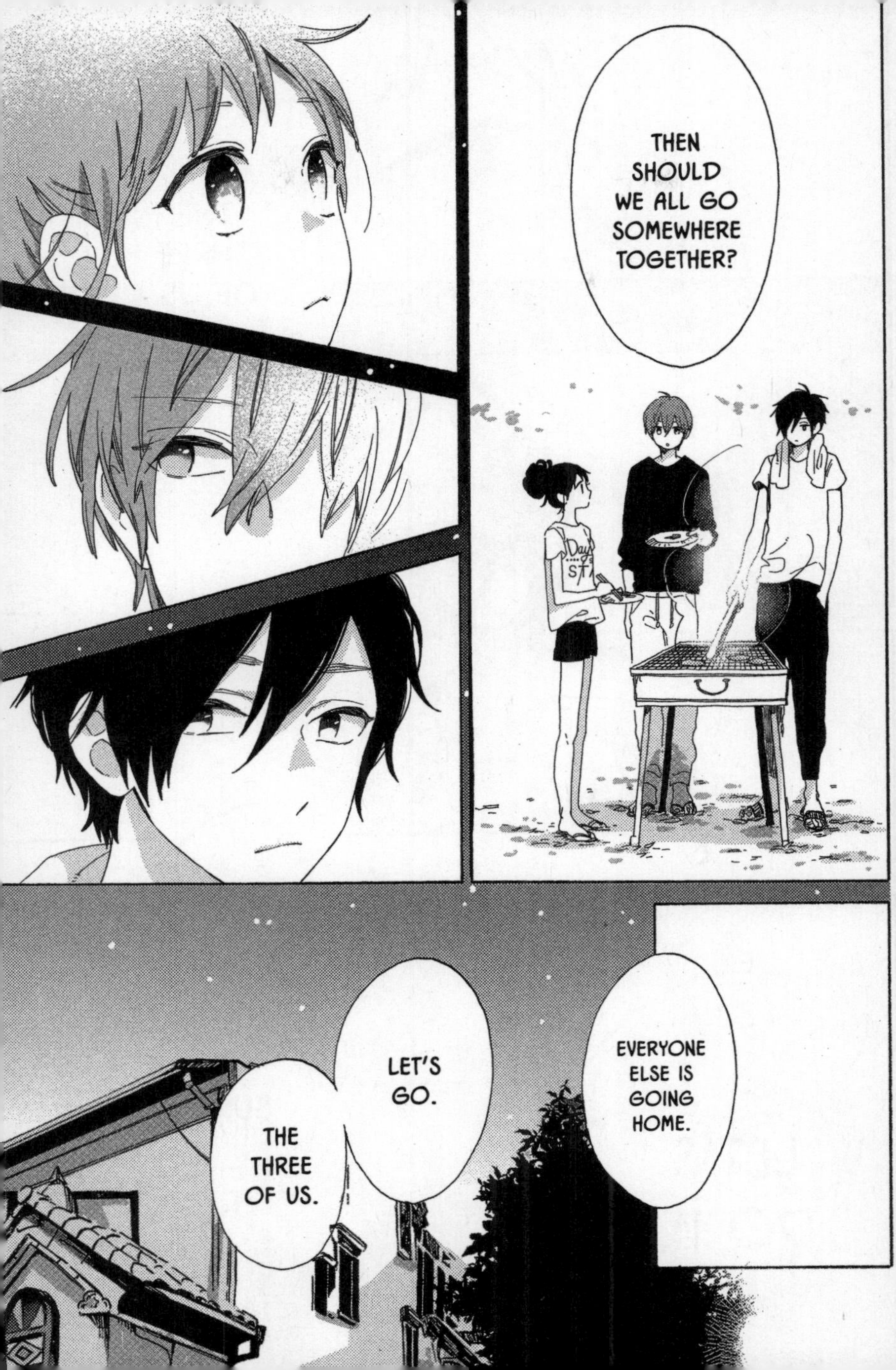
THEN SHOULD WE ALL GO SOMEWHERE TOGETHER?
EVERYONE ELSE IS GOING HOME.
LET'S GO.
THE THREE OF US.

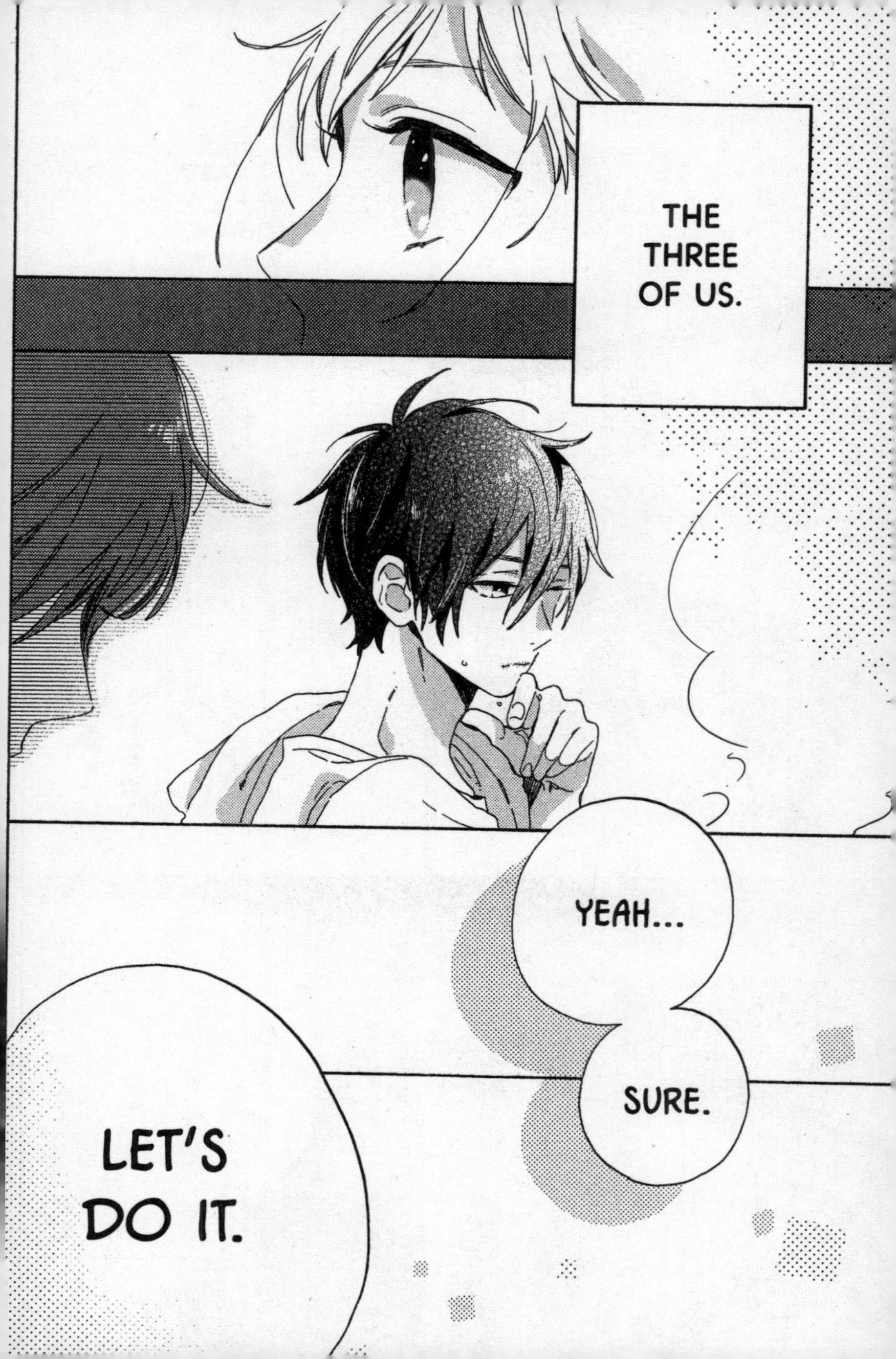
THE THREE OF US.
YEAH...
SURE.
LET'S DO IT.

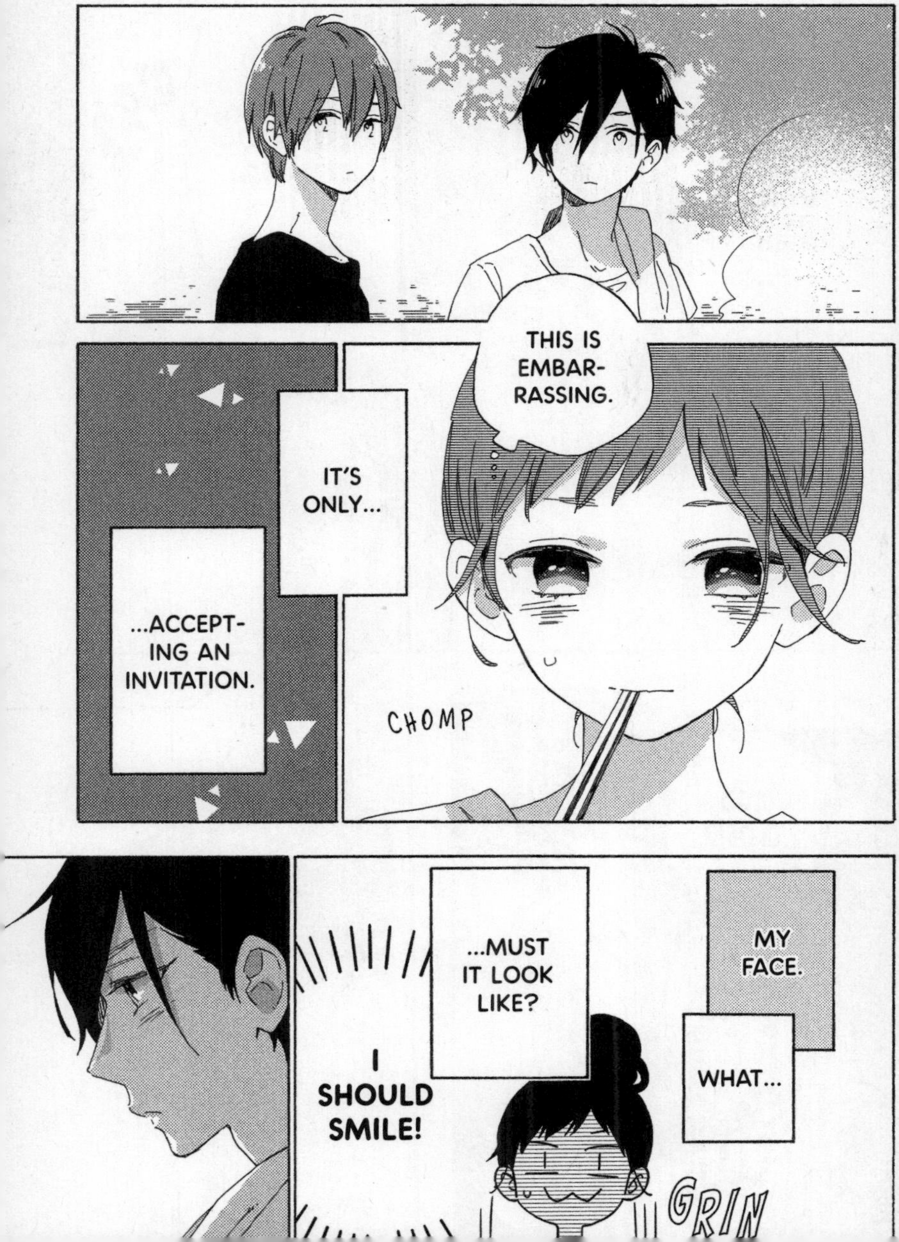
THIS IS EMBARRASSING.
IT'S ONLY...
CHOMP
...ACCEPTING AN INVITATION.
MY FACE.
WHAT...
...MUST IT LOOK LIKE?
I SHOULD SMILE!
GRIN

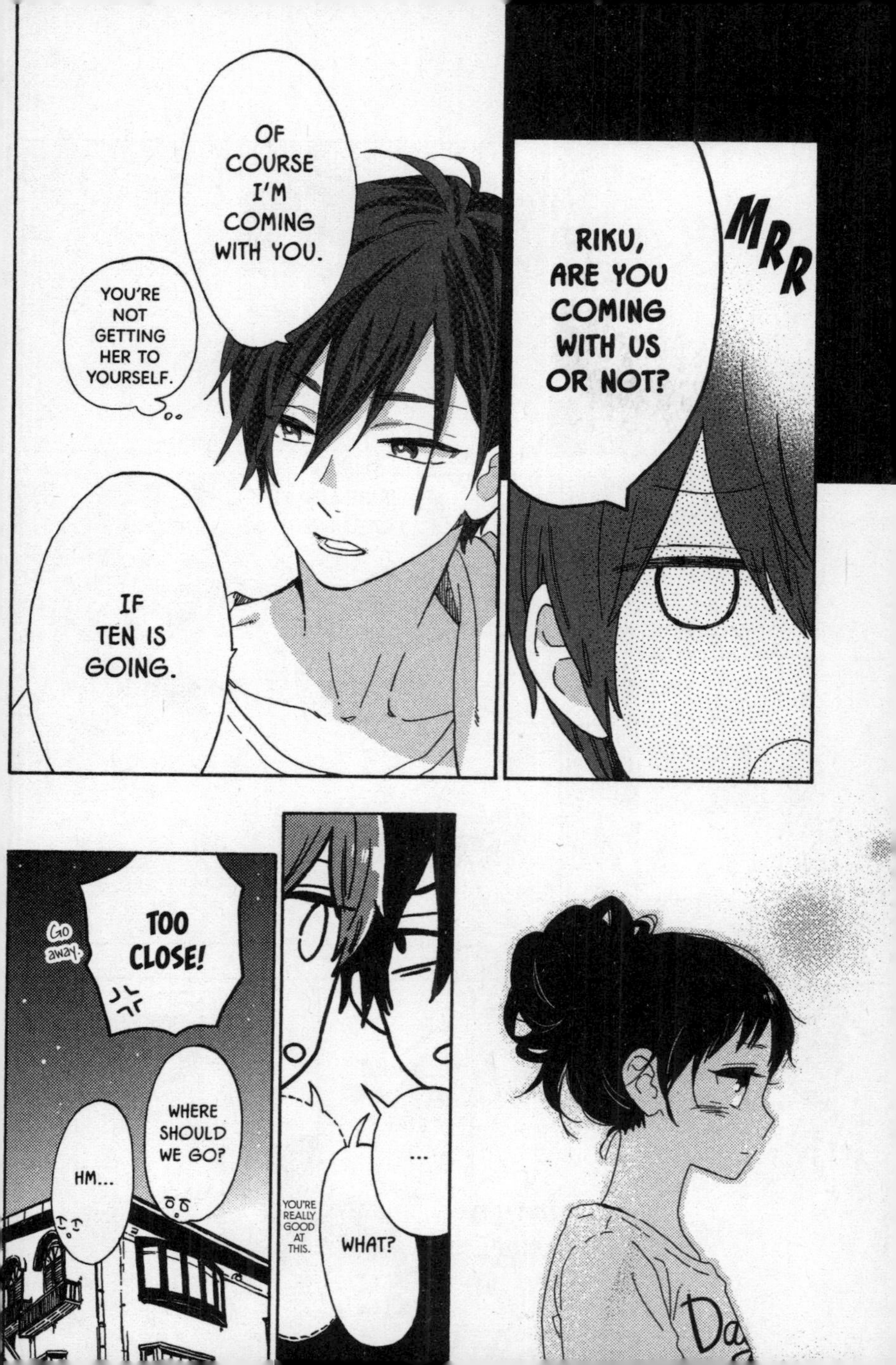

MRR
RIKU, ARE YOU COMING WITH US OR NOT?
OF COURSE I'M COMING WITH YOU.
YOU'RE NOT GETTING HER TO YOURSELF.
IF TEN IS GOING.
...
WHAT?
YOU'RE REALLY GOOD AT THIS.
TOO CLOSE!
Go away.
WHERE SHOULD WE GO?
HM...

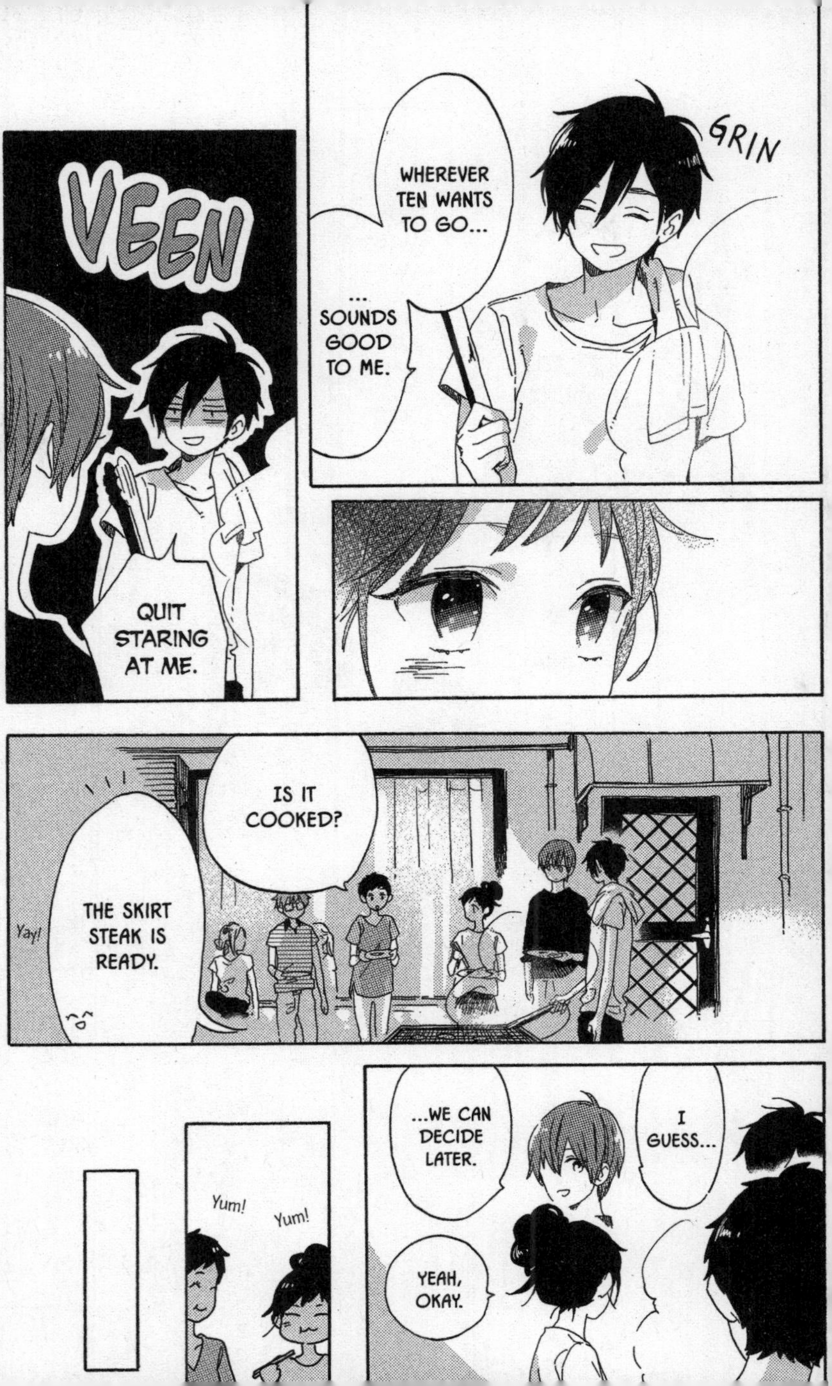
WHEREVER TEN WANTS TO GO...
GRIN
... SOUNDS GOOD TO ME.
VEEN
QUIT STARING AT ME.
IS IT COOKED?
THE SKIRT STEAK IS READY.
Yay!
I GUESS...
...WE CAN DECIDE LATER.
YEAH, OKAY.
Yum!
Yum!

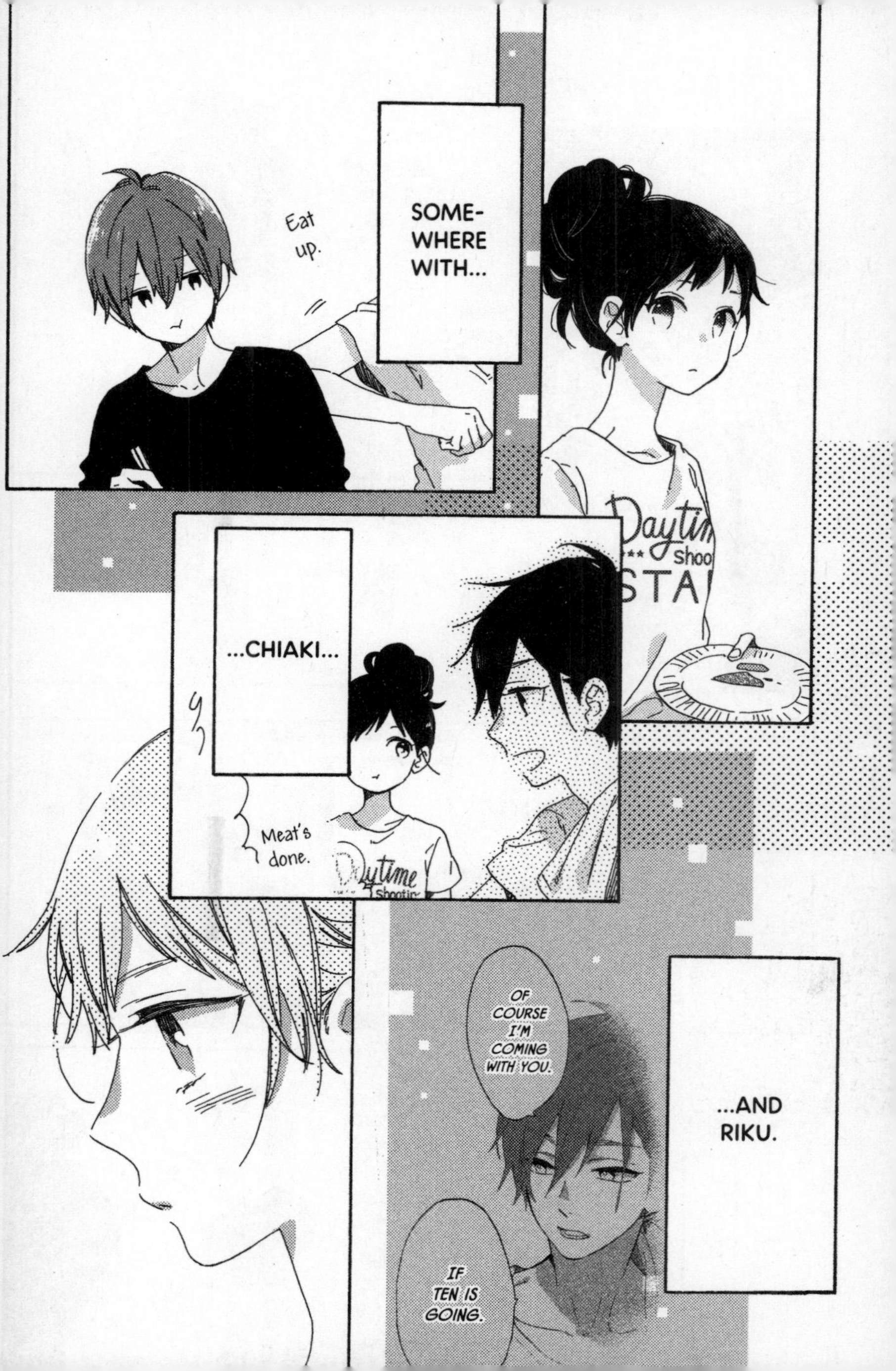
SOME-WHERE WITH...
Eat up.
...CHIAKI...
Meat's done.
...AND RIKU.
OF COURSE I'M COMING WITH YOU.
IF TEN IS GOING.

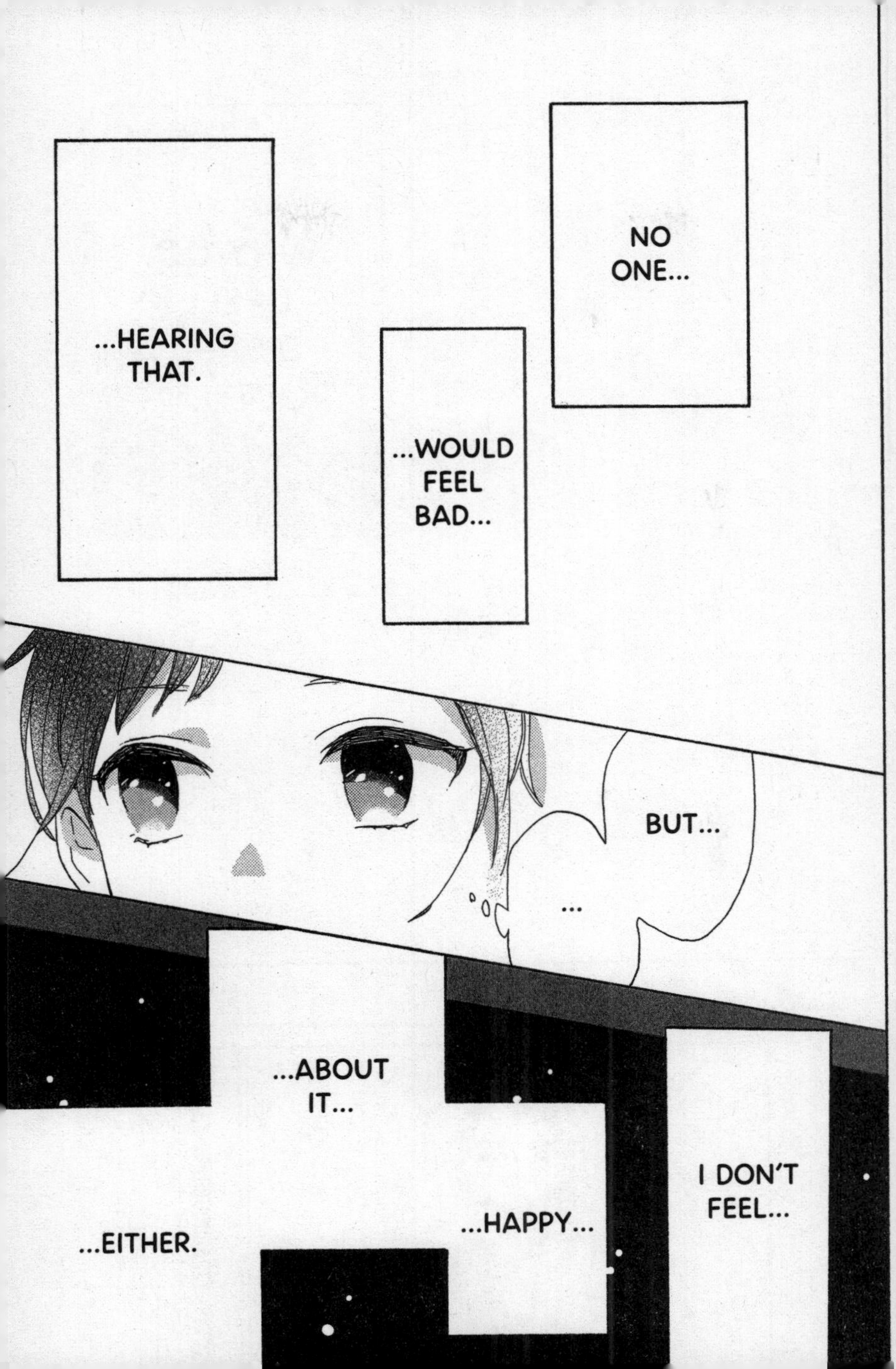
NO ONE...
...WOULD FEEL BAD...
...HEARING THAT.
BUT...
...
I DON'T FEEL...
...HAPPY...
...ABOUT IT...
...EITHER.

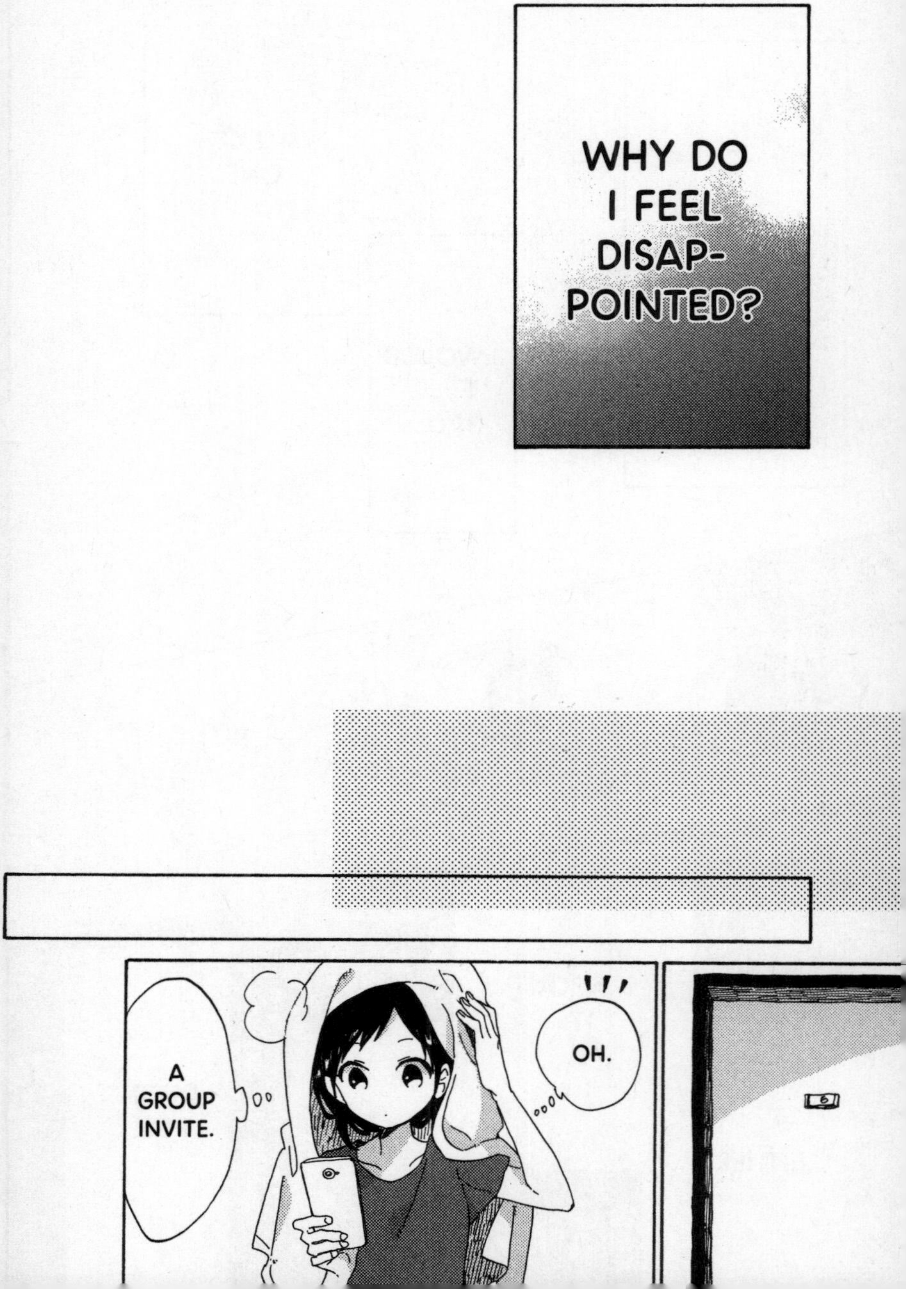
WHY DO I FEEL DISAPPOINTED?
OH.
A GROUP INVITE.

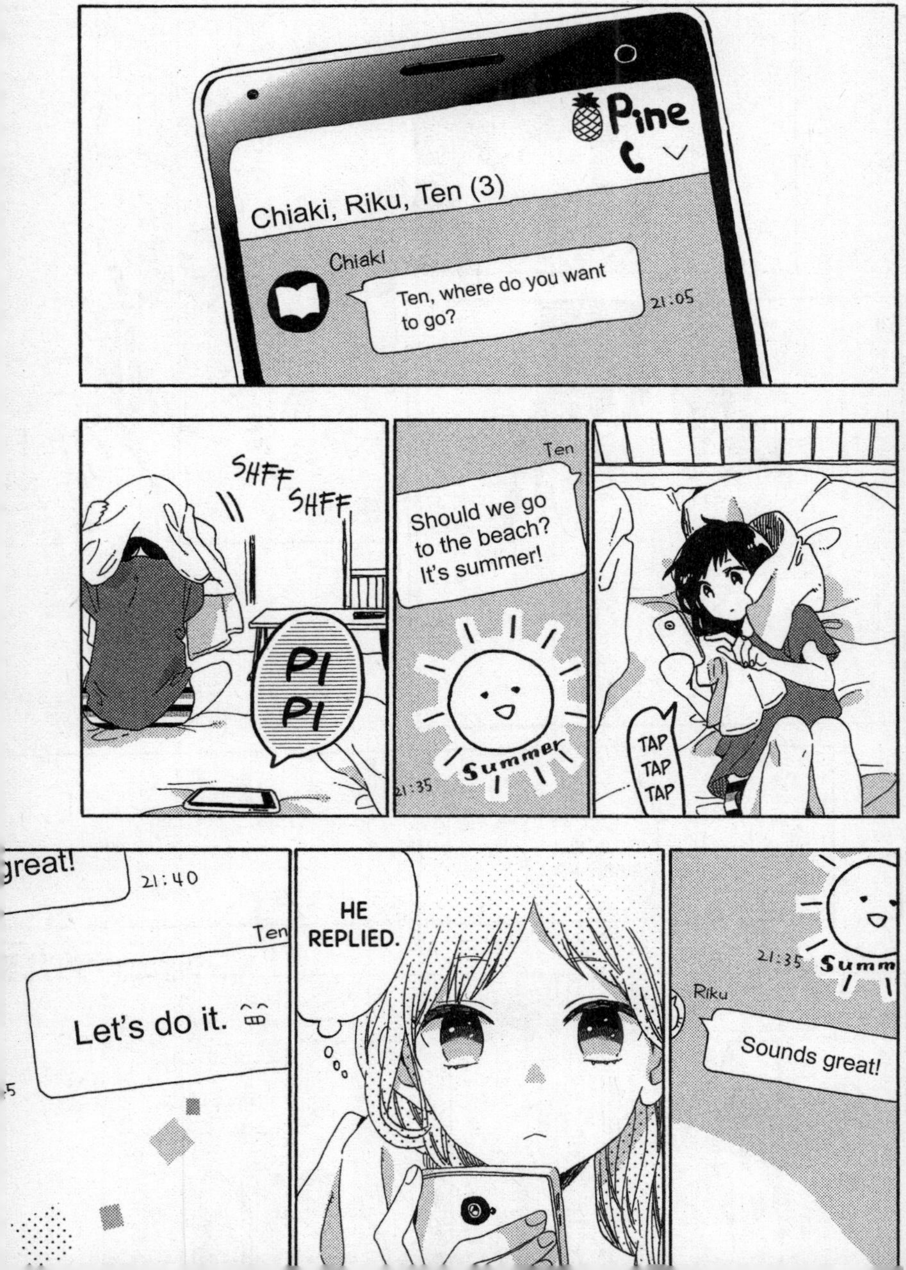

Pine
Chiaki, Riku, Ten (3)
Chiaki
Ten, where do you want to go?
21:05
TAP TAP TAP
Ten
Should we go to the beach? It's summer!
Summer
21:35
SHFF SHFF
PI PI
21:35
Riku
Sounds great!
HE REPLIED.
great!
21:40
Ten
Let's do it.

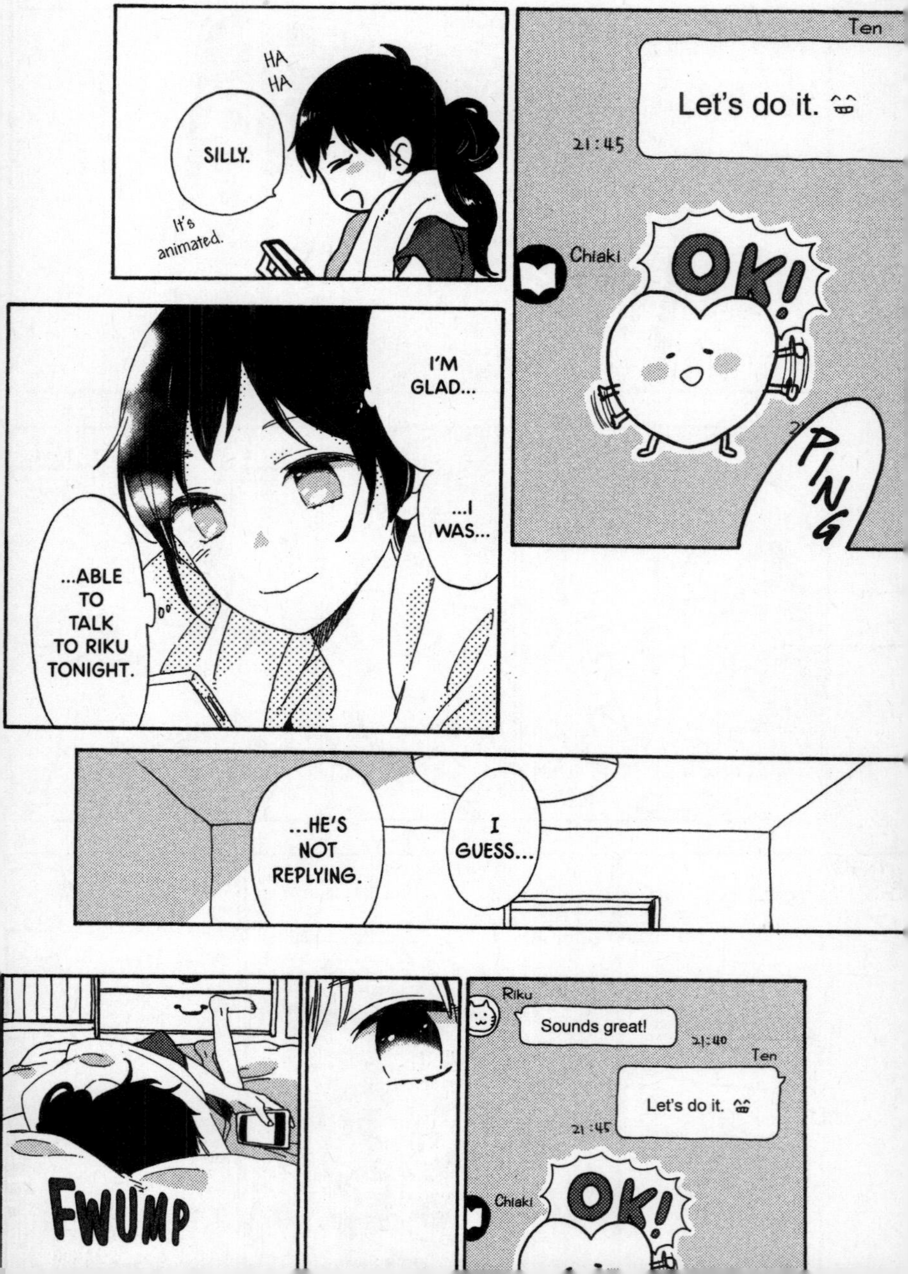
Ten
Let's do it.
21:45
Chiaki
OK!
PING
HA HA
SILLY.
It's animated.
I'M GLAD...
...I WAS...
...ABLE TO TALK TO RIKU TONIGHT.
I GUESS...
...HE'S NOT REPLYING.
Riku
Sounds great!
21:40
Ten
Let's do it.
21:45
Chiaki
OK!
FWUMP

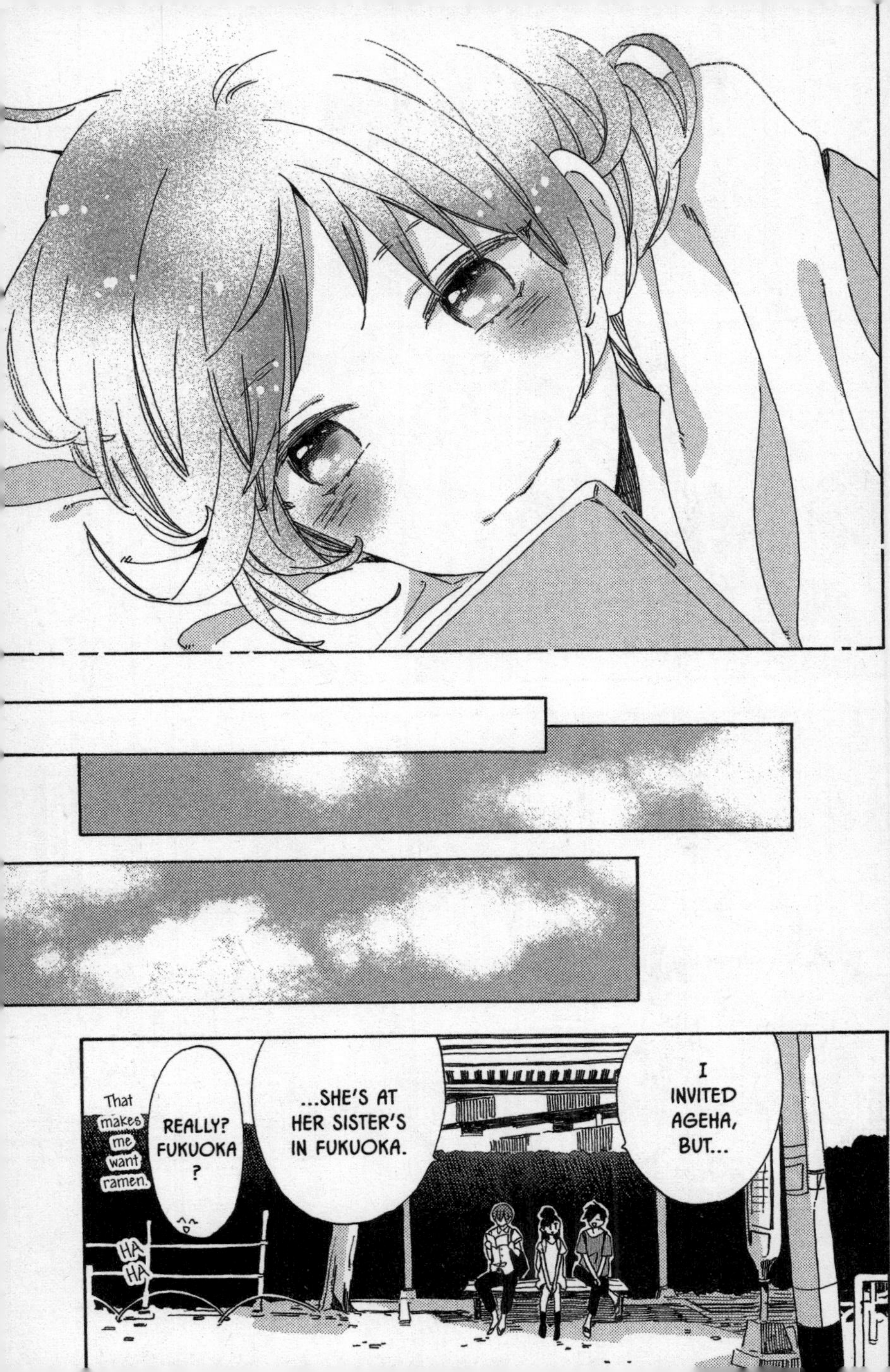
I INVITED AGEHA, BUT...
...SHE'S AT HER SISTER'S IN FUKUOKA.
REALLY? FUKUOKA?
That makes me want ramen.
HA HA

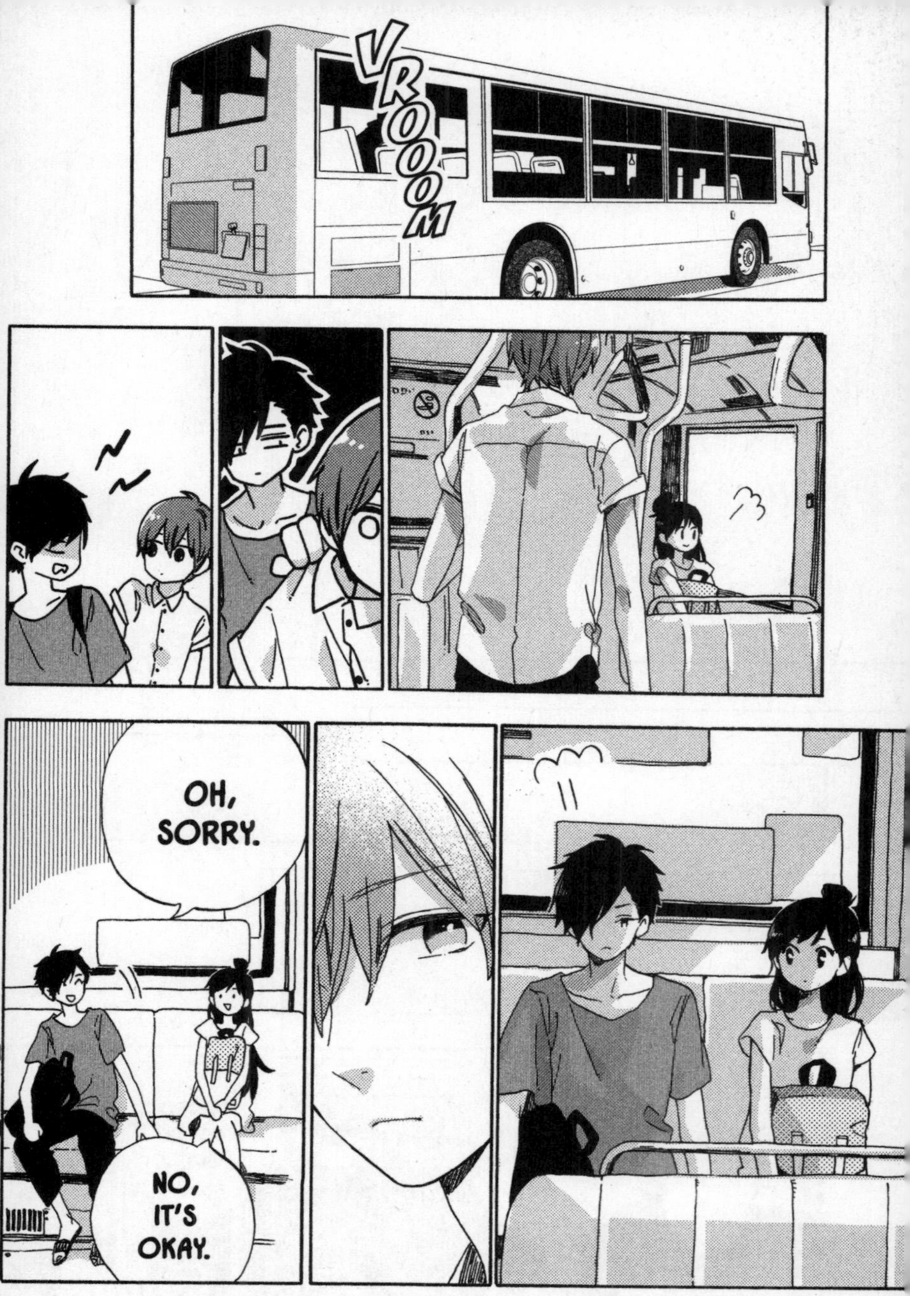
VROOOOM
OH, SORRY.
NO, IT'S OKAY.

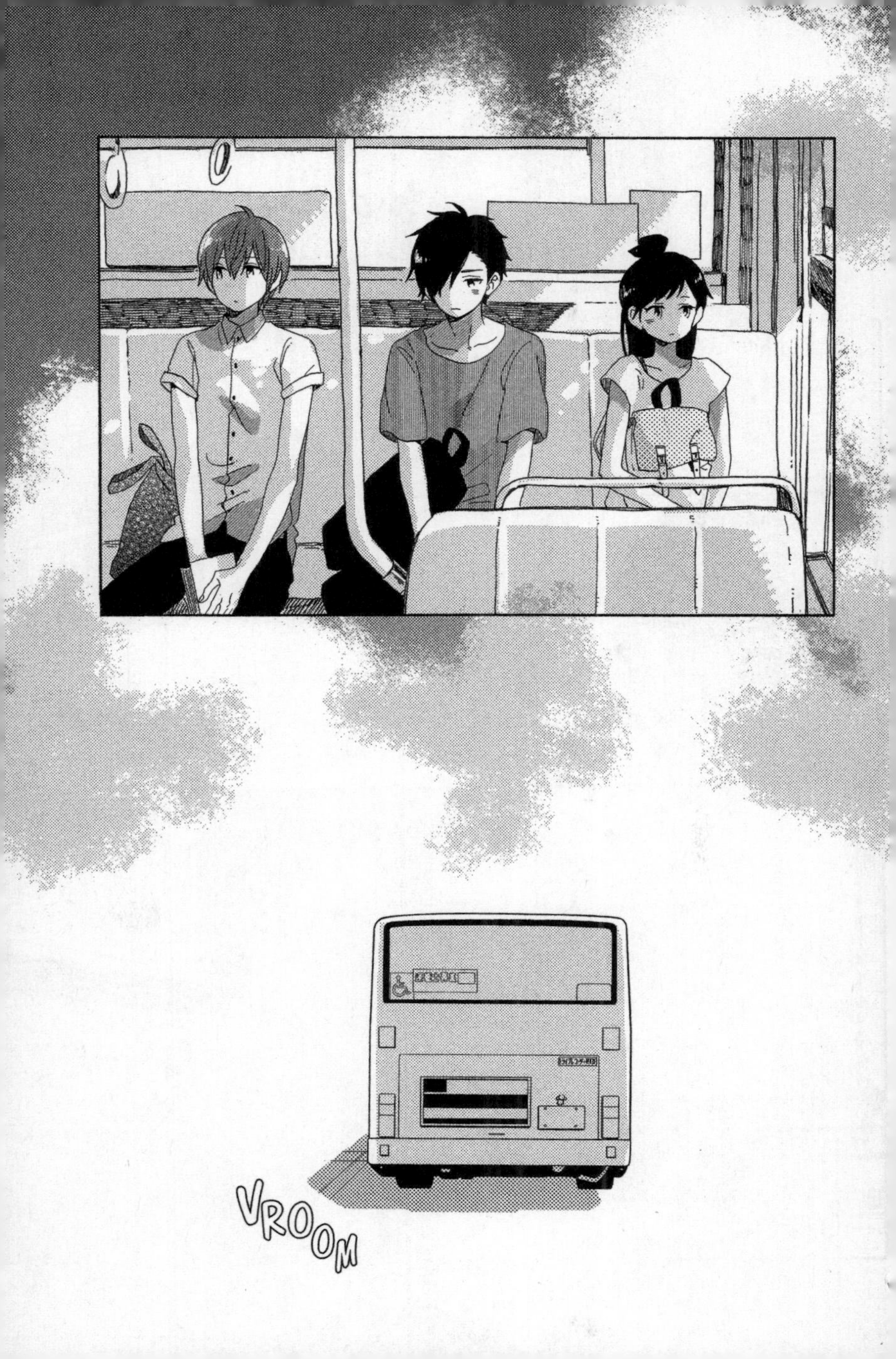
VROOM

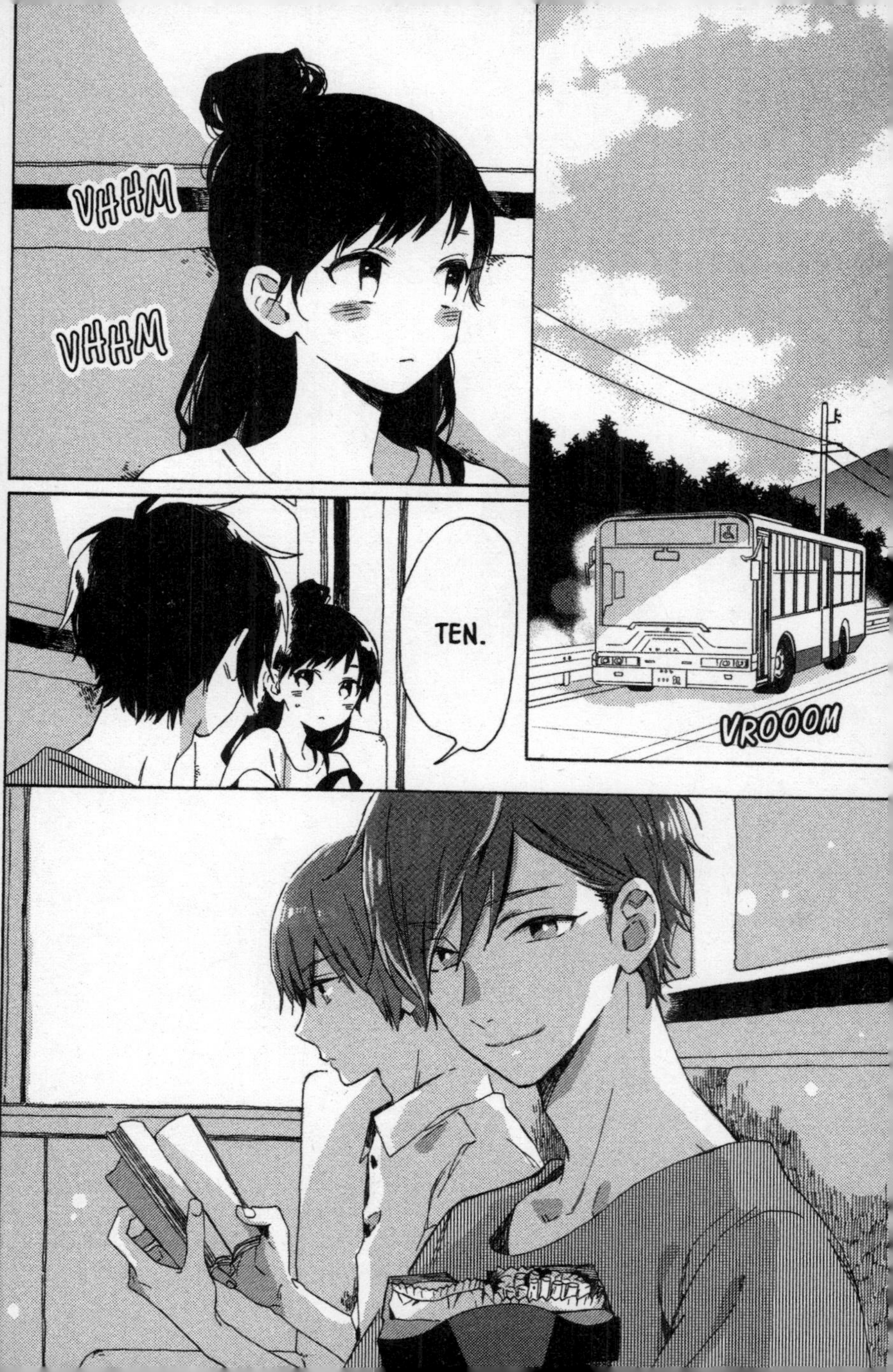
VHHM
VHHM
VROOOM
TEN.

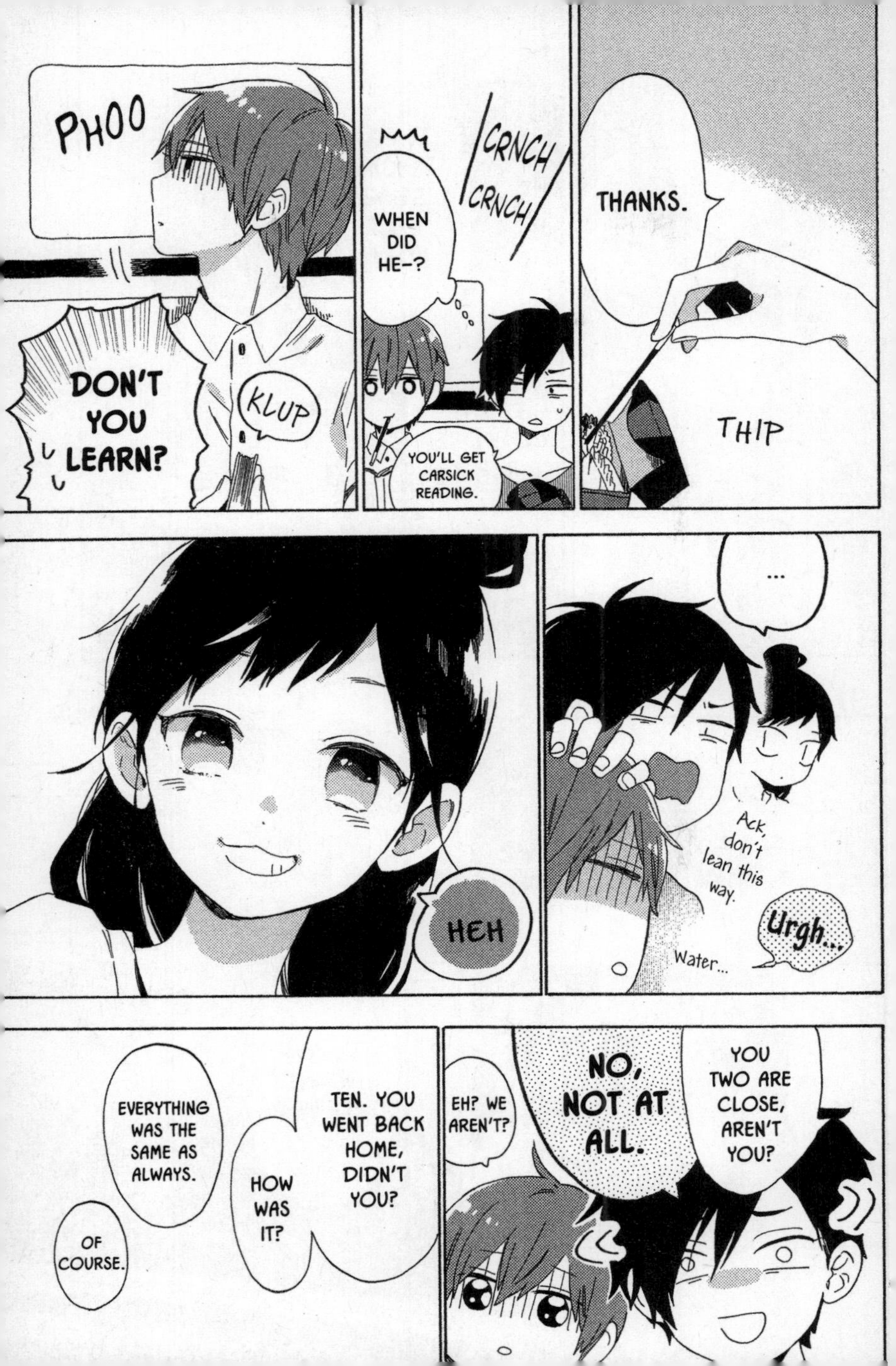

THANKS.
THIP
CRNCH
CRNCH
WHEN DID HE-?
YOU'LL GET CARSICK READING.
PHOO
DON'T YOU LEARN?
KLUP
...
Ack, don't lean this way.
Urgh...
Water...
HEH
YOU TWO ARE CLOSE, AREN'T YOU?
NO, NOT AT ALL.
EH? WE AREN'T?
TEN. YOU WENT BACK HOME, DIDN'T YOU?
HOW WAS IT?
EVERYTHING WAS THE SAME AS ALWAYS.
OF COURSE.

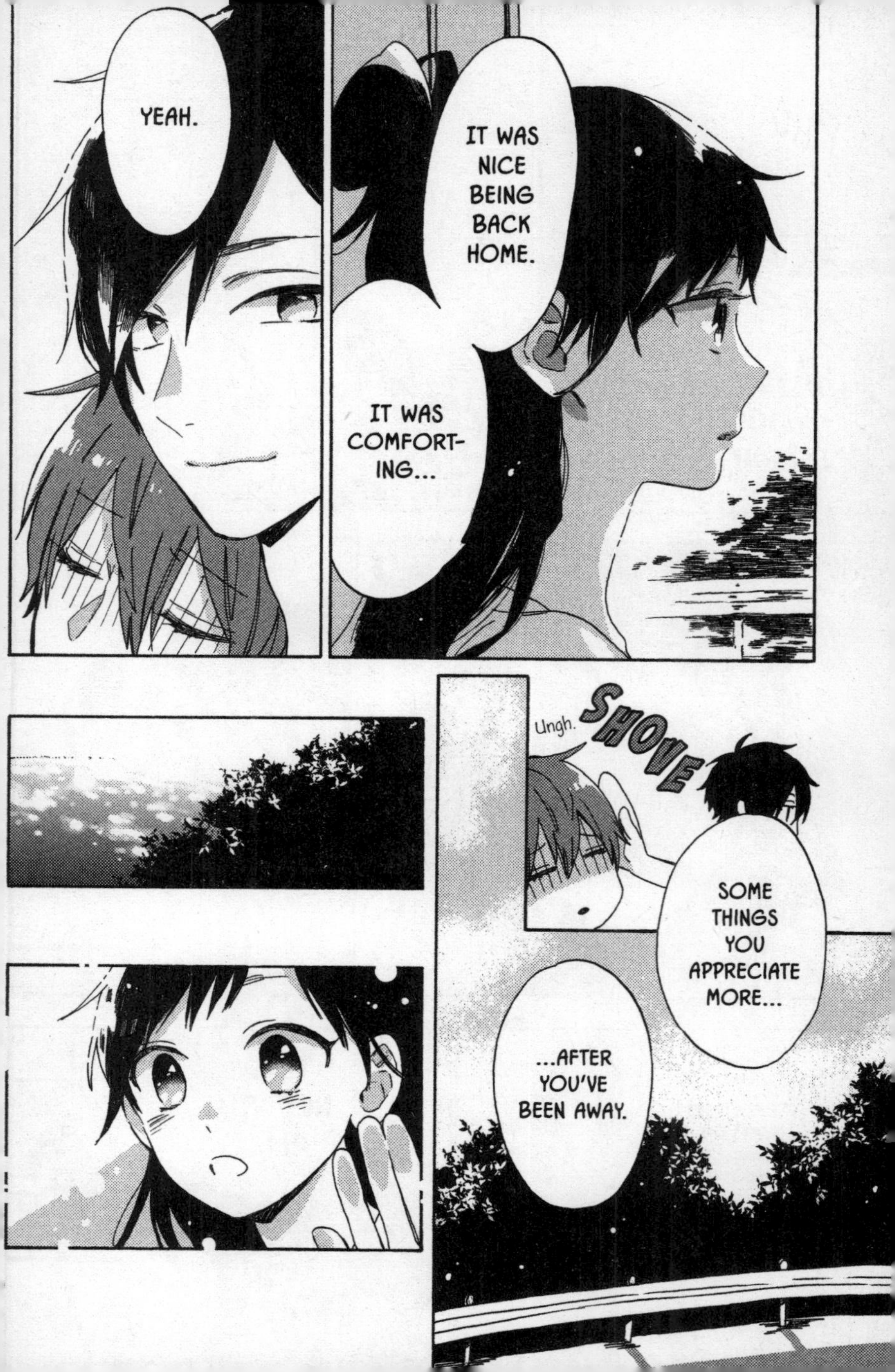
IT WAS NICE BEING BACK HOME.
IT WAS COMFORT-ING...
YEAH.
Ungh.
SHOVE
SOME THINGS YOU APPRECIATE MORE...
...AFTER YOU'VE BEEN AWAY.

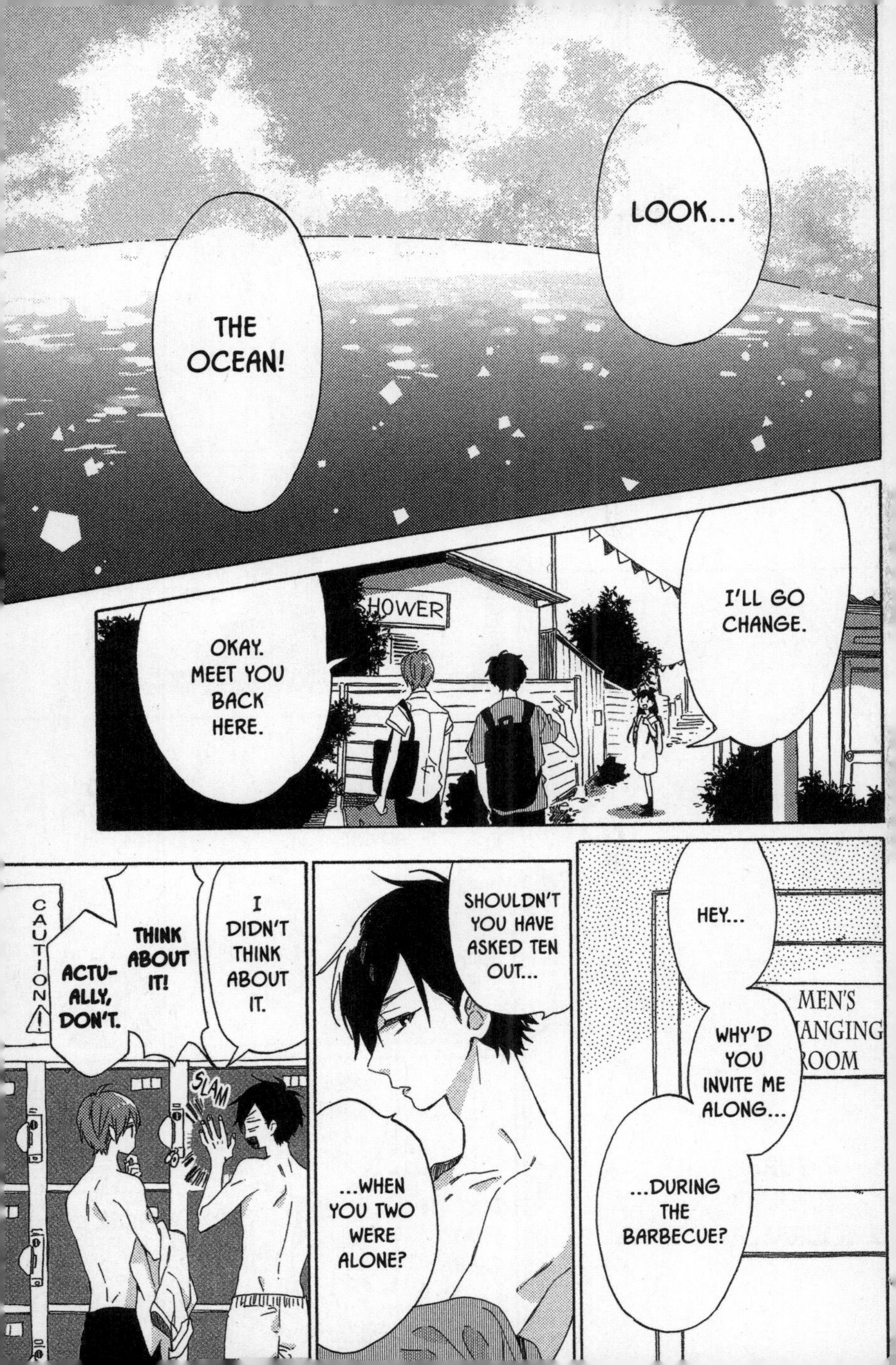
LOOK...
THE OCEAN!
I'LL GO CHANGE.
SHOWER
OKAY. MEET YOU BACK HERE.
HEY...
MEN'S HANGING ROOM
WHY'D YOU INVITE ME ALONG...
...DURING THE BARBECUE?
SHOULDN'T YOU HAVE ASKED TEN OUT...
...WHEN YOU TWO WERE ALONE?
I DIDN'T THINK ABOUT IT.
THINK ABOUT IT!
ACTU-ALLY, DON'T.
SLAM
CAUTION !

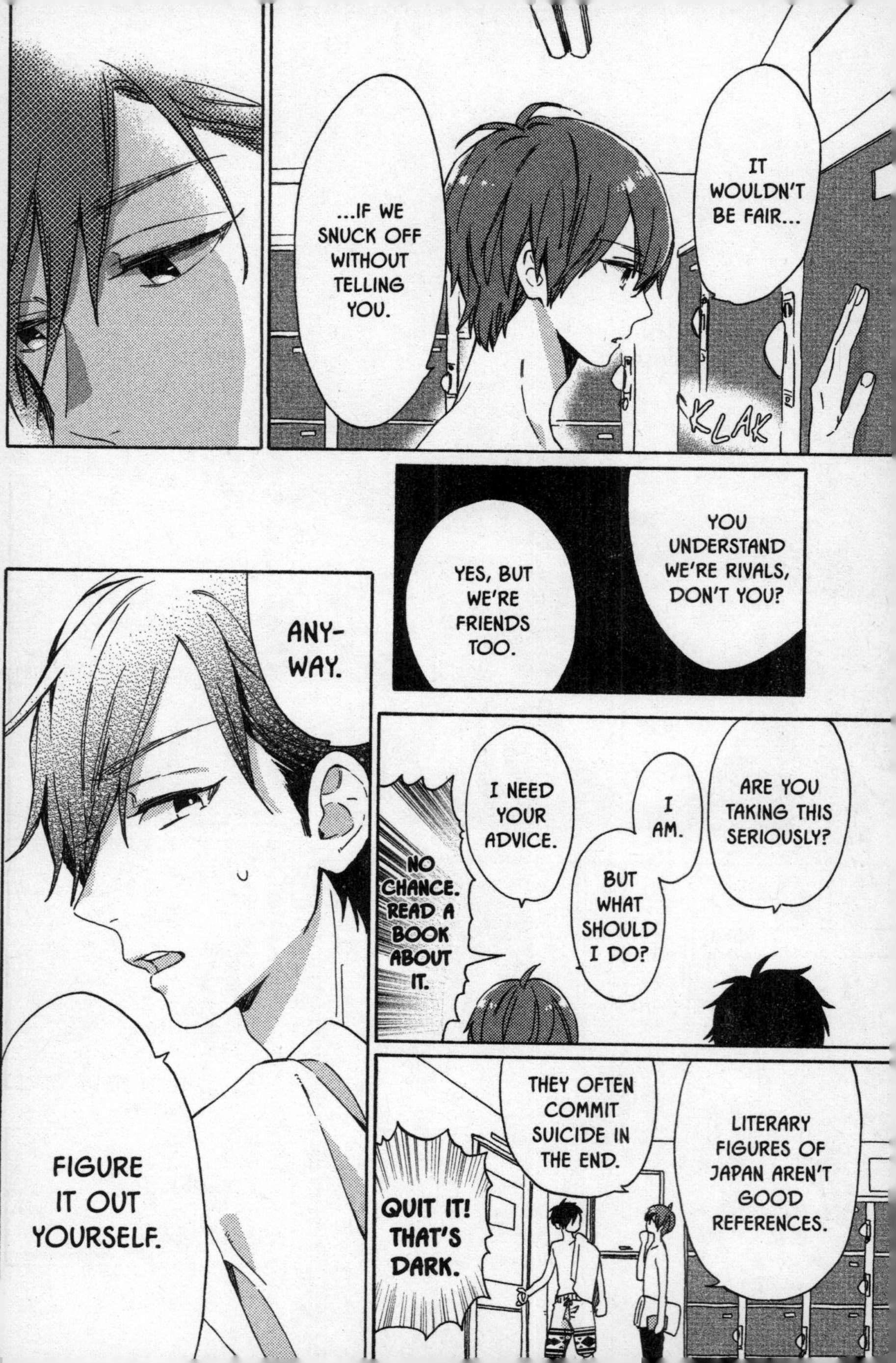
IT WOULDN'T BE FAIR...
...IF WE SNUCK OFF WITHOUT TELLING YOU.
KLAK
YOU UNDERSTAND WE'RE RIVALS, DON'T YOU?
YES, BUT WE'RE FRIENDS TOO.
ARE YOU TAKING THIS SERIOUSLY?
I AM.
BUT WHAT SHOULD I DO?
I NEED YOUR ADVICE.
NO CHANCE. READ A BOOK ABOUT IT.
LITERARY FIGURES OF JAPAN AREN'T GOOD REFERENCES.
THEY OFTEN COMMIT SUICIDE IN THE END.
QUIT IT! THAT'S DARK.
ANY-WAY.
FIGURE IT OUT YOURSELF.

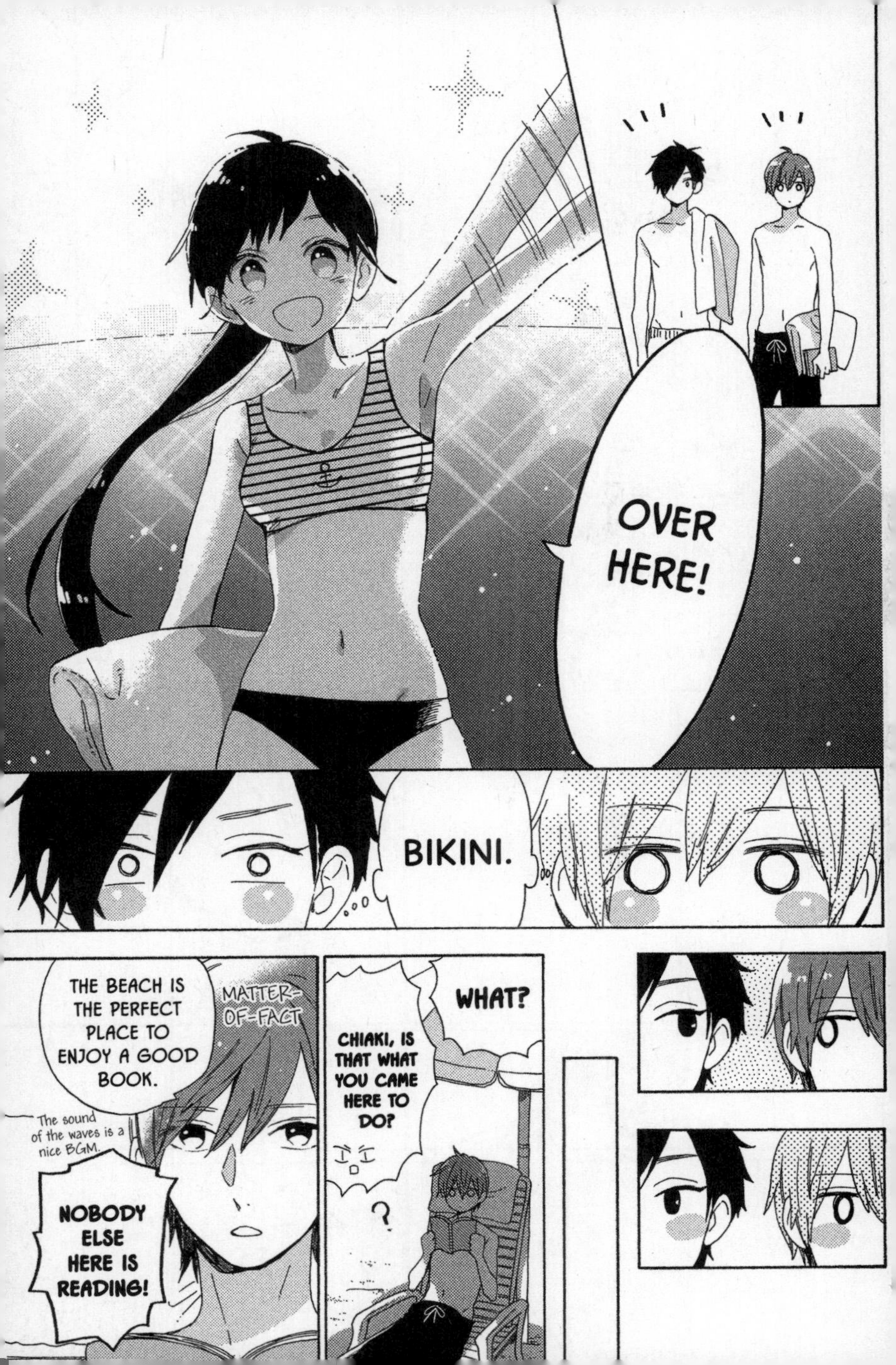
OVER HERE!
BIKINI.
WHAT?
CHIAKI, IS THAT WHAT YOU CAME HERE TO DO?
MATTER-OF-FACT
THE BEACH IS THE PERFECT PLACE TO ENJOY A GOOD BOOK.
The sound of the waves is a nice BGM.
NOBODY ELSE HERE IS READING!

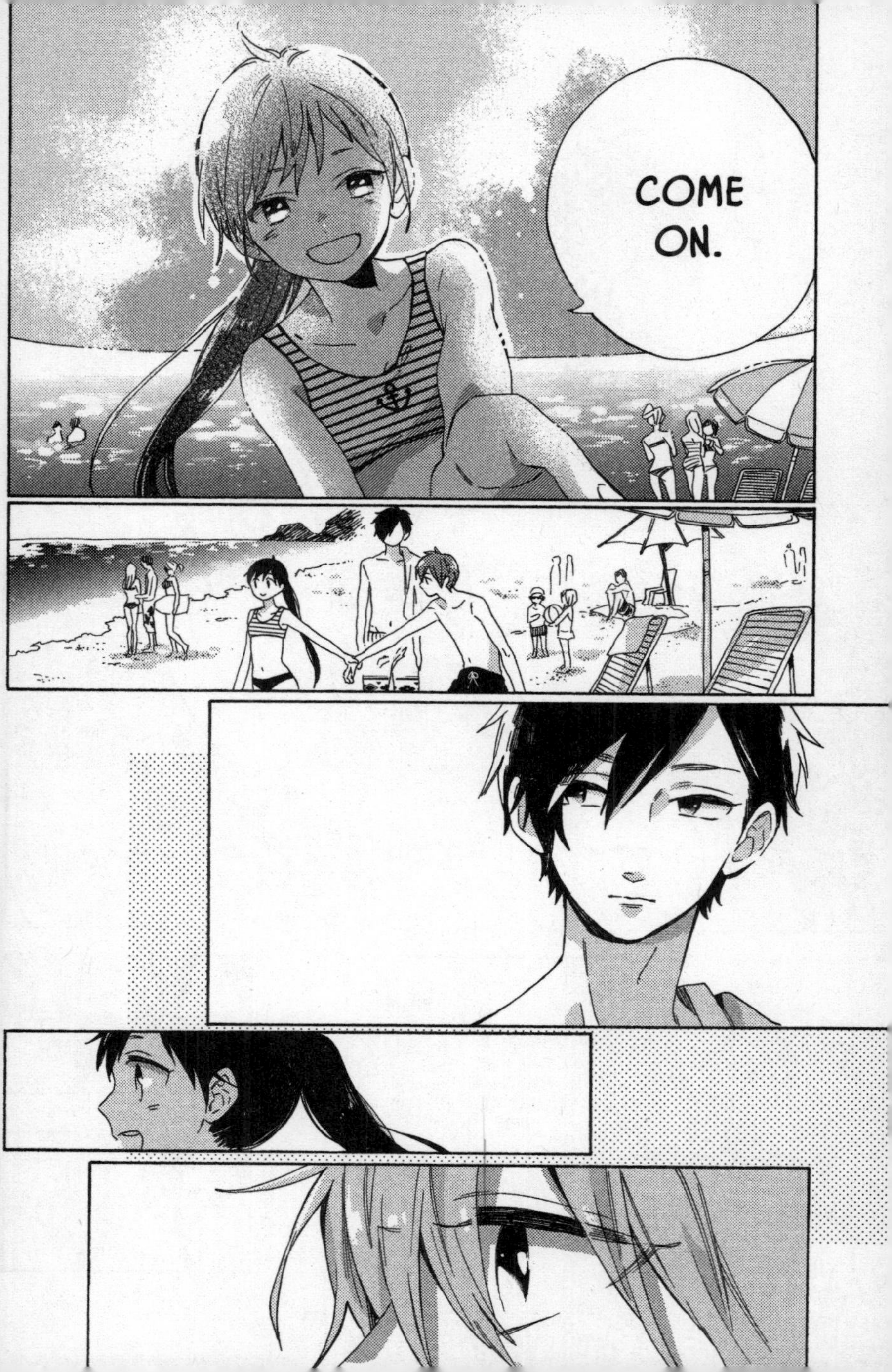
COME ON.

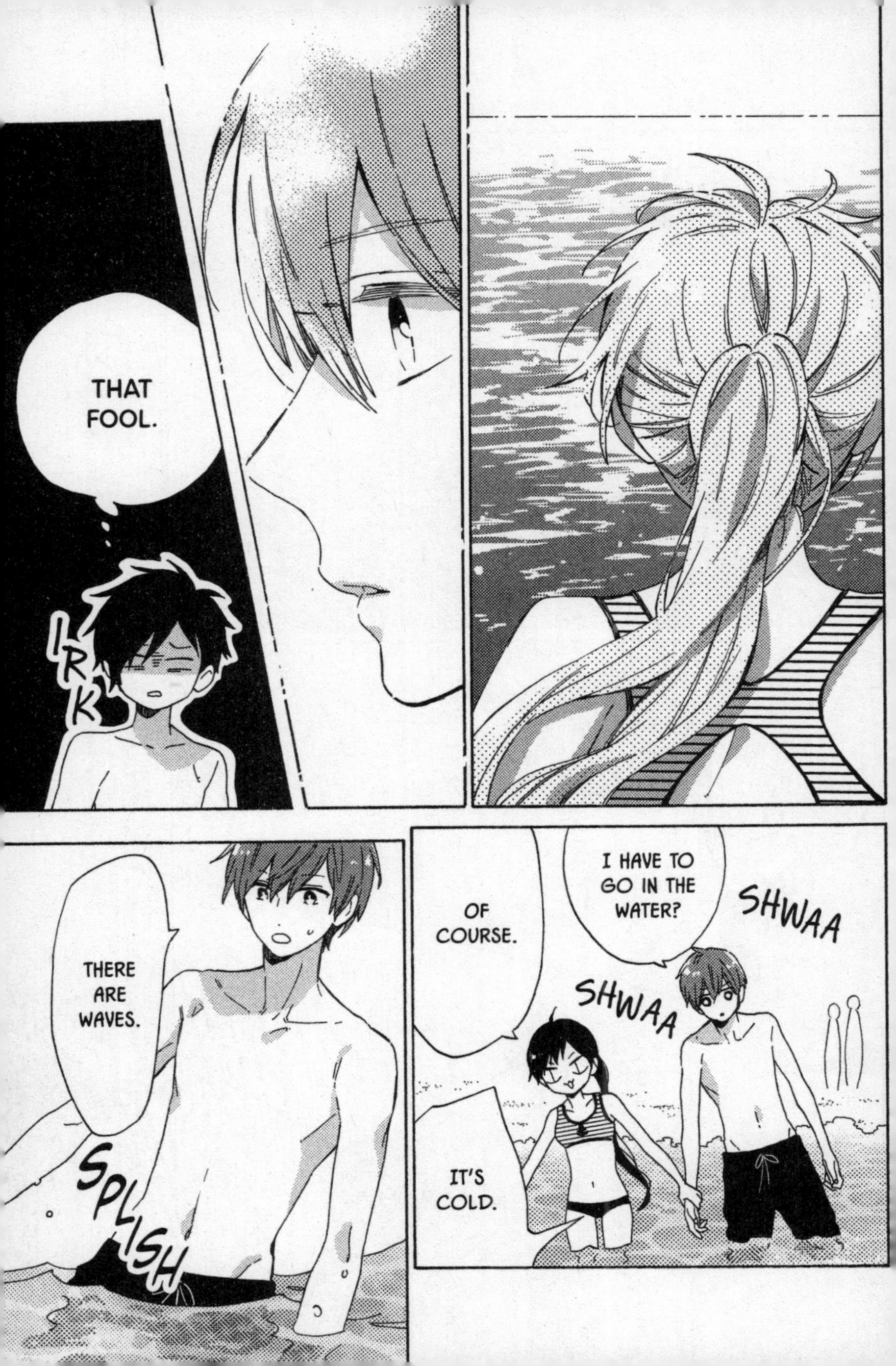
THAT FOOL.
IRK
SHWAA
I HAVE TO GO IN THE WATER?
OF COURSE.
SHWAA
IT'S COLD.
THERE ARE WAVES.
SPLISH

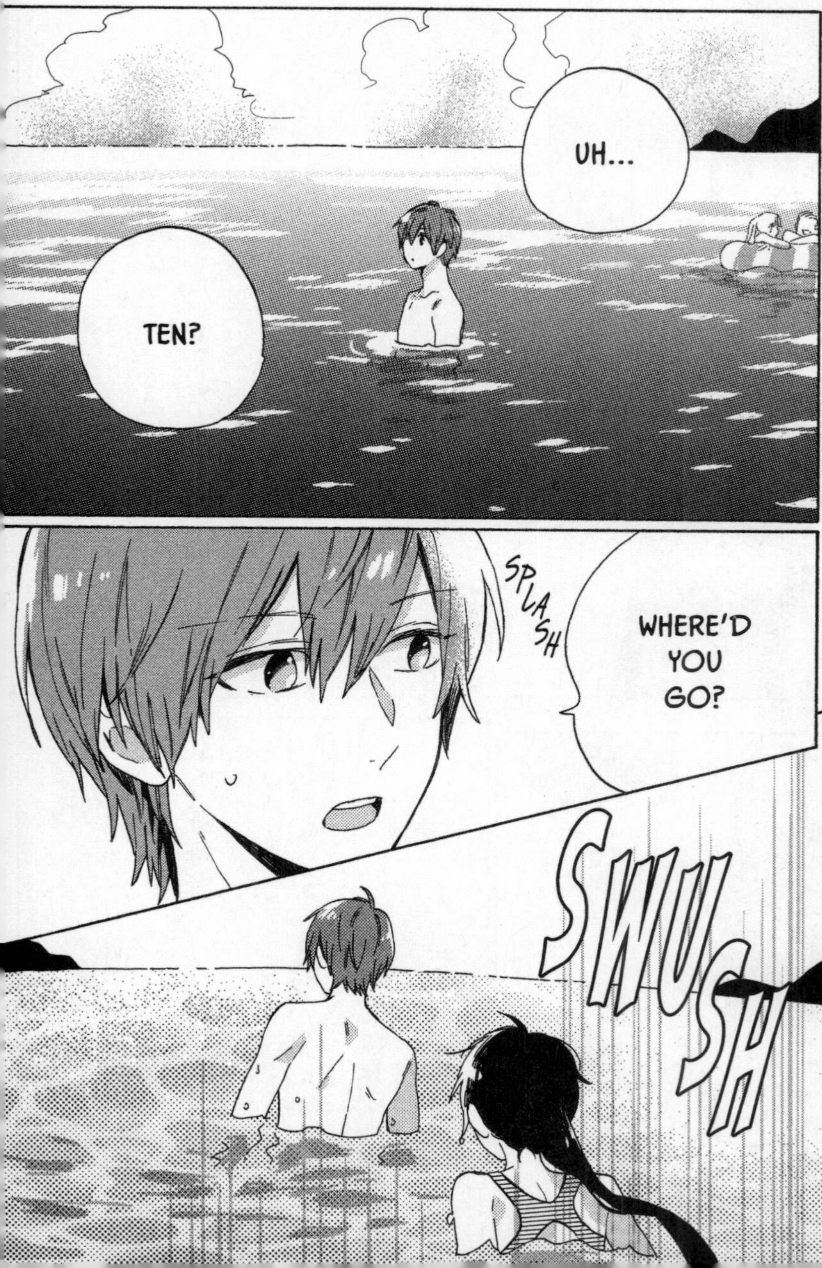
UH...
TEN?
SPLASH
WHERE'D YOU GO?
SWUSH

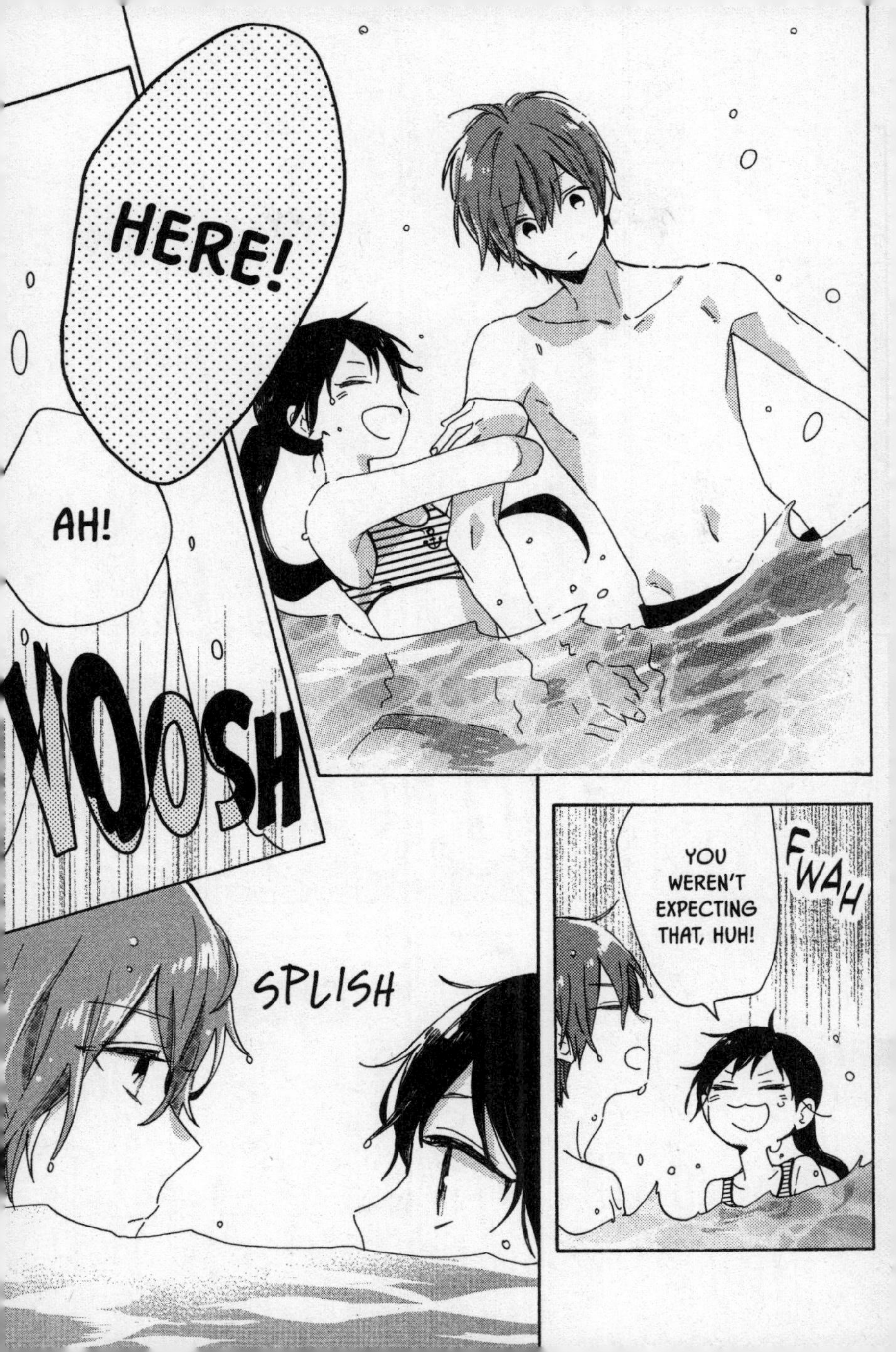

HERE!
AH!
WOOSH
YOU WEREN'T EXPECTING THAT, HUH!
FWAH
SPLISH

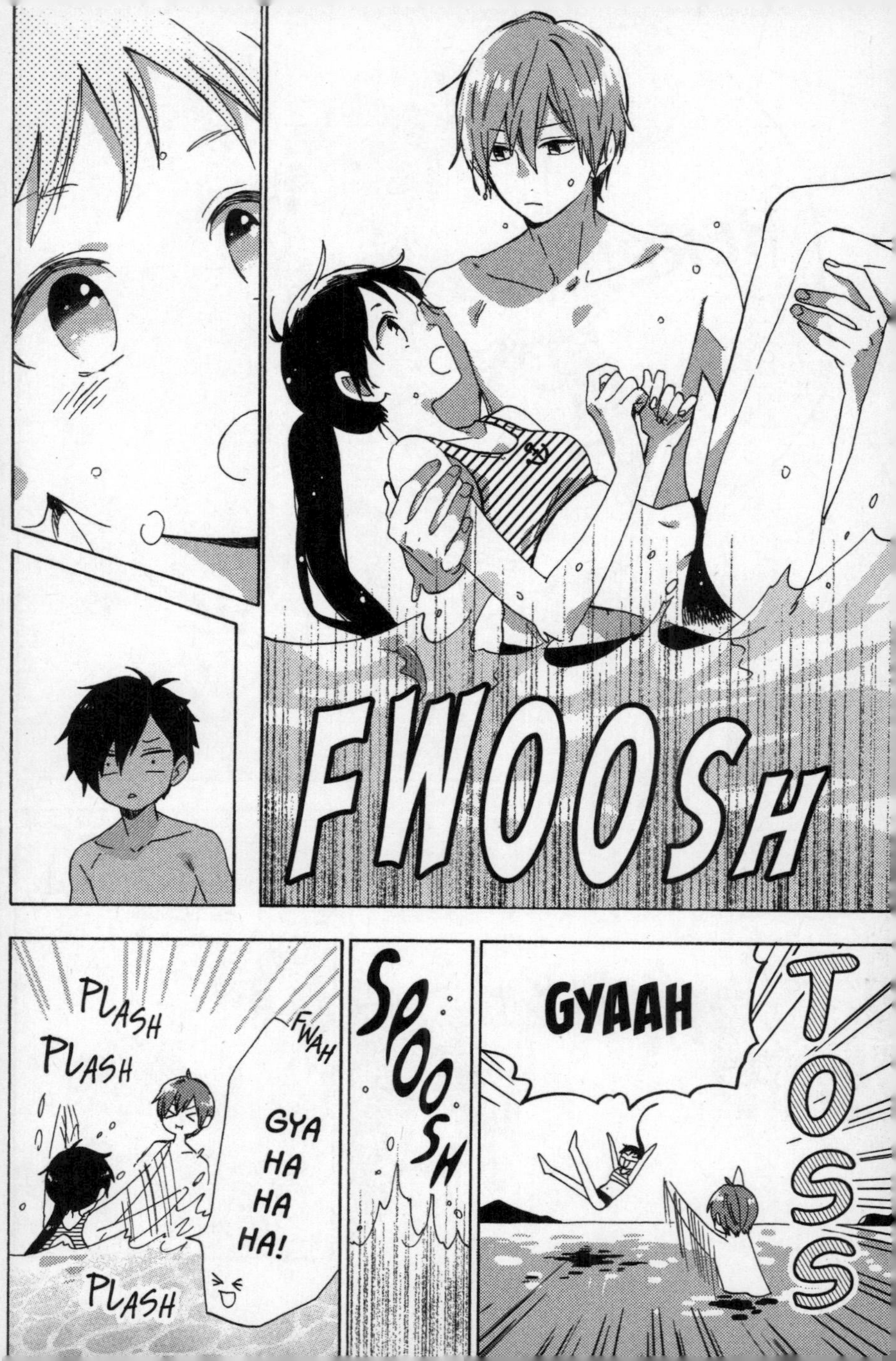
FWOOSH
TOSS
GYAAH
SPOOSH
FWAH
PLASH
PLASH
GYA HA HA HA!
PLASH

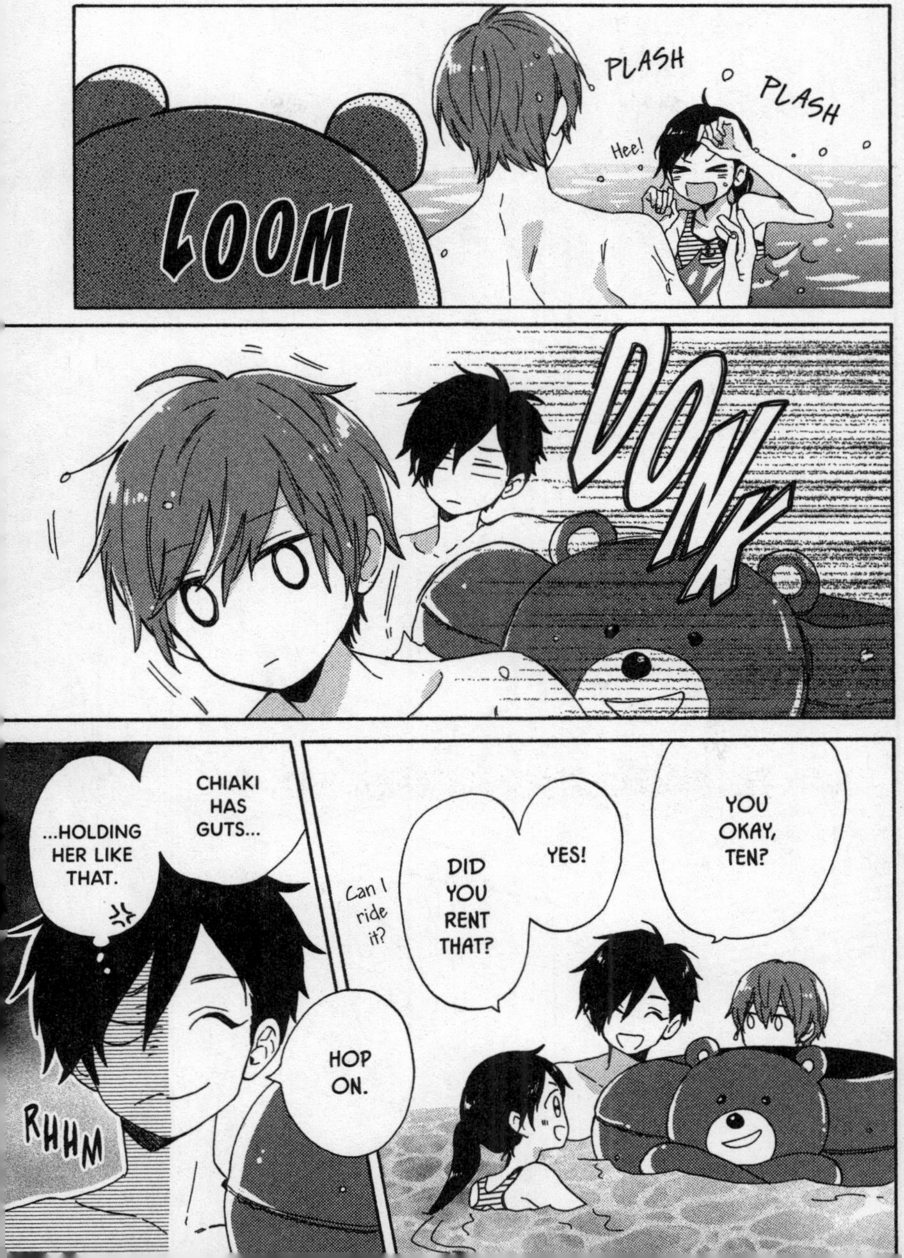
PLASH
PLASH
Hee!
LOOM
DONK
YOU OKAY, TEN?
YES!
DID YOU RENT THAT?
Can I ride it?
CHIAKI HAS GUTS...
...HOLDING HER LIKE THAT.
HOP ON.
RHHM

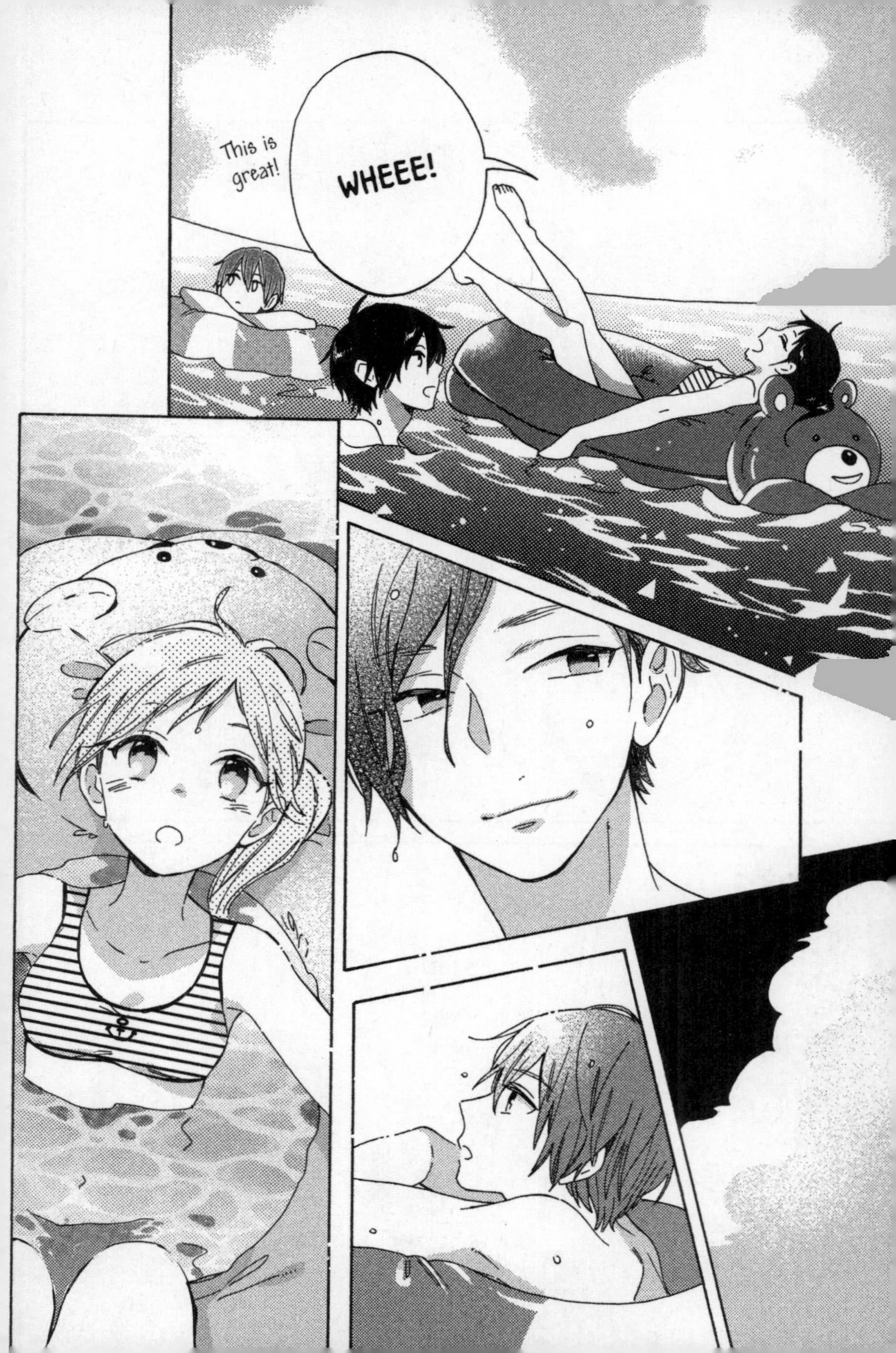
WHEEE!
This is great!

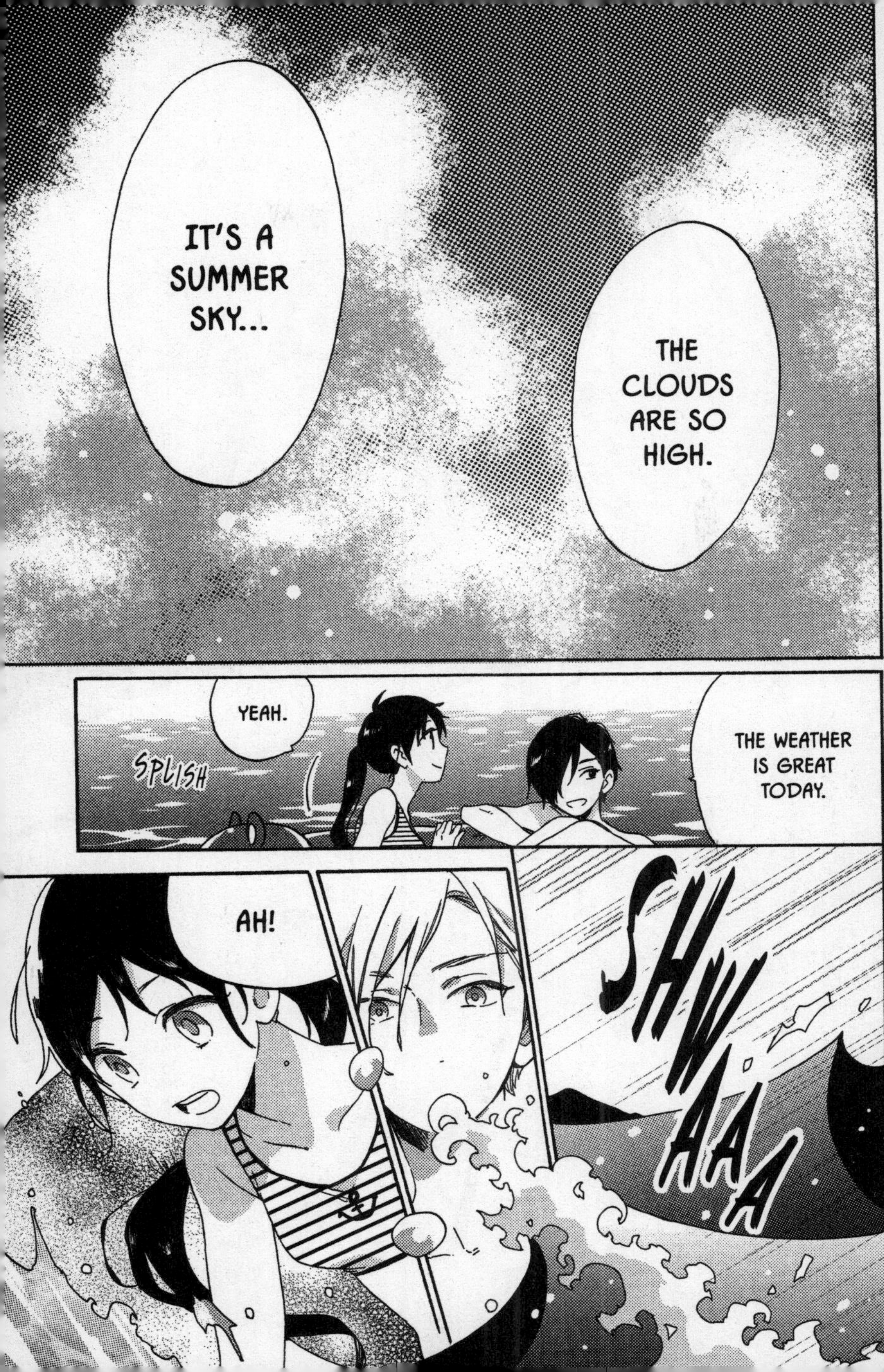
THE CLOUDS ARE SO HIGH.
IT'S A SUMMER SKY...
THE WEATHER IS GREAT TODAY.
YEAH.
SPLISH
SHWAAAA
AH!

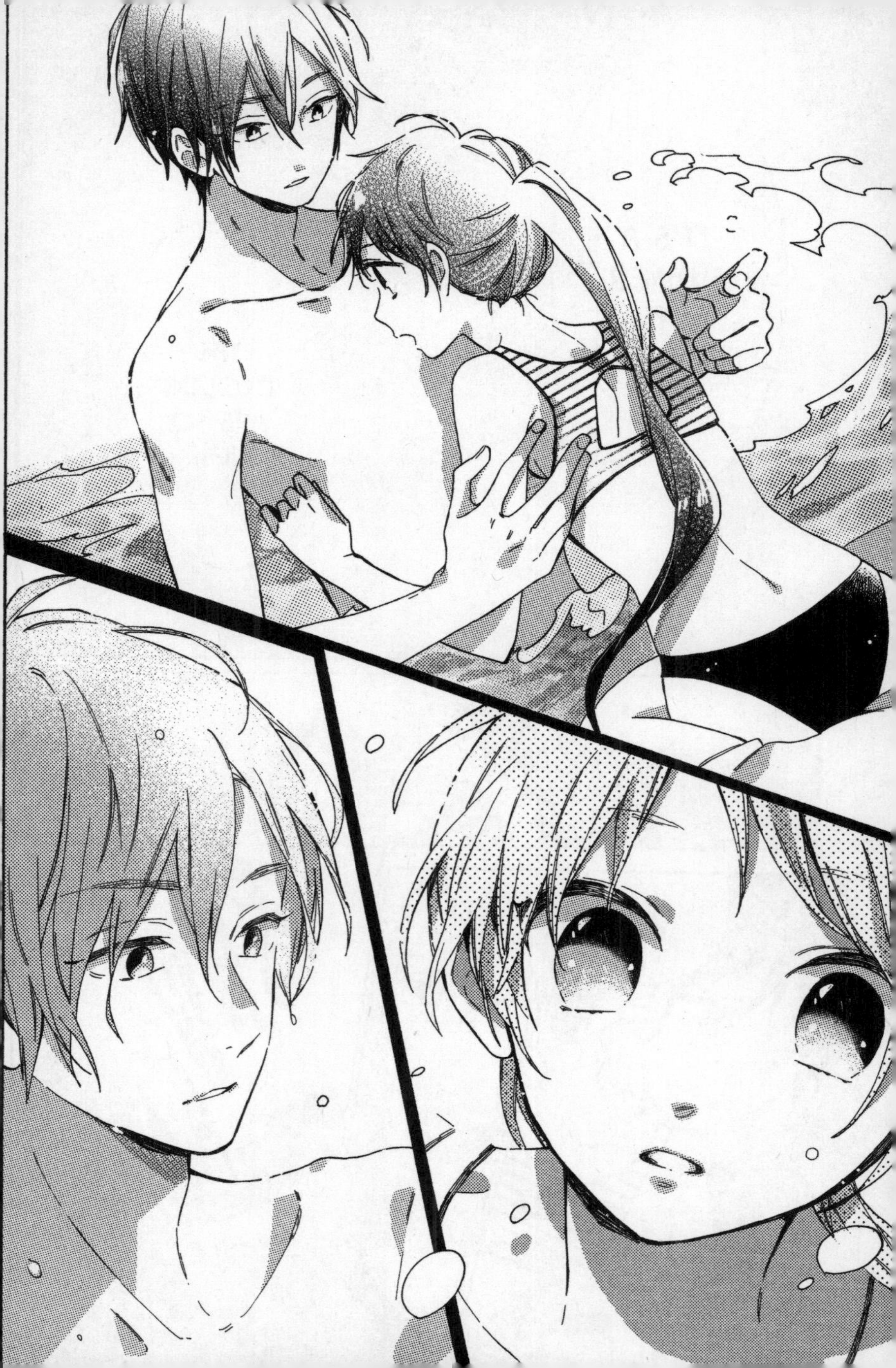

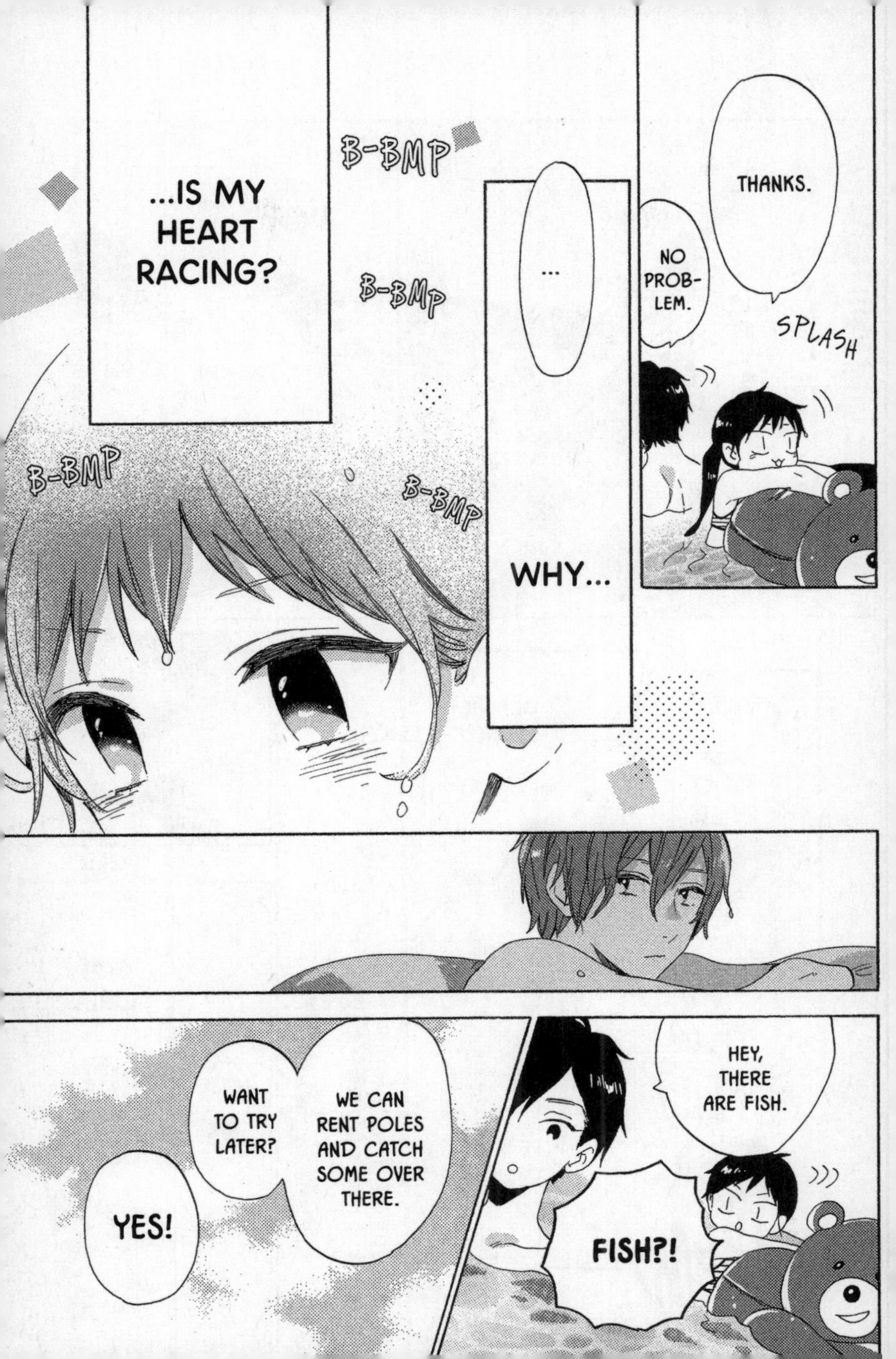

THANKS.
NO PROB-LEM.
SPLASH
...
WHY...
B-BMP
B-BMP
...IS MY HEART RACING?
B-BMP
B-BMP
HEY, THERE ARE FISH.
FISH?!
WE CAN RENT POLES AND CATCH SOME OVER THERE.
WANT TO TRY LATER?
YES!

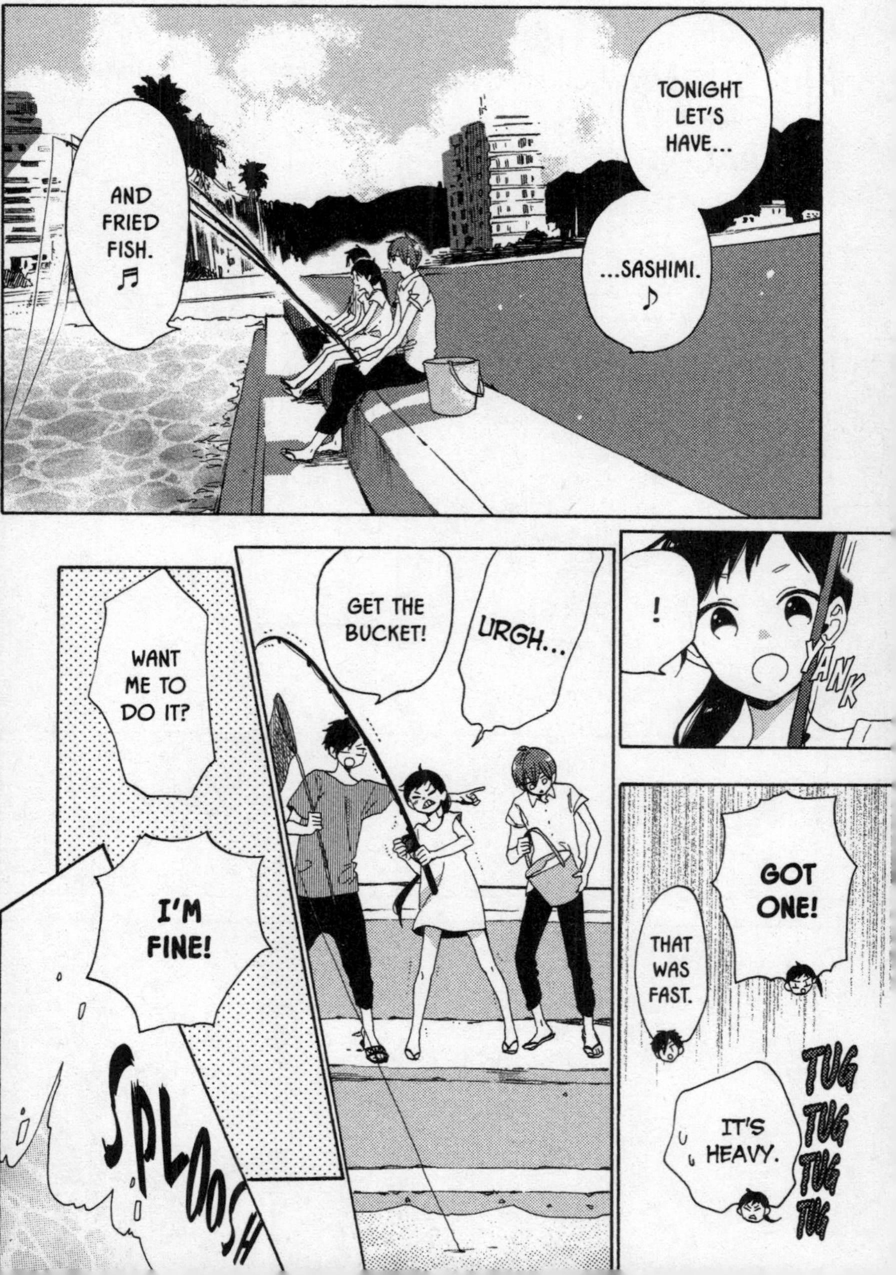
TONIGHT LET'S HAVE...
...SASHIMI. ♪
AND FRIED FISH. ♬
!
YANK
GOT ONE!
THAT WAS FAST.
TUG TUG TUG TUG
IT'S HEAVY.
URGH...
GET THE BUCKET!
WANT ME TO DO IT?
I'M FINE!
SPLOOSH

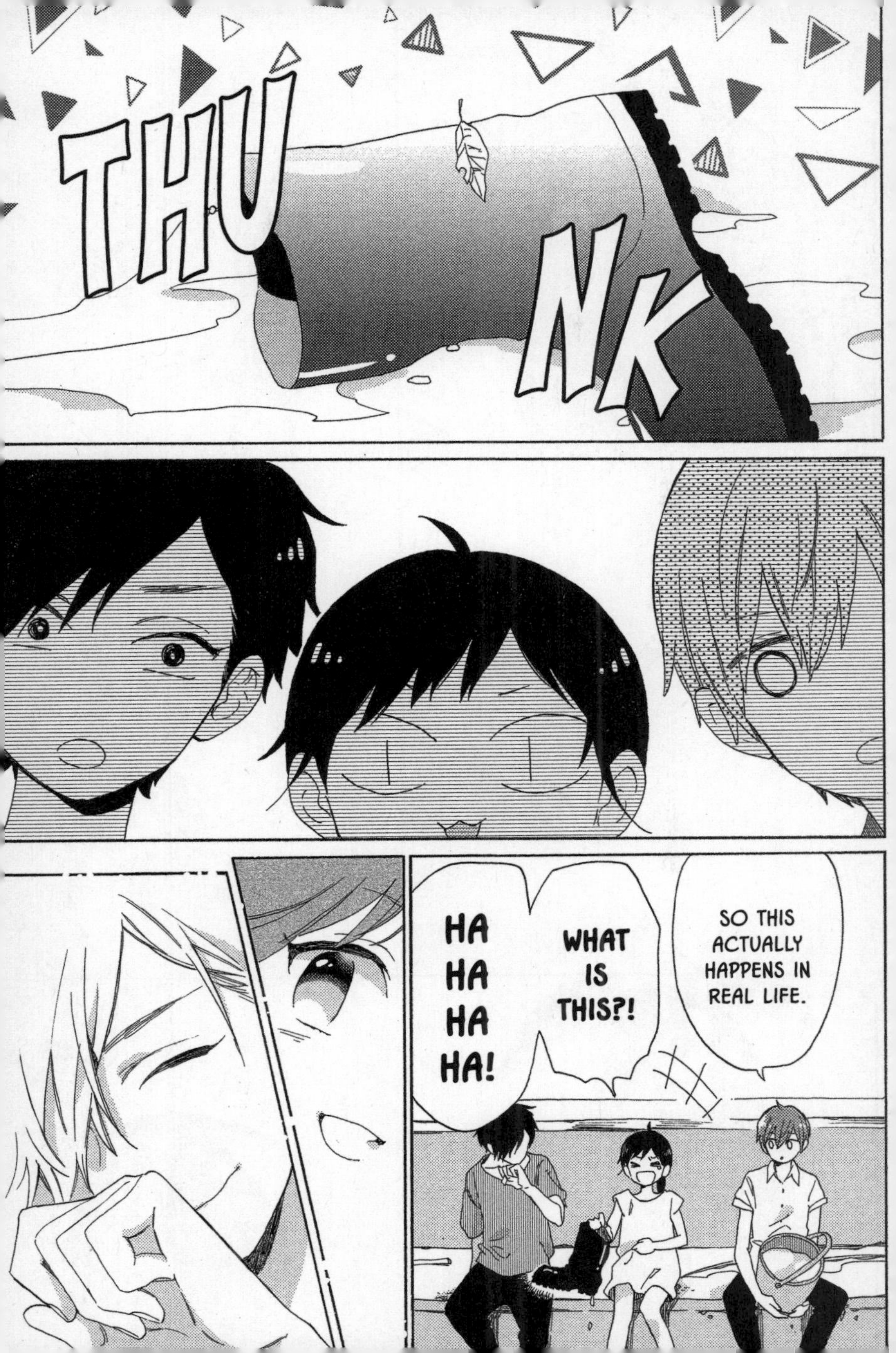
THUNK
SO THIS ACTUALLY HAPPENS IN REAL LIFE.
WHAT IS THIS?!
HA HA HA HA!

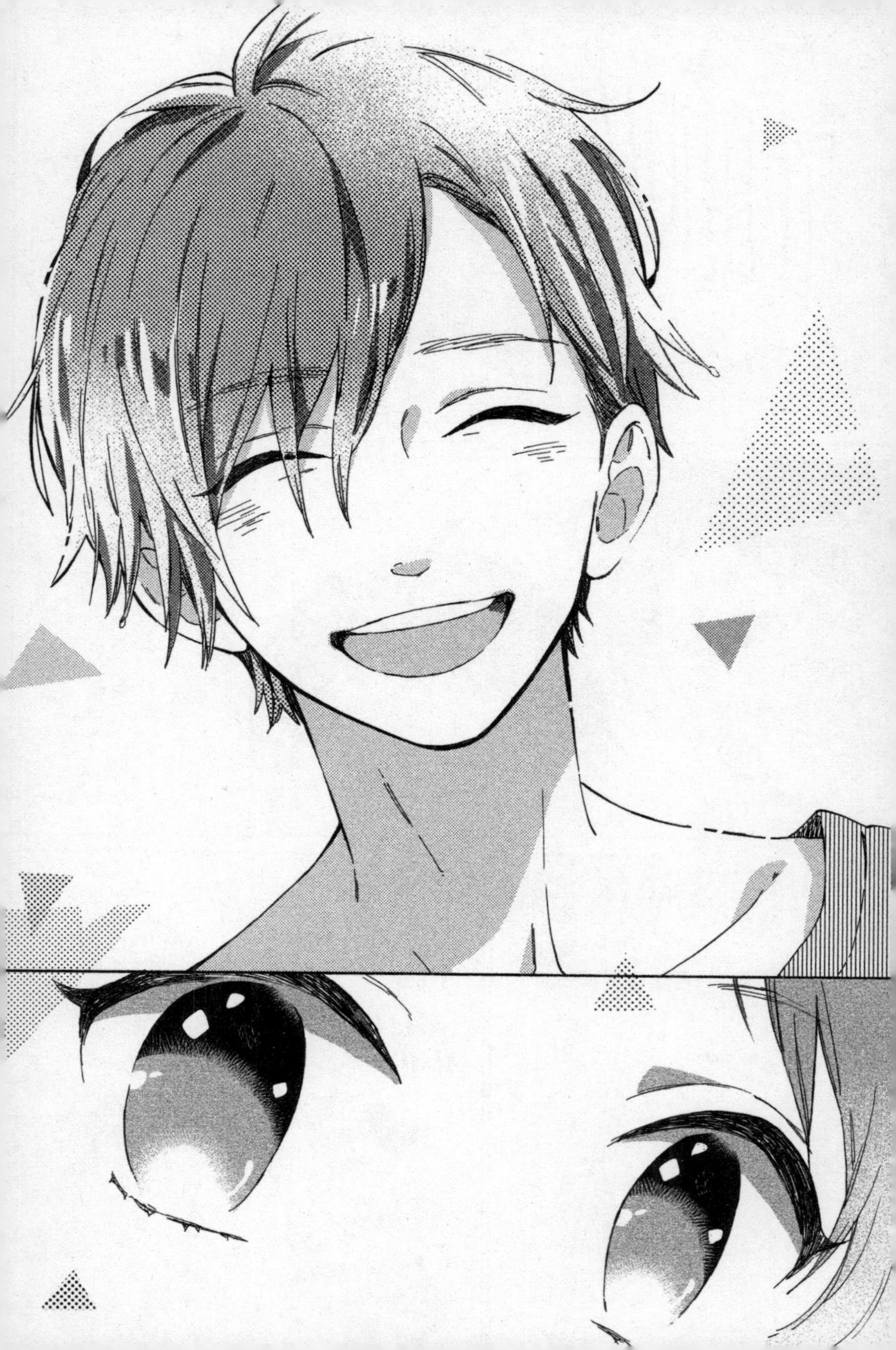

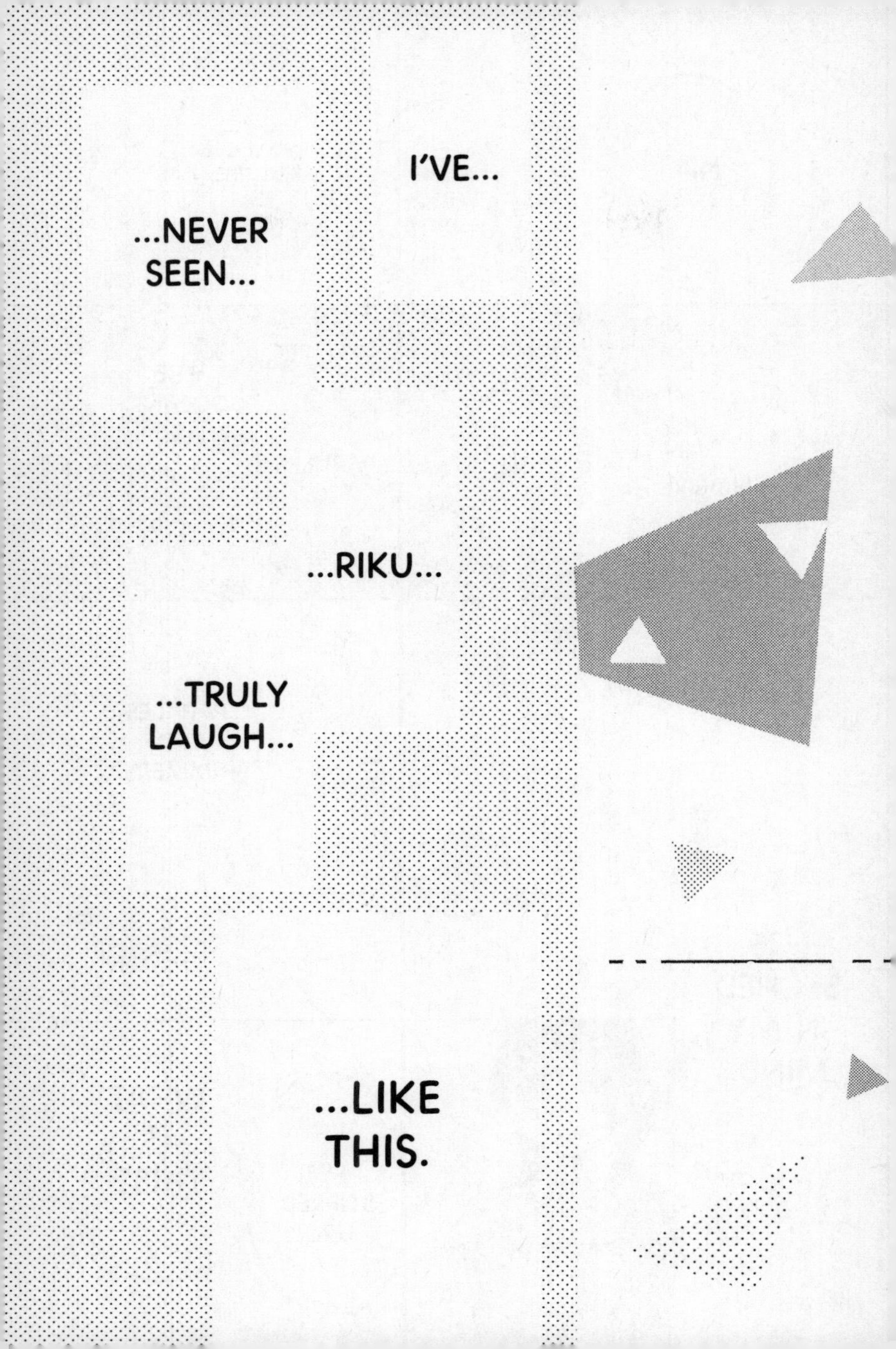
I'VE...
...NEVER SEEN...
...RIKU...
...TRULY LAUGH...
...LIKE THIS.

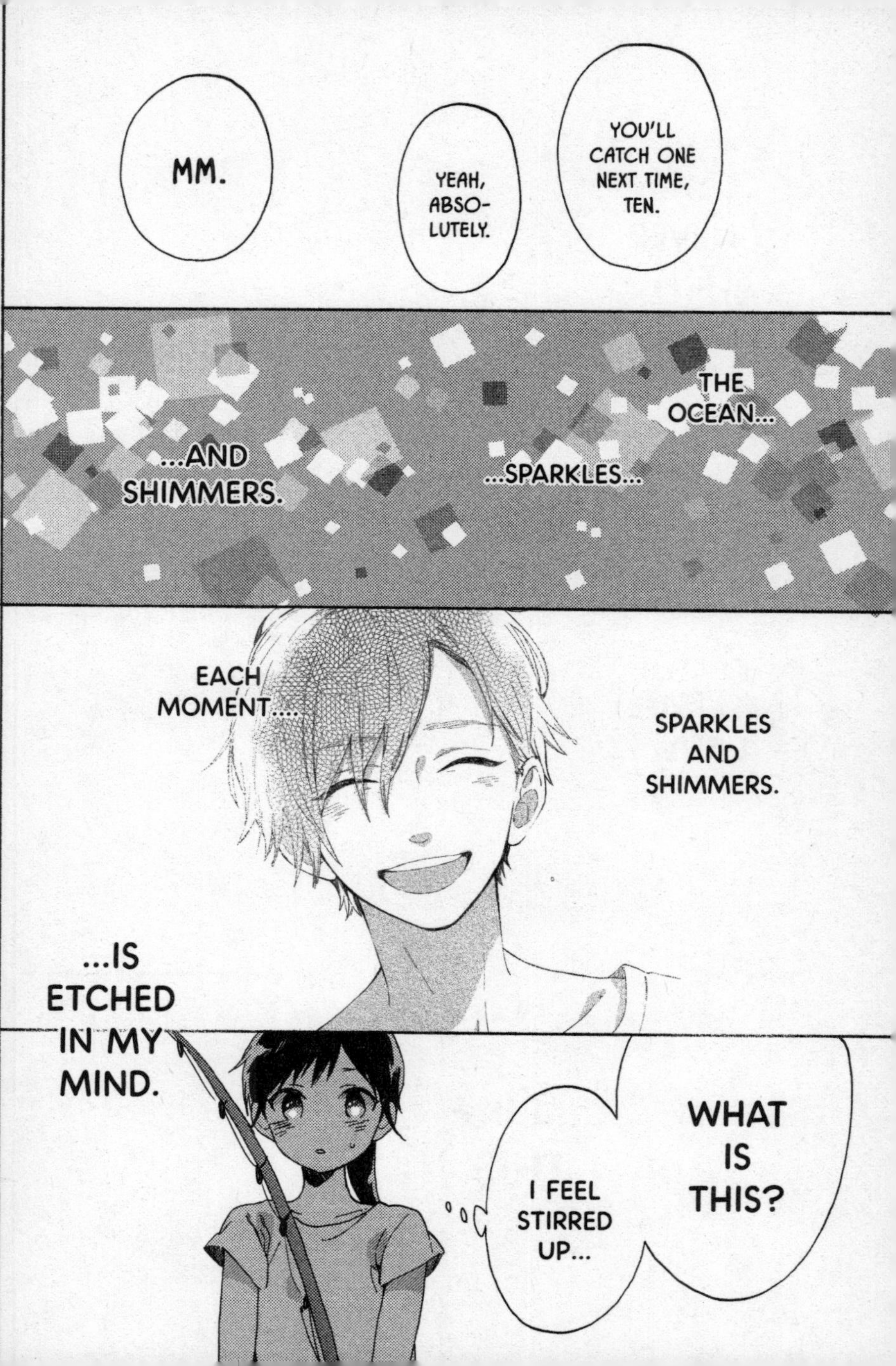
YOU'LL CATCH ONE NEXT TIME, TEN.
YEAH, ABSO-LUTELY.
MM.
THE OCEAN...
...SPARKLES...
...AND SHIMMERS.
EACH MOMENT....
SPARKLES AND SHIMMERS.
...IS ETCHED IN MY MIND.
WHAT IS THIS?
I FEEL STIRRED UP...

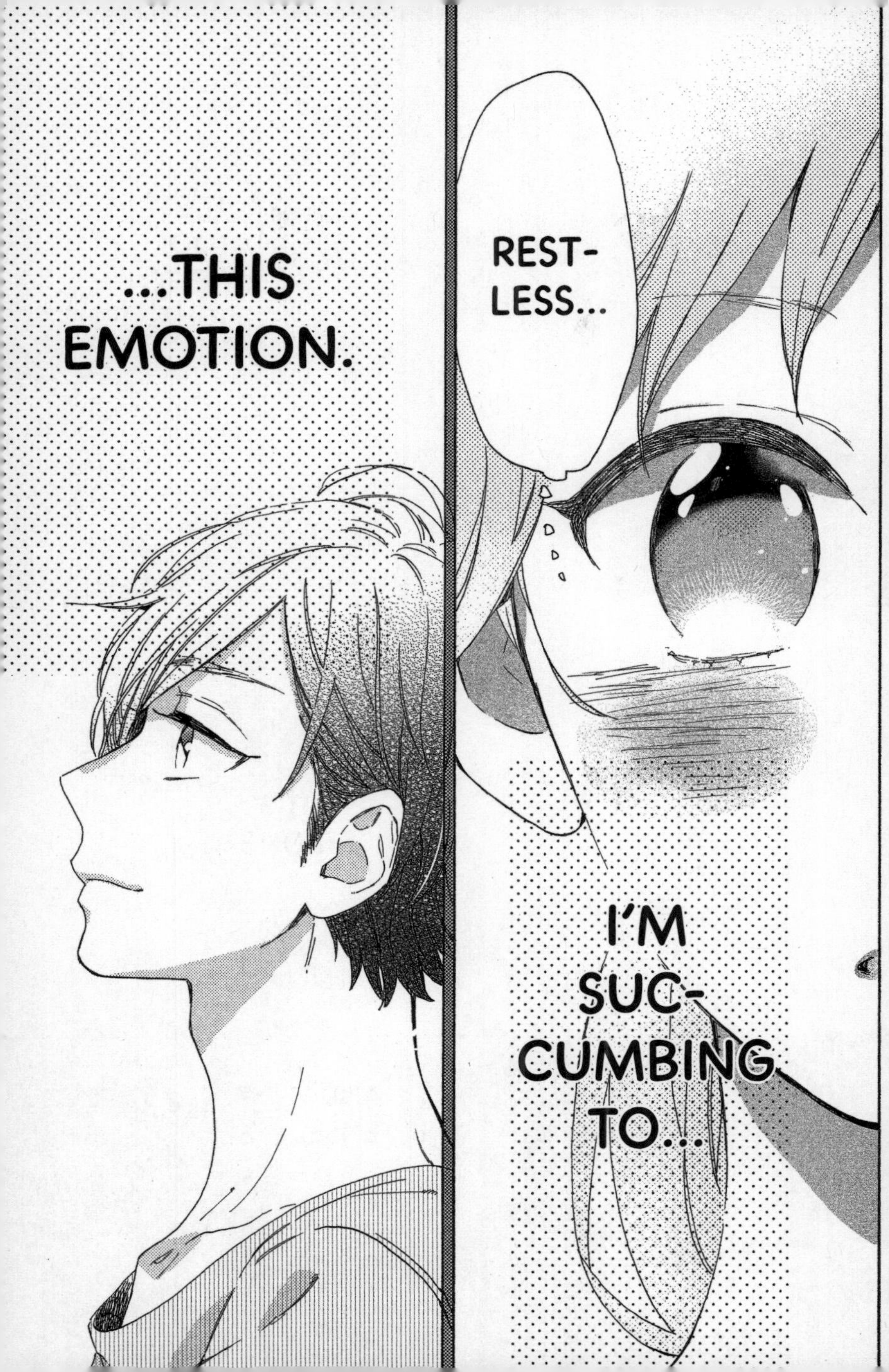
REST-
LESS...
I'M
SUC-
CUMBING
TO...
...THIS
EMOTION.

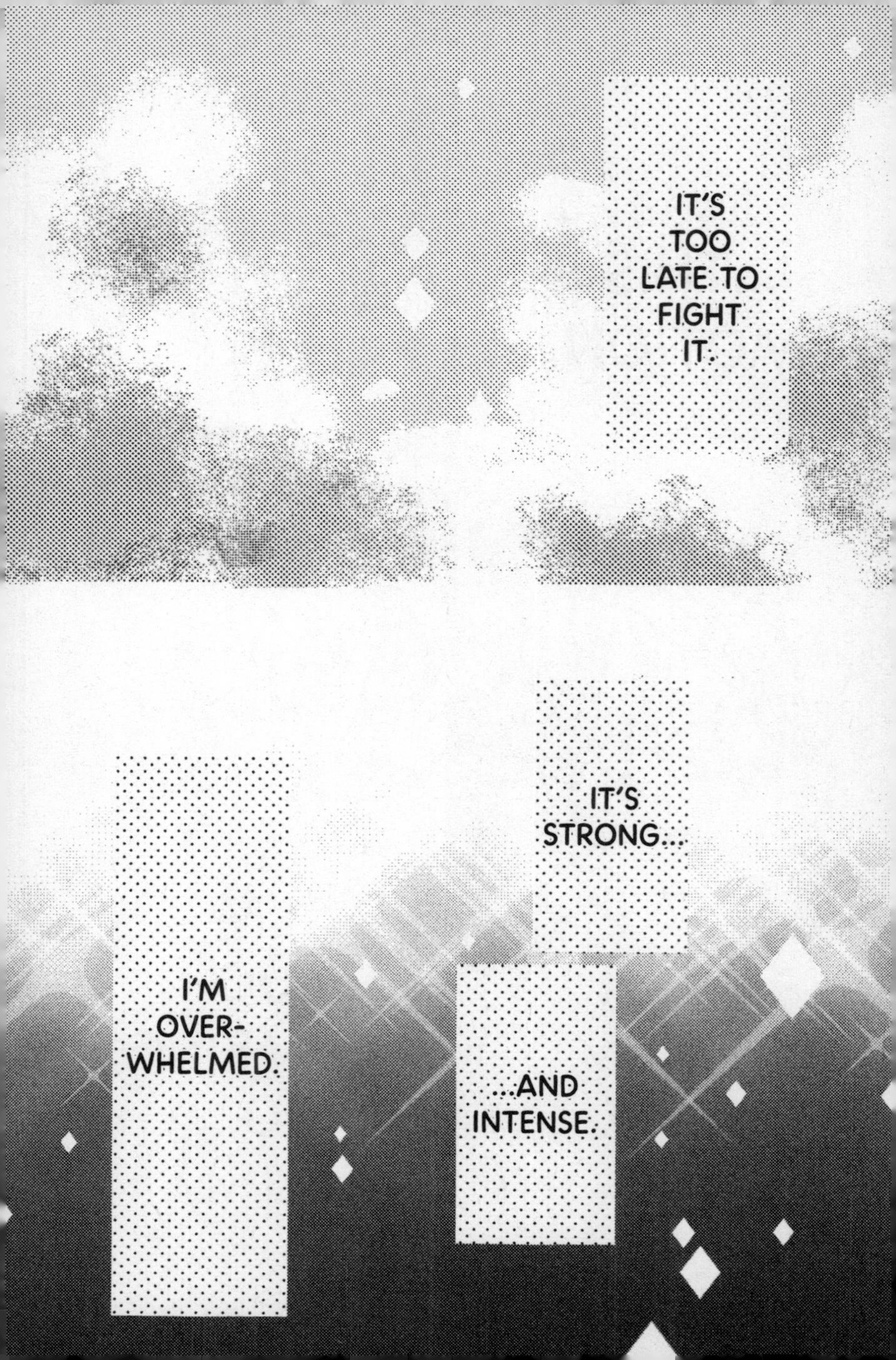
IT'S TOO LATE TO FIGHT IT.
IT'S STRONG...
...AND INTENSE.
I'M OVER-WHELMED.

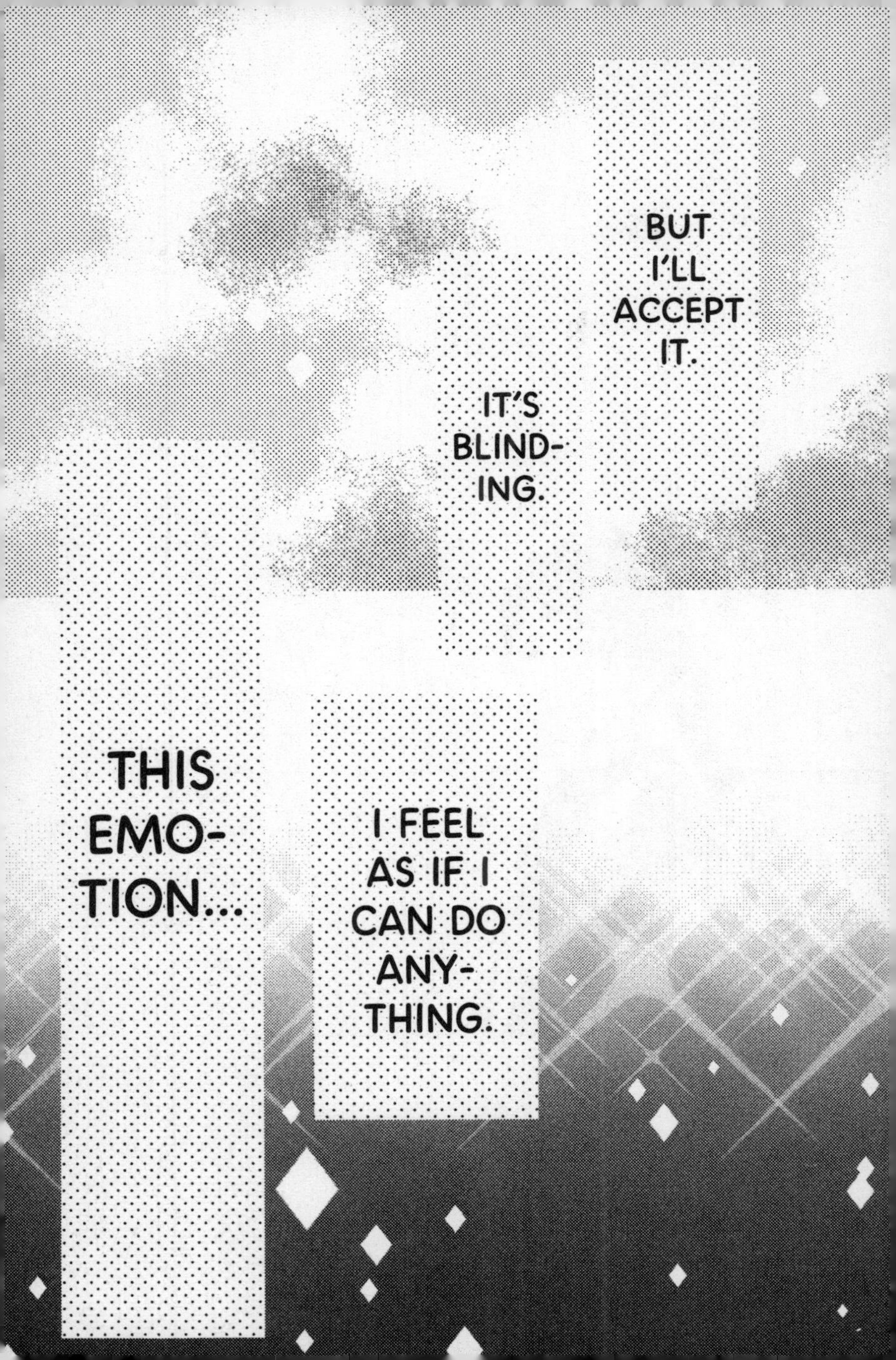
BUT I'LL ACCEPT IT.
IT'S BLIND-ING.
THIS EMO-TION...
I FEEL AS IF I CAN DO ANY-THING.

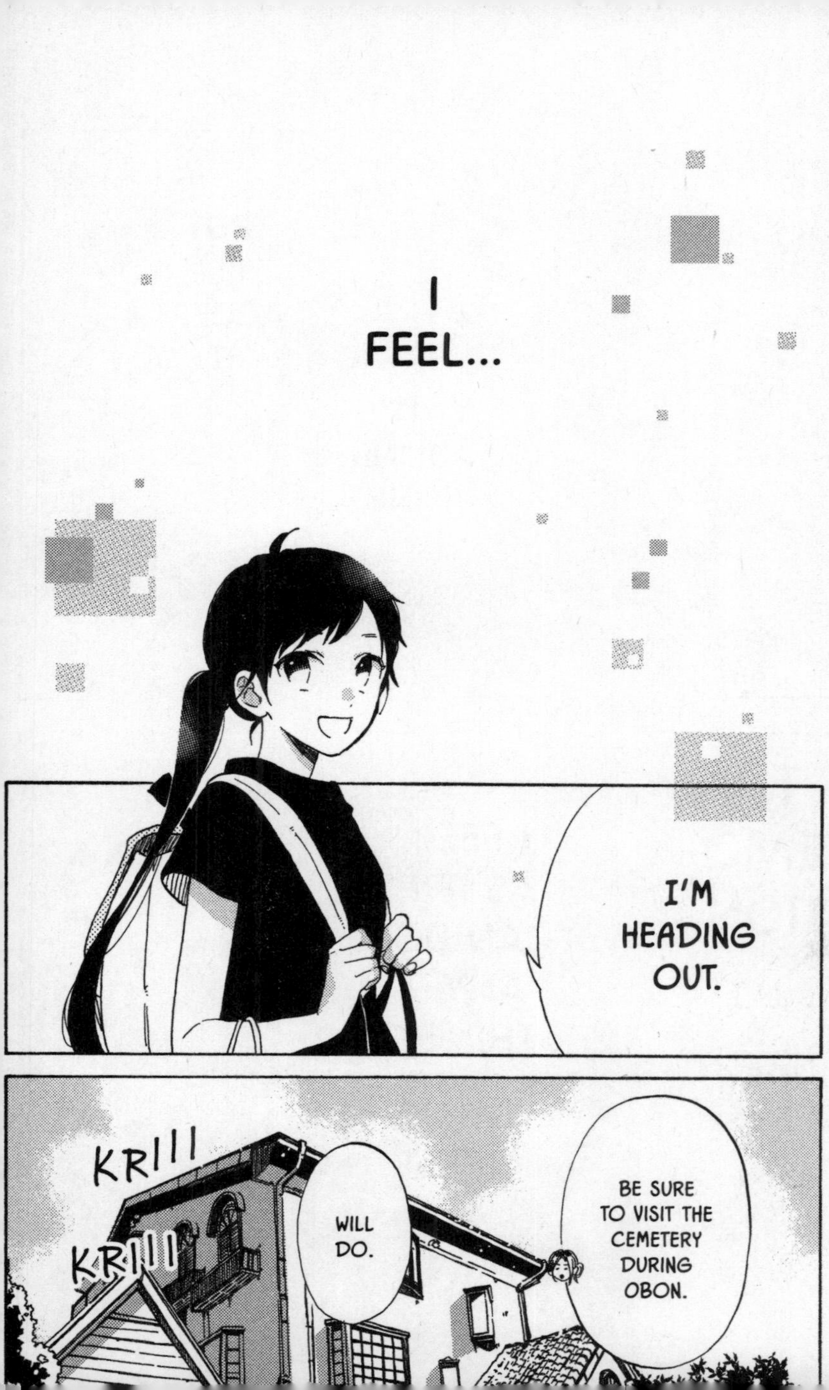
I FEEL...
I'M HEADING OUT.
BE SURE TO VISIT THE CEMETERY DURING OBON.
WILL DO.
KRIII
KRIII

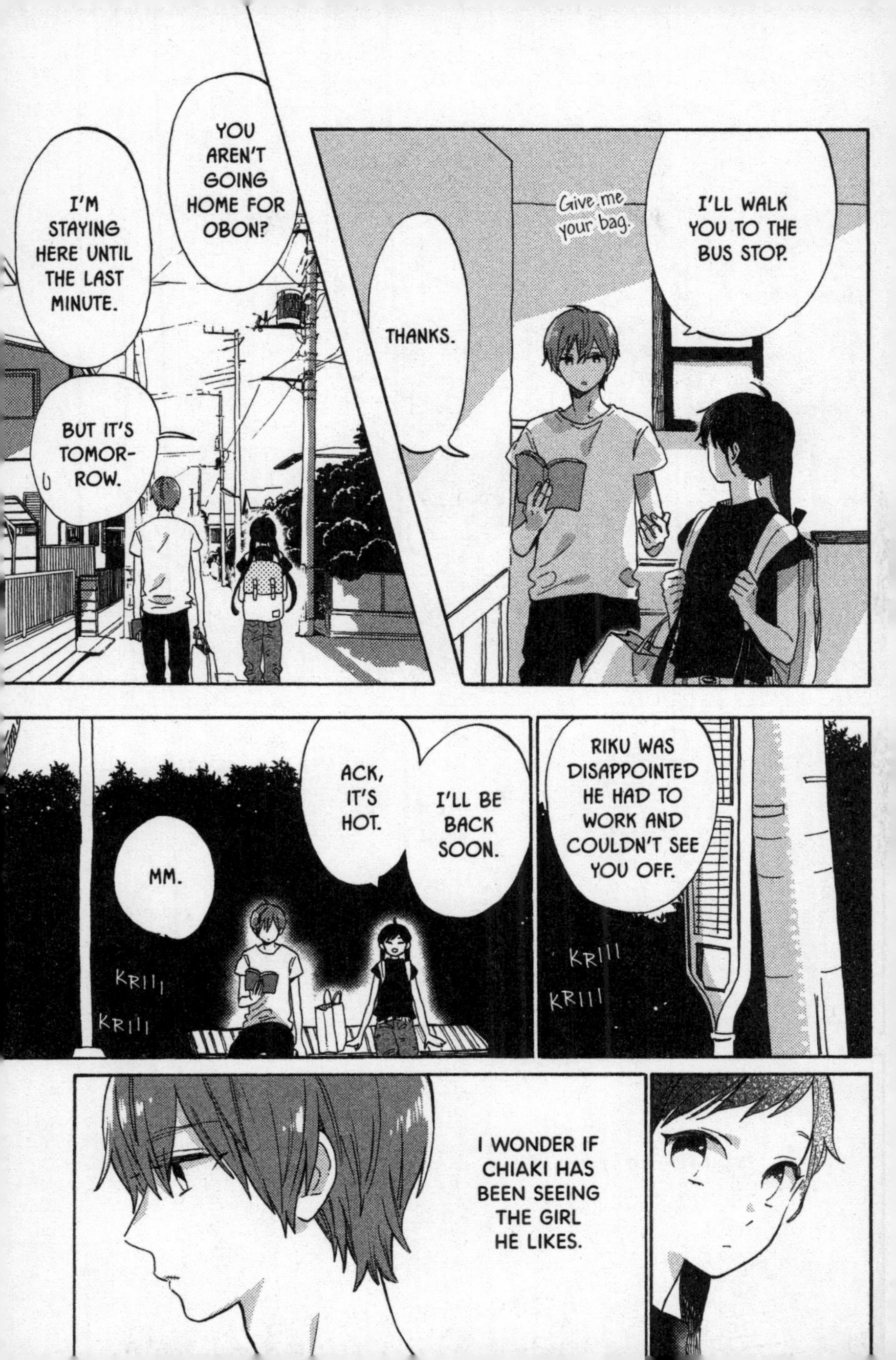
I'LL WALK YOU TO THE BUS STOP.
Give me your bag.
THANKS.
YOU AREN'T GOING HOME FOR OBON?
I'M STAYING HERE UNTIL THE LAST MINUTE.
BUT IT'S TOMOR-ROW.
RIKU WAS DISAPPOINTED HE HAD TO WORK AND COULDN'T SEE YOU OFF.
KRIII
KRIII
I'LL BE BACK SOON.
ACK, IT'S HOT.
MM.
KRIII
KRIII
I WONDER IF CHIAKI HAS BEEN SEEING THE GIRL HE LIKES.

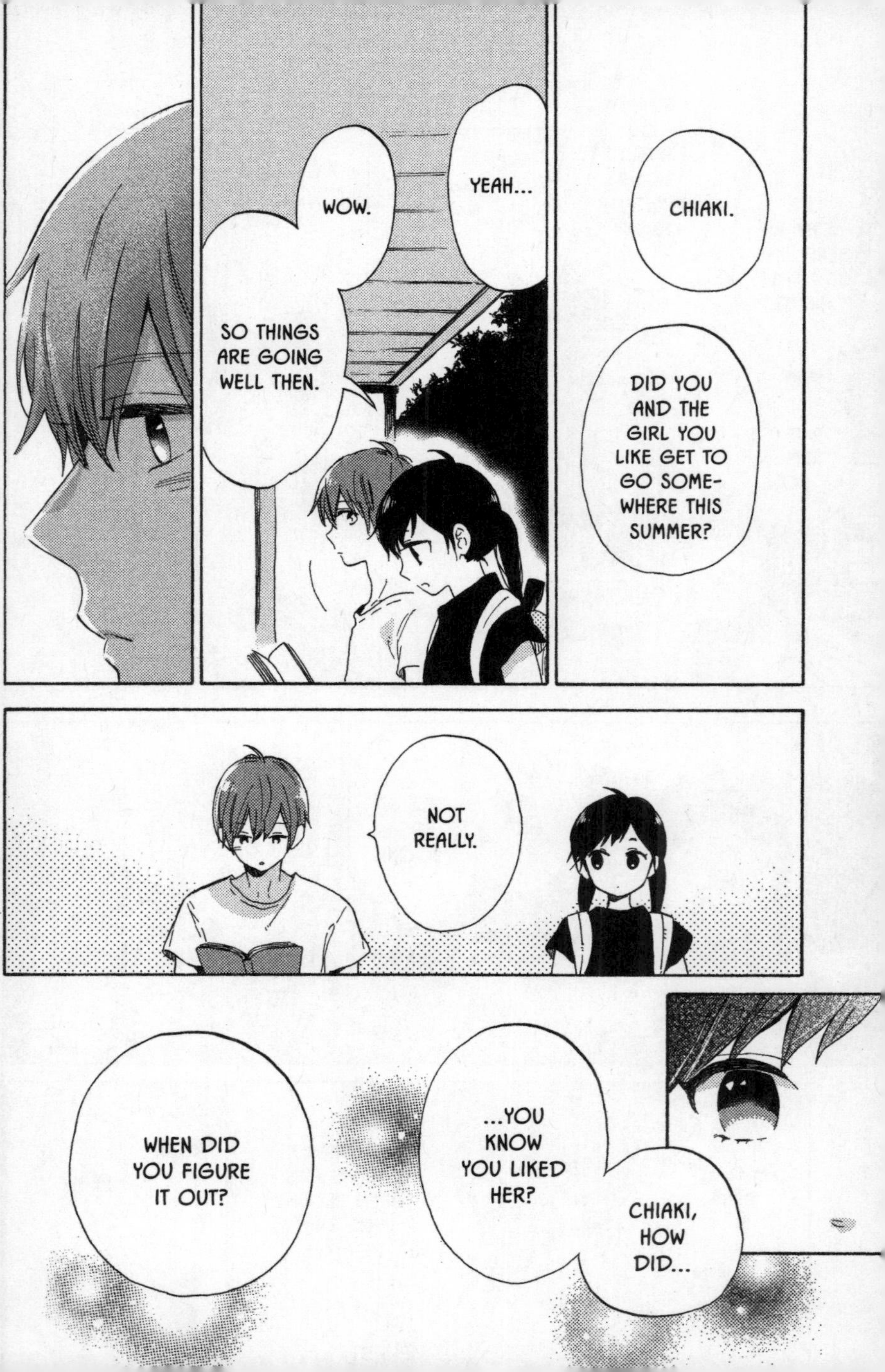
CHIAKI.
DID YOU AND THE GIRL YOU LIKE GET TO GO SOME-WHERE THIS SUMMER?
YEAH...
WOW.
SO THINGS ARE GOING WELL THEN.
NOT REALLY.
CHIAKI, HOW DID...
...YOU KNOW YOU LIKED HER?
WHEN DID YOU FIGURE IT OUT?

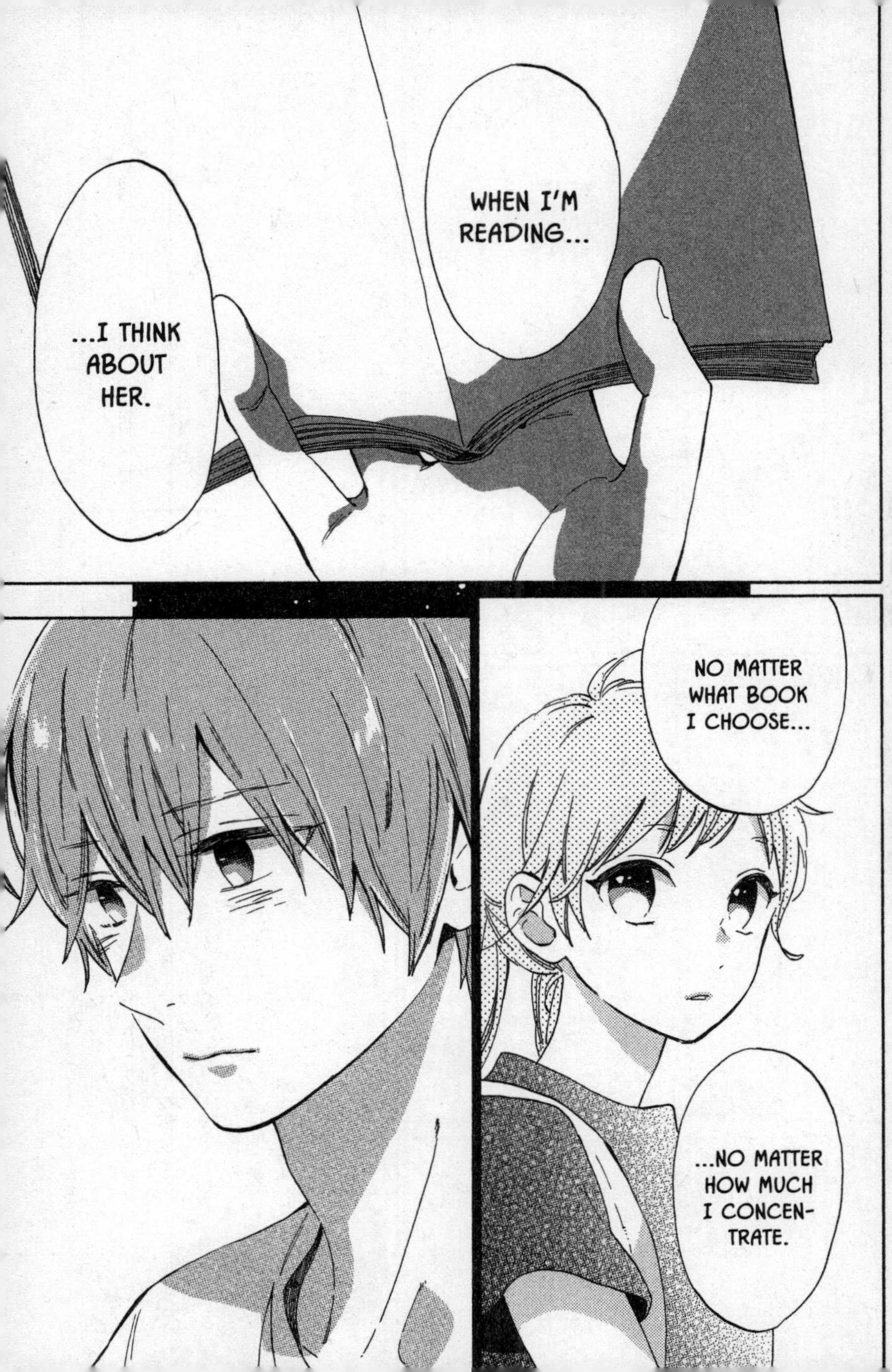
WHEN I'M READING...
...I THINK ABOUT HER.
NO MATTER WHAT BOOK I CHOOSE...
...NO MATTER HOW MUCH I CONCENTRATE.

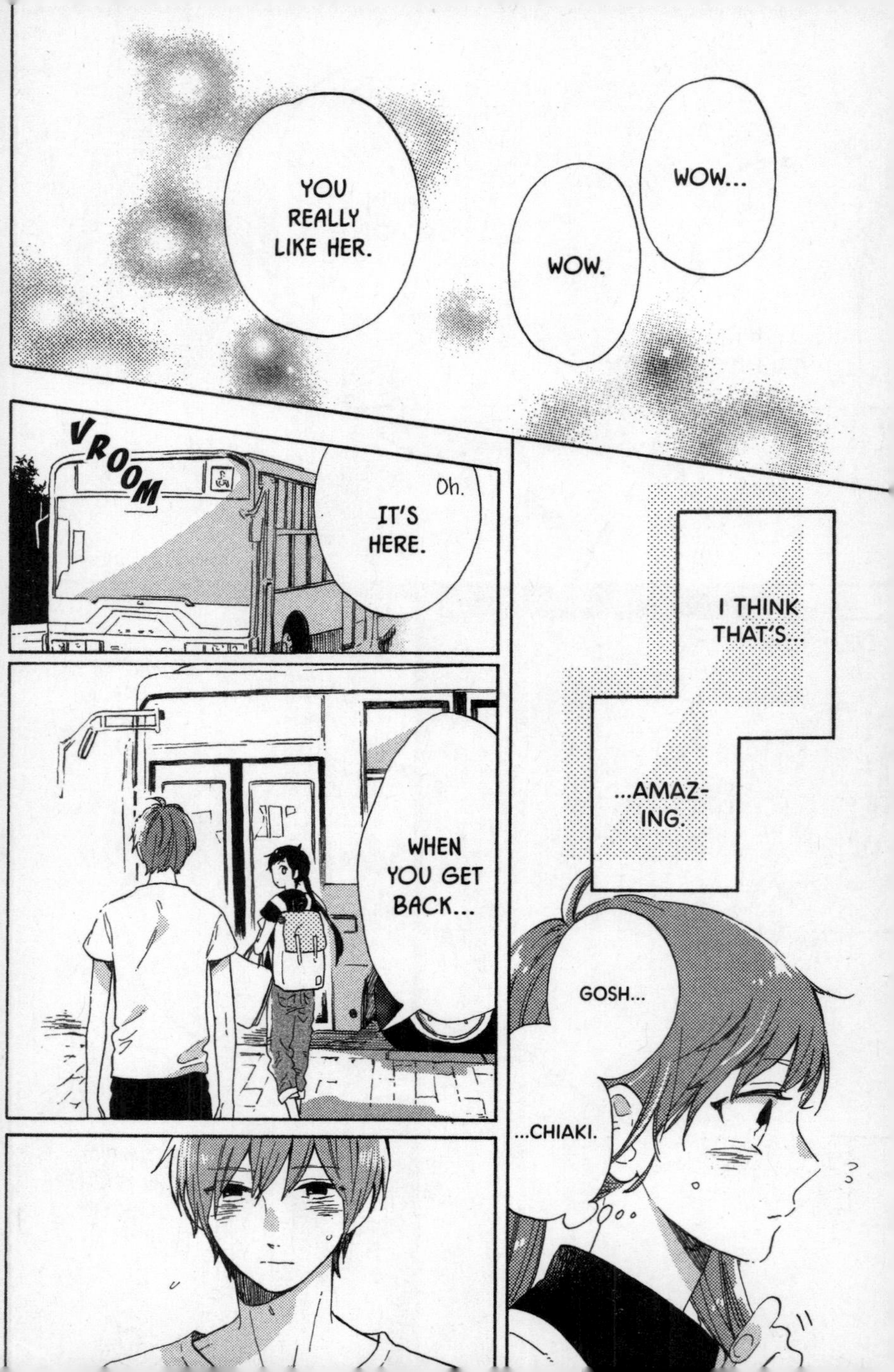
WOW...
WOW.
YOU REALLY LIKE HER.
I THINK THAT'S...
...AMAZ-ING.
GOSH...
...CHIAKI.
VROOM
Oh.
IT'S HERE.
WHEN YOU GET BACK...

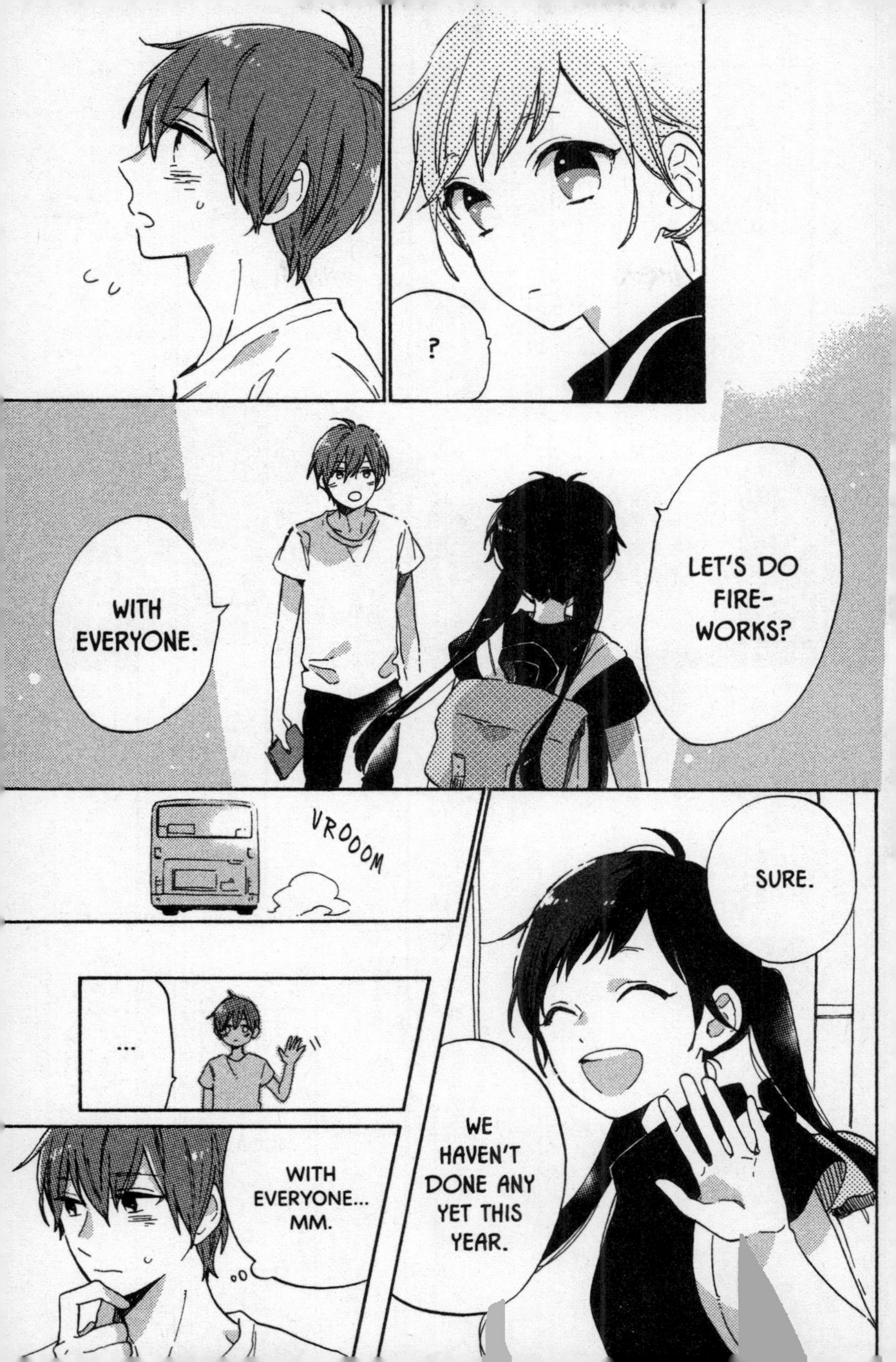
?
LET'S DO FIRE-WORKS?
WITH EVERYONE.
SURE.
WE HAVEN'T DONE ANY YET THIS YEAR.
VROOOM
...
WITH EVERYONE... MM.

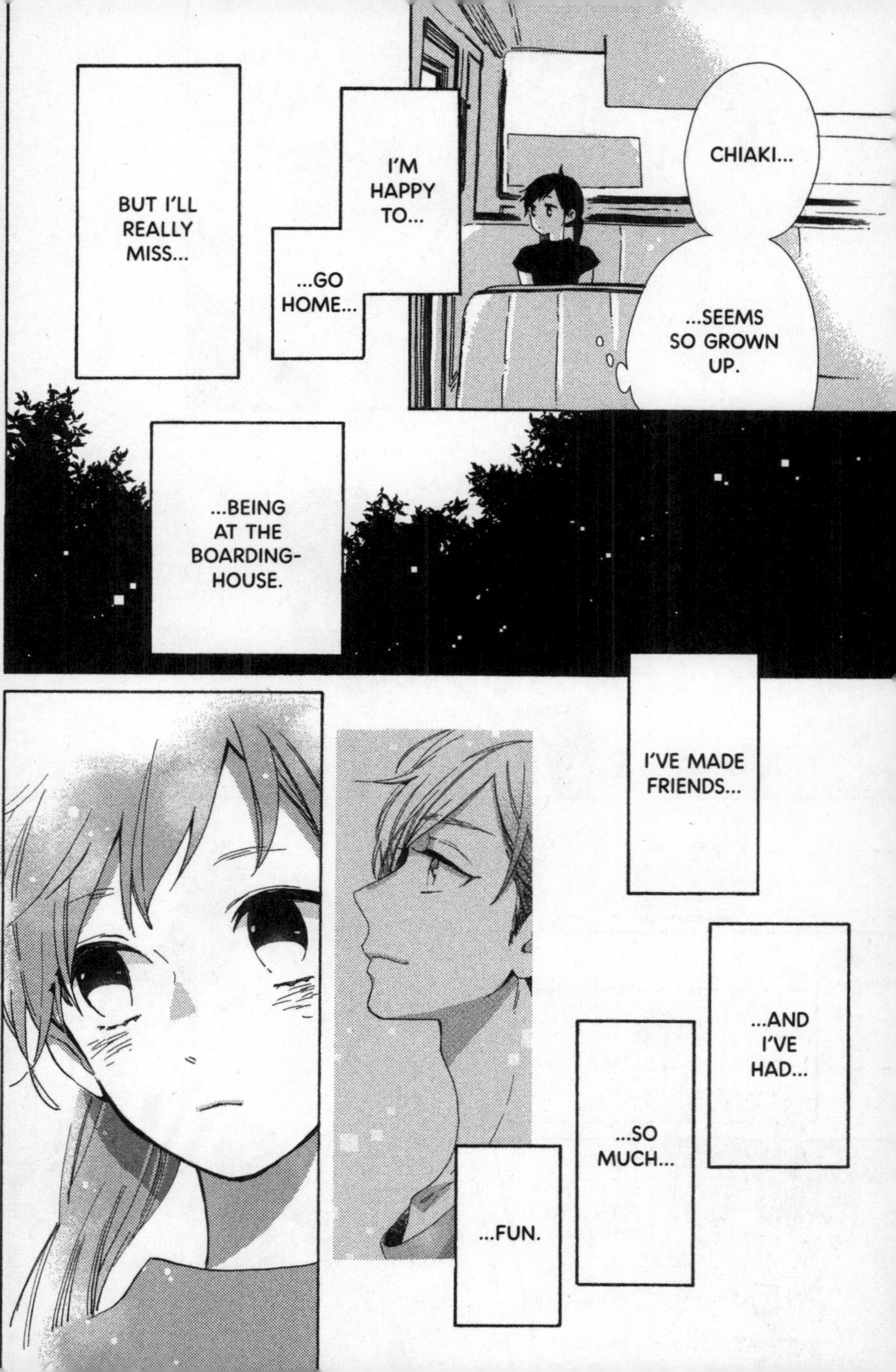
CHIAKI...
...SEEMS SO GROWN UP.
I'M HAPPY TO...
...GO HOME...
BUT I'LL REALLY MISS...
...BEING AT THE BOARDING-HOUSE.
I'VE MADE FRIENDS...
...AND I'VE HAD...
...SO MUCH...
...FUN.

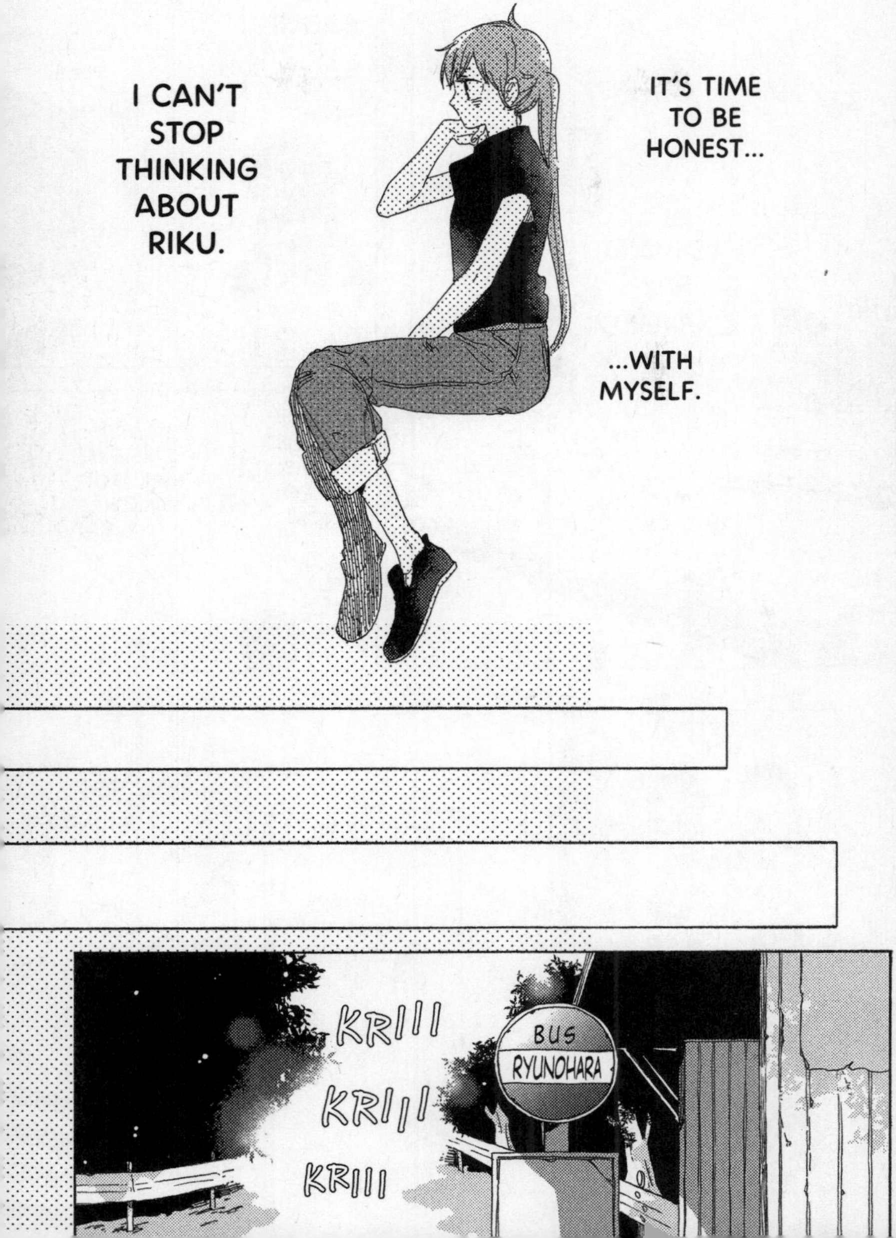
IT'S TIME TO BE HONEST...
...WITH MYSELF.
I CAN'T STOP THINKING ABOUT RIKU.
BUS
RYUNOHARA
KRIII
KRIII
KRIII

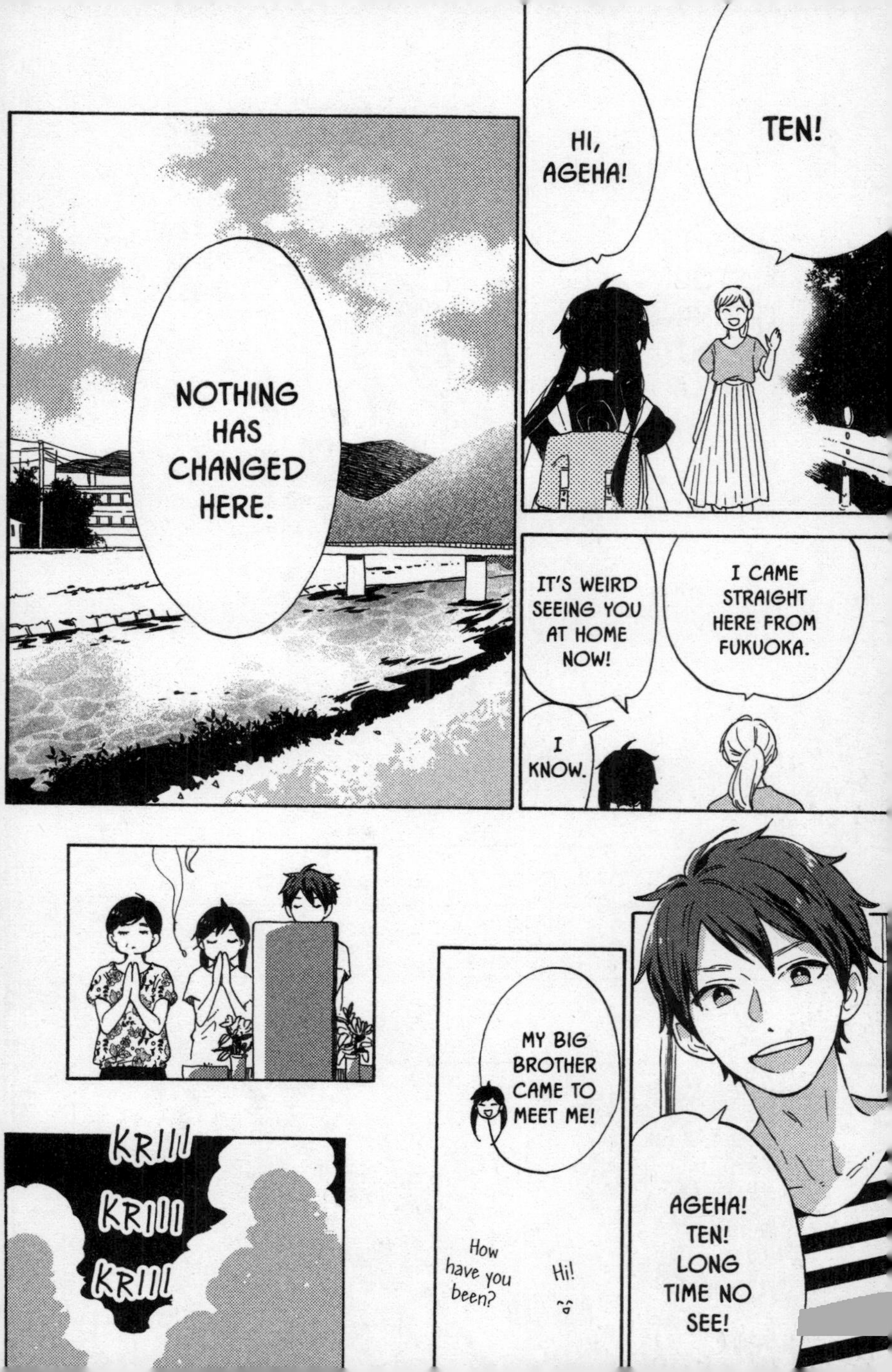
TEN!
HI, AGEHA!
I CAME STRAIGHT HERE FROM FUKUOKA.
IT'S WEIRD SEEING YOU AT HOME NOW!
I KNOW.
NOTHING HAS CHANGED HERE.
AGEHA! TEN! LONG TIME NO SEE!
MY BIG BROTHER CAME TO MEET ME!
Hi!
How have you been?
KRIII
KRIII
KRIII

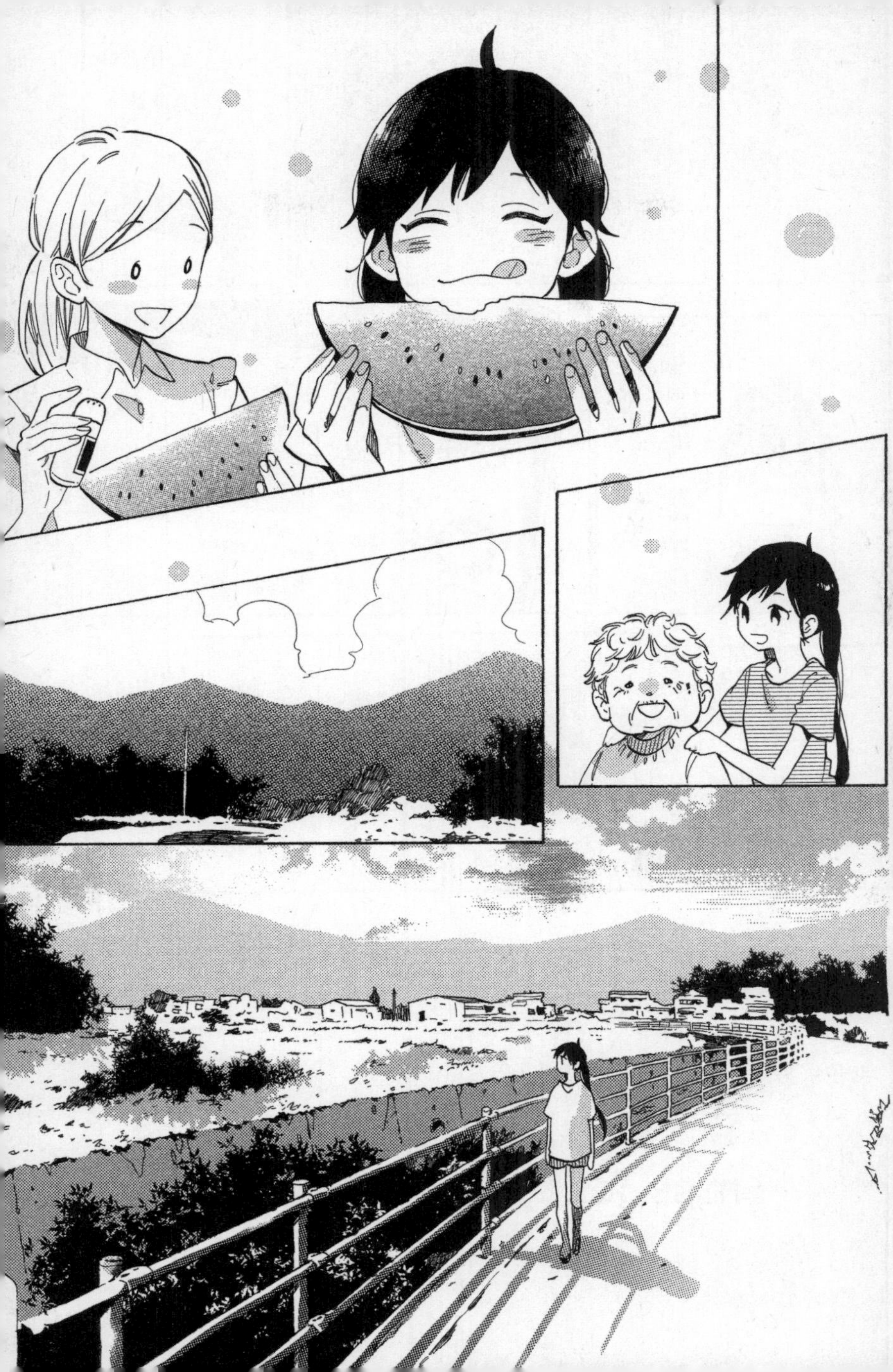

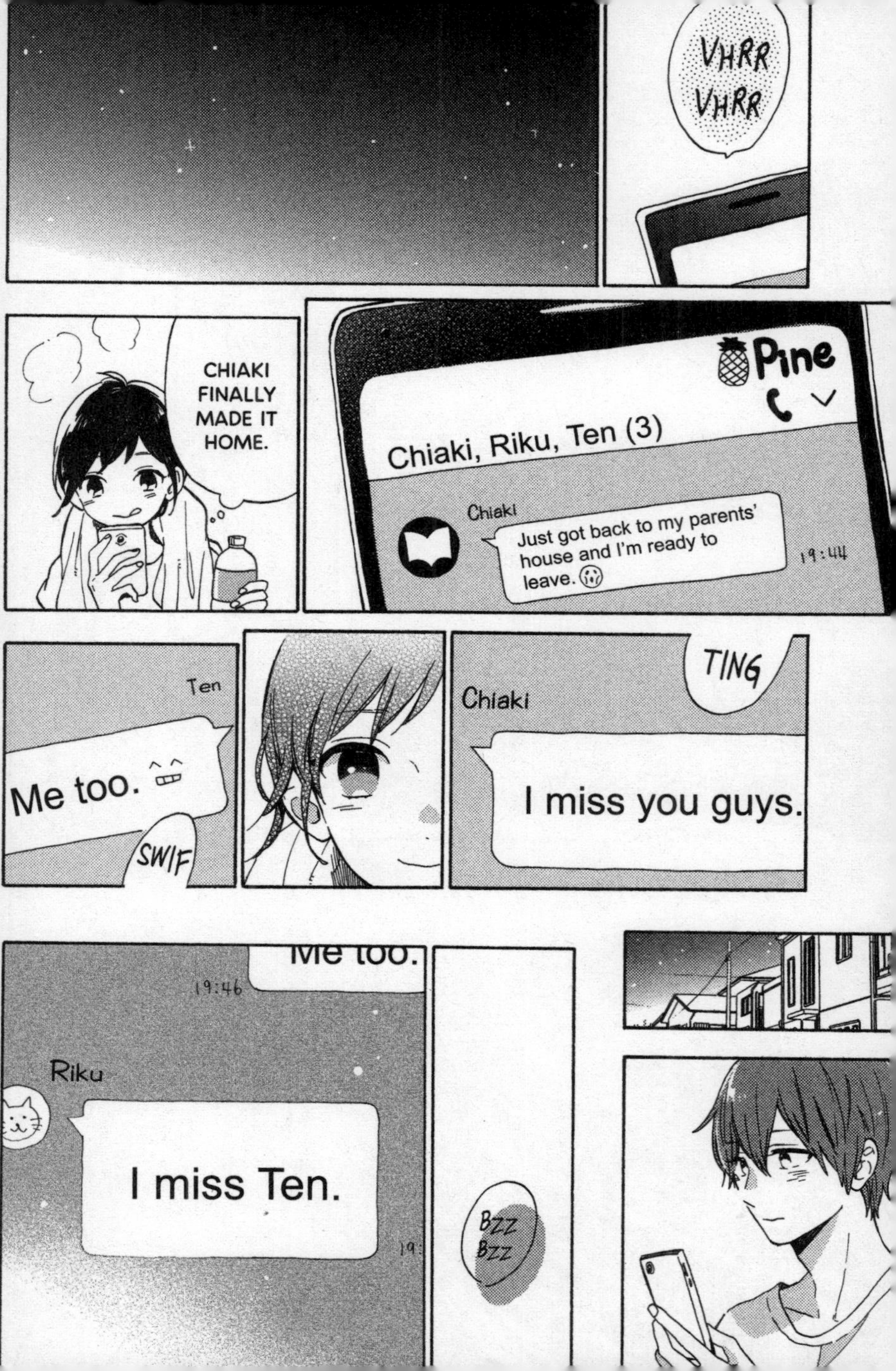
VHRR VHRR
Pine
Chiaki, Riku, Ten (3)
Chiaki
Just got back to my parents' house and I'm ready to leave.
19:44
CHIAKI FINALLY MADE IT HOME.
TING
Chiaki
I miss you guys.
Ten
Me too.
SWIF
BZZ BZZ
Me too.
19:46
Riku
I miss Ten.

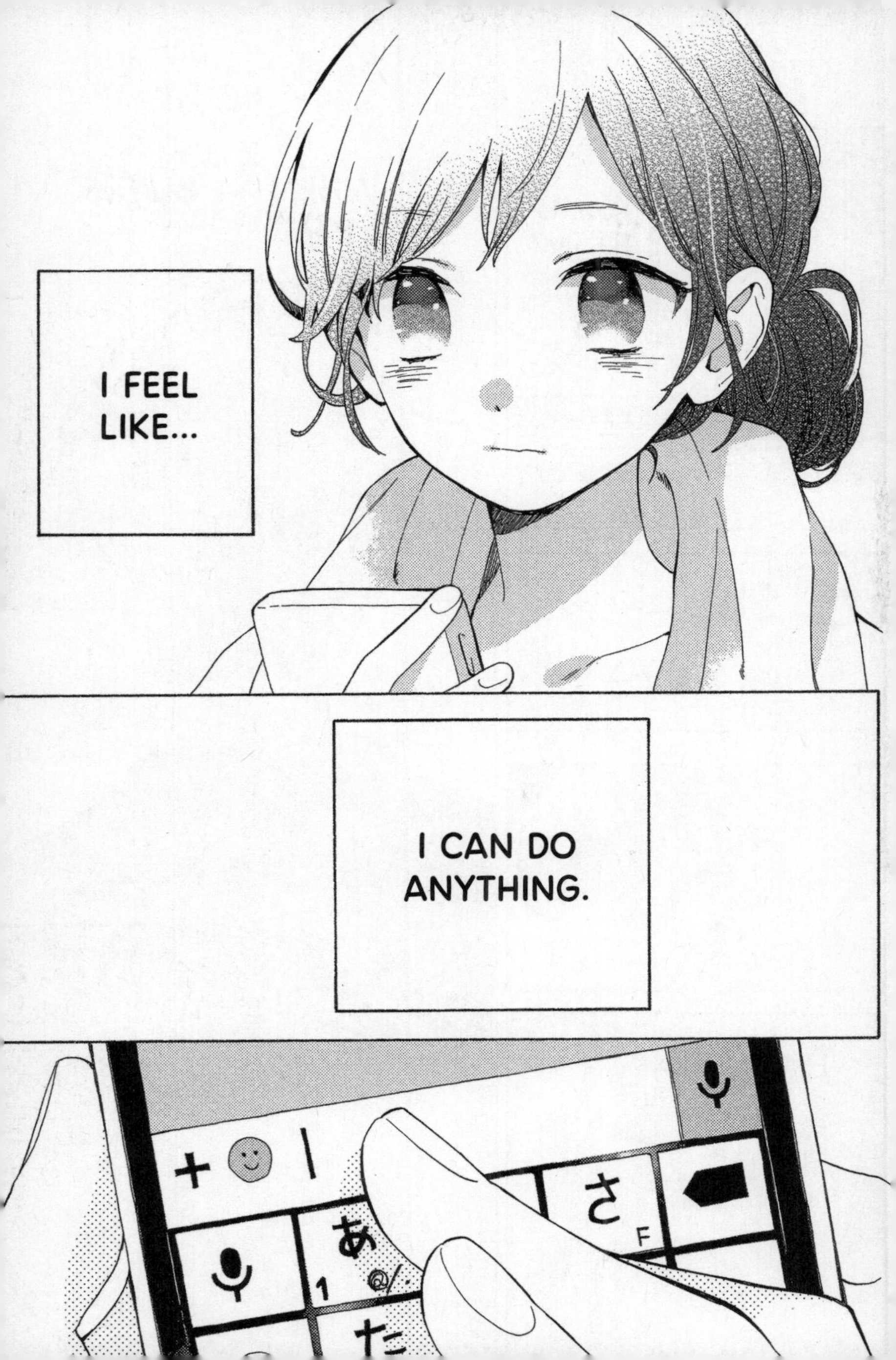
I FEEL LIKE...
I CAN DO ANYTHING.
さ
あ
た

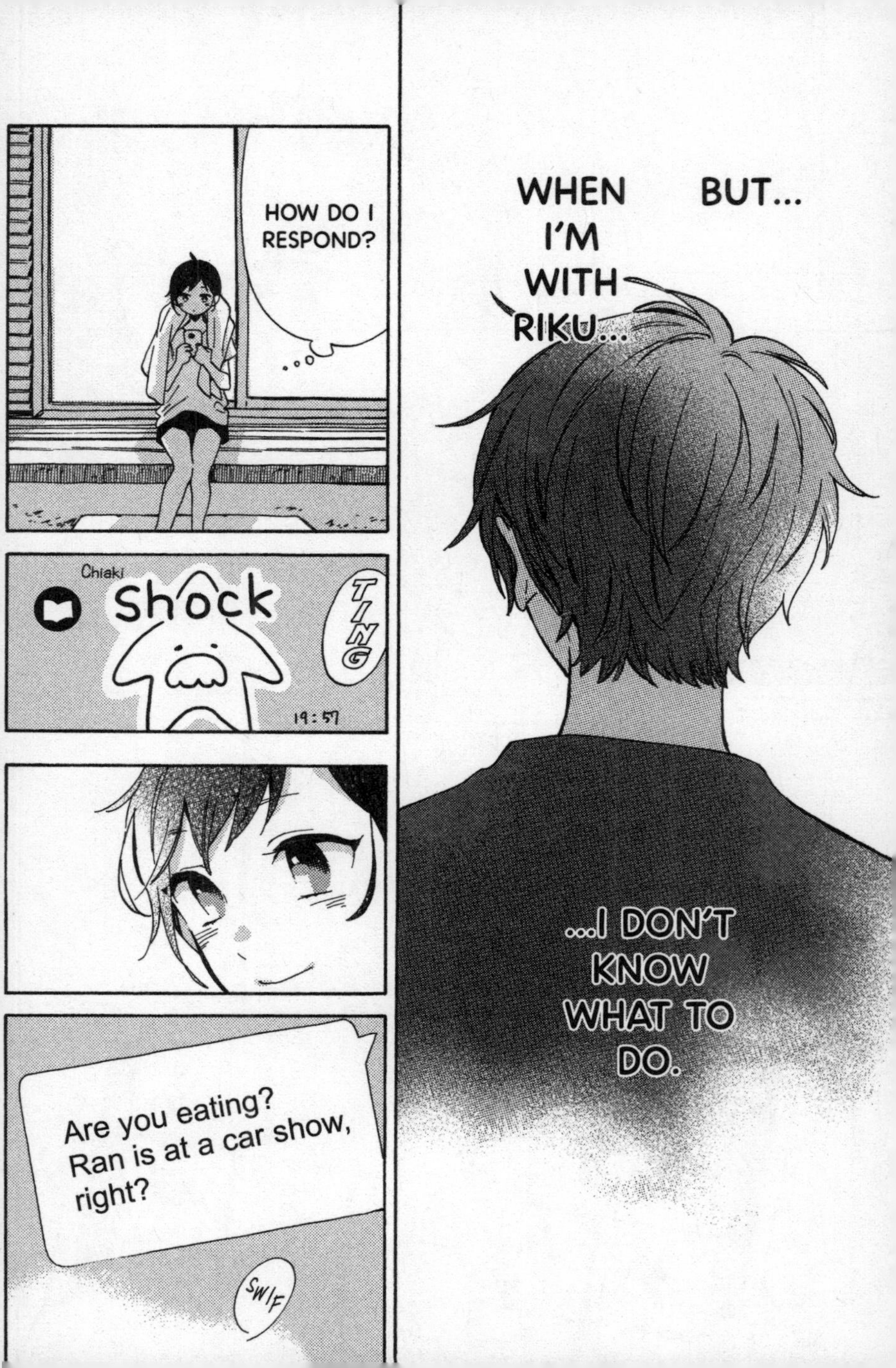
BUT...
WHEN I'M WITH RIKU...
...I DON'T KNOW WHAT TO DO.
HOW DO I RESPOND?
TING
Chiaki
Shock
19:57
Are you eating? Ran is at a car show, right?
SWIF

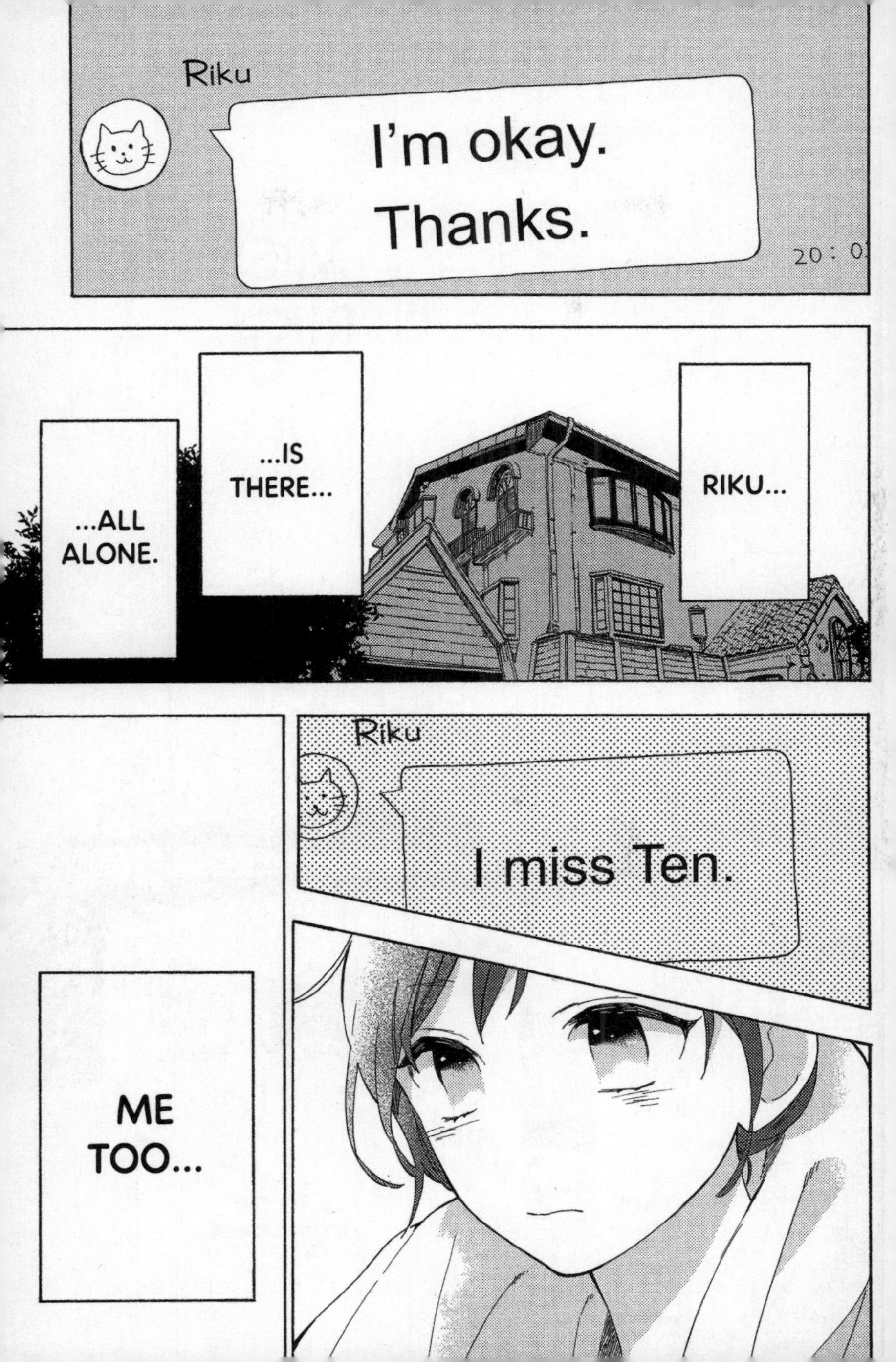
Riku
I'm okay. Thanks.
20:0
RIKU...
...IS THERE...
...ALL ALONE.
Riku
I miss Ten.
ME TOO...

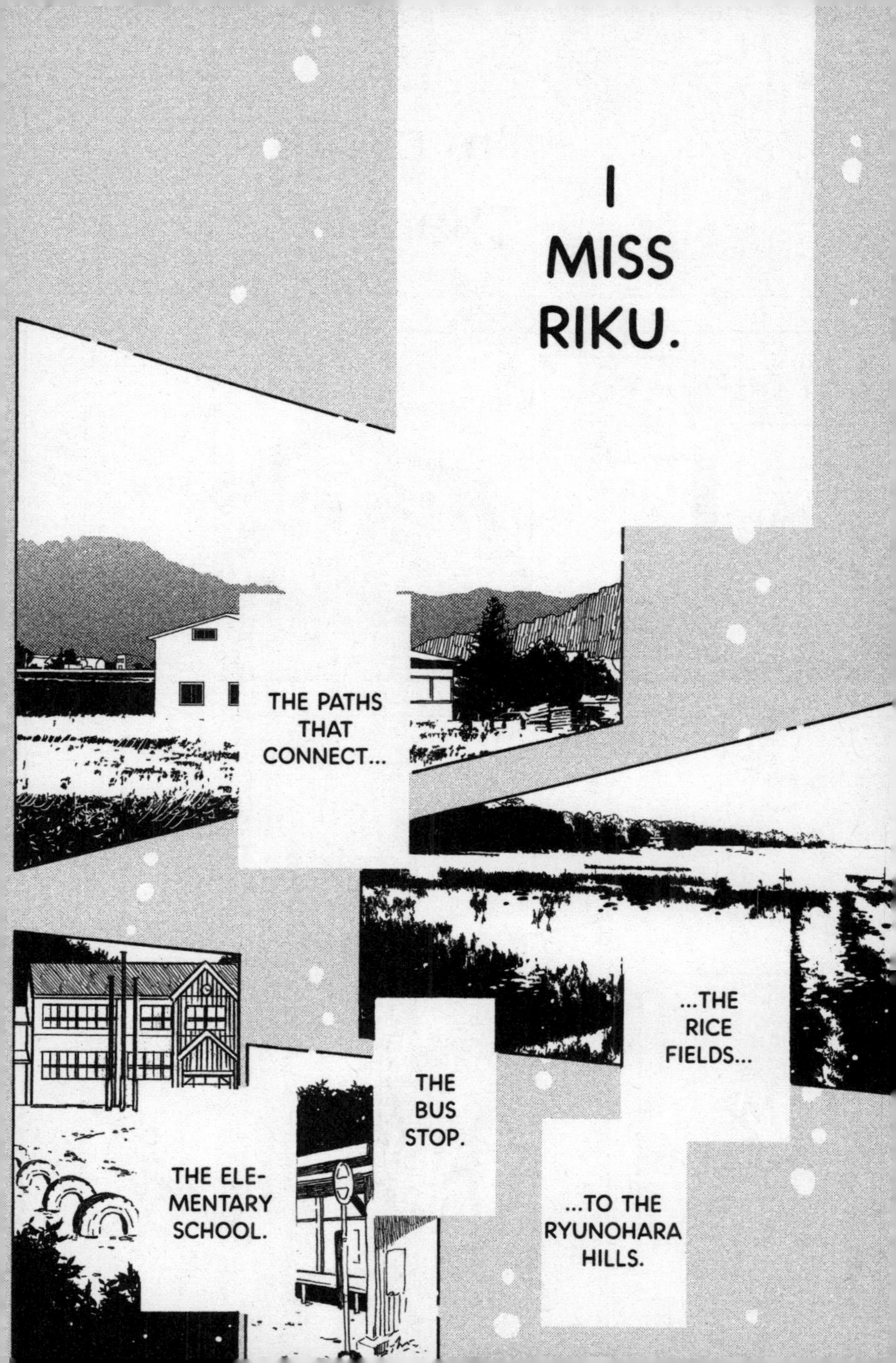
I MISS RIKU.
THE PATHS THAT CONNECT...
...THE RICE FIELDS...
...TO THE RYUNOHARA HILLS.
THE BUS STOP.
THE ELE-MENTARY SCHOOL.

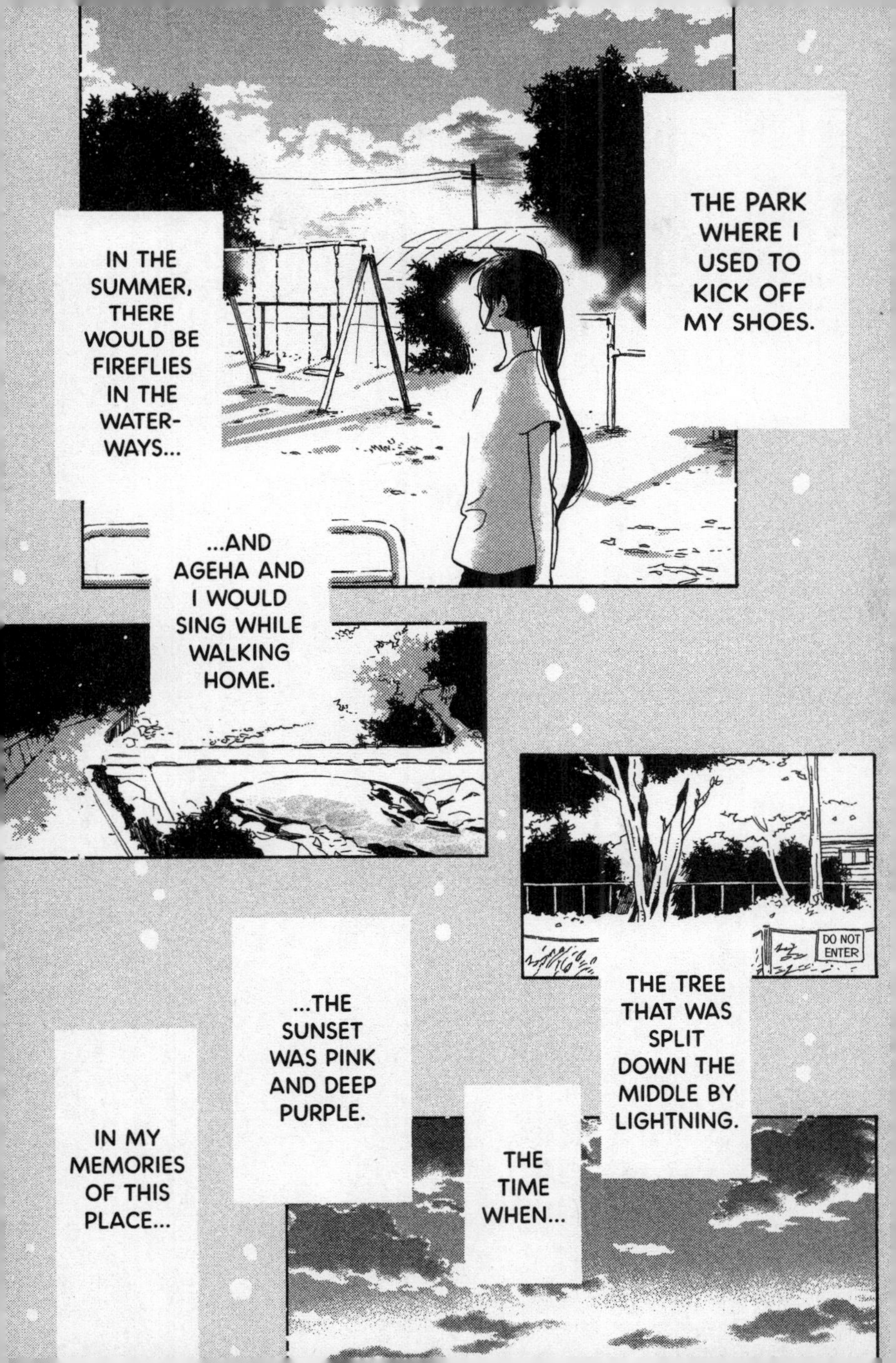
THE PARK WHERE I USED TO KICK OFF MY SHOES.
IN THE SUMMER, THERE WOULD BE FIREFLIES IN THE WATER-WAYS...
...AND AGEHA AND I WOULD SING WHILE WALKING HOME.
DO NOT ENTER
THE TREE THAT WAS SPLIT DOWN THE MIDDLE BY LIGHTNING.
THE TIME WHEN...
...THE SUNSET WAS PINK AND DEEP PURPLE.
IN MY MEMORIES OF THIS PLACE...

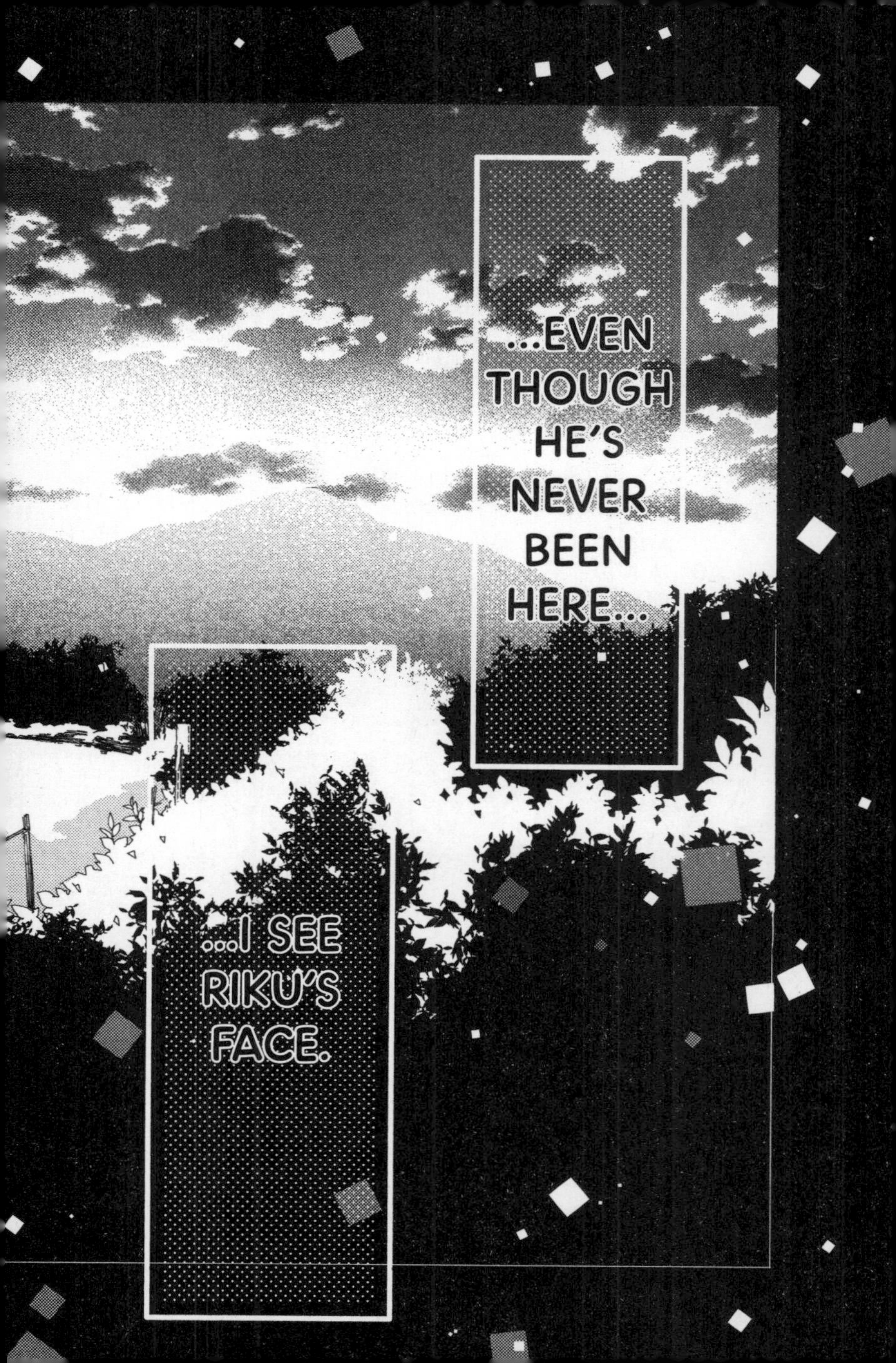
...EVEN THOUGH HE'S NEVER BEEN HERE...
...I SEE RIKU'S FACE.

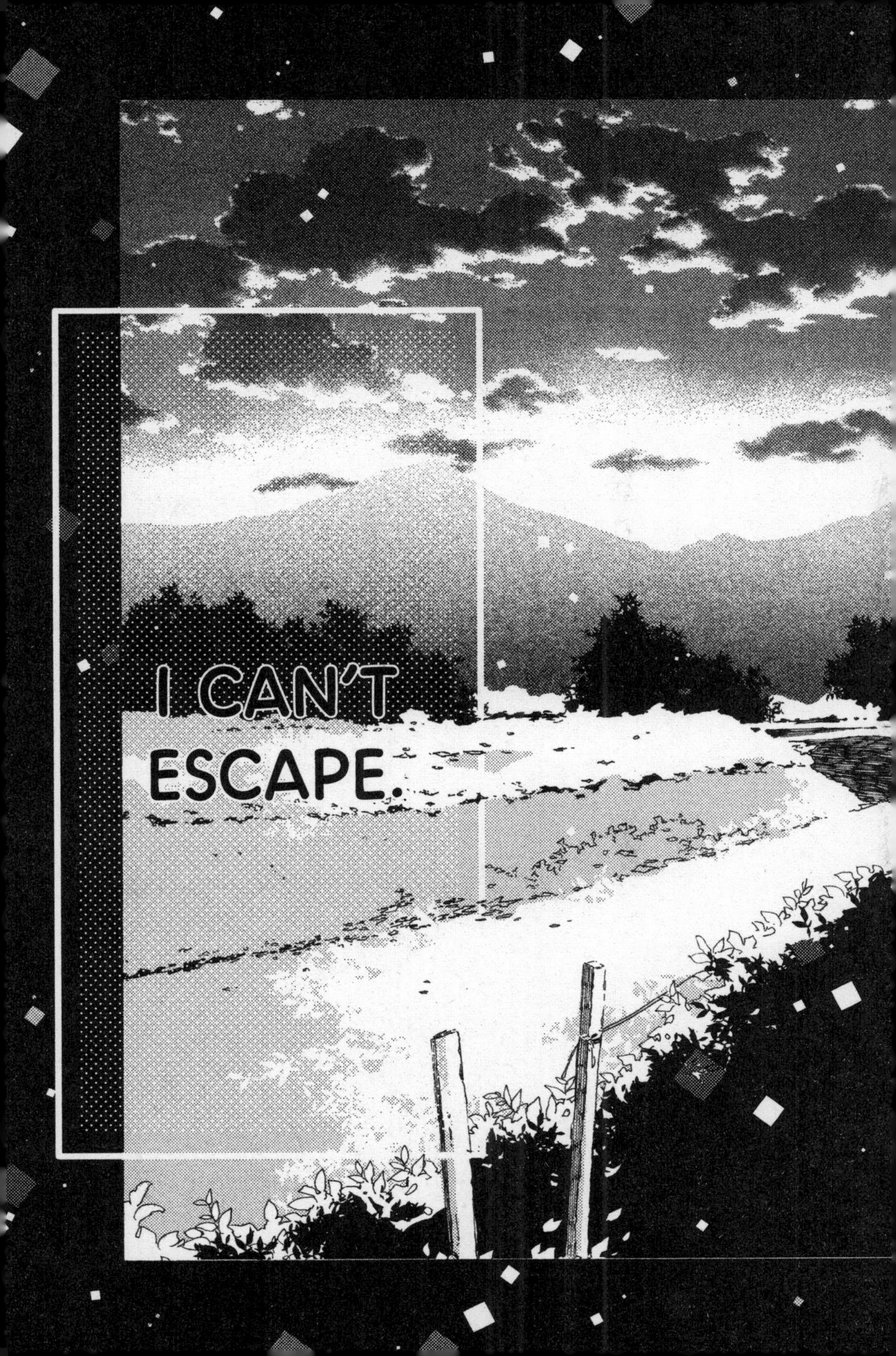
I CAN'T
ESCAPE.

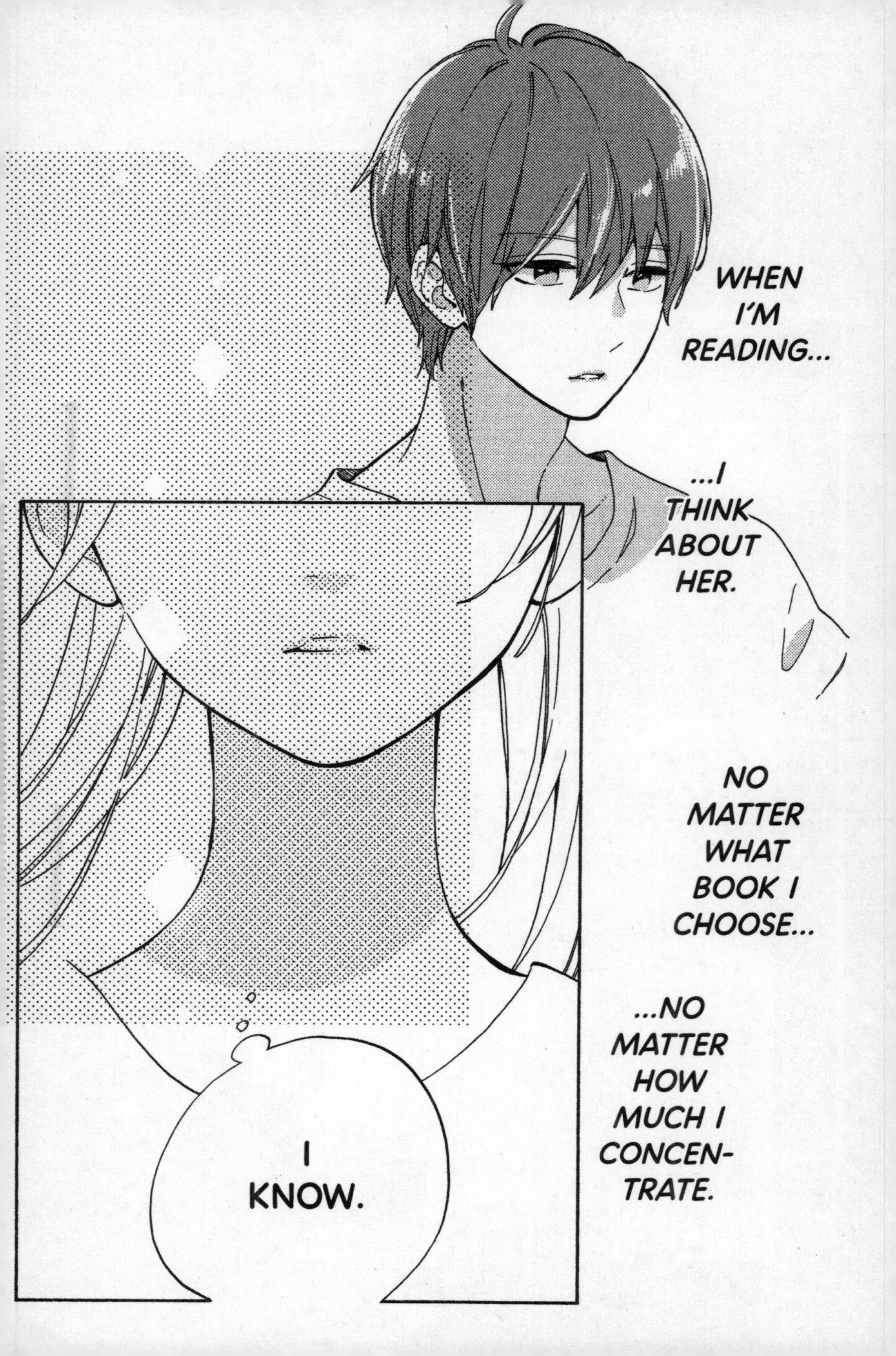
WHEN I'M READING...
...I THINK ABOUT HER.
NO MATTER WHAT BOOK I CHOOSE...
...NO MATTER HOW MUCH I CONCENTRATE.
I KNOW.

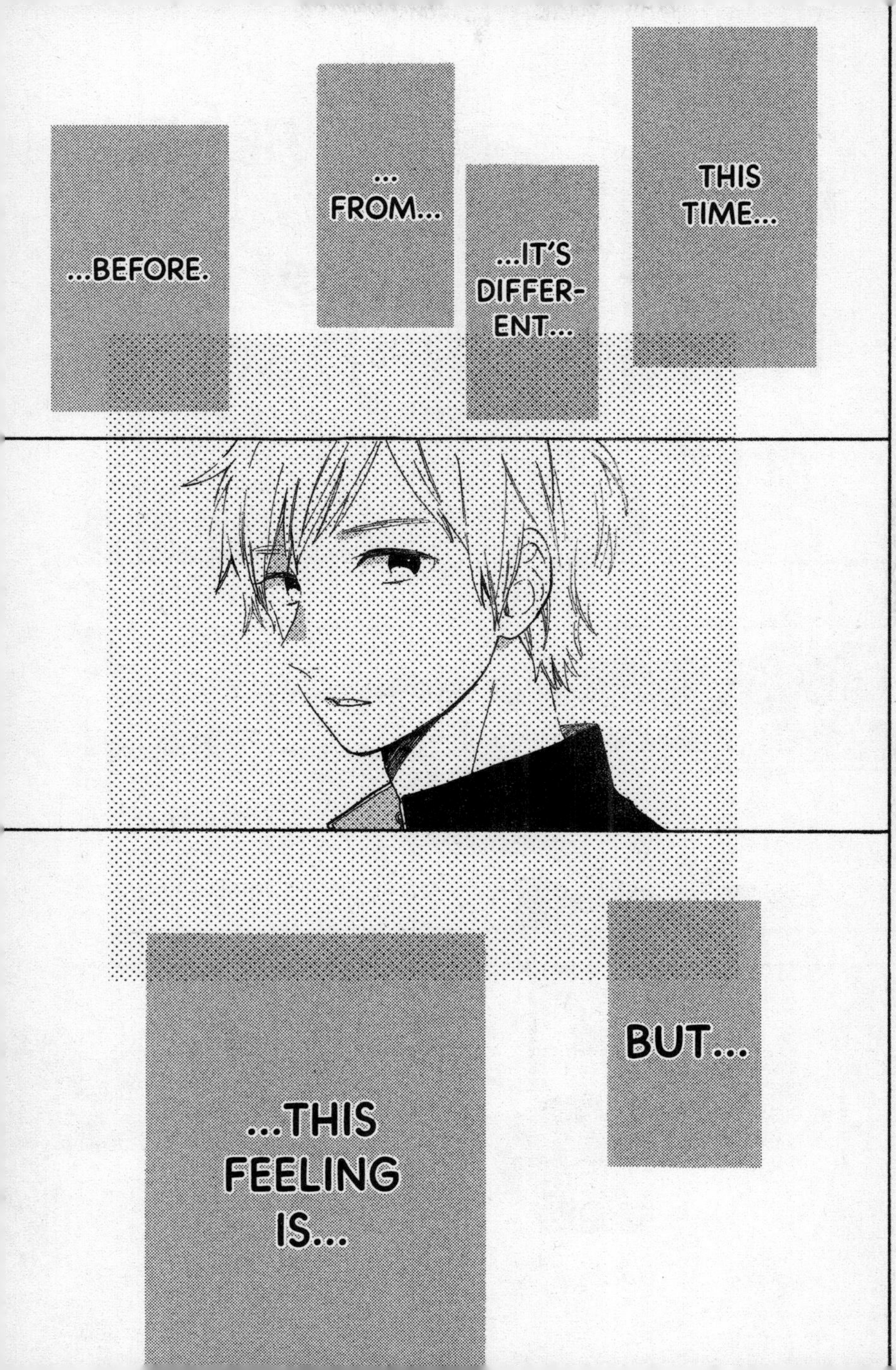
THIS TIME...
...IT'S DIFFERENT...
...FROM...
...BEFORE.
BUT...
...THIS FEELING IS...

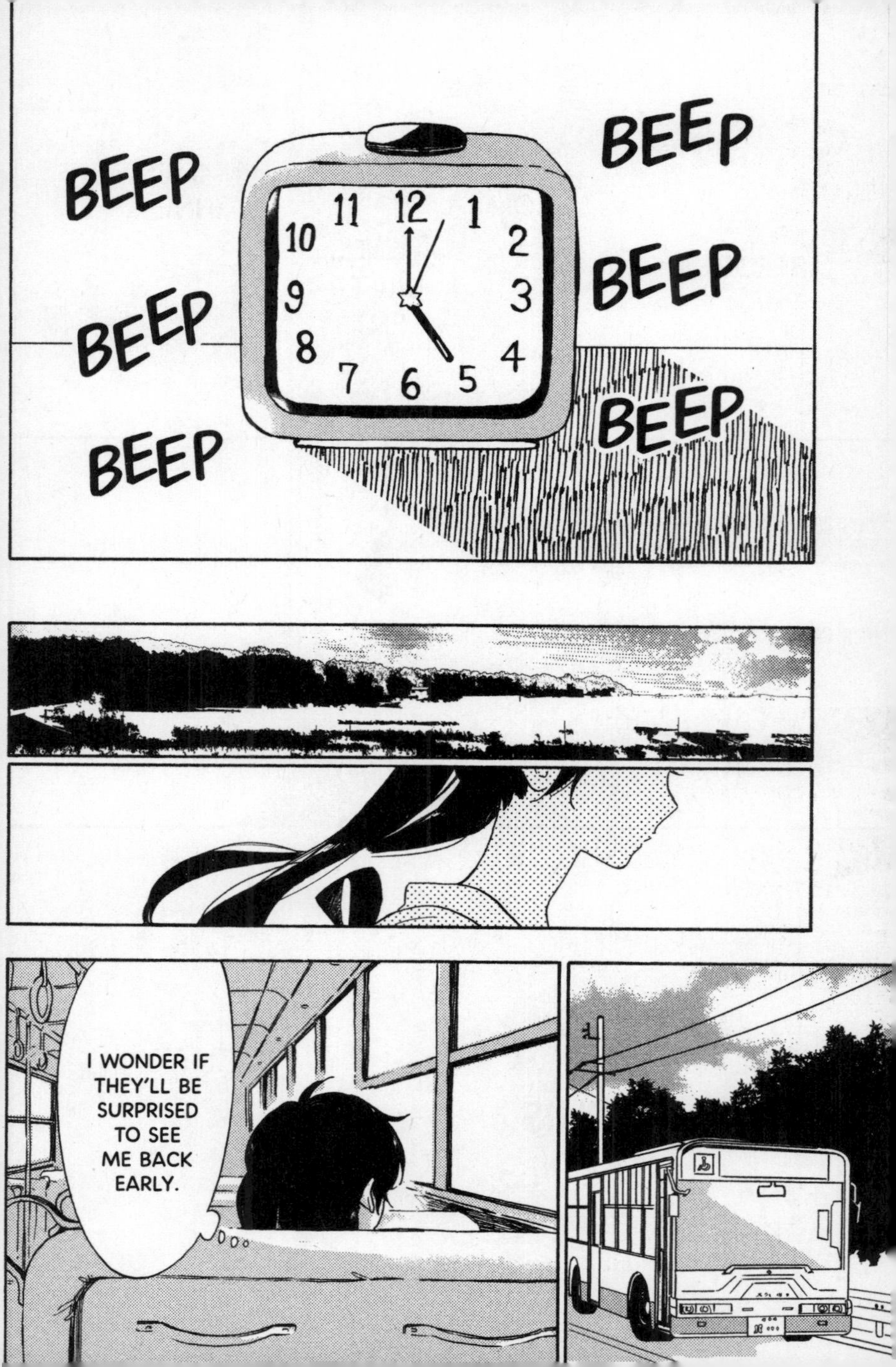
BEEP
BEEP
BEEP
BEEP
BEEP
BEEP
I WONDER IF THEY'LL BE SURPRISED TO SEE ME BACK EARLY.

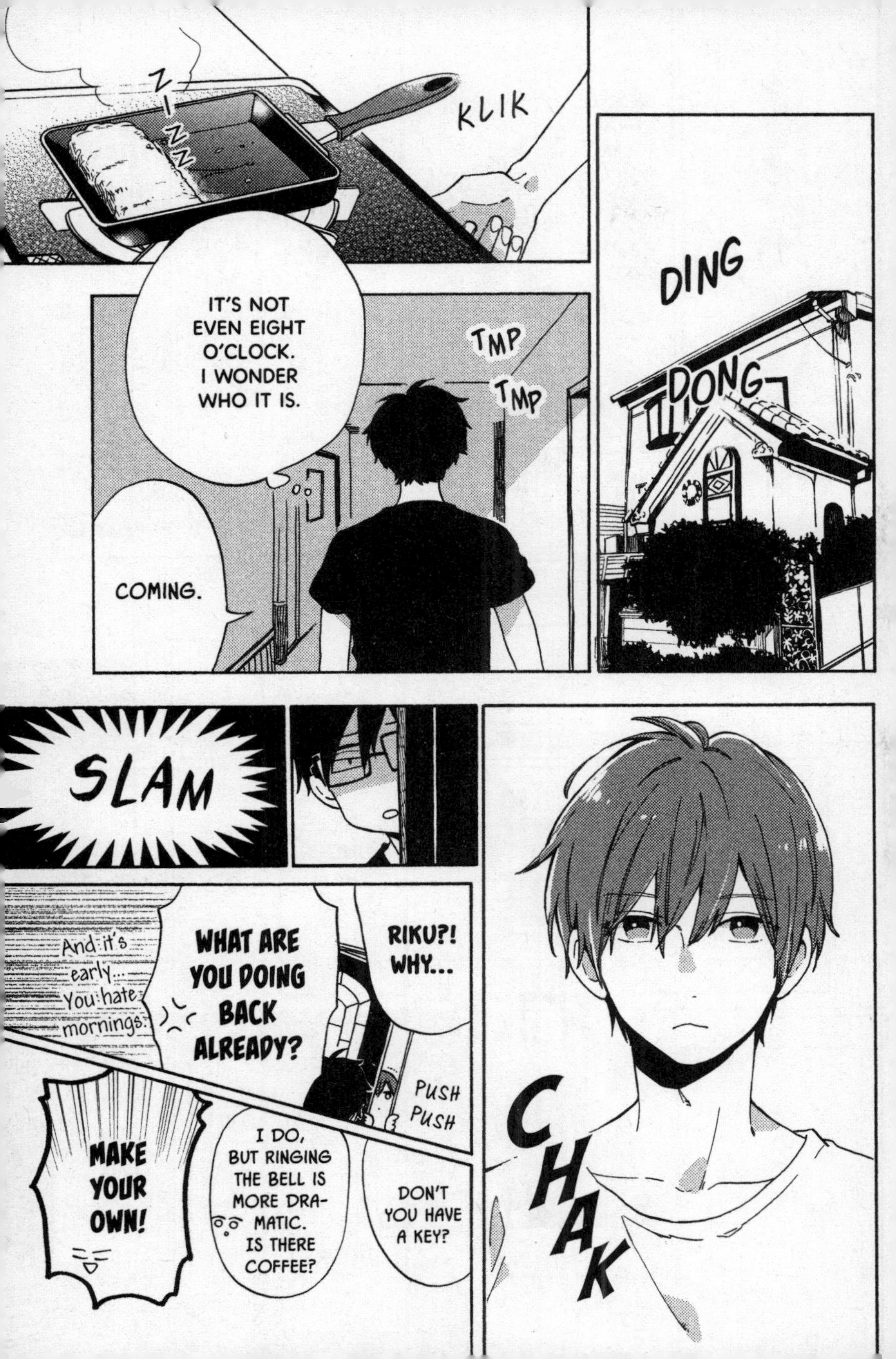
DING
DONG
ZIZZZ
KLIK
TMP
TMP
IT'S NOT EVEN EIGHT O'CLOCK. I WONDER WHO IT IS.
COMING.
CHAK
SLAM
RIKU?! WHY...
WHAT ARE YOU DOING BACK ALREADY?
And it's early... You hate mornings.
PUSH PUSH
DON'T YOU HAVE A KEY?
I DO, BUT RINGING THE BELL IS MORE DRAMATIC. IS THERE COFFEE?
MAKE YOUR OWN!

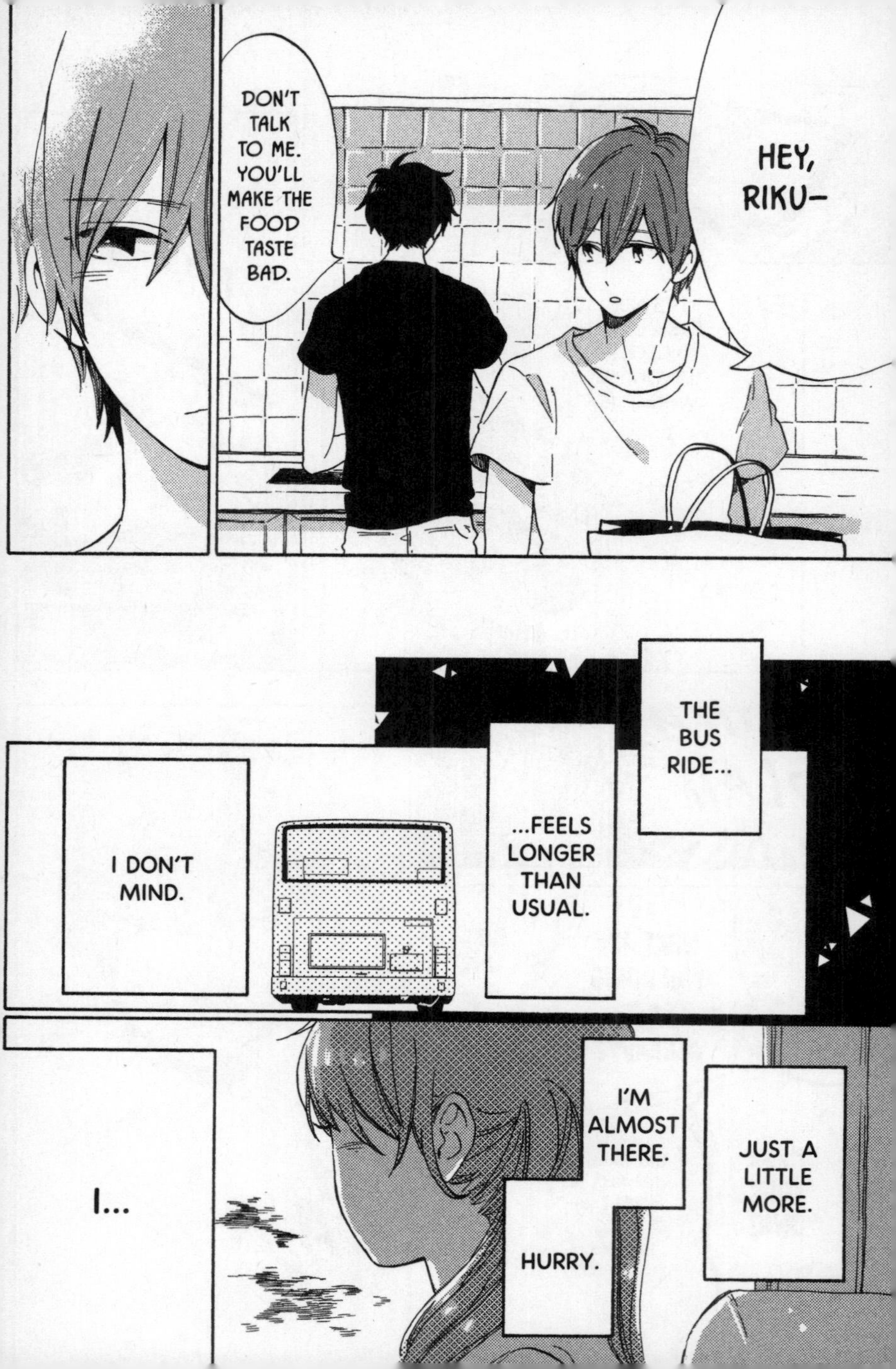

HEY, RIKU—
DON'T TALK TO ME. YOU'LL MAKE THE FOOD TASTE BAD.
THE BUS RIDE...
...FEELS LONGER THAN USUAL.
I DON'T MIND.
JUST A LITTLE MORE.
I'M ALMOST THERE.
HURRY.
I...

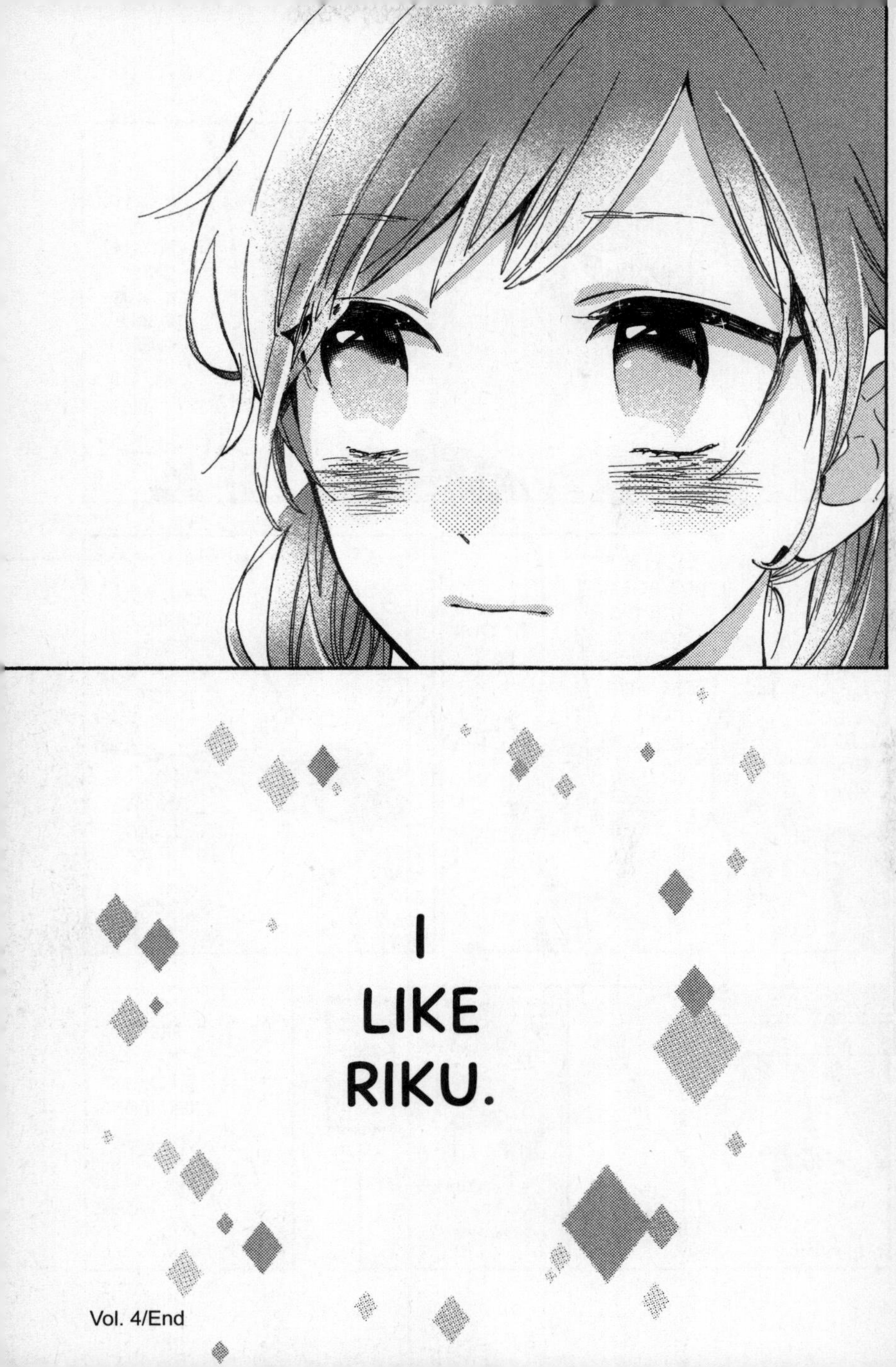
I LIKE RIKU.

Vol. 4/End

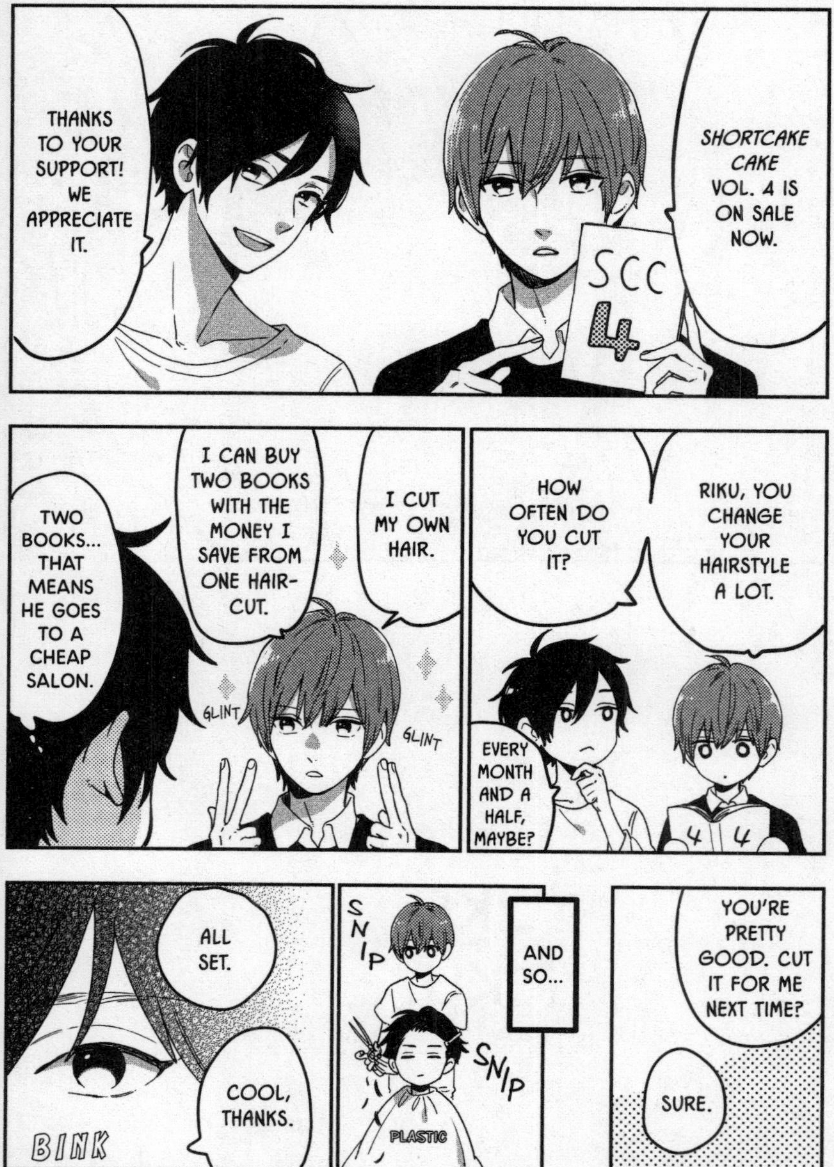
SHORTCAKE CAKE VOL. 4 IS ON SALE NOW.
SCC 4
THANKS TO YOUR SUPPORT! WE APPRECIATE IT.
RIKU, YOU CHANGE YOUR HAIRSTYLE A LOT.
HOW OFTEN DO YOU CUT IT?
EVERY MONTH AND A HALF, MAYBE?
4 4
I CUT MY OWN HAIR.
I CAN BUY TWO BOOKS WITH THE MONEY I SAVE FROM ONE HAIR-CUT.
GLINT
GLINT
TWO BOOKS... THAT MEANS HE GOES TO A CHEAP SALON.
YOU'RE PRETTY GOOD. CUT IT FOR ME NEXT TIME?
SURE.
AND SO...
SNIP
SNIP
PLASTIC
ALL SET.
COOL, THANKS.
BINK

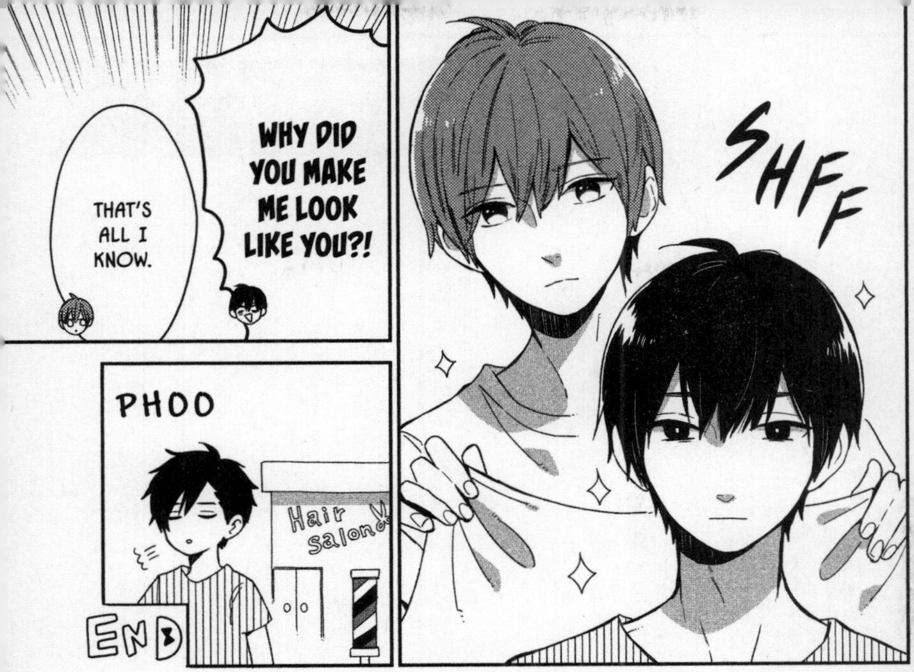
SHFF
WHY DID YOU MAKE ME LOOK LIKE YOU?!
THAT'S ALL I KNOW.
PHOO
Hair Salon
END

AFTERWORD

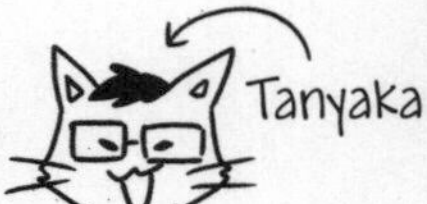
Tanyaka

Hello. Thank you for reading volume 4. Recently, our longtime editor, Nyakacchi, left... And now we're working with **Tanyaka**. Thank you and goodbye, Nyakacchi...and welcome, Tanyaka...

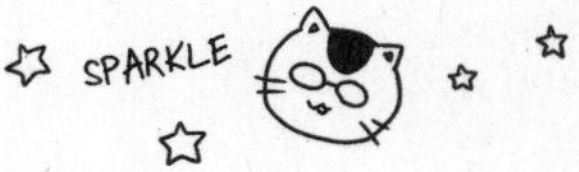
SPARKLE

Thanks for your support!

SPECIAL THANKS

- Nyakacchi & Tanyaka
- The Margaret editorial team
- Our designer, Yasuhisa Kawatani
- Our assistant, Nao Hamaguchi
- Our assistant's helper, Kame-chimu

And all our readers

SHORTCAKE CAKE
Title Page Collection
Chapter 18

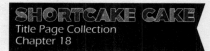

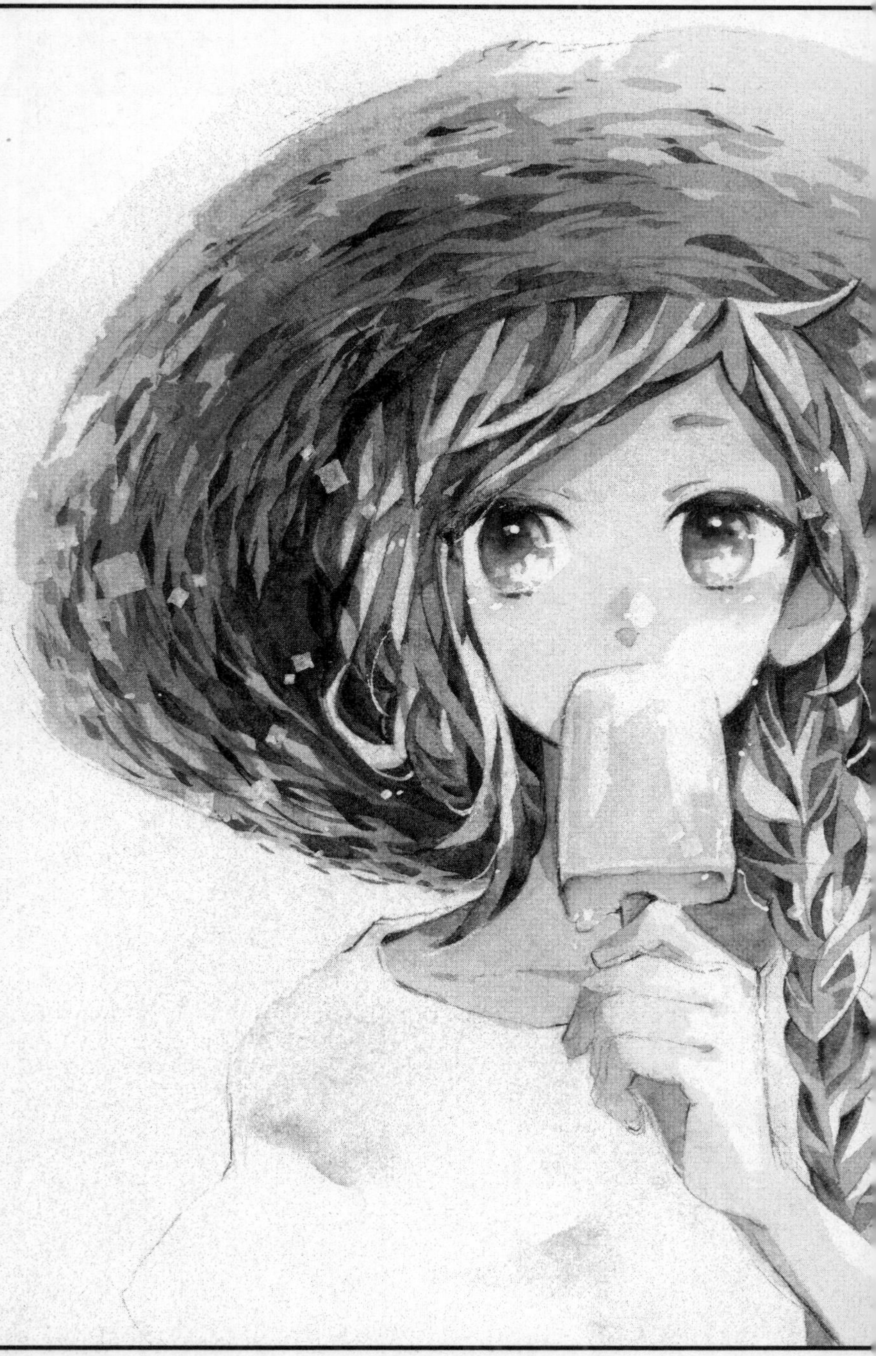

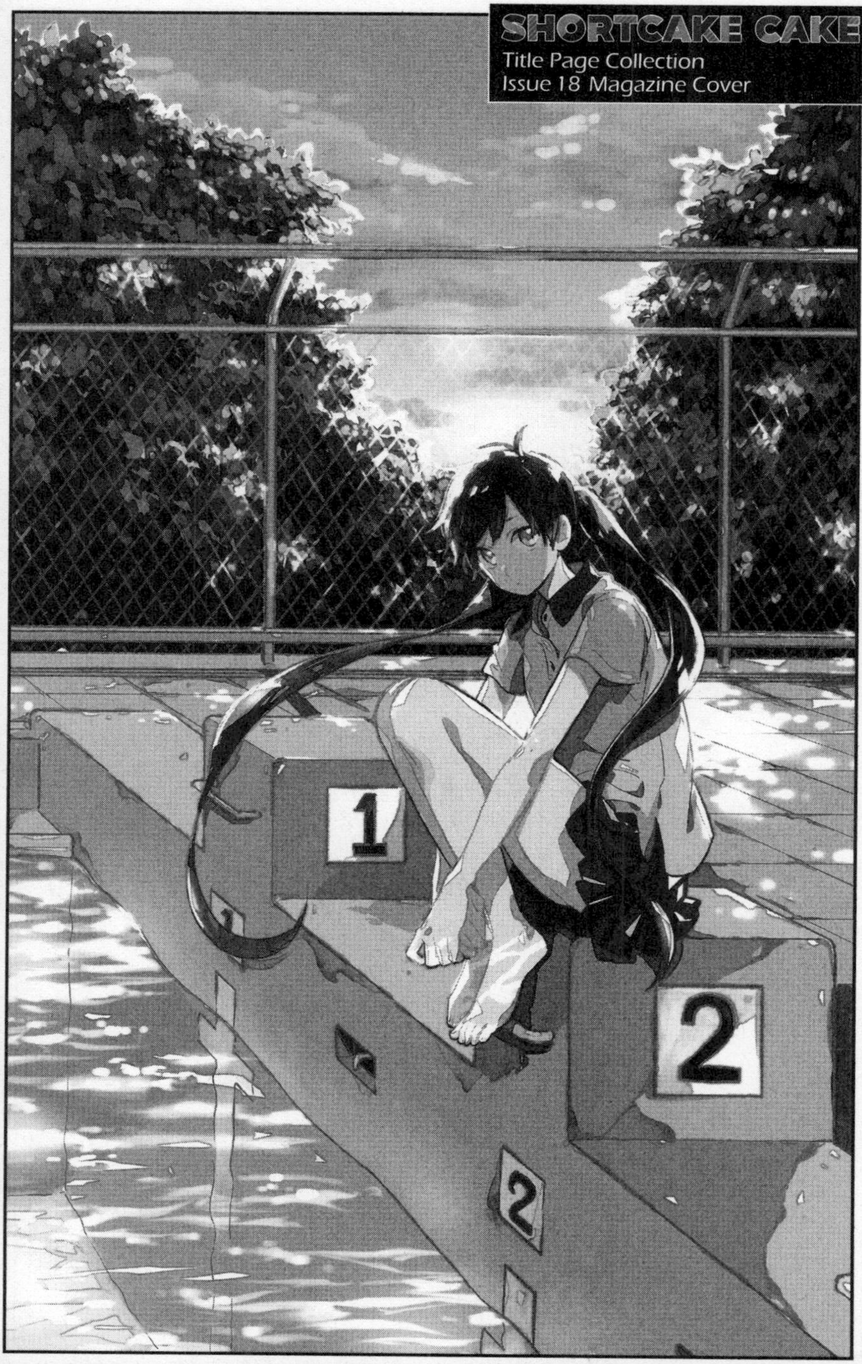
1
2
2

SHORTCAKE CAKE
Title Page Collection
Issue 18 Magazine Cover

SHORTCAKE CAKE
Title Page Collection
Chapter 19

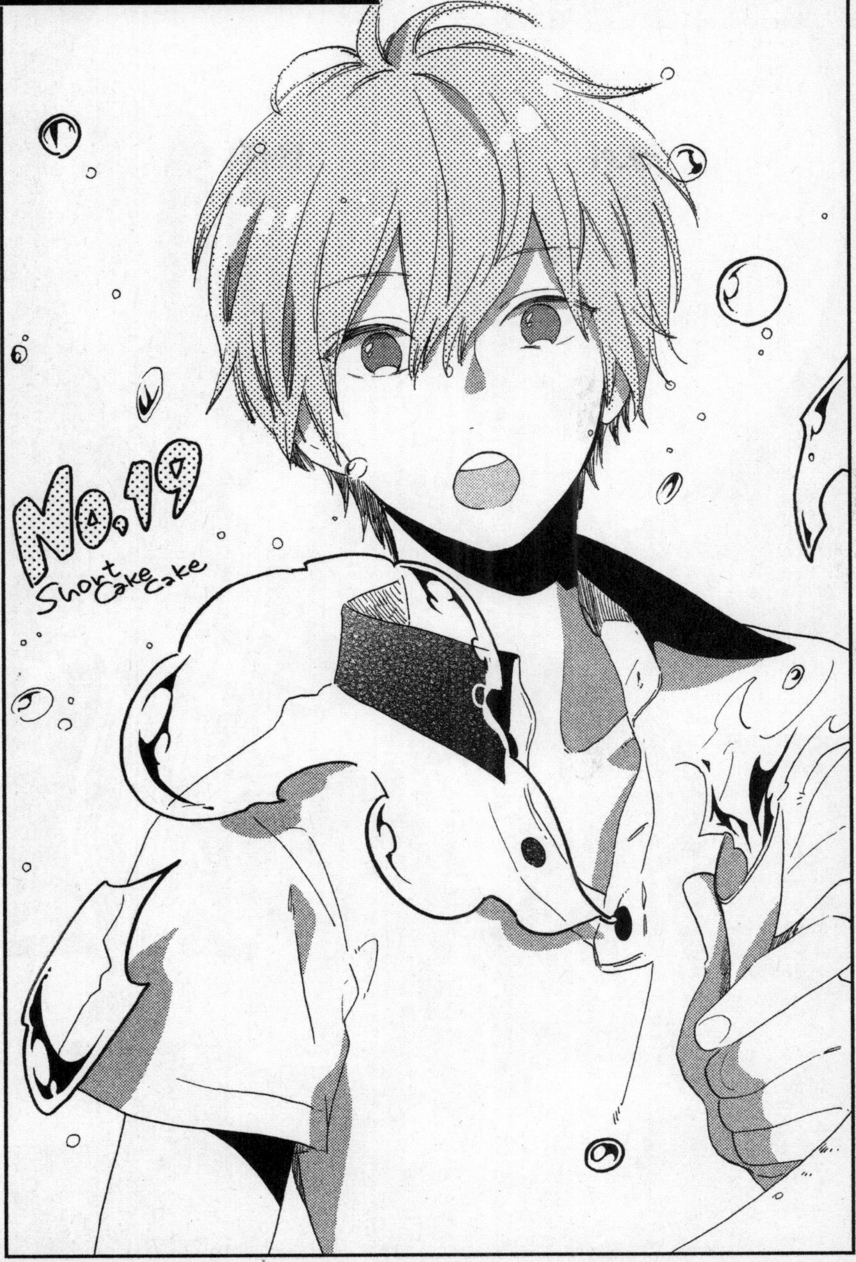
No.19
Short Cake cake

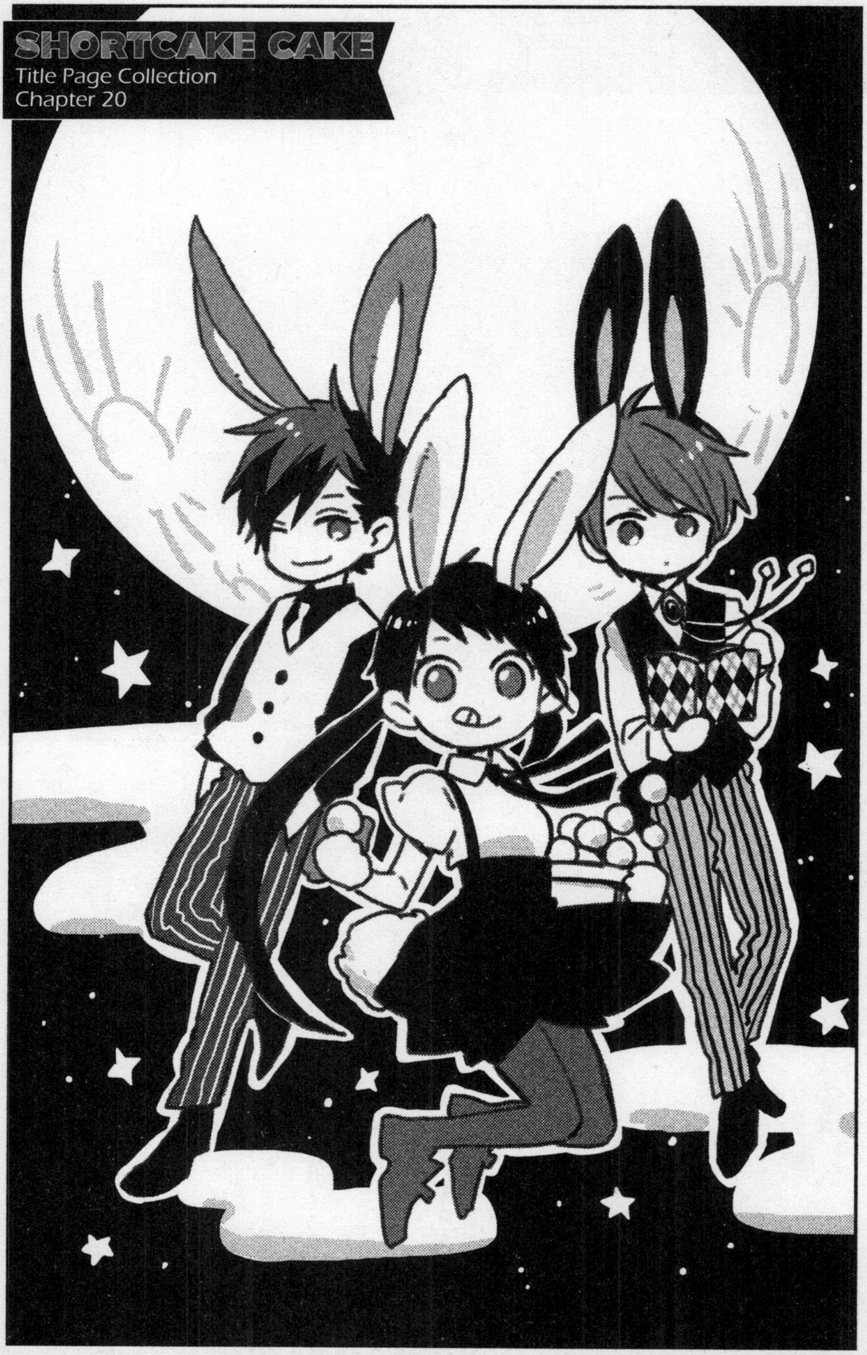
SHORTCAKE CAKE
Title Page Collection
Chapter 20

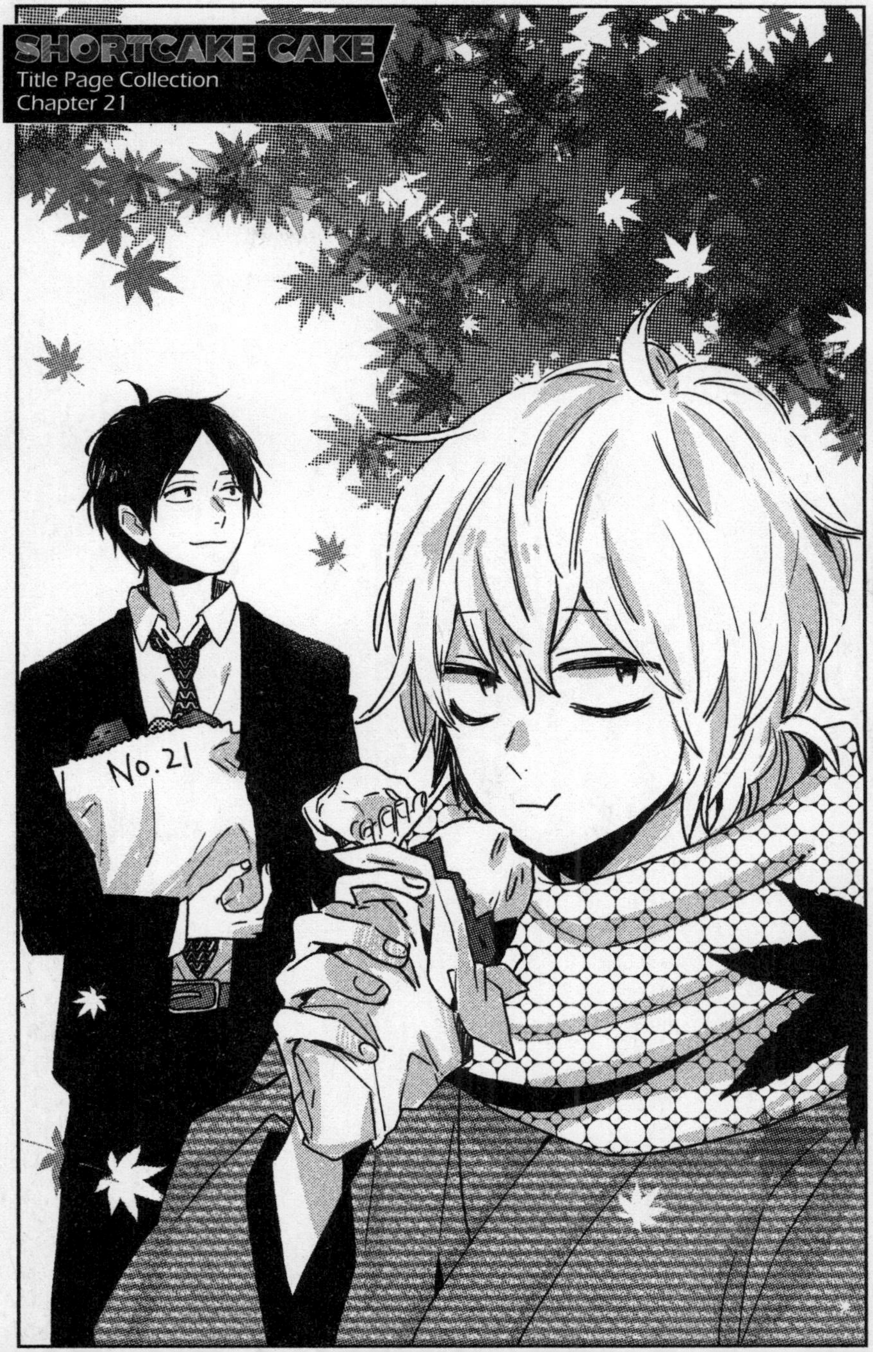
SHORTCAKE CAKE
Title Page Collection
Chapter 21
No.21

SHORTCAKE CAKE
Title Page Collection
Chapter 22

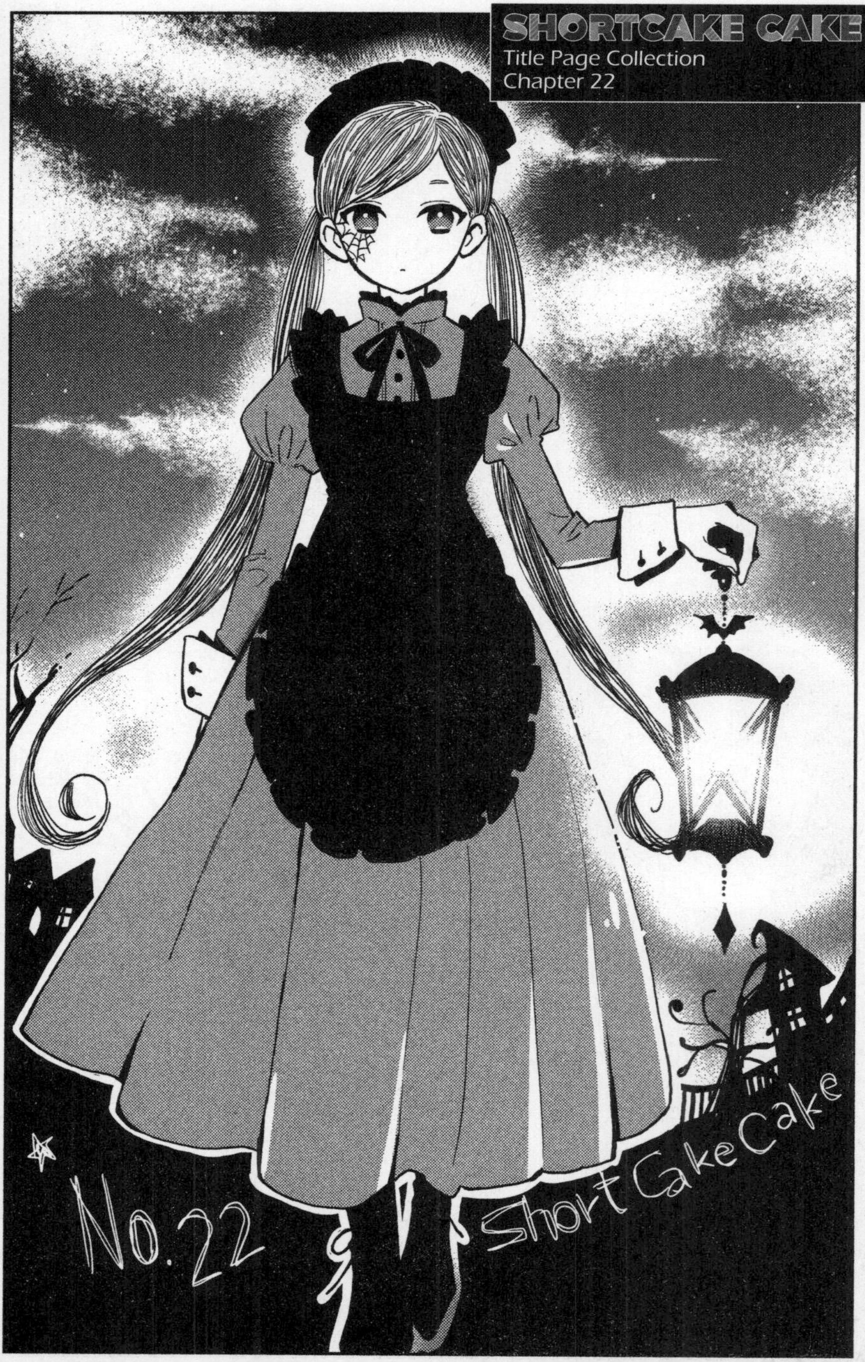
No.22
Short Cake Cake

SHORTCAKE CAKE
Title Page Collection
Chapter 23

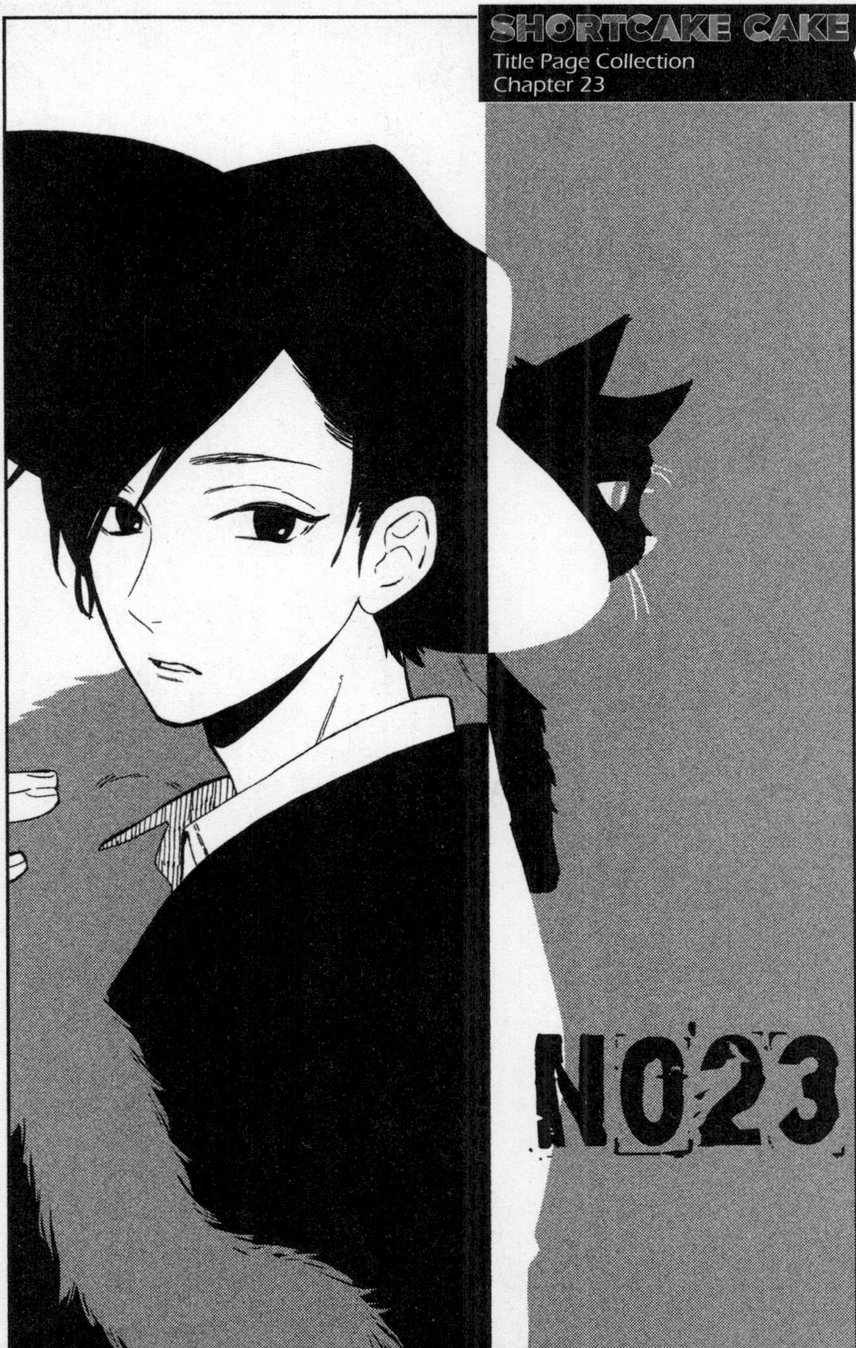
NO23

I want to go to Hawaii.
I hope you'll enjoy volume 5 as well.

—suu Morishita

suu Morishita is a creator duo.
The story is by Makiro, and the art is by
Nachiyan. In 2010 they debuted with the
one-shot "Anote Konote." Their works include
Hibi Chouchou and *Shortcake Cake*.

VOLUME 4
SHOJO BEAT EDITION

STORY + ART BY **suu Morishita**

TRANSLATION **Emi Louie-Nishikawa**
TOUCH-UP ART + LETTERING **Inori Fukuda Trant**
DESIGN **Shawn Carrico**
EDITOR **Nancy Thistlethwaite**

SHORTCAKE CAKE © 2015 by Suu Morishita
All rights reserved.
First published in Japan in 2015 by SHUEISHA Inc., Tokyo.
English translation rights arranged by SHUEISHA Inc.

Printed in the U.S.A.

Published by VIZ Media, LLC
P.O. Box 77010
San Francisco, CA 94107

10 9 8 7 6 5 4 3 2 1
First printing, May 2019

viz.com

shojobeat.com

Honey
So Sweet

Story and Art by Amu Meguro

Little did Nao Kogure realize back in middle school that when she left an umbrella and a box of bandages in the rain for injured delinquent Taiga Onise that she would meet him again in high school. Nao wants nothing to do with the gruff and frightening Taiga, but he suddenly presents her with a huge bouquet of flowers and asks her to date him—with marriage in mind! Is Taiga really so scary, or is he a sweetheart in disguise?

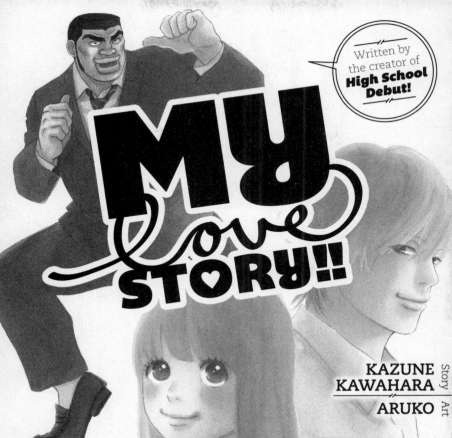

MY love STORY!!

KAZUNE KAWAHARA — Story

ARUKO — Art

Takeo Goda is a GIANT guy with a GIANT *heart*

Too bad the girls don't want him!
(They want his good-looking best friend, Sunakawa.)

Used to being on the sidelines, Takeo simply stands tall and accepts his fate. But one day when he saves a girl named Yamato from a harasser on the train, his (love!) life suddenly takes an incredible turn!

Ao Haru Ride

Takane &* Hana

STORY AND ART BY
Yuki Shiwasu

After her older sister refuses to go to an arranged marriage meeting with Takane Saibara, the heir to a vast business fortune, high schooler Hana Nonomura agrees to be her stand-in to save face for the family. But when Takane and Hana pair up, get ready for some sparks to fly between these two utter opposites!

shojobeat.com

viz.com

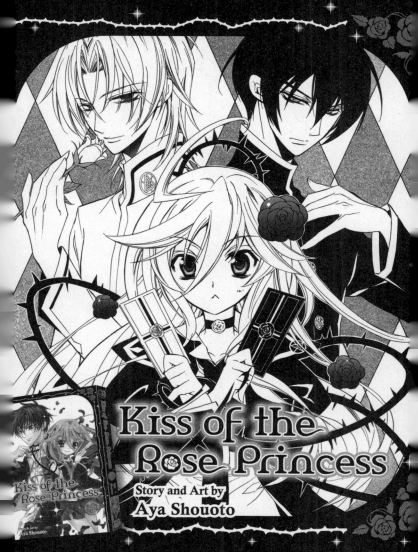

Kiss of the Rose Princess

Story and Art by Aya Shouoto

Anise Yamamoto has been told that if she ever removes the rose choker given to her by her father, a ter~~~ punishment will befall her. Unfortunately she loses that choker when a bat-like being named Ninufa fa~~~ from the sky and hits her. Ninufa gives Anise four cards representing four knights whom she can summ~~~ with a kiss. But now that she has these gorgeous men at her beck and call, what exactly is her quest?!

QQ sweeper

Story & Art by
Kyousuke Motomi

By the creator of *Dengeki Daisy* and *Beast Master*!

One day, Kyutaro Horikita, the tall, dark and handsome cleaning expert of Kurokado High, comes across a sleeping maiden named Fumi Nishioka at school... Unfortunately, their meeting is anything but a fairy-tale encounter! It turns out Kyutaro is a "Sweeper" who cleans away negative energy from people's hearts—and Fumi is about to become his apprentice!

QQ sweeper

1

Story & Art by KYOUSUKE MOTOMI

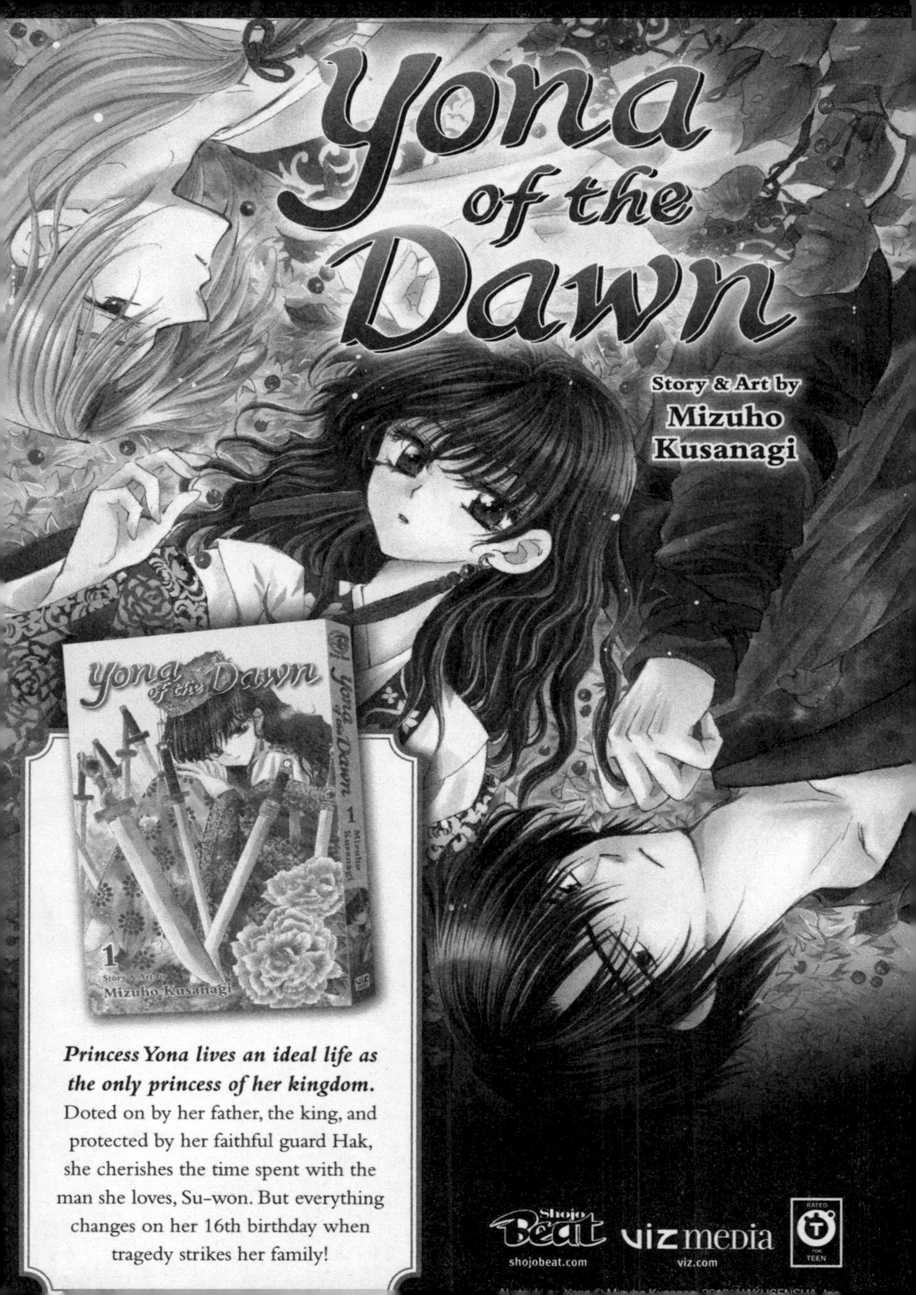
Yona of the Dawn
Story & Art by
Mizuho Kusanagi
Yona of the Dawn
1
Story & Art by
Mizuho Kusanagi
Princess Yona lives an ideal life as the only princess of her kingdom.
Doted on by her father, the king, and protected by her faithful guard Hak, she cherishes the time spent with the man she loves, Su-won. But everything changes on her 16th birthday when tragedy strikes her family!
shojobeat.com
viz.com
RATED T FOR TEEN

THE YOUNG MASTER'S REVENGE

When Leo was a young boy, he had his pride torn to shreds by Tenma, a girl from a wealthy background who was always getting him into trouble. Now, years after his father's successful clothing business has made him the heir to a fortune, he searches out Tenma to enact a dastardly plan—he'll get his revenge by making her fall in love with him!

viz.com

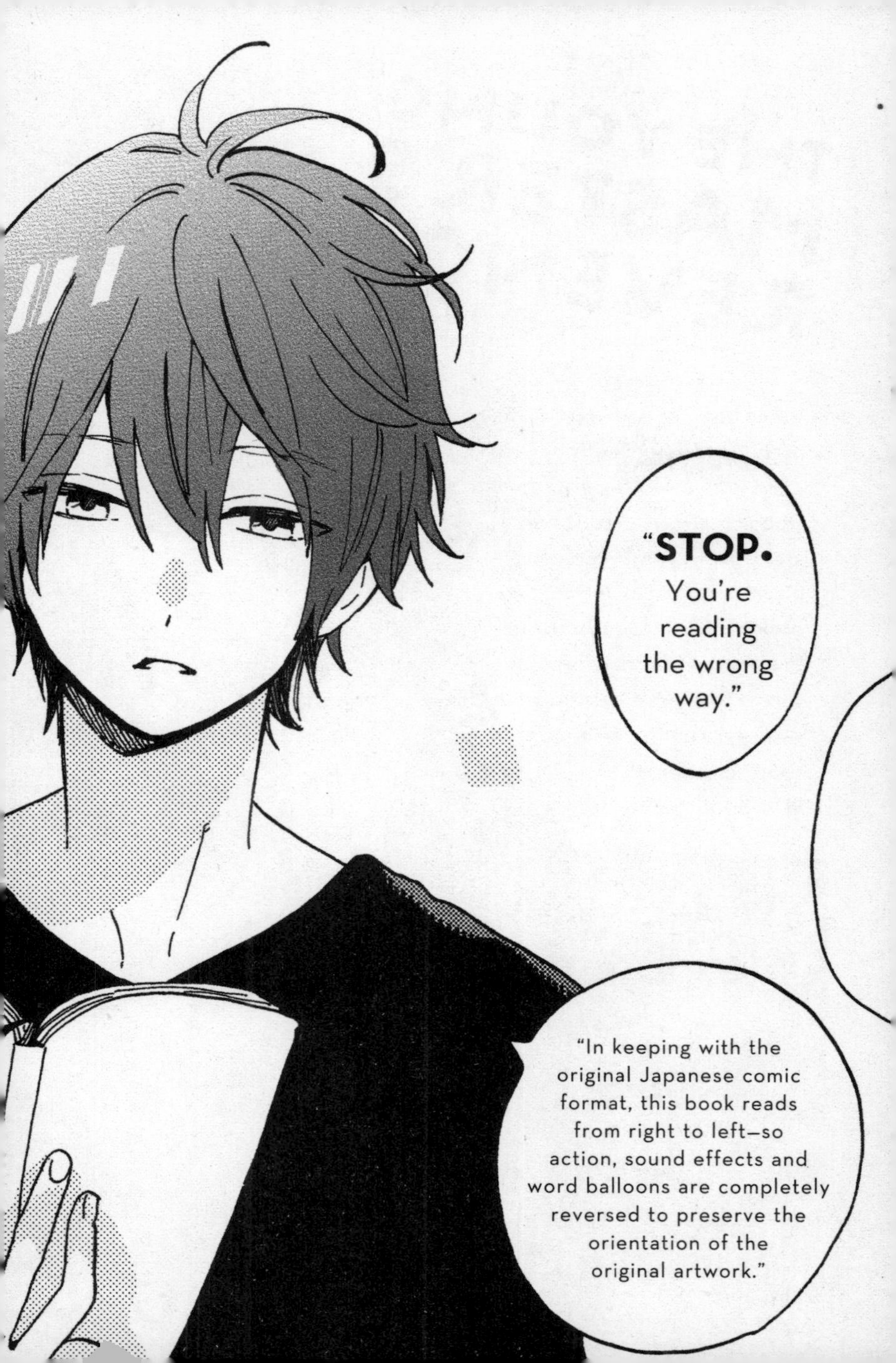
"STOP. You're reading the wrong way."
"In keeping with the original Japanese comic format, this book reads from right to left—so action, sound effects and word balloons are completely reversed to preserve the orientation of the original artwork."